Amazon Conservation in the Age of Development

Amazon Conservation in the Age of Development

The Limits of Providence

Ronald A. Foresta

University of Florida Press
Center for Latin American Studies
Gainesville

Library of Congress Cataloging-in-Publication Data

Foresta, Ronald A., 1944–
    Amazon conservation in the age of development : the limits of
providence / Ronald A. Foresta.
        p.   cm.
    Includes bibliographical references and index.
    ISBN 0-8130-1092-6
    1. Biological diversity conservation—Amazon River Region.
    2. Rural development—Environmental aspects—Amazon River Region.
    I. Title.
    QH77.A53F67   1991   91-94
    333.7'2'09811—dc20   CIP

The University of Florida Press is a member of University Presses of Florida, the
scholarly publishing agency of the State University System of Florida. Books are
selected for publication by faculty editorial committees at each of Florida's nine
public universities: Florida A&M University (Tallahassee), Florida Atlantic
University (Boca Raton), Florida International University (Miami), Florida State
University (Tallahassee), University of Central Florida (Orlando), University of
Florida (Gainesville), University of North Florida (Jacksonville), University of
South Florida (Tampa), University of West Florida (Pensacola).

Orders for books published by all member presses should be addressed to
University Presses of Florida, 15 Northwest 15th Street, Gainesville, FL 32611.

To the memory of George Swope Mirick, naturalist
1909–1983

CONTENTS

PREFACE

Writing this book was a perverse and unpleasant task from beginning to end. During the years it took up, I felt trapped by my own shortcomings as a scholar and betrayed by some of the more perfidious and shabby inhabitants of the districts I passed through. As human nature would have it, now that the task is finally behind me, the extent of my debts to others is beginning to dawn on me. It was the good friends, gracious informants, and fine associates who made it possible for me to see it through. I will never be able to repay them for their help but I can at least gratefully acknowledge it.

Roger Sedjo was a source of advice and hard-nosed yet positive criticism from the earliest stages of the project. His responses to my evolving ideas were important measures of my progress.

Kent Redford had an uncanny knack giving exactly the right counsel. It seemed to come so naturally to him that I'm not sure he was even aware of it.

Gary Wetterberg showed a constant interest in the project and gave it much of his valuable time. He generously shared his documents with me and patiently clarified points when needed, which was often.

Paulo Nogueira-Neto gave me access to his agency's staff, records, and field stations, and even more important, to his own insights on Brazilian conservation, which were always perceptive and frequently profound.

Maria Tereza Jorge Pádua took the project under her wing and made me the beneficiary of her knowledge and observations from the earliest formative stages to the final writing.

Kenton Miller was similarly willing to share his experiences and insights with me.

Those Brazilian conservation administrators whom I interviewed were unfailingly generous with their time and insights. I am in debt to all of them, especially Heloiso Figueiredo and Raquel Milano.

The many American conservationists whom I interviewed and

from whom I otherwise sought advice showed the same consistent generosity.

Mike Wright gave the first draft of the manuscript a critical yet sympathetic reading. In doing so, he forced me to think hard about the broader implications of what I had found.

Alan Moore made me the beneficiary of his vast pool of practical knowledge about Latin American park planning and management.

Marianne Schmink's knowledge of Amazon politics and field conditions—and her skepticism about my conclusions concerning the Brazilian sociopolitical system—improved the manuscript immeasurably.

An anonymous reader's detailed criticism forced me to think through many of the logical tangles and discontinuities of the first draft.

Steve Sanderson's advice, faith in the project, and willingness to go to great lengths to keep the book's production on track were greatly appreciated.

Phil Martin was the consummate editor, by turns supportive, conspiratorial, and informative.

Emery Castle's early faith in the project meant much to me, as did his willingness to secure an RFF grant for the field work.

Will Fontanez, who did the maps, met difficult deadlines with superb work.

Becky Fontanez prepared the tables and provided secretarial support with unfailing competence and good humor.

The University of New Mexico's Latin American Institute graciously included me in its Summer Institute on Brazil, where I was exposed to the literature of Brazilian history, politics, and economy by a superb group of teachers.

Ricardo Paiva and Kate Craven instructed me in Portuguese, although I will not embarrass them by claiming to be their student.

Ruth Haas was a source of consistently good advice. When I did not follow it, I regretted it.

My department provided the supportive environment in which the writing was done. Sid Jumper, the chairman, silently watched me let scores of little things slide by, even if he had to pick up the slack himself.

Sally Mirick put up with an absent or stressed-out husband far beyond the call of duty, even for a professor's wife.

Finally, given my debt to others, it is important to emphasize that responsibility for the errors of fact and interpretation, as well as for all other shortcomings of this book, are mine alone.

INTRODUCTION

Although a vast normative literature has grown up around biological conservation, its analytic traditions are weak. Perhaps because of conservation's great moral freight, it has tended to attract acolytes rather than critical scholars. Those who have studied the evolution of conservation thought or the rise of the organized conservation movement have tended to be active conservationists themselves, and, perhaps because of their insiders' perspective, they have treated these processes as endogenic. Students of conservation also have generally preferred to address conservation issues in restricted, local contexts rather than grapple with the question of how conservation has been shaped by its wider sociopolitical environment, again perhaps because they are usually insiders. This has left biological conservation with a set of ideals, a storehouse of tactics, and even a fairly well understood sense of its own history as a sequence of events, but it has also left its relationship to the main currents of twentieth-century history, its place in the ideological and political world of the late twentieth century, and even its relationship with the biological science of our era only poorly understood. Likewise, it has left its complexion as a political force largely unknown.

Biological conservation takes place within a vast temporal and moral context. The current wave of human-induced extinctions might surpass that at the end of the Mesozoic Era, 65 million years ago.[1] Insuring that the products of billions of years of evolution get through the narrow passage of the present into a future that will, it is hoped, be more hospitable to them is one of the basic aims of today's conservation movement.[2] Yet, in spite of this temporal depth of concern, its lack of a broad sociopolitical perspective leads to an exaggerated sense of immediacy. Extremes of hope and despair abound among those close to biological conservation, often giving way to each other with startling speed. An environmentally sensitive administrator is appointed to an important post in a third world government and optimism surges. A new dam is announced in a biologically sensitive area and despair replaces optimism. Because signs of conservation gain and loss have no common roots in a historical perspective or in a sense of conservation's niche in contemporary public life, they cannot be related to each other. The announcement of every new policy, appointment, or program becomes a new beginning, every setback an ending. Events cannot fuse into trends; a sense of the ground covered or yet to be covered cannot emerge.

Preservation of biological diversity has recently become a major global issue, and the resources being made available to conservation groups and causes are greater than ever before. Yet without a deep perspective, conservationists are forever positioning themselves to take advantage of transitory opportunity and forever changing their tactics to fit the changing shape of that opportunity. This reduces conservation action to a series of disjointed, reactive moves—tactics, in other words. However, progress toward the ambitious, long-term goals of conservation will require deeply reasoned strategies that transcend the moment. Optimal allocation of conservation resources will depend on distinguishing ephemeral or illusory advantages from the solid ones. Fashioning successful programs will require an understanding of the basic shape of the political space within which conservation operates.

Brazilian Amazonia is a good place to begin constructing such an understanding. Perhaps no area of human affairs so taxes the present's capacity for provident action as does the management of the world's tropical rainforests. Their importance to posterity is undeniable; they contain perhaps 50 percent of all living species, and a future without them would have far fewer options for maintaining the commonweal. The effect of massive forest clearing on global weather patterns and chemical cycles is dimly understood but likely to be enormous. The loss of the indigenous cultures the rainforest supports would reduce the sum of human knowledge and adaptability. And as Lovejoy and Oren write, the loss of the rainforest would help reduce future biology to "paleontology, the biology of weedy species, laboratory and zoo biology and...the science of pickled parts."

The problem is unique to our era. Before the mid-twentieth century, most of the world's tropical rainforests were protected by their remoteness, vastness, and inhospitality to civilization. In fact, the biome served as a metaphor for those qualities, as it did in Conrad's

Heart of Darkness. But advances in science and technology reduced the rainforest's natural defenses, while population growth caused increased migration into it. The result has been accelerated rainforest clearing and species loss; one source estimated that loss of rainforest habitat accounts for 70 to 90 percent of all present-day extinctions. If these trends continue, rainforest clearing could reduce global species diversity by a seventh or a fifth within decades. In our time, the tropical rainforest has become a metaphor for civilization's, not nature's, destructive power.

The South American forests are the most species-diverse of the world's rainforests, and the scale of clearing in them cannot be compared to anything in history.[3] Millions of hectares have been transformed into cattle ranches, sugar plantations, and soybean farms. Millions of landless peasants have made their way into the forest, where they have cleared plots for themselves. Enormous lakes have formed behind new dams, drowning thousands of square kilometers of forest. The forest has been diminished with each new project and population surge.

Most of South America's rainforest is found in Brazilian Amazonia, placing that nation in the eye of the issue.[4] Like most of the biome, the forest of Brazilian Amazonia has undergone extensive clearing in recent decades. But it also saw considerable conservation activity in the 1970s and 1980s. Brazil's Secretariat of the Environment (SEMA) and the Institute for Forest Development (IBDF) established extensive conservation programs. Foreign conservation organizations expended much time and energy in Brazilian Amazonia. Perhaps nowhere else in the world has such a serious, principled effort been made to fold current science into conservation policy. These efforts brought millions of hectares of rainforest under public protection and led to the promulgation of environmentally sound laws. In fact, Brazilian efforts to preserve its natural patrimony were estimable enough to win the Getty Prize, given for outstanding contributions to global conservation, for two of Brazil's leading conservationists.

During this period Amazonia also saw the expression of some of the deepest normative impulses of our era: the promotion of regional development, the search for national independence, the harnessing of science to human welfare, and the struggle for social equality and a stable political system. Conservation, therefore, had to find its niche amid all the conflicts and contradictions that arose from this tangle of values. Doing so involved a constant search for allies and unceasing efforts to discern the shape of conservation's space in the modern world. Brazilian Amazonia thus provides a rich and important ground for an analysis of biological conservation's complexion as a sociopolitical force.

In spite of this, conservation in Amazonia has inspired even less analysis than elsewhere; change in Amazonia has attracted almost all the scholarly attention. It is easier to see than conservation: forest clearing means dams under construction, settlers on the move, and bulldozers at work; conservation is often only the silence of the forest. Billions of dollars have been spent promoting change in Amazonia, and thousands of administrators and entrepreneurs have been involved. Conservation agencies are few, small, and located on the margins of power. They are led by middle-level administrators presiding over small staffs and operating on relatively small budgets. The importance of conservation to the federal government waxes and wanes. Because of its modest scale and its location on the periphery of the national political agenda, Amazon conservation appears to be a less likely source of insights into national life than development programs and their managing agencies.

This lack of an analytic tradition has given rise to a disjointed, often contradictory perspective on conservation's achievements in Amazonia. Even more than conservation events elsewhere, those in Amazonia seem to lack antecedents, descendants, or connections to concurrent events in the region. As a consequence, a fabulous, mythic perspective has arisen and obscured Amazon conservation's real past. Conservation and opposition to it have become an episodic play of good and evil in which conservation action is the domain not of administrators, scientists, and politicians, but of heroes: a few wise Nestors, a few Horatii manning lonely bridges. The agents of change in Amazonia have also become caricatures, usually ones acting out of immediate, base motives: greed, desperation, and willful ignorance.

This perspective encourages indignation and enthusiasm—both necessary for rallying support to conservation causes, perhaps—but discourages the extraction of lessons from the past. Moral myth seldom focuses on the context of human action. People are greedy and ignorant everywhere; they are also noble and capable of foresight and self-sacrifice everywhere. It takes values, institutions, and what might loosely be called history to shape human actions into constructive and destructive forms, and to allow them to form interpretable patterns.

The intention here is not to strip conservation of its moral dimension, but rather to expand our understanding of conservation's relationship to some of the broader sociopolitical currents of our world: the progress of science, the implementation of the development ideal, the elaboration of the international capitalist system. Only once a solid understanding of such relationships has been achieved will it be possible to see conservation action as more than a bundle of tactics in a play of good and evil, whose outcome can always be the object of faith, but never of the reasoned interpretations on which successful strategies for biological conservation will need to be built.

CHAPTER 1

Nature and the Practice of Development

The vision of the future in the early twentieth century was part bright and part dark. In the West, the maturing industrial revolution and the advance of civilization made life, in H. G. Wells's words, "heavy with the promise of greater things."[1] Beyond the industrialized states were cultures that discouraged invention and economies incapable of productively using capital. The scarcity and stagnation that the classical economists had predicted, and that the West had avoided through science and inventiveness, were their likely fate, and only imperial rule brought a measure of well-being to them. But this dichotomy, like the imperial order it fitted and legitimized, was swept away by the Second World War. Those who would reconstruct the world on the rubble of the old imperialism were determined to create a new order of modern, prosperous states. The promotion of global development became central to what Adler called "the agenda of the Brave New World" that emerged after 1945.[2] Everyone would become heir to Wells's vision of heavy promise.

The instruments of universal progress were built into the institutional framework of the postwar order.[3] The creation of "conditions of economic and social progress" was one of the United Nations' basic goals, and specialized UN agencies—the Food and Agriculture Organization, the International Monetary Fund, the UN Development Programme, the World Health Organization—were set up to carry out the development mandate. North American and then Western European nations established development-promoting agencies to supplement the UN's efforts. Private philanthropic foundations turned their attention to the problems of underdevelopment.

A broad consensus was eventually reached on the basic prescription for national development: the complete restructuring of national economies and a massive expansion of their material output.[4] The old colonial economies based on the export of agricultural products and extractive resources had proved poor engines of progress; they were subject to rapid, unpredictable price fluctuations, and the terms of trade had steadily turned against them. They had few multiplier effects within the national economy. An economy of progress had to be built upon an advanced industrial sector that made full use of national resources and forced all other sectors along the path to modernity; it drove the economies of the already-developed nations of the world, and it would do the same for the rest of the world.[5]

Development theorists viewed such fundamental change as possible only with active state participation.[6] The state had to wrench the economy out of its ingrained routines by matching fiscal policy with national objectives. It had to adopt policies that insured the rapid acquisition and efficient use of modern technology. It had to generate large amounts of capital through the management of savings and the creation of attractive conditions for foreign capital. Equally important, the state had to force fundamental changes on society.[7] It had to turn peasants and campesinos into citizens of a modern state. It had to educate people for new jobs and give them motives for participating in the national transformation. It had to create what Meier called an ideology of progress.[8] These economic and cultural tasks required a greatly expanded state apparatus and a shift of power within the state from traditional politicians to technocrats and professional administrators.

In few countries were the ideals and practices of national development woven more tightly into public life than in Brazil. A planning mentality permeated the federal government after 1945, and development plans were a regular feature of the national economy by the end of the decade.[9] A national development bank was created, and a sophisticated federal planning structure evolved in the early 1950s. Brazil worked closely with many of the UN's development agencies and received aid from the bilateral development programs of the industrialized nations, especially those of the United States.

Juscelino Kubitschek, who began his five-year term as president in 1956 when the ideal of development was reaching its full ascendance as an international vision, made national development the ideological centerpiece of his administration, launching his presidency with the promise of "fifty years progress in five." He established the Council of Development, a planning and advisory body that reported directly

to him, and under him specialized government planning groups
directed the growth of key industries: autos, computers, metallurgy,
even motion pictures. He built Brasília to be the new capital of his
new Brazil, and the Belém-Brasília Highway to draw more of the
nation into the modern national core. Although Kubitschek was not
fully successful in meeting his specific goals, he instilled in Brazilians
a new confidence in the nation's future and made economic development a performance criterion against which all future governments
would be judged.[10]

The military government that came to power with the coup of
1964 was as willing to embrace developmentalism as its predecessors
had been, and acted quickly to rekindle the development process
according to its own lights. The old politicians were replaced as top
ministers by professional administrators, frequently economists or
military men, many of the latter with training as engineers. They in
turn began sweeping personnel changes in their ministries, replacing
old officials loyal to the civilian parties with technocrats created in
their own image. A similar process occurred in state governments,
whose independence was now severely reduced. Politicians and
administrators with allegiances to the old system were replaced by
professionals loyal to the generals and their ideas of development.[11]

Before the end of its first year in power, the military government
began reforming the structure of the administration to make it more
capable of promoting development. The next year, it introduced the
Plano Decenal, which laid out general performance goals for the
economy over the next decade. The ministries of planning and
finance were given the power to set long-term policy for the rest of
the federal bureaucracy, in effect making them superministries and
making their ministers national development czars. The Minister of
Planning, Roberto Campos, became the chief architect of Brazilian
economic development during the early years of the military government, and Antônio Delfim Neto, as the Minister of Finance, later
succeeded him in this role.[12] Under these men and their advisors, the
principles of development came to completely dominate Brazil's economic life.[13] More state-owned corporations were created to give
direction to what remained essentially an entrepreneurial and market-
oriented economy. Public policies strongly favored industrialization
and arranged the rest of the economy around it so as to make industry the engine of modernization.

These efforts were successful beyond any reasonable expectation.[14] Annual rates of economic growth ranged between 8 and 12 percent during the years 1967–1972, almost doubling the gross national product during the period. Manufacturing had an average annual growth rate of almost 13 percent, with the value of exports expanding at twice that rate. The Brazilian press and much of the public were mesmerized by the nation's economic performance, referred to simply as "the miracle." Roett wrote, "Suddenly, Brazil's economic role in world affairs was no laughing matter."[15] Far from it, in surpassing the ambitious performance goals set by the United Nations for its development decade of the 1960s, Brazil became a model for other developing nations.

***

There had always been doubt about the developmental ideal and the progressive vision of material abundance that undergirded it. By the early twentieth century, natural scientists had become aware of the profound impact of human action on the natural world, and they understood that modern humanity eclipsed its ancestors in potential for destruction.[16] A zoologist, Alexander Carr-Saunders, first treated the human population as a biological force of great destructive potential in his 1922 work, *The Population Problem*.[17] A negative view of human impact on the natural world became common within the natural sciences as the century progressed, so much so that Sauer could write in 1957 that "to the biologist, man's role often seems to be that of a creature who...spoils the balance of the ecosystem." Perhaps Wells and development theorists saw modern humans in the image of Hephaestus and Athena, but to Sauer, we belonged in the lineage of Daedalus.[18]

The accumulated work of scientists with an ecological perspective was slow to have an impact on mainstream thinking about the human condition, however.[19] Ecological relationships often had a complexity that precluded the precise measurements that had become the accepted standards of evidence.[20] Arguments of ecological damage based on imputed general relationships and imprecise data fared poorly when placed against precise engineering specifications or estimates of economic benefit. The concepts necessary to fuse the concerns of scientists into a broad critique of the norms of development were also lacking. Without them, the record of human damage to the environment remained fragmented by discipline and could not be fused into a coherent image of mankind's ecological relationship to nature.[21]

Perhaps most importantly, ecology-based questions about the wisdom of development practice had little intrinsic appeal to those who shaped the postwar world. They appeared negative and cautionary when optimism and a willingness to take risks and to pull out all stops seemed called for. They offered no clear, simple path to the universal betterment with which the international order was so bound up.

A coherent ecological critique was fusing beneath the hegemony of the development ideal, however. The concept of biosphere, steadily refined and increasingly rigorous, became available to serve as a focus for thought about the dynamics of the natural world.[22] "Ecosystem" came into general use, making it possible to lift studies of individual species or small groups of organisms out of the narrow confines of their subdisciplines and to unify research on human impacts on the natural world. With the introduction of the term "ecosphere" in the late 1950s, ecosystem and biosphere were fused into a useful concept that combined the integrating elements of the former and the universality of the latter.[23] Once these terms became accepted frames of analysis, concepts like carrying capacity, subsistence density, limiting factor, and systemic stability transcended the hundreds of local contexts in which they had been used and became powerful tools for understanding basic characteristics of human-nature relations.

The capacity of the natural sciences to measure the impact of human activity on the ecosystem steadily improved while the analytic concepts took shape.[24] By the 1960s, instrument refinements made it possible to detect human-placed substances in the environment at very low concentrations. The discovery that contaminants such as DDT and organochloride pesticides were widely present quickly followed, and so did the realization that global carbon, nitrogen, and phosphorus cycles were being altered by human actions. Satellites allowed more efficient monitoring of the earth and its atmosphere, and computers made possible an unprecedented accumulation and manipulation of environmental data.

As ecologists armed with new concepts and instrumentation probed modern development, a list of projects gone awry for ecological reasons began to be accumulated.[25] The deforestation associated with agricultural development schemes caused landslides that swept away highways and caused erosion that filled reservoirs with sediment. Dams spread schistosomiasis and created a favorable habitat for the tsetse fly. The resistance of insects to pesticides led to large crop failures and a scattered resurgence of malaria. High levels of industrial and agricultural contaminants accumulated in soils and water throughout the developing world. Anthropologists and allied social scientists added to the critique of modern development with their detailed, critical scrutiny of the impact of development programs on the social structure, diets, and general welfare of their intended beneficiaries.[26]

Critics of development practice began to argue that there had been a failure to distinguish between the mere increase in a society's material assets and what they saw as true development: an increase in a society's capacity to sustain itself at a high level of well-being.[27] They held that as the scale of modern economic activity increased and came to dominate more of the earth's surface, this failure had become one of mankind's greatest problems. As the realization that economics had grossly underestimated the size and pervasiveness of externalities steadily grew, so did the feeling that development theory had inherited this flaw.[28] Development, like its core discipline, seemed too caught up in linear, monetary relationships to model the world or the commonweal in a sufficiently complete fashion, and this had led it away from accurate measures of human welfare.[29]

The implications of this environmental critique for the human future were profound. Within the progressive vision, the masterline of history was human inventiveness and technological achievement. Early civilizations progressed from lower to higher stages with the accumulation of what Childe called "significant achievements": art, pottery, metal working, writing, etc.[30] During the industrial revolution, the accumulation of significant achievements speeded up, allowing for a more rational reorganization of the material world. There was nothing to prevent these trends from continuing and leading to increased mastery over nature in the future.

High regard for science had led to a relaxed view of the present's responsibility for its own posterity. Roberts and others argued that previous generations, employing new technology, had turned resources into capital and knowledge, whose benefits to the future outweighed their costs in depleted resources.[31] The present was doing the same for its posterity. Tullock rhetorically asked if we "must look to the prospectively wealthy future for a source of worthy recipients of our bounty?" Baumol argued that, if anything, the present should try to share in the affluence of the future.[32]

The accepted dissent to this vision came primarily from intellectuals in the scholarly tradition of Spengler and Toynbee. Some dissidents doubted human capacity to keep technology harnessed to proper ends; others questioned Western civilization's ability to maintain itself in good order, even with an ever-increasing stock of technology.[33] By the 1950s such dissent was usually dismissed as unreasonable in the face of recent progress; Van Doren accused it of being "isolated from social realities" and of reflecting arid, relict academic traditions. He saved his admiration for economists, whose optimism about progress "allowed them to concentrate single-mindedly on the means of achieving it."[34]

The ecological perspective radically altered practically everything connected to the future, including its antecedents, its likely shape, and, perhaps most importantly, the present's responsibility for it. Increasing manipulation and exploitation of the environment, rather than any detached process of technological elaboration, became the masterline of material history. The capacity of human cultures to expand into diverse ecological niches became a convincing explanation for the rise of early civilizations.[35] The industrial revolution became a period in which a switch from a renewable resource base to a largely nonrenewable one took place. Within this perspective, the material transformations that had taken place over the past two hundred years, and from which current development theory took its models, had been based on conditions unlikely to prevail indefinitely into the future. Global systems modelers projected past trends of population increase, resource use, and pollution into the future and saw a world characterized by overpopulation, intolerable levels of pollution, and industrial collapse.[36] This view resembled that of the classical economists, but now it had underpinnings in a powerful, coherent interpretation of the past and in solid evidence of current, increasing environmental disruption.

A future facing serious ecological constraints was not one capable of getting along on the scraps of the present. It would be less, not more capable of guaranteeing its own prosperity than the present, making Baumol and Tullock's sanguine view appear improvident. Thus while the relationship of the present to the progressive future could be what Page called "self-administering," the new future placed heavy moral burdens on the present and demanded active concern.[37]

The ecological perspective also brought great expanses of the future into the moral pale of the present. Within the progressive vision, the distant future was a very vague place. Its problems were not easy to foresee, but the technologies and scientific resources available for solving them were likely to be so powerful that the far future was an even less worthy object of the present's concern than the more immediate one.[38] Within the new view, however, the further one looked into the future, the more likely it was that trends of increasing material prosperity would play themselves out. In fact, the scale of the future's problems, and the paucity of its resources for dealing with them, seemed directly related to how far into it one was inclined to look.[39] Keynes's offhand comment that "in the long run we're all dead" seemed to sum up the smugness and the shortsighted-ness of past thinking about the future.

As the environmental critique coalesced in the 1960s, what McNeill called "a noisy concern for the future" arose in the developed world.[40] Its press devoted increasing space to environmental issues and its citizens began paying attention to them. Governments of the developed world responded with new environmental laws and pro-tection agencies. The environment became a global issue.[41] The UN's 1972 Stockholm Conference on the Human Environment attracted widespread attention and had a profound influence in the developing world, causing scores of less-developed countries to establish mecha-nisms for protecting their environments.[42]

Brazil had not been in the forefront of the environmental move-ment. It had heard only praise for its development policies from abroad, and its accumulation of polluting industries and its destruc-tion of biological resources had not mitigated that praise.[43] The pro-fessionals to whom national development had been entrusted were not led to a concern for the environment by their calculus of costs and benefits. Furthermore, several of the UN agencies with which Brazil interacted closely were slow in reacting to rising concern for the biosphere. The UN's Economic Commission for Latin America (ECLA), for example, showed no serious interest in environmental matters in the 1960s or early 1970s, and as late as 1970, the UN's Advisory Committee on the Application of Science and Technology to Development was asserting that the resources of the entire world had to be developed to the fullest extent possible.[44]

When environmentalism emerged as an important issue in the industrialized nations, Brazil responded with some token environ-mental measures. Several Brazilian states passed legislation and a few established agencies for environmental oversight, but the laws lacked enforcement mechanisms and the agencies had little real power. The national government established a Council for Pollution Control and wrote some antipollution passages into the National Sanitation Policy of 1967, but neither the federal laws nor the council were taken seriously.[45] In fact, Brazil hoped to attract some of the industries facing stringent anti-pollution restrictions elsewhere. A Brazilian cabinet minister argued that large and relatively underdeveloped Brazil could be more flexible than smaller, more crowded nations like Japan in accommodating polluting industries.[46]

The Brazilian government's position on the environment shifted dramatically after the Stockholm Conference, however. The Brazilian ambassador to the United States explained that his government favored environmentally responsible development, not growth at any cost. In line with this assertion, the national government insisted that a new factory being built in Brazil by the Japanese be equipped with advanced antipollution safeguards. The federal government enacted antipollution legislation to toughen the mild environmental measures already on the books and established a federal Secretariat of the Environment (SEMA) to enforce the new legislation. Brazil's Second Amazon Development Plan, which appeared in 1974, asserted that development would not be allowed to cause the "deterioration in the quality of life," or to "devastate the country's patrimony of natural resources."[47] With this passage, concern for the environment was embedded at the core of the national planning process.

***

Biological conservation had been a part of the imperial system of the early twentieth century: most metropolitan states were under commitments to protect the flora and fauna of their colonies; international conservation treaties were in effect; private conservation organizations flourished. But the Second World War destroyed the edifice of prewar conservation just as it destroyed the imperial order on which it was based.[48] The new international order of the postwar era did not particularly value nature for itself. The primacy of economics within development theory led to a view of nature as a stock of resources, and the era viewed natural resources as a relatively unimportant factor in the global economy. The values assigned to nature were derived from its employment as a factor of production. The important distinctions within nature were those of potential use. The subtle and reticulate character of human-nature relations practically guaranteed they would be lost in the rigorous calculus of development's costs and benefits. Such reasons to value nature as rarity, aesthetics, and popular enjoyment did carry over from earlier eras, but they were diminished by their lack of alignment with the key values and perspectives of the early postwar era.

Steps to protect nature on an international level were further complicated by conservation's imperial past. Many among the elites of the newly independent nations saw nature protection as an element of colonialism to be swept away with the rest of the structure of the colonial era. Perez Olindo, a prominent Kenyan conservationist, noted that the native elite of the immediate pre-independence era thought of wildlife as a "bloody nuisance."[49] At best, biological conservation could wait until more immediate problems of development had been tended to.

The lack of importance accorded nature and its colonial associations condemned biological conservation to marginal status in the international order during the first two postwar decades. Although an International Union for the Conservation of Nature (IUCN) was established after the war, neither it nor conservation in general received much support from the UN or national governments, or much attention from the press or the publics of the developed world. International conservation organizations were strapped for funds and unable to carry out such basic tasks as keeping track of endangered species and protected natural areas. Even in developed nations, including the United States, the conservation issues of earlier eras seemed to have burned out and the old organizations seemed moribund.[50]

Protected nature assumed a new importance with the coalescence of the ecological critique. Unaltered nature's capacity to absorb pollution made it a buffer against environmental disruption. Nature also came to be viewed as an ecological control, what Leopold described as "a base datum of normality, a picture of how healthy land maintains itself."[51] The more development projects that went awry for ecological reasons, the more important this seemed. The new humility about human capacity to understand the long-term effects of technology gave nature an important new dimension. As Odum later summed up the argument, "Until we can determine more precisely how far we may safely go in expanding [human activity] at the expense of the [natural] landscape, it will be good insurance to hold inviolate as much of the latter as possible."[52] The argument conferred on protected nature a central role in mediating between the present and posterity.

The importance of nature's role as insurance against the self-serving calculations of the present grew as distant posterity became an object of concern. Discounting future values at some market-determined rate, while perhaps a satisfactory way of mediating between the present and the near future, appeared unsatisfactory in ordering the present's relationship with the distant future: any but the most minuscule discount rates would reduce any far-distant benefits of today's actions to a current trivial value.[53] It seemed more provident to pass to distant posterity a natural world little diminished in biological options than to trust market-determined calculations, which might convert the future's biological endowment into technology or sunk capital inappropriate for future needs.

The increasing theoretical fit of protected nature and the goals of universal human betterment drew many development-oriented agencies into international conservation in the 1960s. The Rockefeller Brothers Fund supported the establishment of two schools of wildlife management in Africa. The Food and Agriculture Organization (FAO), which, beyond some interest in the preservation of plants and animals of obvious economic value, had considered conservation outside its sphere of responsibility, began to promote wildlife and natural area protection. The UN Development Programme (UNDP), which had previously thought conservation programs incompatible with economic development and had displayed an outright hostility toward biological conservation in the world's poorer nations, changed its attitude and began supporting them. By 1972, FAO, usually with UNDP support, was operating an advisory program in park and wildlife management in twenty-two countries around the world.

Bilateral aid agencies of the United States, Great Britain, and West Germany followed suit and began providing support for conservation planning in countries around the world. Financial help and technical advice from the British Ministry for Overseas Development, for example, was important in drawing up an ambitious Peruvian national park plan of the mid-1960s. The American Peace Corps sent scores of its volunteers to third world parks and wildlife refuges, where they wrote management plans and trained native personnel. The Inter-American Institute of Agricultural Sciences (IICA), a facility of the Organization of American States, began training Latin Americans in wildlife management on its campus in Costa Rica.

Conservation agencies in the developed world expanded their range of operations beyond national boundaries. The U.S. National Park Service established an office of international liaison and through it forged links with conservation agencies in Asia, Africa and Latin America. The U.S. National Park Service joined its Canadian equivalent in sponsoring an annual International Seminar on National Parks for conservation officers from developing nations. A crossflow of consultants and advisors created regional conservation networks and kept conservation administrators in touch with their counterparts in other countries, creating a sense of camaraderie among native managers and keeping them abreast of the latest developments elsewhere.[54]

While the new importance of nature greatly expanded the niche for biological conservation in the international order, advances in science expanded the pale of conservation's concern. Early twentieth-century biology had placed great value on the unique and the exceptional: nature most clearly revealed its inventiveness and genius at its extremes. It was assumed that most advances in scientific knowledge would take place by studying these extremes, and by contemplating them, laymen would most quickly develop an appreciation of nature's majesty. The lingering romantic aesthetic canons of the nineteenth century, which assigned great value to the spectacular and the dramatic, reinforced this tendency to find value in the extreme and unique.[55] Biological conservation undergirded by such views was easy to formulate and relatively easy to execute. Conservation could, and did, focus on unique areas and a few magnificent species.

As knowledge accumulated about hundreds of less spectacular plants and animals, they were deemed worthy of protection.[56] Advances in population genetics made it clear that the preservation of species, even the spectacular species on which traditional conservation had focused, would be difficult without maintaining breeding populations in their natural habitats. With the emergence of ecology as a recognized biological science, the ecosystem became an entity worthy of protection in and of itself. For example, whereas just the migratory birds that used wetlands were originally seen as worth protecting, now entire wetland ecosystems became valid objects of protection.[57]

* * *

The new, expanded canon of biological importance and the new niche of conservation in the international order demanded a new operating doctrine for organized conservation. One of the leaders in the effort to forge such doctrine was Kenton Miller. Although Miller was only one of many conservationists out of whose work a general synthesis arose, and although many of the ideas he espoused were already prevalent in the international conservation community by the time he expressed them, his work did represent perhaps the most ambitious distillation of conservation thought into explicit operational principles. Miller's connections with Latin America were strong, and his writing was especially influenced by the conditions he observed there.

Miller, an American, was exposed to the recent conservation thought in his formal education: as a master's degree candidate at the University of Washington in the early 1960s, he worked under Frank Brockman, a conservationist with long associations with the IUCN; while pursuing a doctorate in wildlands planning at Syracuse University, he became steeped in the new environmental movement's basic literature and struggled with the question of how to apply it to conservation practice.[58] Miller began his involvement with Latin American conservation in 1962, when he drew up a development plan for Canaima National Park in Venezuela as part of his master's work. After receiving his doctorate in 1968, Miller returned to Latin America in the employ of the FAO to work on a number of management plans for protected areas. Gradually, his academic training, field experience, and participation in the regional network of Latin American conservationists fused into a coherent, ramified approach to biological conservation.[59]

Miller reasoned that conservation could be effective only if ideologically linked with the basic goals of universal human betterment at the core of the development ideal, and institutionally linked with the organs of development. Miller had observed the great increase in state power in South America in the 1960s and had seen that power funnelled into development planning. With support from the American-led Alliance for Progress, central planning by the national states had increased (by the mid-1960s nine South American nations had established central planning agencies) and the development of many of the continent's backward and underpopulated areas had come under state management. With lending countries and foreign assistance programs insisting on state planning as a condition for financial aid, such planning seemed likely to become even more important in the future, both as a government activity and a determinant of landscape change.[60]

Recent history supported the logic of the argument. South America had long been a lagging continent with regard to nature protection. It was of marginal importance in prewar international conservation, and in the first two postwar decades, indigenous disinterest was reenforced by the lack of importance accorded conservation by development theory. Stillwell noted the lack of a strong conservation tradition on the continent in the early 1960s.[61] Yet there had been a quickening of Latin American conservation activity in that decade, mostly, as Miller had observed, in connection with regional development programs. Colombia's Agrarian Reform Institute and the Magdalena Valley Corporation proposed a network of parks for the lower Magdalena basin in the early 1960s.[62] Peru developed a national park system plan between 1966 and 1969 as part of regional development efforts and with the assistance of international development agencies. A number of Latin American nations established wildlife and wildlands management programs as parts of forestry development programs.

Miller reasoned that conservation programs in South America could be effective only if broad lines of communication were forged between conservation planners and agronomists, economists, and others involved in national planning. Conservation, he argued, had to be recognized as a tool of development.[63] Linking conservation to national development would also insure that conservation planners would be exposed to the broader goals of national planning, and that other planners would be kept mindful of the benefits that conservation programs could provide. Miller wrote that, "As conservation becomes integrated into development, the conservationist will move from being the beggar on the street to a consultant, advisor and regular associate of the national planning board."[64]

Such a strategy demanded professionalism. Conservation planners could take their place among the other planning professionals only if they were as educated in their profession as the others were in theirs. Miller understood how shared values and occupational mobility had molded foresters into a powerful profession in the United States and other developed nations, and he thought it important that the same thing happen with biological conservation. Miller therefore stressed the need to develop a cadre of professional conservationists and advocated making training programs a prominent part of national conservation efforts.[65]

Because national planning was demanding greater professionalism throughout government and a corresponding decrease in the role of politics in day-to-day public decisions, professionalism would also link conservation to the future world of the rational discharge of the public's business, not the past one of ideology and petty political intrigue. Miller thought circumstances demanded an even greater commitment to apolitical professionalism from conservation than from other sectors of state planning: only by emphasizing the professional and technical could biological conservation keep clear of the political controversies of the era, while retaining its positive referents (in the abstract) all along the political spectrum.[66] Avoiding political controversy was essential, since only by implementing similar programs in countries of widely differing ideological casts could all the continent's endangered species and samples of all its important ecosystems be protected.

Conservation programs had to be comprehensive and national in scope if they were to provide a wide enough range of tangible benefits—watershed protection, resource management, education, tourism, recreation—to appeal to those who directed national planning.[67] They had to be systematic and geographically comprehensive if they were to include the diversity of species and ecosystems that had become the benchmark of modern conservation. To this latter end, Miller thought it important to decide a priori and systematically what an ideal national conservation program should consist of, and what the criteria for selecting the natural areas included in it should be.

He stressed the importance of building national or regional conservation programs on a scientifically credible biogeographic base. This would link conservation to science-derived values and would give conservation programs added credibility with other planning professionals. Throughout the 1960s, conservationists had devoted much energy to the creation of such a base. The IUCN underwrote the development of a global zoogeography, a mapping system for the world's coastal and marine environment, and a world-wide biome classification scheme.[68] By the end of the decade, the scientific base for systematic conservation was much improved.

In line with his systematic approach, Miller stressed the importance of placing each protected area in the appropriate management category. The IUCN had worked through the 1960s to establish a clearly defined, standardized set of categories for protected nature.[69] Each of the IUCN categories—national park, biological reserve, natural monument, national forest reserve, etc.—served a specific end. An area in the wrong category would not provide maximum benefits.[70]

Miller stressed the need for extensive documentation and record keeping: each nation should have a fully articulated approach to biological conservation; each policy should be explicitly documented; each protected area should have documents showing how it fit into national conservation goals and containing plans for its management. This advocacy of documentation reflected the professional cast of prevailing development doctrine, but it also reflected Miller's personal experience. His work at Conaima and elsewhere had convinced him that one of the biggest obstacles to conservation in South America was lack of continuity; the elaboration of a major program of nature protection was a long, step-by-step process. Too frequently he had seen managers and planners trying to deduce the intentions of their predecessors and endlessly reinventing policy and procedures.[71] Only with careful documentation could this waste of energy be avoided and the continuity of intent be maintained.

Conversely, Miller opposed wholly opportunity-driven approaches, arguing that programs pieced together over time without the benefit of a master policy were unlikely to be satisfactory conservation instruments, either biologically or politically. But he was also a pragmatist who knew that circumstances sometimes called for speed in decision making and for compromise. Indeed the sense of history that led Miller to advocate comprehensive planning also led to his occasional willingness to cut corners in the name of expedience. He was part of a generation of conservationists that felt itself weighed down by responsibility for all of posterity and therefore under great pressure to act quickly. David Brower, executive director of the Sierra Club, had suggested in 1960 that most of what would be saved for the future would have to be set aside during the coming decade. At his opening address to the First World Conference on National Parks in 1962, Stewart Udall, the American Secretary of the Interior, suggested that his generation would likely be the last with an opportunity to set aside large areas of protected nature anywhere on earth.[72] The weight of such a future meant that sometimes conservation planners had to, in Miller's words, "take the best they could get."

This "taking the best they could get" applied to science. In spite of a decade's progress in forming a scientific base for conservation decisions, that base was still incomplete, especially at the level of the region or nation. One could not wait for science to answer all the questions with certainty; decisions had to be made on the basis of the best work available. In his own work, Miller used whatever biogeographic systems he could find: Holdridge's in Costa Rica, Tosi's in Peru, and Di Castri's in Chile.[73] If political obstacles or established uses prevented the protection of the most biologically valuable area, as they often did, conservationists should turn to more attainable areas.

Miller, unlike many policy theorists, had the opportunity to put his ideas into large-scale practice. He assumed a teaching position on the faculty of IICA in Costa Rica and from there spread his ideas among the expanding conservation network in Latin America. Then, in 1969, Nelson Rockefeller visited the institute, which his family's philanthropies supported. Miller discussed his ideas with Rockefeller and suggested a project to upgrade nature protection throughout Latin America. The suggestion, and the reasoning behind it, hit three sweet notes for Nelson and his tribe—development, conservation, and Latin America—so Miller was invited to the New York headquarters of the Rockefeller Brothers Fund to formally propose the project he had suggested to Nelson.[74] The fund agreed to support the project, which was eventually named the Regional Project on Wildlands Management. The FAO agreed to cosponsor it and the UN Development Programme lent support.[75]

Under Miller's direction, a national wildlands plan was drawn up for Cuba, and the codification of Colombia's wildlife protection laws was undertaken. Work was begun on national park system plans for Ecuador, Costa Rica, and Colombia. Chile, in collaboration with the regional project, began a major overhaul of its national park system. Over the next several years, new parks were established in Chile, old ones deemed unnecessary were decommissioned, and the entire system was brought in line with the model Miller advocated.[76] As Miller had hoped, the regional project's stress on professionalism and service to development goals shielded it from Latin America's political turbulence and allowed compatible national conservation programs for countries as different politically as Cuba and Colombia to be drawn up. The emphasis on professionalism even allowed the Chilean program to survive the military coup of 1973 with little alteration.

Miller's project brought a new cohesion to Latin American conservation, while his approach brought it a new measure of respect and vigor. Thanks largely to Miller's efforts, the number of protected areas in South America meeting the criteria for inclusion on the UN List of National Parks and Protected Areas rose from 98 in 1968 to 126 in 1972 and to 161 in 1975. The total area under protection rose even more steeply, from 13.7 million hectares to 18.3 and then to 25.9. Scores of management plans for individual protected areas were prepared in the early 1970s under the project. The national environmental legislation of several nations was streamlined and strengthened.

***

Brazil had gradually accumulated a disparate collection of pro-tected natural areas, but it remained without a systematic approach to conservation during the early 1970s (see figure 2.1, below). Miller tried to draw it into the regional project in 1970 and 1971, and although the state of São Paulo surveyed state-held natural areas with technical advisors from the project, the Brazilian federal gov-ernment seemed little interested;[77] it feared participation in multi-national initiatives might threaten its sovereignty in its lightly settled frontier areas.[78] As more countries were drawn into the project, Brazil's lack of participation weighed heavily on the project's staff; no program of biological conservation for South America could be wholly successful without Brazil's participation, whatever its achieve-ments elsewhere.

Miller's frustration was most acute in connection with Brazilian Amazonia. The interest of early conservationists in large mammals and other spectacular fauna had not led them to prize the tropical rainforests, which were relatively poor in such animals, but as esti-mates of the percentage of the world's species found in the tropical forests rose, so did the importance scientists and conservationists accorded the biome.[79] The rainforests were also among the world's least protected biomes in the 1960s, and those of South America, especially those of Amazonia, were no exception.[80] Although some protected areas on the periphery of the basin had been established in the late 1960s and early 1970s, many in connection with the Regional Wildlands Project (figure 1.1, table 1.1), the Brazilian heart of the forest remained without protected areas or a coherent conser-vation plan; it was the largest geographical gap in South American nature protection, and Miller and his associates were anxious to fill what he called the "hole in the doughnut."[81]

Miller's comprehensive, development-related approach seemed ideal for Amazonia. The region was so vast, and past human assaults on it had been so minor and intermittent, that most of the rainforest

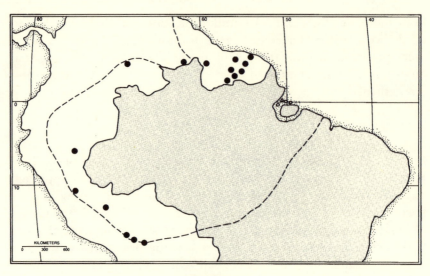

FIGURE 1.1
Protected Natural Areas in Non-Brazilian Amazonia, 1973

was still undisturbed at the beginning of the 1970s. It would therefore be possible to plan in the comprehensive fashion Miller felt was
optimal.

Moreover, Amazonia had long been the object of regional planning efforts, which Miller saw as the ideal vehicle for biological conservation. After the Second World War, the federal government
began its efforts to overcome the isolation and poverty that had characterized Amazonia since the collapse of the rubber boom in the
early twentieth century.[82] Although only a modest amount of federal
money was allocated to Amazonia in the first postwar decade, the
institutions of regional development were gradually put in place in
those years. The Credit Bank of Amazonia was established and given
a mandate to support development projects. A regional development
authority, SPVEA, was set up with headquarters in Belém.

In the late 1950s, Amazon development became a part of President
Kubitschek's ambitious plans. New federal highways linked
Amazonia to the rest of Brazil for the first time. The federal government sponsored a mix of programs to improve the region's health
and education facilities, communication network, and electric grid.
More federal credit was made available for agriculture, and farms
and ranches began to dot the southern and eastern margins of the
region by the end of the 1950s.[83] Under federal guidance, the pace of

TABLE 1.1

Protected Areas (10,000 Hectares or Larger) Established in Amazonia by 1973

Country	Unit	Date Established	Size in Hectares (× 1000)
Bolivia	Bella Vista National Park	1946	90
	Isiboro Secure National Park	1965	1,100
	Ulla Ulla Wildlife Reserve	1972	240
Colombia	El Tuparro Faunal Reserve	1970	290
Guyana	Kaieteur National Park	1929	12
Peru	Tingo Maria National Park	1965	18
	Pacaya-Samiria National Reserve	1972	1,388
	Manu National Park	1973	1,533
Surinam	Eilerts de Haan Gebergte Nature Reserve	1966	220
	Raleighvallen-Voltzberg Nature Reserve	1966	56
	Tafelberg Nature Reserve	1966	140
	Wia Wia Nature Reserve	1966	36
	Coppename Nature Reserve	1966	10
	Brownsberg Nature Reserve	1969	11
	Sipaliwini Nature Reserve	1972	100
Venezuela	Canaima National Park	1962	3,000

Source: Wetterberg et al., "Conservation Progress," p. 8.

natural resource exploitation in Amazonia quickened in the 1950s. In Amapá territory, Brazilian business interests joined with Bethlehem Steel in developing an enormous manganese-mining complex. Tin mining began in Rondônia and gold production throughout Amazonia steadily increased. When Brasília became the nation's capital in 1960, Amazonia seemed even less remote and its development seemed an even more important national concern.

The military formulated its own prescriptions for Amazon development when it came to power.[84] A new regional agency, the Superintendency for Amazon Development (SUDAM) was created and ordered to draw up a new five-year plan for the region. The federal government enlisted the aid of the U.S. Air Force in the Radar Amazonia or RADAM project, an extensive aerial survey to map the region's topography, geology, soils, and mineral deposits for the first time. In accord with the new government's preference for managed development by private capital, new fiscal incentives for private investment in Amazonia were instituted. Roberto Campos, the first architect of development policy under the generals, persuaded American businessmen to invest in Amazonia, and in 1967, Daniel

Ludwig, the American shipping magnate, committed to the Jari Project, which would produce vast amounts of wood and pulp for world markets. In that same year, the discovery of the Serra dos Carajás iron deposits allowed for collaboration with foreign capital on another giant exporting project.

Then, in 1970, a new initiative with the potential to eclipse all former ones was instituted: President Médici announced the ambitious Program of National Integration (PIN).[85] The spine of the plan would be a network of roads, the most important being the Transamazon Highway crossing Amazonia from the arid Northeast to Peru in the far west. Large colonies, called Integrated Colonization Projects, or PICs, would be developed along the highway. Colonists would be offered free land, credit at attractive rates, agricultural advice, and guaranteed access to markets. Towns and small cities providing the services a developing area would need would be be placed at regular intervals along the highway. Thirty percent of all federal funds earmarked for Amazonia between 1971 and 1974 would go to the PIN program, which was to provide farms for 100,000 families within five years, and perhaps for a million within ten.

The road building associated with the PIN program proceeded according to schedule in the early 1970s. The Transamazon Highway was opened as far west as Itaituba in 1972 and the long stretch between Itaituba and Humaitá was completed in 1974. Colonies along the highway started taking shape, and in 1972, the program, scheduled to run to 1975, was extended to 1978.[86] Work on the Northern Perimeter Highway, a second great east-west road through Amazonia and another spine of colonization, was begun in 1973.

Amazon planning, especially PIN, was not the kind of vehicle for conservation Miller had in mind. The compatibility of conservation and development assumed that the latter would be based on a sensitivity to the innate biological and physical potential of the region. Development would be focused on those areas that had the greatest potential for agriculture, resource extraction, or other wealth-producing activities. Conservation would then protect the interstices, offering a range of environmental services that would complement the development efforts and make it a net plus in the eyes of regional planners.

Thus, while Brazil's new environmentally sensitive attitude following Stockholm was an encouraging sign, there was little of substance to show for it in Amazonia, where planning provided little purchase for conservation. Given the indifference of the Brazilian government to Miller's previous overtures, and the turn development in Amazonia had taken with the PIN program, the near future threatened to do what four centuries of European presence had failed to do: substantially alter the region, perhaps destroying the rainforest that dominated it.

Prospects for Amazon conservation changed in 1974: the PIN program was abandoned. The National Institute of Colonization and Agrarian Reform's (INCRA's) settlements had fared poorly after 1970: the agency had settled fewer than 6,000 families by 1974.[87] Many of those who did come reverted to subsistence agriculture, drifted to the cities, or left the region entirely. The program suffered from inadequate supplies, bad professional advice, delays in land titling, and inadequate access to markets and credit, but the main cause of failure seemed to lie deeper than operational shortcomings.

As an expression of the logic of conventional development, PIN seemed flawless. A developing nation's agricultural sector was to hold surplus populations until the other sectors of the economy were ready to absorb them. It was to provide ample, inexpensive, and increasingly high-quality food for a rapidly increasing urban population. Eventually the rural work force would have to become a source of effective demand for the products of the industrial sector.[88] Private forces in agriculture were too inefficient and undercapitalized to accomplish these goals, however, so government had to take a hand.[89] Brazil was fortunate; it had vast, fresh Amazonia, where it could build new agricultural regions, create a class of prosperous farmers, and quickly raise agricultural production.

Yet on an ecological level, PIN, like much of conventional development theory, seemed lacking. The PIN program was established in ignorance of Amazonia's development possibilities, but rather than restrain planners, the ignorance had exactly the opposite effect: it allowed them to fall back on the vague myths of soil fertility and only the most tentative soil surveys. ECLA, from which so much Brazilian planning doctrine was derived, did not stress caution. Rather it emphasized action and placed great stock in the trial-and-error learning that came from implementation.[90] Such was the era's faith in technology and the capacity of public planning that it was assumed any unforeseen problems could be overcome as they arose. Nor did the Brazilian geopolitical tradition stress caution; Humboldt had once speculated that Amazonia would become "the granary of the world," and Brazilian nationalists assumed such a future was only a matter of time and planning. Physical conditions had defeated past settlement efforts in Amazonia, but such conditions were part of the "tyranny of geography" that modern technology had broken.[91]

By 1974 the ignorance of Amazonia upon which the program had been founded was being dispelled by new data, much produced by the RADAM project, and the emerging picture was of isolated patches of arable land surrounded by vast areas with little potential for commercial agriculture. It became clear that a uniformly settled and prosperous Amazonia was an ill-founded dream. The publication of RADAM soil data for Amapá and northern Pará, showing how poor were the soils of the region, produced immediate disillusionment with plans for the Northern Perimeter Highway.[92] Scientific work in the early 1970s added to the disillusionment by resolving the contradiction between the apparently poor soils and the luxuriance of the rainforest: The trees of the forest recycled nutrients from dead organic litter on the forest floor through the action of mycorrhizal fungi. The cycle excluded the soil. Subsequent analysis indicated that 90 percent of the soils of Amazonia were deficient in nitrogen and phosphorus, and more than 75 percent were deficient in potassium. A like percentage contained toxic levels of aluminum and calcium, and sulphur and magnesium deficiencies were present in more than half the region's soils.[93] Moreover, the poorest soils were in the uplands, where road-based PIN concentrated most of its settlement efforts.[94]

While RADAM data was disproving the myth of ubiquitous soil fertility, the pace of mineral discoveries in the basin increased (table 1.2). These discoveries coincided with the increasing importance primary resources were assuming in the calculations of economic planners around the world. Whereas previous decades had assumed that overabundance of natural resources would characterize the future world economy, a steep rise in the price of several metals in the early 1970s was taken as a sign that an era of resource scarcity was ahead. Amazonia took on the appearance of an archipelago of development opportunities based on metals such as iron, gold, tin, magnesium, and bauxite set in a matrix of very limited agricultural potential. The mystique of the conquest of Amazonia lingered on in the popular imagination, but those who were directing the economy now knew better.[95] Rather than lead Brazil to greatness, the region was better suited for the prosaic role of generating foreign exchange and fueling the industries of the South, the real engine of Brazil's recent rise.

TABLE 1.2
Major Resource Discoveries in Amazonia to 1973

Year	Locale	State or Territory	Resource	Discoverer
1612	Gurupi	Pará	Gold	Prospectors
1855	Calçoene	Amapá	Gold	Prospectors
1912	Maú-Tacutú	Roraima	Diamonds	Prospectors
1915	Upper Solimões	Amazonas	Lignite	Unidentified
1937	Araguaia-Tocantins	Pará	Diamonds	Prospectors
	Tepenqúem	Roraima	Diamonds	Prospectors
1941	Serra do Navio	Amapá	Manganese	Mario Cruz/ Bethlehem Steel
1952	Unspecified	Rondônia	Tin	Prospectors
1955	Middle Amazon	Pará/Amazonas	Sodium chloride	PETROBRAS
	Nova Olinda	Amazonas	Oil/gas	PETROBRAS
1958	Middle Tapájos	Pará	Gold	Prospectors
1963	Tropas	Pará	Tin	Prospectors
1966	Sereno	Pará	Manganese	Union Carbide
	Trombetas	Pará/Amazonas	Bauxite	ALCAN
1967	Carajás	Pará	Iron	U.S. Steel
	Buritirama	Pará	Manganese	U.S. Steel
1968	Morro do Felipe	Amapá	Kaolin	Ludwig group
1969	Maraconái	Pará	Titanium	Union Carbide
	Maicuru	Pará	Titanium	U.S. Steel
1970	Velho Guilherme	Pará	Tin	IDESP/ PROMIX
	Mocambo	Pará	Tin	PROMIX
	Paragominas	Pará	Bauxite	Rio Tinto Zinc
	Capim	Pará	Kaolin	CPRM/Mendes Júnior
1971	Carajás	Pará	Manganese	AMZA[1]
	Quatipuru	Pará	Chrome	DOCEGEO[1]
1972	Jabuti	Pará	Bauxite	DOCEGEO
	Almeirim	Pará	Bauxite	DOCEGEO
1973	Onça-Puma	Pará	Nickel	INCO

[1]Subsidiary of the Rio Doce Valley Company (CVRD)
Source: Santos, *Amazônia, Potencial Mineral,* pp. 12–13.

The change in planning perspective was embodied in the Second Amazon Development Plan, PDAM II, unveiled in 1974 and scheduled to run from 1975 to 1979. Its centerpiece was the Polamazonia program, which comprised investment plans for fifteen "development poles," areas of Amazonia with special economic potential (figure 1.2).[96] In one, Serra dos Carajás, the largest iron mine in the world would be developed. An enormous new hydroelectric dam would supply electricity to the mine, and the longest railroad constructed in modern times would carry its ore to new export facilities near São Luis in Maranhão. A development pole in Amapá would be

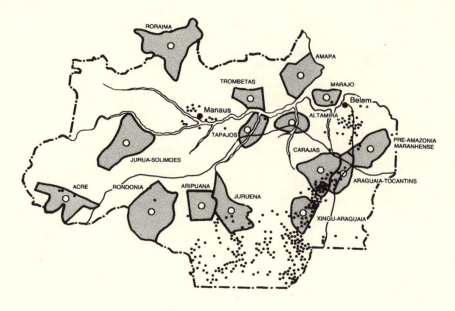

FIGURE 1.2
Amazon Development Poles and Subsidized Livestock Operations. Adapted
from Kleinpenning, "Evaluation of the Brazilian Policy." Small dots show
location of subsidized ranches. Hatched areas are development poles.

based on the already-extant manganese mines in the territory. The
large bauxite deposits along the Rio Trombetas would be the base
resource of another pole, while one in the far northern territory of
Roraima would be based on gold deposits. Large-scale ranching,
plantation agriculture, and wood harvesting would play an important role in many of the poles.

The transition from PIN to Polamazonia seemed like a triumph of
the rational: plans based on ignorance of nature and the distribution
of natural resources were replaced by those based on knowledge.
With that triumph, conservation appeared compatible with state-
directed development. The new, more archipelagic view of Amazonia's development opportunities devalued the interstices, those
vast areas where the soils were poor and no valuable minerals were
found. Leaving many of them in a natural state would have little
impact on the national or regional economy and, in fact, seemed like
a reasonable complement to the development planned for the poles.
Polamazonia's planners apparently saw it the same way: the
Polamazonia decree of 1974 stated that conservation should be con-

sidered a key part of development and that the "designation of lands for forest and biological reserves [and] national parks" should be part of the Polamazonia program.[97]

While the shift in planning emphasis was taking place, the Brazilian government requested the FAO's help to modernize its forest industry. The FAO, which had been intermittently active in Brazilian forestry since the early 1950s, consented. The project, the Forest Development and Research Project (PRODEPEF), would assess Brazil's forest industry, develop commercial uses for unused tree species, and conduct a forest inventory. The FAO, however, sensitized to the new international mood by the Stockholm Conference, recommended that an assessment of Brazil's nature preservation needs be included in the program. Brazil consented and the FAO asked Miller, then completing the Regional Wildlands Project, to oversee the assessment. Miller accepted, signaling the beginning of systematic planning for biological conservation in Brazilian Amazonia.

CHAPTER 2

Tracing the Landscape of Biological Value

Gary Wetterberg, who was selected to do the actual PRODEPEF field work in Brazil, had much experience in South American conservation and a long exposure to Miller's ideas. He had met Miller in 1968, while serving as a Peace Corps volunteer in a Chilean national park, and the careers of the two remained intertwined for years afterward. When Wetterberg returned to the United States to complete a doctorate, Miller served on his dissertation committee. Later, Wetterberg was drawn into the Regional Wildlands Project and developed a set of national environmental codes for Colombia under Miller's direction. During the long association, Wetterberg became imbued with Miller's approach and Miller formed a high opinion of Wetterberg's skills as a conservation planner.[1] Wetterberg joined the PRODEPEF project as a consultant in early 1975, and Miller arranged for him to be stationed at Brazil's National Institute of Amazon Research (INPA) in Manaus. Wetterberg's specific charge was to evaluate the overall needs of Brazilian conservation, with particular emphasis on Amazonia, and produce a detailed set of recommendations on which a concrete conservation program could be based.

When Wetterberg arrived at INPA in May 1975, he understood the significance of his task. A conservation program for Brazilian Amazonia would fill the last great geographical gap in South American nature protection, capping a decade of international conservation work.[2] He also appreciated its uniqueness. Miller had stressed how, ideally, plans for biological conservation should be sketched onto a landscape before human occupation reduced freedom of action, but it was already too late in most areas of the world; conservationists normally had to choose from among a few policy options and among the few natural areas that remained on a settled landscape. Amazonia, however, had been so little altered that it presented a nearly clean slate of conservation opportunities; here ambitious, systematic conservation principles could be applied to a major bioregion, an opportunity Miller never had, and perhaps no one but Wetterberg ever would.

Wetterberg also appreciated the strategic advantages of the scientific, systematic conservation Miller advocated.[3] The fate of the first major conservation initiative in Amazonia, a group of forest reserves established by President Quadros in 1961, offered a lesson (figure 2.1). The idea of the reserves was a whim, as were many of Quadros's ideas, and the task of identifying suitable areas caught SPVEA unaware. Uncertain of the intended purpose of the reserves, the agency arbitrarily made river accessibility the key selection criterion.[4] After the formal establishment of the reserves, no administrative machinery was set up for them. Undemarcated, unmanaged, and without any clear purpose, they were invaded by *posseiros* (squatters) and subjected to speculative schemes. By the time Wetterberg arrived in Brazil, there was little outside the statute books to show they existed at all.

The recent history of the Brazilian national park system also underscored the point in Wetterberg's mind. He had discussed Brazil's few extant national parks with Alceo Magnanini, then director of the IBDF's National Parks Department (DN), at the Second World Conference on National Parks in 1972, and had been struck by the weakness of the director's position.[5] Magnanini had inherited no overall strategy for managing or expanding the park system, nor had he been able to forge a clear set of norms on which a policy could be based. Although Wetterberg thought Magnanini was a competent administrator, his lack of a strategy meant he was constantly forced to, in Wetterberg's words, "deal with the cards that had been dealt him; he was always reacting."

A new national park had been added to the system in 1971 and another in 1972, but they were the result of local initiatives behind which the right political coalitions had accumulated.

The first major protected natural area in Amazonia, a million-hectare national park on the banks of the Tapajós River in eastern Pará, was established by presidential decree in 1974, but the event was anomalous. The park's location and shape had been decided by regional planners with no input from conservationists, and it was unconnected to any wider conservation plans. When Wetterberg

FIG 2.1
Brazilian National Parks, Biological Reserves, and Forest Reserves, 1961.
Triangles indicate forest reserves.

arrived in Brazil, he quickly deduced that this passivity and lack of direction still characterized the IBDF's conservation efforts, and that changing this was essential; whatever plan he developed would have to "permit those public agencies responsible for nature conservation to gain an offensive position."[6] This would require a consistent set of principles that focused departmental energies on clear, practical goals.

Those principles would also have to align conservation policy with the dominant values of the administration as a whole. The cast of the administration established by the military was technical and professional. The second plan for Amazonia (PDAM II) had accepted the need for biological conservation, but insisted such conservation be systematic and, according to Wetterberg, based on "solid biological criteria."[7] Any conservation plan that appeared capricious or based on specious, facile arguments would be out of alignment with both the dominant sentiments of the federal government and the norms to which it expected future planning for Amazonia to conform. Thus the only politically viable approach seemed to be the systematic, comprehensive one Miller advocated and Wetterberg inherently preferred.

* * *

Such an approach required a firm base in scientific knowledge. Without one, it would be impossible to defend choices or bring professionalism fully into play. Comparatively little scientific work had been done on the world's tropical rainforests, however. Most were located in poor nations with only modest scientific capacities. The forests were inhospitable and frequently inaccessible, and funding for research in them was difficult to obtain. Studying the forest canopy, where much of the insect and other animal life was concentrated, was especially difficult. Ignorance about the rainforest had recently begun giving way before scientific initiatives like the UN's Man and Biosphere Program, but the unknown was still vast.

Of the world's great equatorial rainforests, that of Amazonia was the least known. Its vastness and continental location made it the least accessible of the major rainforests. Research in Africa and Southeast Asia benefitted from colonial rule during Europe's great age of scientific exploration, but that in Amazonia did not. After the breakup of the empires, the scientific interests of the metropolitan powers tended to remain focused on their former colonies, so except for the Guianas, Amazonia continued to be left out. New knowledge had begun to accumulate here too as a result of INPA's research efforts and the UNESCO-sponsored Flora Neotropica project, but so much remained unknown that Prance discovered twenty-two new species in the Chrysobalanaceae family in Amazonia in the early 1970s, and even what turned out to be common trees in the Manaus region were still being discovered when Wetterberg arrived. One conservationist wrote with casual certainty that most of the species in Amazonia had never been seen by a scientist.[8] This meant that one of Wetterberg's most important and formidable tasks was forging the little scientific knowledge available into a firm base for Amazon conservation policy.

For Wetterberg, the first specific problem arising from this scientific ignorance, or what Lovejoy called "unplumbed biology," was the lack of regional differentiation. Tree species were difficult to dif-

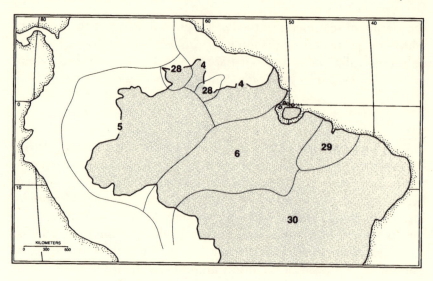

FIGURE 2.2
Biogeographic Subdivisions of Amazonia According to Udvardy. Adapted from
Wetterberg et al., "Conservation Progress"

ferentiate through casual observation, and the morphology of the
forest was strikingly uniform. Miller wrote that to most observers,
Amazonia was a "giant sea of homogeneous green jungle."[9] Scientists were beginning to understand that this was not so; they knew
that rainforest species composition could vary greatly from one
locale to another, but there had been little systematization of this
knowledge. The lack of information might not hinder conservation
planning in Ecuador or Bolivia, which had relatively little rainforest
within their boundaries, but since almost half of the basin's forests
were within Brazil, finding a convincing set of regions was essential
for systematic representation.[10]

Extant biogeographies were of little use. The new global biogeographies were too general. Udvardy's recently completed scheme,
for example, placed most of Brazilian Amazonia into two vast
provinces (figure 2.2), hardly an improvement on the popular view
of the region as homogeneous green jungle; if anything, it seemed to
support that view. The biogeography the IUCN adopted in 1974 was
worse: it placed most of Brazilian Amazonia in one province.
Schemes developed specifically for Amazonia were too uncertain.
Ducke and Black had delineated seven rainforest regions in

Amazonia in 1953 and 1954, but their scheme was based on very limited sampling and was too tentative to bear the weight of policy. Rizzini divided the region into eight subregions in 1963, but his scheme, which differed greatly from Ducke and Black's, was also based on very limited field sampling.[11] The large differences between the two schemes discredited both of them and pointed out how much more work had to be done. Holdridge's "life zone" scheme, which Miller had used and advocated, was useless in Amazonia because its differentiations relied on more extreme variations in climate and elevation than were present.

Fortunately, current scientific work held promise. Ghillean Prance, a plant taxonomist, was developing a new phytogeography of Amazonia. His scheme, which used the distribution of eight frequently occurring plant species, divided Amazonia into eight regions (figure 2.3).[12] Prance's scheme was backed by more evidence than any of the older ones—he had spent years collecting Amazon flora and examining herbarium collections—but since it was generally similar to Ducke and Black's scheme, it drew authority from the convergence. After its publication, it quickly became the standard phytogeography of Amazonia.

Prance was the director of INPA's graduate program when Wetterberg arrived in Manaus, and Wetterberg quickly learned about Prance's work. Prance was sensitive to the conservation implications of his work (as were others—it had been supported by the World Wildlife Fund [WWF]) and argued that unless a portion of each region was put under public protection before development altered it, a unique component of Amazon biota would be lost. Wetterberg realized that Prance's scheme, unlike earlier Amazon biogeographies, had the scientific credentials necessary to dispel the idea that Amazonia was a homogeneous green jungle. Unlike Udvardy's scheme, it also set out enough regions to serve an ambitious program. Wetterberg would therefore propose Prance's phytogeography as the scientific core of Amazon conservation policy.[13]

A focus on Amazonia's upland rainforests was a logical outgrowth of this choice; Prance's scheme was based on species from these forests, so it was only a useful guide if conservation policy focused on them. Wetterberg also felt this decision was scientifically justifiable and provident. Recent surveys showed these upland forests comprised approximately 90 percent of the forests of Amazonia, and research was beginning to reveal their full complexity, diversity, and

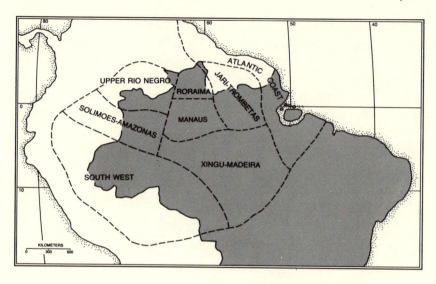

FIGURE 2.3
Phytogeographic Subdivisions of Amazonia According to Prance. Adapted from
Wetterberg et al., "Conservation Progress"

degree of endemism.[14] The other major forest types in Amazonia—
the inundated and semi-inundated forests of the wetlands, with their
lower species diversity and composition that changed little from one
area to another—could be adequately represented in relatively few,
small reserves.

Once the decision to use Prance's scheme was made, the specific
areas most worthy of protection—those whose diversity or other
characteristics gave them a special biological value—had to be
identified. In principle, such a task could arise in connection with any
region-based conservation program, but human activity so limited
the choices in most areas of the world that it almost never arose in
practice. Amazonia was different; because so much of the region's
biota remained undisturbed, this was a pressing task with few fore-
closed options. The selection criteria had to be solid if they were to
pass muster at higher levels of government, but little was known
about any discrete parts of Amazonia, except for those few small
places where research had been carried out. Gathering such information would be a mammoth, time-consuming task, and, as Wetterberg
wrote, "the luxury of extensive or detailed studies of entire floras
and faunas" was out of the question.[15] Reprising the situation later,

Thomas Lovejoy observed that "some sort of shortcut was needed: some emerging biogeographic pattern on which conservation planning [could] depend."[16]

Before leaving the United States, Wetterberg had sought advice on his task from several conservationists and tropical biologists, including Lovejoy, program director of the World Wildlife Fund-US, who suggested that the recently coalesced Pleistocene Refuge Theory might be useful. Conventional scientific wisdom up to the late 1960s held that the equatorial rainforests were among the world's oldest and most stable bioregions. The Pleistocene glacial periods, which had profoundly altered the biogeography of the temperate regions, were thought to have little affected the equatorial regions except for changes in sea levels. Biologists assumed the great species diversity of the rainforest was due to this stability—that it had permitted the undisturbed evolution of a great many specialized organisms.[17]

Haffer, in 1969, deduced from bird species distribution in Amazonia that the region had been much drier during the late Pleistocene.[18] This, he argued, had caused savannas and dry woodlands to take over most of the area while the forest fragmented and survived only in the wettest parts of the basin. Other biologists found evidence for a fragmented and diminished Pleistocene rainforest in the distribution of other taxa. Vanzolini identified several former forest islands from his work on lizards, and Prance identified several from the distribution of plant species. The argument from species distribution was tentatively corroborated by pollen core analysis.[19]

During the drier epoch, rainforest species would have fragmented into separate populations as the forest contracted and fragmented. Allopatric speciation—that caused when a formerly unified breeding population is split—would have then taken place in the forest islands, producing a large number of new species. With the return of a wetter climate at the end of the Pleistocene and the expansion and eventual fusion of the forests, individual forest species that had evolved in the fragments would have expanded their ranges at different rates, depending on their intrinsic dispersal capacities. The more rapid dispersers would have reestablished contact with their former cospecifics. Slower dispersers might not yet have reclaimed all their former ranges.

Haffer saw Pleistocene Refuge Theory as having strong conservation implications.[20] He argued that only the sites of the former forest fragments were certain to contain the full richness of the Tertiary forests, so their preservation would the surest way of preserving maximum species diversity in a region where so little was known about individual species distribution. It also seemed like the most efficient way to proceed for a program with deadlines and limited resources. As Myers summarized the argument, protecting these species-rich refuges "could yield a greater return for the conservation dollar than setting aside much larger areas elsewhere."[21] Wetterberg concluded that refuge theory could serve as the guide he needed to the high-value areas within Prance's phytogeographic regions.

All the Pleistocene forest islands were large, however, and some were enormous. (Smaller fragments might have existed, but dispersal dynamics would have erased all trace of them since the return of a wetter climate.) One occupied most of the Brazilian state of Rondônia, and another stretched westward from Belém for hundreds of kilometers. Wetterberg knew the practical restraints on Amazon conservation made these areas far too large to protect in their entirety, but how much less would do?

There was little in the conservation literature from which an answer could be fashioned. Conservationists had grappled with the question of reserve size for decades, and as the goals of biological conservation became more ambitious the question became more problematic. Advances in community ecology made it clear that preserving certain species required areas large enough to preserve the species on which they were dependent.[22] Preserving large predators in the wild, for example, meant setting aside areas large enough to maintain sufficient prey populations. Preserving species in symbiotic relationships with other species required that enough territory be allowed for their symbionts.

Once maintaining more abstract entities like ecosystems became a major conservation goal, the size question became even more complicated. It was easy to formulate a general answer from ecological principles: a protected area had be large enough to allow the system to perpetuate itself in all its complexity,[23] but such abstractions, even if widely agreed upon, were of little use in making decisions about actual reserve size. Was it better to set aside several small reserves or one large one of the same total area? The question lacked a scientific or even intuitive answer. Naturalists had known since the early nineteenth century that bigger reserves were likely to contain more species than small ones simply by chance,[24] but they also knew that several smaller reserves spread over a large region would likely include a greater number of habitats than a single protected area. The lack of size guidelines became a pressing matter for conservationists; when Richards asserted at the 1972 World Conference on National Parks that the problem of the minimum size of protected areas was of great practical importance few disagreed.[25]

Island Biogeography Theory offered an answer when Wetterberg needed one. The biology of islands has fascinated biologists ever since Darwin visited the Galapagos,[26] but the subject was first approached with theoretical rigor by Robert MacArthur and E.O. Wilson in 1963, and over the next several years they laid the foundations of what they called Island Biogeography Theory.[27] MacArthur and Wilson argued that, assuming a uniform habitat, small islands would have fewer species than large ones because they had fewer resources with which to sustain minimum breeding populations, and the smaller populations they did sustain would be more subject to extinction through random misfortune. MacArthur and Wilson also argued that very isolated islands would have fewer species than less isolated ones of the same size because the former were more difficult for colonizing species to reach. All other things being equal, an island's species richness would thus be a function of its size-dependent species maintenance capacity and its isolation-dependent colonization rate. Its biota would be in equilibrium when its rates of extinction and colonization were equal—although the actual species composition might vary over time. They expressed these relationships in a series of equations that, given an island's area and degree of isolation, could be solved for the expected number of species.[28]

By logical extension, the theory predicted that if the isolation of an area were to increase—for example, if a peninsula became an island through a seismic upheaval—it would now have too many species to be maintained with its now-reduced accessibility to new stock. The number of species would begin to decline, a process MacArthur and Wilson called "relaxation," and eventually a new and lower equilibrium would be reached. The same process of species reduction would occur if an island were suddenly reduced in size; it would be in a state of "superequilibrium," without the resources to support populations of all its inhabitant species.

MacArthur and Wilson saw their theory as applicable to far more than literal islands. They argued that since "insularity is a universal feature of biogeography, [and it] applies to a lesser or greater degree in all natural habitats," their work might provide the foundation for a general theory of community diversity.[29]

Field tests of MacArthur and Wilson's construct began soon after it was formulated. The species diversity of islands in the Caribbean and in the Bismarck Sea off New Guinea produced a good agreement with the theory's basic predictions with regard to island size and degree of isolation. Studies of recently isolated islands also found higher diversity than might have been expected from island size and isolation, supporting the theory's predictions with regard to super-equilibrium. Following up on MacArthur and Wilson's claims of universal applicability for their theory, scientists began testing it in different types of isolated habitats, and here too results were encouraging. The species diversity of patches of savanna woodland in the moist rainforest on New Guinea exhibited the island-like characteristics the theory predicted. Isolated mountain-top communities in the Andes seemed island-like in the relationship of their species diversity to their area and isolation from like communities. Even the aquatic communities on isolated patches of reef showed the predicted diversity.[30]

The theory implied that establishing many small reserves would be unwise because a small, isolated area would almost immediately lose those species requiring a large territory: they would not have the space to maintain breeding populations, and random extinction events would then quickly take their toll on other species.[31] Moreover, the same species would be at greatest risk in all the reserves. Therefore it was better to concentrate as much protected acreage as possible in very large reserves so as to reduce loss rates. Field work had enabled scientists to calculate historical rates of species loss from areas of a known size once they were isolated; Terborgh, for example, estimated that the island of Trinidad had lost 0.6 percent of its avifauna during its first hundred years as an island.[32] This fixing of the rate of loss meant that whereas ecological principles gave only general prescriptions for the size of protected areas, Island Biogeography Theory offered specific guidelines.

Wetterberg was vaguely aware of the theory before he took on the Brazil assignment, but Lovejoy pointed out its conservation implications and informed him of the recent field work it had inspired.[33] Once in Brazil, Wetterberg delved into the literature and realized that here was the third major prop of a scientific, systematic approach to Amazon conservation. Prance's phytogeography gave him the regions to represent. Pleistocene Refuge Theory pointed him toward the best areas to protect within those regions. Now Island Biogeography Theory gave him a guide to the size of the reserves.

* * *

Wetterberg was fortunate to have this recent bloom of scientific work to guide him, but science is seldom useful to policy makers in its pure form: it is seldom as conclusive as policy demands, and it frequently points to politically improvident actions. The science Wetterberg wished to use was no exception. One problem was with Pleistocene Refuge Theory. Scientists using different life forms had found evidence of greatly restricted distributions during the Pleistocene, findings that seemed to support refuge theory. Yet each of those life forms indicated a different pattern of refuges (figure 2.4). Working with lizards, Vanzolini found evidence of four large refuges located on the periphery of the Amazon basin—three, in fact, on the eastern slopes of the Andes. Prance's botanical evidence led him to discern fourteen refuges scattered widely throughout the basin and varying widely in size. Haffer's pattern based on bird distribution had little spatial overlap with the others.

If the forest had retreated to the few wet parts of the basin during the Pleistocene, the evidence should have pointed to the same places. The simplest explanation for the discrepancy was that the theory was wrong: the forest had not retreated and fragmented. The mass of evidence, however, seemed too substantial for it to have been wholly wrong. Two other explanations allowed for the correctness of the theory in spite of the spatial incongruity of the evidence. One was that the rainforest had fragmented during the Pleistocene, but time had erased the traces of the fragments, and the present distribution of the supposed indicator species was due to not-yet-understood ecological causes.[34] The other was that the forest fragments had existed and were reflected in present species distributions, but understanding of the distributions was still too tentative to produce a coherent picture of the forest during the Pleistocene. Such inconsistencies were common early in the development of general theory, and presumably a coherent pattern of refuges would emerge with more species distribution studies.[35]

Wetterberg could not wait for further research to clear up the uncertainty, so he decided to accept areas identified by two or more scientists as valid Pleistocene forest fragments. Wetterberg knew that

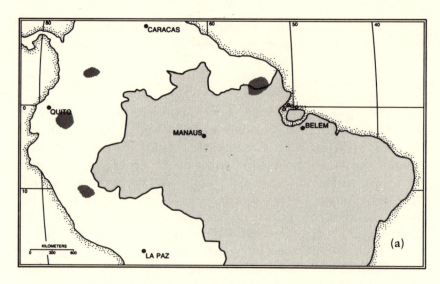

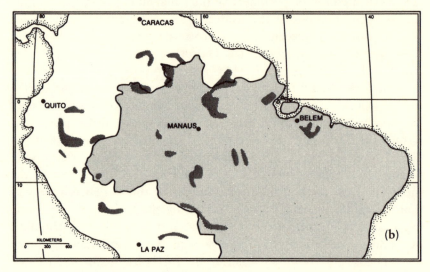

FIGURE 2.4
Postulated Pleistocene Refuges: a. Identified by Vanzolini; b. Identified by
Brown; c. Identified by Prance; d. Identified by Haffer. Adapted from
Wetterberg et al., "Analysis of Nature Conservation"

chance alone would likely cause some overlap in the patterns, but he
assumed that if the forest had been fragmented during the
Pleistocene, areas where there was already some agreement among
scientists were more likely to have been fragments than areas where
there was none. He also reasoned that while the decision may have

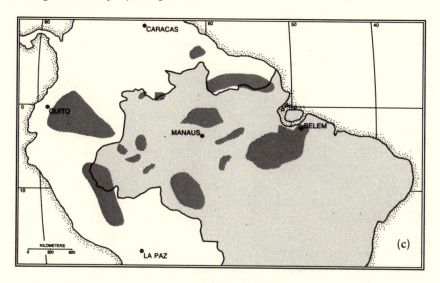

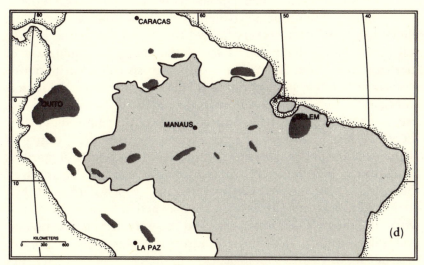

(Figure 2.4, *continued*)

been outside the bounds of strict scientific reasoning, if refuge theory was wrong or if the forest fragments were figments of incomplete data, these areas were still highly diverse parts of the rainforest, so preserving them would still advance biological conservation. In short, Wetterberg assumed he had little to lose and much to gain by using a tentative geography of Pleistocene refuges.

He next took the practical step of matching the eleven areas he assumed were Pleistocene forest fragments against the development poles of the Polamazonia program.[36] He found overlap in only three cases, and the overlap was only partial in all three. Even here, Wetterberg suspected that conflict could be avoided because only some parts of any pole would be transformed by the development program. For example, RADAM judged the high Uopiane and Pacaás Novos massifs, near the very center of the Northwest Development Pole in Rondônia, as unsuitable for almost all economic activities:[37] their elevation and rough topography made them inaccessible, poor soils made them unsuitable for agriculture, and even commercial ranching was deemed unfeasible. Likewise, the spatial requirements of bauxite extraction and processing in the Trombetas Pole in western Pará were modest, and there were no development plans whatsoever for much of the territory within the official limits of the pole. Therefore the preservation in the Pleistocene refuges, even those near areas of planned development, would involve few costs in forgone economic opportunities.

Island Biogeography Theory posed its own problems as a basis of policy. First, it had attracted vociferous criticism from the beginning; Simberloff, Abele, and others faulted the theory for failing to take full account of habitat diversity and the chance accumulation of localized flora and fauna in explaining species distribution.[38] According to Abele and Connor, this failing left the entire theoretical edifice as "simply a formalization of the observation that large areas usually contain more species than small areas."[39] Field studies by the theory's critics found less of a relationship between area, degree of isolation, and species diversity than Terborgh and other supporters of the theory had found. Lynch and Johnson asserted that much of the species loss on the Channel Islands, which Diamond had attributed to relaxation, was due to human action.[40] Armed with this work, the theory's detractors attacked its usefulness as a conservation guide, arguing that in many cases, size was a less important determinant of an area's biological worth than habitat characteristics or the presence of unique species. Conservationists, they concluded, should concentrate on saving as many diverse habitats and unique species as possible, even if this meant smaller protected areas or less total area protected within a region.[41]

Therefore while Pleistocene Refuge Theory appeared to be an immature but basically valid theory, Island Biogeography Theory's inherent capacity to advance understanding of the biological world or to produce useful conservation guidelines was still in dispute among reputable scientists. Using Pleistocene Refuge Theory required some improvising but using Island Biogeography Theory required an act of faith. Also, whereas negative consequences of embracing Refuge Theory were likely to be slight if it turned out to be incorrect, if Island Biogeography Theory was wrong about the optimal size and number of protected areas and the criteria to be used in selecting them, the consequences could be serious.

Second, while the Island Biogeography Theory's posited species-area relationship implied that bigger reserves were better than small ones (as a rough rule of thumb, each tenfold increase in area would double the number of species held in equilibrium) the theory could not say how large a reserve should be; only once it had been decided on some extrinsic criterion how many species should be protected and what were acceptable rates of species loss could the theory be employed to determine how large a protected natural area should be.

Wetterberg weighed the arguments and concluded that those in favor of Island Biogeography Theory were convincing enough to justify giving priority to the establishment of a few large reserves.[42] The decision was almost as much an act of faith as a scientific judgment, but it was buttressed by other lines of reasoning. In 1971 Richards had pointed out that large ranges and low densities of many rainforest animals meant that only large reserves would be able to maintain breeding populations. Two years later Fittkau and Klinge braced that argument when they determined that a typical hectare of upland rainforest contains 900 metric tons of plant biomass but only about 0.2 tons of animal biomass.[43] By the mid-1970s, most conservationists assumed areas that aimed at protecting whole rainforest ecosystems would have to be very large.

The question of acceptable rate of loss ultimately turned on the nature of the future and on the present's responsibility to it. While Island Biogeography Theory did not directly address these questions, its implication that an isolated reserve would become biologically impoverished over time, and its calculation of rates of loss in centuries and millennia, led conservationists to think of the far future, and to think of it as a place where the negative consequences of present actions with regard to the globe's biological endowment would accumulate.[44] There was thus a strong synchrony between the new vision of the future that grew up with the ecological critique and the implicit dictates of Island Biogeography Theory; both forced the long term into the pale of conservation concern.

The literature of Island Biogeography Theory also supplied a use-

ful specific number. Terborgh had calculated from his work on rainforest birds of the neotropics that a forest patch of 259,000 hectares
would lose no more than 1 percent of its bird species per century.[45]
Wetterberg knew of no work on the range of large rainforest mammals, but he inferred from work done on wolves, grizzly bears, and
mountain lions in North America that an area of this size was probably sufficient to maintain breeding populations of large rainforest
fauna such as jaguars, as well as the bird populations on which
Terborgh had made his estimates.[46] Wetterberg also intuitively felt
that Terborgh's rate, which measured appreciable species loss in centuries, was a sufficiently provident basis for policy, and he understood that just the appearance of the number in the scientific literature made it a firm peg on which to hang a policy decision.[47]

He decided to propose 259,000 hectares as the minimum necessary
size for a reserve that would represent a major forest region. Since
Island Biogeography Theory implied that a protected area would better retain its species if the hospitality of its immediate surroundings
was maintained, and recent experience in other Latin American countries had shown the value of a buffer around parks and reserves to
protect them from squatters,[48] he also decided to propose a ten-kilo-
meter protective strip around this 259,000-hectare core area, which
brought the total minimum area to be protected to approximately
500,000 hectares.[49] Wetterberg argued that while this would be a
very large area to set aside in other parts of the world, in Amazonia
there was still room and time to preserve nature on such a scale.

Two other problems arose once the decision was made to use
Island Biogeography Theory as a key policy prop. First, one of points
raised by the theory's critics was an undeniable fact, if not necessarily a damning criticism. It had become axiomatic that samples of all
important biogeographic regions and biological communities should
be placed under public protection, but turning this into operating
principles was difficult.[50] At the level of the species and community,
the natural world seemed more characterized by gradation than by
abrupt breaks, so a conservation planner faced the question of how
many reserves were needed to do justice to variation within a region.
The question was acute in Amazonia, where variation was usually
subtle and so little was known about changes in species composition
over space, but Island Biogeography Theory could not help deal with
it; the logical edifice rested on the assumption of uniform conditions.
Without any guidance from the theory or other elements of the con-

servation literature,[51] Wetterberg decided to propose two representative reserves for each of Prance's regions. He reasoned that a second large reserve, distant from the first, would provide a hedge against chance biological misfortune, as well as protect additional species. He also judged two large reserves politically within reach, while more might not be.[52]

Second, even among Island Biogeography Theory's strongest proponents there was little disagreement on the need to preserve the smaller, biologically special areas so valued by the theory's detractors. Terborgh, who had done much to promote Island Biogeography Theory as a basis for conservation policy, argued that special vegetation communities like bogs, oases, and coastal habitats; areas of special faunal importance like turtle nesting beaches, bird migration funnels, rookeries; and rare, highly localized plants had to be protected in small, sometimes actively managed reserves.[53] Island Biogeography Theory, with its stress on uniform habitat and cosmopolitan species, could provide little insight into how policy for such areas should be formulated. A set of guidelines based on other principles was needed, but there was none in the scientific or conservation literature. Prescriptions for such areas were inevitably individualistic, based on unique biological characteristics, and not useful in fashioning a policy for a whole class of areas a priori. Wetterberg was forced to accommodate the special areas in an intuitive fashion. He decided to propose allowing twenty of these smaller reserves, averaging 100,000 hectares, to protect the important places neither Island Biogeography Theory nor his emphasis on representing the dominant ecosystems of the regions had led him to.

With these decisions Wetterberg had fashioned science into a coherent approach to Amazon conservation squarely within the mainstream of wider conservation thought, but there were two further problems. The first was a logical outgrowth of the science he had used: two of Prance's phytogeographic regions, Jari-Trombetas and Roraima, contained no Pleistocene refuges, and only two of the eight regions had two or more. Since preserving the best representatives of regional ecosystems—not preserving Pleistocene refuges, per se—was the mainspring of Wetterberg's approach, additional selection criteria had to be found for six of Prance's regions.[54]

The second sprang from the fact that Amazonia was not a blank slate from a conservation perspective. One large area, the recently established Amazonia National Park, and several smaller areas, mostly turtle nesting sites along the tributaries of the Amazon River, were already under the protection of the Brazilian forestry institute. There were also the forest reserves President Quadros had established almost fifteen years earlier. Ignored by the forest code of 1967, they were in an administrative limbo, but they did exist on paper. In addition, many proposals for protecting areas of Amazonia had been advanced over the years. The RADAM program had identified areas it deemed appropriate for national parks on its maps of Amazonia. Some proposals had been advanced by individual scientists or had grown out of past surveys of Brazil's conservation needs.

The biological value of many of the areas in question was slight or uncertain, and Wetterberg was led to few of them by his own selection criteria. Amazonia National Park, for example, owed little to ecological values. INCRA, when asked to cooperate with the IBDF in the establishment of the park, decided that it could spare a million hectares from projects in the Itaituba region, so that would be the size of the park. Once this was determined, the park's boundaries were drawn to keep it away from the Transamazon Highway and the Tapajós River, and therefore out of the way of regional economic development.[55] Preservation also tended to be a residual category for RADAM. Although some of the smaller sites it recommended preserving had important biological features, the larger areas were generally picked because they were remote from development projects and unsuited for agriculture. The biological reasons RADAM gave for its larger selections were usually post hoc.[56]

If Wetterberg made allowances for these areas, their mediocrity and ragtag eclecticism would undercut the rigor of his approach, debasing it in the eyes of his primary clients, the military and technocratic elite, and clouding the clear policy trajectory he hoped to establish. On the other hand, it was unwise to ignore them. The IBDF was committed to Amazonia National Park. RADAM was a favored, high-priority project. Some of the proposals enjoyed the sponsorship of prominent scientists or conservationists. Ignoring them would thus risk alienating those whose cooperation might be crucial in implementing his proposals. Furthermore, while many of the proposals had only slight scientific justification, some were more solid, and taken together they did represent a wide range of conservation thought and values. Excluding them from his planning would be at least arrogant.

Wetterberg solved both problems with a priority system. Eleven areas identified as Pleistocene forest fragments by two or more scientists would get top priority for protected status. Five additional areas identified as likely fragments by only one scientist, but suspected of exceptional biological value on the basis of other evidence, were assigned second priority. Third priority went to the old forest reserves and to all areas proposed for protection by a credible source. Twenty-three areas were placed in this category, although Wetterberg intended it to be an open-ended group to which new proposals could be added as they were formulated. Wetterberg stressed that second- or third-priority status did not mean innate inferiority, but rather that an area did not pass muster on the criteria he thought should be at the heart of conservation policy for the region.[57]

The priority system allowed Wetterberg to emphasize the primacy of science in a systematic approach to conservation while at the same time circumventing the practical limits of the approach: the identification of an insufficient number of areas to protect, the alienation of elements of the conservation and scientific communities, and the exclusion of alternative but perhaps valid selection criteria. Combined, the three priority groups contained at least three and as many as eleven areas in each of Prance's regions (table 2.1, figure 2.5). This would mean a surplus to choose from. If Wetterberg's proposal ever led to the actual selection of reserves, it would give play to the pragmatism and flexibility Miller had insisted were necessary in building a successful conservation program.[58]

Wetterberg felt he could not concentrate exclusively on protected natural areas, however; embedding them in a broader regional plan for conservation seemed essential. Miller's argument that conservation would be successful only if its compass included areas beyond parks and reserves had become part of prevailing conservation doctrine in Latin America.[59] Wetterberg thought such measures especially important in Amazonia for several reasons. First, a large number of Amazon species had limited ranges, so any area of the forest was likely to contain a number of species found there and nowhere else.[60] Therefore even the most extensive set of protected areas could not, by itself, prevent a large number of extinctions as the region became developed.

Second, Island Biogeography Theory implied that outside conditions had a great bearing on the capacity of parks and reserves to maintain the species they protected. If the surrounding area became very dissimilar to the reserve, the latter would become the equivalent of a newly isolated island. The process of relaxation would set in and would continue until a new, lower equilibrium and a less diverse

TABLE 2.1
Priority Conservation Areas by Phytogeographic Region

Phytogeographic Region	First Priority Areas	Second Priority Areas	State, Territory or Country	Number of Third Priority Areas
Atlantic Coast	Bacia do Capim		Pará	8
	Oiapoque		Amapá	
		Cabo Orange	Amapá	
		Marabá	Pará	
Jari-Trombetas	Guiana Shield		Surinam/French Guyana	8
Xingu-Madeira	Ponta do Flechal		Pará/Mato Grosso/	
			Amazonas	6
	Altamira		Pará	
	Caxinduba		Pará	
		Upper Xingu	Mato Grosso	
Roraima	None	None		9
Manaus	Jaú		Amazonas	3
	Jatapu		Amazonas	
Upper Rio Negro	Pico da Neblina		Amazonas/Venezuela	12
		Caxiauia	Amazonas	
Solimões-	Cutiuaia		Amazonas	None
Amazonas	Loreto		Amazonas/Peru/Colombia	
	Northern Napo		Colombia/Peru/Ecuador	
		Panaúa	Amazonas	
Southwest	Southern Napo		Ecuador/Peru	5
	Javari		Peru	
	Huallaga		Peru	
	Serra do Divisor		Acre/Peru	
	Ucayali		Peru	
	Inambari		Peru	
	Yungas		Bolivia	
	Eirunepé		Amazonas	
	Purus		Amazonas	
	Marmelos		Amazonas	
	Serra das Onças		Rondônia/Mato Grosso	
		Parecis	Rondônia	

Source: Wetterberg et al., "Analysis of Nature Conservation," p. 23.

complement of species was reached.[61] Diamond recognized this as an especially severe problem in the tropical rainforest, where so many species, adapted to the stable conditions within the forest, were slow dispersers and inefficient colonizers.[62] Maintaining at least an element of similarity between the reserve and surrounding lands would help the protected areas slow the species loss that Island Biogeography Theory argued was the fate of any isolated biological community. It would also allow fauna in the protected areas to forage beyond their boundaries and thereby maintain a larger population than would be possible on just the resources within the protected areas themselves.

Finally, protected natural areas in Amazonia would not be isolated from their surroundings by elevation or other natural barriers; most

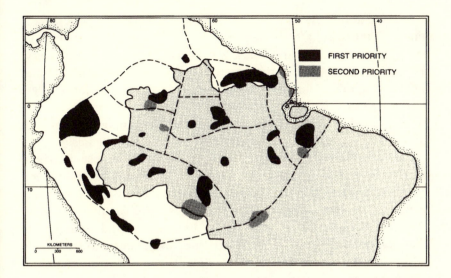

FIGURE 2.5
First- and Second-Priority Conservation Areas. Adapted from Wetterberg et al.,
"Analysis of Nature Conservation"

would simply be demarcated areas. This would leave them greatly
exposed to human activity around them: pesticides and herbicides
could contaminate their air and water; exotic, weedy species that
accompanied agriculture could invade them; increases in the human
population could bring squatter invasions and hunting forays.

Wetterberg therefore concluded that the establishment of protected areas should be accompanied by conservation measures for
the entire region:[63] greater efforts to enforce hunting regulations
throughout Amazonia; the management of Amazonia's commercial
forests on a sustained-use basis; the prohibition of large-scale deforestation or the introduction of exotic species; the institution of a
national bird banding program; and the establishment of incentives
for landowners to manage their land for conservation values. He also
decided to recommend such indirect measures as adding conservation to the public school curriculum and training rural police in the
enforcement of conservation laws.

* * *

Wetterberg had decided on the essentials of his proposal by late
1975, although his doubts about some of the science on which it

rested and about the way he had fashioned science into policy made
him hesitant to fully commit to it.[64] As Miller and his own experience had taught him, however, it was impossible to wait until everything was known; one had to use the best current information and
build enough flexibility into plans to accommodate new knowledge.
Wetterberg satisfied himself that he had done this by early 1976, so
he circulated a short report spelling out his proposed approach
among a few scientists, conservationists, and public officials.

The reception was positive, in large measure because Brazilian
conservationists were ready for its message. The connections between
Brazilian conservationists and the international conservation movement had became substantial in the 1960s; José Candido de Melo
Carvalho became the director of the Brazilian Foundation for the
Conservation of Nature (FBCN) in 1966, and under him the FBCN
became an important link between Brazilians and the international
conservationists.[65] New doctrine flowed into Brazil as a result of
these links, and awareness of Brazilian problems increased abroad.
Sensitized to conservation theory's increasingly ecological perspective, Brazilian conservationists had turned their attention to
Amazonia. This and the Campo Cerrado woodlands south of it were
the only two regions of Brazil where the preservation of major,
undisturbed ecosystems was possible. Elsewhere, the landscape was
largely the product of human activity. It might be possible to protect
small, unique ecosystems or populations of important species on
these altered landscapes, but only through intensive management.[66]

IBDF officials were especially receptive to the report. Amazon conservation was squarely within the agency's pale of responsibility. As
part of a reorganization of the federal bureaucracy in 1967, the old,
ineffectual Forest Service was replaced with the larger and more
powerful Institute of Forest Development. As its name implied, the
new agency was to actively manage the nation's forests to make them
contribute to national development, but responsibility for the
national parks, biological reserves, and several non-site-specific protection programs was also given to it.[67]

Carvalho became one of the chief advisors to the IBDF president,
and through him international conservation doctrine flowed into the
institute as well as into private Brazilian conservation organizations.
The IBDF's 1969 report on Brazil's conservation needs showed the
degree to which the IBDF and international thought were in alignment by that time. It asserted that protecting representative samples

of Amazonia's major ecosystems was a top national conservation priority, and while the report recommended no specific minimum size (there were no firm guides to size yet) it argued that the protected areas had to be large enough to maintain entire biological communities.[68] Because the Brazilian government as a whole gave little attention to biological conservation in the years before the Stockholm Conference, neither the report nor the thinking behind it had any impact on public policy. The report itself sank into obscurity, and the national park system floundered without a sense of direction.[69]

Increasingly, however, signs from elsewhere within the federal government pointed to a more favorable top-level disposition toward conservation: Brazil had signed an accord with Colombia to suppress the pelt trade in endangered species in 1973, and the president of the republic, the minister of interior, and several other high government officials had taken part in the impressive dedication ceremonies establishing Amazonia National Park in 1974. Brazil signed an accord with Peru to suppress the pelt trade and ratified the International Convention on Endangered Species (CITES) in 1975. The IBDF now sensed the time was right for a new, ambitious conservation initiative, and Wetterberg's report was the ideal basis for one. The agency asked Wetterberg to help it develop a specific program based on his report. Since IBDF sponsorship would give him the chance to put his ideas into practice, Wetterberg accepted and shifted his base from Manaus to the institute's headquarters in Brasília.

CHAPTER 3

The Mosaic of Opportunity

When Wetterberg arrived in Brasília in early 1976, he met Maria Tereza Jorge Pádua, a young administrator rising through the IBDF's ranks and a conservation advocate. Politically shrewd, she worked with Wetterberg during 1976, helping him deepen the political and pragmatic dimensions of his work.[1] Aligning conservation with the dominant values of the government was the most important political task during the early, formative stages of conservation planning for Amazonia, but now a more delicate task arose: fitting conservation's ambition to the political space and energy available to it. If the limits of the possible were undershot, conservation might fail to save what was within its grasp. If the limits were overstepped, the opportunity to fill the last great gap in South American conservation might be lost.

To Jorge Pádua and other Brazilian conservationists, the limits appeared broader than ever before. While the military government had not put conservation at the forefront of its concerns, especially in the years before the Stockholm Conference, it did make changes that, while aimed at other ends, laid the administrative and political groundwork for a substantial program of Amazon conservation.

First, as part of a general effort to mold the nation's legal code into an instrument of development, the disjointed and often contradictory forest legislation that had accumulated over the preceding several decades was replaced by a new and strengthened forest code in 1965.[2] The new code's restrictions on deforestation expanded earlier legislation: it was now illegal to clear forest from steep slopes, near springs, along river banks, and on the margins of lakes, even on private land; landowners could clear no more than 50 percent of the forests on their land. A companion faunal protection code was passed two years later.[3] It declared all wild animals government property and outlawed professional hunting, the pelt trade, and the export of any products made from wild animals. These reforms gave biological conservation a strong grounding in federal law.[4]

Second, in 1971, the federal government had assumed ownership of all state lands in Amazonia within 100 kilometers of any federal road and within 150 kilometers of an international boundary, 311 million hectares in all.[5] The move was intended to secure the national frontiers and give INCRA, the newly formed National Institute of Colonization and Agrarian Reform, a sufficient land base for the colonization component of the PIN program; it also gave the federal government an ample land base for an ambitious conservation program.

Finally, the new federal-state relationship that evolved under military government provided a more favorable political climate for Amazon conservation. From the nineteenth century onward, national politics included a large measure of respect for the interests of the regional elites; even the strongman Getúlio Vargas was careful to respect them.[6] This aligned the actions of the federal government within a state with the wishes of the state's politically powerful, or at least insured that such actions seldom went directly against those wishes.

Historically, nature protection was a political issue only in the urbanized South, where there was a substantial middle class and a style of pluralist politics that made politicians somewhat sensitive to middle-class concerns. In Amazonia, the middle class was small and the political system was less open to it. The traditional elite of the region, largely merchants and those who controlled access to Amazonia's natural wealth, had never been particularly mindful of the resources on which their incomes were built.[7] They viewed public protection of nature as irrelevant, or even as a threat to their vital interests. Consequently, most early federal conservation initiatives had been directed toward the South, where they had local support.[8] Lacking such support in Amazonia, the federal government's ability to protect nature in the region was limited.

When the national legislature was vitiated in the aftermath of the 1964 coup, much of the direct political power of the regional elites was destroyed, tilting the federal-state relationship sharply in favor of the federal government.[9] The military regime also instituted a tax reform that concentrated more power over the public fisc at the national level and made the states dependent on the federal government for much of their budgets, and especially for capital spending. With these changes, the power of state interests to determine the nature of federal activities within their states was greatly reduced.

With Jorge Pádua's encouragement, Wetterberg's ambitions for conservation expanded to fill the large political space that appeared open to them. He would recommend three rather than two large reserves for each of Prance's bioregions. He would recommend twenty-four rather than twenty smaller protected areas for Amazonia as a whole.

He also increased his plan's flexibility by adding more candidates for protected-area status. In 1975, Brown delineated a set of Pleistocene forest fragments based on his research on butterflies, adding another voice of support to Pleistocene Refuge Theory and more Pleistocene forest fragments.[10] Brown's fragments allowed Wetterberg to expand his first-priority category to fifteen areas and his second to seven. As Wetterberg uncovered more areas recommended for protection by outside sources, he increased his third-priority category from twenty-three to forty-two areas. The total number of candidate areas for protected status rose to sixty-four.

These refinements were incorporated in a second report, "An Analysis of Nature Conservation Priorities in the Amazon," published jointly by the IBDF, the FAO, and the UNDP in late 1976. "Analysis" was both original and faithful to the principles of mainstream international conservation.[11] The tone of the report was scientific, emphasizing the science used in determining minimum size and selecting the priority areas. The report was biocentric in its values, stressing that all protected-area selections should be made primarily on biological criteria. But "Analysis" was also a politically attuned document, playing down the less systematic elements of the approach so as to not detract from the impression of internal logic it hoped to project.

The report deviated from Miller's principles in one important way. Rather than detailing the broader conservation measures Wetterberg thought should be taken in Amazonia, the report simply asserted that a system of protected areas was but "one aspect of land-use management that must be complemented by other environmentally compatible land uses."[12] Jorge Pádua deemed it unwise to stress conservation measures for all Brazilian Amazonia. Establishing national parks and biological reserves was a clearer part of the IBDF's legal mandate than were more general measures, and therefore a report focusing on the former was more likely to be favorably received by top administrators. Wetterberg was not happy with mere generalities, but he accepted the political need for them. The managers of the IBDF's national park system had become the principal clients for his planning and the instruments of its implementation. As Wetterberg later recounted, "Their mandate...did not extend beyond protected areas. We had to give them the pieces they could use."[13]

Several thousand copies of the report were printed in Portuguese by the IBDF and distributed in Brazil while the FAO published additional copies in English and distributed them internationally. The report was enthusiastically received, especially among scientists. Many of the prominent figures in Amazon research and conservation responded in writing, and while some questioned details, none took issue with the basic approach.[14] Terborgh wrote that if Brazil implemented the plan it recommended, it would take a large step toward the best system of protected natural areas in the world.[15] The proposal received additional credibility and prestige when the Intergovernmental Technical Group on the Protection and Management of Amazon Flora and Fauna (CIT), an international steering body for Amazon conservation representing all the nations with territory in Amazonia, accepted it as a model for conservation planning throughout the basin.

The military government approved the report in late 1976, and its acceptance throughout the federal bureaucracy ensued.[16] The forestry section of the Second Amazon Development Plan was rewritten in 1977 to allow large areas of Amazonia to be set aside "according to the recommendations" of the report. RADAM, pleased by the inclusion of so many areas it had identified for preservation, placed all the priority areas on its own land-use suitability maps of Amazonia. INCRA agreed to delineate the priority areas on its maps of land-use potential and to give the IBDF access to its own data on the areas.[17] Taken together, these actions placed the IBDF's areas of conservation interest in front of those who would plan the region's future.

***

The next step was drawing up a slate of specific proposals. The biological underpinning of "Analysis" was a mix of theory and nonjudgmental eclecticism, in part because so little was known about Amazon biology. Specific proposals for protected areas would have to be grounded in specific knowledge, however. Some high-priority areas probably did not have the outstanding natural qualities they were suspected of having. Some were probably already so altered that protecting them would not be worthwhile. On the other hand, some low-priority areas probably had unsuspected biological virtues. Because the program, even under the best of circumstances, could bring only a small percentage of the region under public protection, the opportunity costs of picking the wrong areas could be high. From this stage onward, natural history would eclipse high-level theory as a factor in the IBDF's conservation decisions.[18]

This stage also posed a new set of political considerations. Those informing "Analysis" were general, focusing on images and orientation and adjusting ambitions to the perceived level of political receptivity. A slate of proposals would involve a far more specific set of political considerations. Parts of Amazonia were already occupied. Much more of it was already the object of powerful interests and ambitions. Each set of actors in Amazonia had its own types of power. The strength and character of these interests, as they expressed themselves in each priority area identified in "Analysis," had to be assessed before conservation plans for Amazonia could take definite forms.

One of the most perplexing elements of the equation was the *caboclos*, or the Amazon peasantry, and the more recently arrived poor settlers from elsewhere in Brazil. Portuguese-speaking and Catholic in belief, but retaining many elements of indigenous material culture, caboclos lived along the watercourses of the region in small family groups. They raised crops in small forest clearings and cattle on wet grasslands and natural upland prairies.[19] They fished the rivers and lakes, and they collected wild fruits, tapped rubber trees, and hunted in the forest around them. Some cut commercially valuable trees on the *várzeas*, the seasonally inundated bottomlands, and in the more accessible parts of the upland forests. They traded forest products for commercial goods at small trading posts or with itinerant merchants who plied the rivers of the basin, but the low population densities meant inefficient, monopolistic collection and distribution and usually kept the caboclos impoverished.

Where new roads and other development initiatives had penetrated, caboclos were joined by poor settlers from other parts of Brazil.[20] The settlement frontier had reached well into the eastern and southern flanks of Amazonia by the 1960s. The lure of the PIN program increased the flow of settlers in the early 1970s, mostly from the closing frontiers in the South and from the poor, overpopulated Northeast. According to one analyst, for every family brought to Amazonia by INCRA, another five came on their own during the

PIN era. In all, perhaps a million and a half migrants came to the region during the early 1970s.[21] The immigration of small-scale farmers was no longer officially encouraged after the demise of PIN,[22] but many came anyway; the promise of available land and the opportunity for a new life remained strong lures.

Some were lucky enough to find places in the remaining government-sponsored schemes. Some were hired for clearing gangs on the new large farms and cattle enterprises. Some made arrangements with ranch managers by which they would be allowed to grow crops for a time in return for clearing the land, and after the arrangement expired, they looked for a similar arrangement elsewhere. Most simply found unoccupied land and begin farming it. Secondary roads in developing areas were dotted with the untitled homesteads of poor, recent arrivals.

Fitting caboclos and small settlers into conservation planning was a problem with many dimensions. They could not be ignored because native lifeways were destructive to wildlife, which like the land itself, was viewed as common property. Manatee populations were a fraction of what they had been a century earlier, a testament to the hunting pressure that even relatively small numbers of caboclos could bring on a species. Thanks also to caboclos (and to the markets they served), the large turtles were now gone from the Amazon River and most of its major tributaries, and many fish species were becoming rare. Selective cutting of commercially valuable tree species such as rosewood (a source of linalool, a perfume ingredient) had led to widespread depletions. New settlers presented a similar threat because they frequently adopted similar attitudes and behavior toward the region's wildlife.

On the other hand, caboclos and poor settlers could not simply be removed; a law prohibiting the uncompensated expulsion of caboclos from the land they occupied "by custom" had been in effect since the nineteenth century.[23] The military government and its economic advisors were disdainful of squatters' rights (which devalued land as a market commodity, impeded accumulation of the large blocks of land necessary for commercial agriculture, and discouraged the capital investments on which modern agriculture relied) but they were careful not to tamper with them. Historically, the frontier had been a safety valve for those dissatisfied with the socioeconomic order elsewhere in rural Brazil, and squatters' rights were an essential part of this function of the frontier.[24] A vague responsibility for the security of small farmers and caboclos went along with INCRA's management of rural colonization, so these groups also had some measure of formal representation in the federal bureaucracy.[25]

Rights and administrative protection were often vitiated by political reality. The suspension of democracy deprived poor rural people of their vote, and the military had moved against the rural unions that had formed in the years before it came to power. These steps deprived caboclos and small settlers of what little political leverage they had. Low-density settlement patterns, an atomized social structure, and the absence of institutions that might have served as a catalyst for collective action compounded the problems of political articulation for the caboclos. Small settlers were further hindered by a landscape that made few provisions for them and, in the case of the newest arrivals, by their lack of legal rights to the land they occupied. Accordingly, INCRA and other settlement agencies in Amazonia seldom vigorously discharged their responsibilities to small settlers or caboclos, especially when they got in the way of well-funded private development initiatives. INCRA predictably sided with large owners when they were in conflict with small settlers. Whenever possible, the agency found alternate lands for settlers, but it was not above forcible expulsion.[26]

Nevertheless, caboclos did have the power to create what the government euphemistically called "social tensions" by violently protesting their treatment at the hands of government or private forces of development. Government agencies, especially INCRA, could find themselves in trouble if they allowed such tensions to develop. When settler unrest on the Araguaia-Tocantins frontier in the late 1970s boiled over into violence, INCRA's responsibilities in the area were transferred to a special agency, which took over INCRA personnel and answered directly to the National Security Council.[27] The slap in the face demonstrated that sometimes government agencies had to be mindful of even lowly small farmers and caboclos.

The problem of finding these people further complicated all calculations. Unlike most peasants worldwide, caboclos seldom had strong attachments to particular sites and frequently moved along the watercourses of Amazonia in search of better opportunities. The lack of extensive kin ties or complex social organization among caboclos heightened the problem of determining their numbers or exact locations: there were few local informants with an extensive knowledge of a region's inhabitants.[28] Frequently the little information available was inaccurate or, given the mobility of caboclos, out of date. Similar problems prevailed with regard to more recently arrived small settlers, many of whom also relocated frequently. Moreover, many of the newcomers did not have rights to their lands, and were not anxious to make their presence known to government officials.

Tribal Indians were another important and, from a conservation perspective, perplexing element of the human landscape of Amazonia. When Europeans penetrated Amazonia in the sixteenth and seventeenth centuries, they destroyed the advanced Indian cultures they found along the major rivers, but less advanced Indian groups survived for centuries in more remote areas. The twentieth century was even less hospitable to Indians than previous ones had been: whole tribes were eliminated through deculturation or extirpation. The number of extant tribes had been reduced to 143 by 1957, and that number had been halved by the mid-1970s. Yet tribal life continued in areas distant from the main axes of transportation and development. In some cases, the tribes formed tenuous commercial links to the national economy (through pelt traders, for example) but others had no contact with whites, or only fleeting, intermittent contact.[29]

The idea of allowing indigenous peoples to remain in protected natural areas was being discussed with enthusiasm in international conservation circles in the 1970s; Indians left in protected areas would, so the argument went, be protected against the depredations of settlers, while the Indians, in turn, would protect the natural areas.[30] Such an arrangement went against the conventional norms of development, however, which viewed indigenous cultures as prisons of backwardness.[31] This was the orthodox thinking in South America, even among conservationists. At the Second World Conference on National Parks in 1972, Carvalho argued against mixed Indian and nature reserves because they would retard integration and thus be unfair to the Indians.[32] They also seemed unwise from a conservation perspective. Latin American history seemed to teach that Indians were inevitably deculturated by contact with national culture and that such contact was inevitable. Latin American conservationists felt that deculturation, even in its early stages, made Indians a threat to nature. The Argentine Italo Constantino had argued in 1972 that modern weaponry made it easier for natives to kill animals, and the intrusion of the national economy and culture into their lives was "an inducement to kill and capture more of them."[33]

While the integrationist policies Carvalho espoused lost favor with many in Latin America, just as they had elsewhere, objections to mixing Indians and conservation remained. Brazilian conservationists had seen pelt and hide merchants establish commercial links with tribes in the remotest areas of Amazonia and felt it was only a matter of time before all Indians became what Carvalho called "authentic predators and destroyers of the environment." Nogueira-Neto, secretary of the environment, felt that once Indians were exposed to whites, they became "bellicose, unreasonable, and impossible to deal with."[34]

Thus, prevailing opinion among Brazilian conservationists in the late 1970s was that the protection of indigenous cultures and biological conservation, while perhaps having a conceptual symmetry, did not mix in Amazonia.

Therefore, like the caboclos and small settlers, Indians were seen as a threat to the region's biota and conservationists could not ignore them. Yet dealing with Indians, like dealing with caboclos and small settlers, was not simple. Indians had their own rights to land outside the legal titling process. Brazil had ratified the convention of the International Labor Organization in the 1950s, which stated that aboriginal peoples should be left in control of their ancestral lands. The right was embedded in the Brazilian constitution of 1967, which guaranteed Indians exclusive use of the lands they occupied. The Indians also had a federal agency, the National Indian Foundation (FUNAI), charged with protecting their rights. Shortly after the agency's establishment in 1967, its leadership, with strong connections to the anthropological community and sensitive to the plight of Indians in Amazonia, instituted a program to find all Indians and identify and protect their lands.[35]

Here too political reality often vitiated official rights. The policy of protecting Indian lands aroused broad opposition: public planners feared that large demarcated Indian reserves throughout Amazonia would threaten their ability to acquire unfettered control of the vast acreage needed for their development schemes; land speculators feared it would reduce their field of operation. Moreover, FUNAI's ministry, Interior, saw economic development as its job and was not intrinsically sympathetic with the agency's goal of setting off Indian lands. Within a few years of FUNAI's founding, its progressive, university-based leadership had been replaced by military men for whom national security and development were more important than Indian welfare.[36]

In this political environment, identification and demarcation of

Indian lands fell hopelessly behind schedule, leaving many—perhaps most—Indians in Amazonia still without the benefit of protected lands in the mid-1970s. Moreover, FUNAI seldom had sufficient personnel or political power to defend even demarcated Indian lands. They were invaded with impunity, and when this provoked violent resistance, FUNAI moved the Indians elsewhere.[37] It could seldom resolve disputes with development-promoting agencies in favor of Indians; in one case, legal obstacles to the construction of a road through an Indian reserve were overcome by simply extinguishing part of the reserve. An impotent FUNAI was prey to corruption: its program of certifying that no Indians were present in an area, a prerequisite for conveying public lands to a private owner, was routinely undermined by bribery and other illegal entreaties.

FUNAI's performance, plus the fact that assimilation doctrine remained popular at high levels of the federal government (the Geisel administration proposed new measures in 1978 to speed assimilation)[38] made the tribal Indians of Amazonia appear to be a modest and diminishing political force. Nevertheless, because their rights to land were embedded in the federal constitution and Brazil's international treaty obligations, Indians were not wholly without weight in regional political equations. The question for conservationists was how seriously those rights should be taken and how long they would last.

The well-capitalized players in Amazon development—speculators, large ranchers, commercial farmers—also had to be considered. Ranching in Amazonia was little hampered by the shortage of labor or lack of a large local market. The price of beef was usually high enough to sustain the cost of transporting cattle to distant markets on poor roads from isolated settlements on the frontier, and bulldozers and power saws made clearing forest for pasture far easier than it had been in the days of the ax and handsaw.[39] Moreover, the FAO had estimated that global demand for beef would increase by more than a third during the 1970s, and international development agencies were heavily promoting cattle projects in tropical Latin America.[40] As Brazilian ranchers were joined by international corporations and their Brazilian subsidiaries in establishing new ranches, a huge ranching region stretching from the eastern fringe of the rainforest in Pará westward along the southern margin of the forest in Mato Grosso began to form.

Large-scale commercial agriculture also made inroads into

Amazonia during the 1970s. Although agriculture did not have all the inherent advantages of cattle ranching as a frontier activity—it was more capital intensive and it needed better roads and access to markets—well-capitalized farmers from other parts of Brazil rushed to take advantage of Amazonia's low land prices. As a result, large areas near Amazonia's new roads were transformed into agricultural districts producing soybeans, sugar, and other plantation crops.

Speculators complemented and lubricated commercial land development. During the early 1960s investment in the newly accessible areas of Amazonia seemed like a good hedge against the political uncertainties and inflation of the era. Many of those investments paid off spectacularly, as land on the margins of Amazonia rapidly appreciated in value with the stability and economic growth in the late 1960s. During the miracle of the 1960s and 1970s, speculation in Amazon land was an outlet for profits made in southern industry, and it remained a hedge against inflation, which was never fully brought under control.

The private forces of development in Amazonia could bring considerable power to bear on local decisions. Ranchers, commercial farmers, and speculators had the money and connections to make their way in the unsettled arena of local-interest conflict. They bribed state officials into registering false claims, hired gunmen to take land they wanted by force, and exercised strong influence on the local judiciary. More power came from the conformity of their goals to what the government saw as important public ones. Brazil's economic planners hoped to double Brazil's beef production, enabling the country to become the world's leading beef exporter by 1980, and Amazonia had a large role in meeting these goals. Farming in Amazonia was producing soybeans for export and sugarcane to be turned into the biogas that reduced Brazil's costly dependence on foreign petroleum. The conversion of Amazonia into a settled region secured the nation's claims to it.

Government supported these interests. The federal government sold public land at low prices to ranchers, allowed them liberal tax write-offs for their investments in land and stock, and subsidized the construction of meat packing plants in Amazonia. Cattle ranching was allowed to capture more than half of the economic development incentives offered by SUDAM between 1970 and 1973, and additional incentives were captured by commercial crop raising.[41] The state of Pará offered its own incentives for opening new lands to commercial ranching and farming.

Yet government had a large say in determining where and how these interests would express themselves. State and federally constructed roads gave speculative value to land and permitted farmers to market their crops. Government subsidies set the parameters of investment and profit. Federal officials used infrastructure planning and fiscal incentives to funnel private investment into areas where they thought it would do the most good. Thus, from a conservation perspective, the key question with regard to these interests was not how much power they had—that was clear—but rather how government action would shape the expression of that power.

A final consideration—and further uncertainty—arose from land ownership in Amazonia. Although much of Amazonia was already in private hands, which parts were in whose hands was not always clear. Most of Amazonia was originally given over to private owners in enormous patents by the Portuguese crown, but land ownership was relatively unimportant to any of the participants in the economy that evolved there in the eighteenth and nineteenth centuries; access to the caboclo as producer and consumer, not the ownership of land, drove the system. Land was so plentiful it was treated like a free good.[42] As a consequence, title records were allowed to fall into a chaotic state. Several national land inventories were conducted in the nineteenth century, and although they only noted de facto possession, they assumed a quasi-legal status over the years. The states of Amazonia had accumulated vast amounts of land through patent cancellations and other types of ownership lapses, but they seldom had a good idea of exactly which lands they owned. Even as late as the decade after the Second World War, land in most of Amazonia had so little market value this confusion caused little concern.[43] By the early 1960s, however, inflation and increasing accessibility caused demand for titles to swamp titling mechanisms.[44] Two or more titles to the same tract were sometimes issued out of incompetence or corruption. Sometimes overlapping titles were issued. Sometimes dubious old titles suddenly appeared. Investment and development pressure was so great that it simply overflowed the confused titling process: many large holdings without clear title were the object of capital improvement loans made by the Amazon development bank; others received tax breaks under SUDAM's development incentive programs. When the federal government took control of large amounts of public land in Amazonia in 1971, another set of bureaucratic actors and another layer of confusion were added.[45]

Although complex and sometimes ambiguous, these factors were not abstract. Each interest expressed itself in a concrete fashion: Indians, small settlers, and caboclos were present in some areas and absent in others; land speculation had reached some areas of Amazonia but not others. Some areas were being rapidly transformed into ranching and agricultural districts, while others were untouched by these processes. This meant a unique political calculation had to be made for each area under consideration. Jorge Pádua and Wetterberg assumed that the strong hand of the federal government, with its ascending power and its commitment to rational regional planning, would eventually impose a high degree of order on the Amazon landscape, but for now, conservation planners had to take this interest, uncertainty, and conflict into account in every specific decision they made. Neither conceptual shortcuts nor political generalizations would be useful at this stage.

* * *

The IBDF sent out evaluation teams to gather the large amounts of human and biological information that selecting the best areas would require, and Wetterberg and Jorge Pádua drew up formal evaluation criteria to guide the teams in their work (table 3.1). Non-theoretical and practical, they were the bridge between the detached elegance of theory and the reality of Amazonia. As befitted the now-favored status of the conservation initiative, the military provided logistical support. A large number of institutions with a stake in the future of Amazonia, including INPA, FUNAI, the FAO, the FBCN, and several Brazilian universities, joined in the evaluations.

Evaluation typically began with an overflight to assess the general characteristics of the area and perhaps identify features that would serve as boundaries for a park or reserve. This was followed by surface exploration to confirm details or investigate anything of interest spotted from the air. The expedition to the lower course of the Trombetas River in August 1977 was typical in most ways (see figures 3.4, and 7.4, below). Although Wetterberg had given the area only a third-priority rating, it seemed like a prime candidate for protection: RADAM had suggested it as a park; Russell Mittermeier, an American primatologist, had suggested protecting it for the primates found in the area; and it contained some of the most important turtle nesting beaches remaining in Amazonia. The evaluation began with an overflight to confirm RADAM's identification of the major vege-

TABLE 3.1
IBDF Criteria for Selecting Protected Areas in Amazonia

For Biological Reserves

1. Area should contain those biological characteristics that led to its inclusion in "An Analysis of Nature Conservation Priorities."
2. Area should be unoccupied by settlers; if settlers are present, their removal should be possible.
3. Area should be large enough to assure the self-perpetuation of the ecosystem and meet other management objectives. Areas intended to represent phytogeographic regions of Amazonia ought to contain at least 250,000 hectares and be surrounded by a buffer strip 10 kilometers in width.
4. Area should not contain Indians.
5. To the extent possible without sacrificing important biological phenomena, areas known to contain commercially valuable mineral deposits should be avoided.
6. Area should have easily identifiable and defendable natural boundaries—i.e., those that follow rivers, drainage divides, or other notable topographical features.
7. Area should be compact.
8. When possible, area should include a variety of landscapes and plant communities.

For National Parks:

1. In addition to the above criteria, area should contain some unique element of the nation's natural or cultural patrimony.
2. Area should have scenic beauty, recreation potential, and/or good accessibility.

Source: Wetterberg and Jorge Pádua, "Preservação da Natureza," pp. 39–40.

tation types and to look for previously unknown areas of unique vegetation. (The team discovered several patches of savanna, which it recommended including in any reserve established.) The team then traveled by boat up the Trombetas River and into the lakes north of the river to observe the turtle nesting areas close up, determine the number of caboclos present, and assess the degree of disturbance they had caused.

The expedition to the upper Xingu River region of northern Mato Grosso was similar in scale but different in specific objectives.[46] The area had been included on the third-priority list on the basis of a FUNAI agent's report that it contained a large population of giant river otters (*Pteronura brasiliensis*). The preservation of this species was one of the Brazilian conservation movement's top priorities, which gave the area a special significance.[47] The team spent four days in small boats trying to determine the size of the otter population. They sighted enough individuals to confirm the Indian agent's report.

When possible, several areas were assessed at once. The four promising areas Wetterberg had identified in the small territory of Amapá—Cabo Orange, Cabo Norte, Oiapoque, and Lago Piratuba —were relatively close to each other, so one expedition sufficed for all four. In all, IBDF teams surveyed thirty-four of the areas Wetterberg had identified during 1977 and 1978.

The expeditions were complemented by information gathered in Brasília and Amazon state capitals. The land ownership picture was clarified as much as possible by searching through land office records. The intentions of other federal agencies toward each area were probed, as was the possibility of special sources of support for a protected area (through the Polamazonia program, for example). The question of whether an area's protection was likely to cause any political problems for the forest institute was explored, and finally the powerful central organs of the military government, especially the National Security Council, were sounded out for any objections.

As information from the field and government offices accumulated, whittling Wetterberg's list of prospective areas into a set of proposals began. Sometimes reports from the field indicated so many Indians or squatters that a prospective area was immediately ruled out. This was the case for the old Gurupi Forest Reserve, an area of considerable biological appeal.[48] Sometimes the survey teams discovered that the commercial frontier had already reached the area, degrading it or making a fierce fight over its protection likely. Some promising areas were found not to have the expected biological characteristics. For example, the field team visiting the Bacia do Capim, a first-priority area, discovered it was not dominated by the rainforest it expected to find, but by more xeric vegetation, making the area a poor choice to represent the bioregion.

Sometimes promising areas were scuttled by high-level politics. Prance had placed most of the northern territory of Roraima into a distinct phytogeographic region, and Wetterberg had identified eight promising areas in the territory in "Analysis," many of which received favorable reports from the field evaluation teams. The boundary between the territory and Venezuela was tense, however, and the National Security Council feared the presence of parks or reserves near it might compromise national security. Furthermore, rich mineral resources had recently been discovered in Roraima, and the territorial and federal governments feared that protected natural areas might impede access to them. Jorge Pádua considered it prudent to avoid Roraima entirely for the time being.[49]

Sometimes INCRA or FUNAI objected. Normally, if INCRA had no plans for the area in question, it would go along with the IBDF's wishes; such cooperation cost the colonizing agency little, while advancing a program with high-level approval and accommodating a fellow agency within the Ministry of Agriculture. If, however, it had plans for settlements in the area, or thought the removal of squatters might lead to social unrest, it would oppose the transfer, or it would at least insist that any protected area exclude the land in question. Likewise, if FUNAI thought Indians were present, it would oppose the establishment of a protected area.[50] The IBDF had no uniform response to such objections. If it thought it could bring power to bear on the decision, or if it thought it had allies elsewhere in government, it might attempt to override them by appealing to a higher authority. Normally, INCRA's objections carried more weight than FUNAI's: INCRA had considerable power in Amazonia, while the Indian agency was politically weak and, given the state of its program to identify Indian lands, often unable to back up its assertions about the presence of Indians with conclusive evidence.[51]

As the list was pruned, tentative proposals were shaped for those still-promising areas. There was no fixed upper size limit:[52] the IBDF reasoned that the larger the area, the more species it was likely to include, the slower the rate of species loss, and the more likely it was to be a self-regulating ecosystem. On the other hand, Terborgh's 259,000 hectares was adhered to as a rough lower size limit, although the idea of a buffer zone was dropped. The retention of this number from Island Biogeography Theory might seem surprising in light of the scant attention otherwise paid to the dictates of theoretical biology at this stage, but it retained a practical value. Abele and Connor had argued that Island Biogeography Theory was little more than a restatement of an obvious fact: large areas usually contained more species than smaller ones.[53] While meaning this as a criticism, Abele and Connor pointed out one of the theory's virtues as a policy guide: even if the specific numbers Diamond, Terborgh, and their associates had attached to the relationship of size to diversity proved wrong, the relationship itself would remain. Very small areas would contain fewer species than large ones and thus be less satisfactory in representing a region's biota. Terborgh's number itself was not scientifically special, but there was cause for believing it was approximately the minimum necessary size for maintaining viable populations of large predators.

Shape and boundaries were another area where theory and practicality converged. Ecological theory indicated that the best shapes for reserves were compact ones, which reduced destructive edge effects.[54] Compactness also reduced a reserve's exposure to unauthorized incursion and made management easier. Natural boundaries also made both ecological and management sense. A river was a barrier to human and nonhuman invaders and was easily demarcated and patrolled. A boundary at the edge of a watershed prevented the area's penetration by boat while protecting its water from the effects of outside activity.

In some cases, the presence of natural features made the proper shape of a protected natural area seem obvious from the start. By using as boundaries the rivers that paralleled the Jaú River, a small tributary of the Negro River, a large, compact natural area with an easy-to-guard perimeter could be delimited (see figure 3.5, below). A large, compact protected area in the Oiapoque region of northern Amapá could be almost completely delimited by placing boundaries along convenient rivers (figure 3.1).

Sometimes there was little choice with regard to boundaries, however. The Machado River was the ideal western boundary of a protected natural area carved out of the old Jaru Forest Reserve, but a large cattle ranch had been established on its eastern bank, and INCRA was considering the establishment of an agricultural settlement there. The IBDF would have to settle for a surveyed boundary east of the river if it wanted a reserve in the area (see figure 7.8, below). Elsewhere, the boundaries of established Indian reserves or agricultural settlement schemes were the necessary limits of any protected area; they had to be accepted as they were.[55]

Ideally, a protected area would be free of privately owned land, in which case a simple property transfer from a state government or another federal agency to the IBDF could be effected. Amazonia National Park had been established quickly and with little objection because the land was almost entirely under INCRA's control. The presence of private land or clouded titles made this impossible in many areas, however.

Land prices in Amazonia were still very low relative to the rest of Brazil (table 3.2), so even large purchases were economically possi-

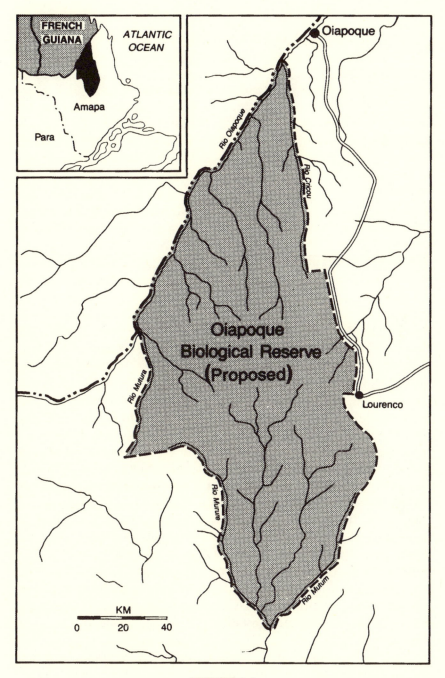

FIGURE 3.1
Proposed Oiapoque Biological Reserve

TABLE 3.2
Estimated Average Cost of Unimproved Land in Protected Areas—1977
(Cruzeiros per Hectare)

Region	Protected Area	Cost
Amazonia	Amazonia NP	20
	Trombetas BR	52
Center-NE	Sete Cidades NP	108
	Chapada dos Veadeiros NP	131
	Emas NP	260
	Serra da Canastra NP	600
South-SE	Serra da Bocaina NP	2,152
	São Joaquim NP	5,100
	Iguaçu NP	5,200
	Aparados da Serra NP	1,700
Urban	Tijuca NP	67,660

Source: IBDF/FBCN *Plano do Sistema: Primera Etapa*, p. 8.

ble, but the IBDF preferred to minimize the amount of private land it had to buy and to avoid conflict over clouded titles.

These considerations produced inherent tension; on one hand was the desire to protect as much land as possible, and on the other was the desire to avoid management problems, acquisition expense, and conflicts with other interests. The contrary pulls produced an ideal size and shape for each area under consideration, one at which the conservation benefits of protecting more acreage were offset by the additional problems this would entail. Determining where the equilibrium lay was unsystematic because it depended on many imprecise calculations: the presence of squatters or Indians, the extent of private lands, the probable effectiveness of boundaries, intrinsic manageability, and, in some areas, the compatibility of conservation and development goals. Nevertheless, finding it was important because it produced a conservation optimum. If areas were underdrawn, they would be less effective conservation instruments, protecting fewer species and less complete ecosystems. If overdrawn, establishing them might be impossible, and if established, they might be impossible to defend.

While local considerations were important in determining where the equilibrium for each area lay, the master determinant was the strength of biological conservation as a goal within the IBDF, the government, and Brazilian society as a whole. Recent events made Jorge Pádua and her associates optimistic. Her conservation message

TABLE 3.3

Proposed Stage One IBDF Protected Areas

Unit	Priority Category	Phytogeographic Region	State or Territory	Date Established	Proposed Size	Size as Established
Cabo Orange	2	Atlantic Coast	Amapá	July 15, 1980	526,000	619,000
Lago Piratuba	2 (Cabo Norte)	Atlantic Coast	Amapá	July 16, 1980	571,000	395,000
Oiapoque	1	Atlantic Coast	Amapá	Not established	1,473,000	
Marajó	3	Atlantic Coast	Pará	Not established	89,000	
Rio Trombetas	3	Jari-Trombetas		September 21, 1979	385,000	385,000
Upper Xingu	2	Xingu-Madeira	Mato Grosso	Not established	520,000	
Jaú	2	Jari-Trombetas	Amazonas	September 24, 1980	2,321,000	2,272,000
Pico da Neblina	1	Upper Rio Negro	Amazonas	June 5, 1979	2,200,000	2,200,000
Abufari[1]	3	Southwest	Amazonas	September 20, 1982		288,000
Guaporé	2 (Parecis)	Southwest	Rondônia	July 11, 1979	1,498,000	600,000
Jaru	1 (Serra das Onças)	Southwest	Rondônia	September 21, 1979	268,000	268,000
Pacaás Novos	2 (Parecis)	Southwest	Rondônia	September 20, 1982	765,000	765,000
				Median Proposed Size	571,000	

[1] Not included in original group
Source: IBDF/FBCN, *Plano do Systema: Primera Etapa.*

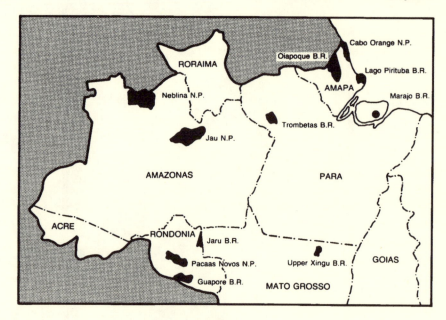

FIGURE 3.2
IBDF Stage One Protection Proposals

had found favor among the IBDF's top administrators, and an ambitious conservation plan had been ratified in principle at the highest levels of the federal government. Agencies involved in Amazon development had shown a willingness to cooperate with a conservation program for the region. Moreover, ample financial resources seemed likely. The Brazilian economy was booming and the budgets of government agencies reflected this; further prosperity and increased budgets seemed to lie ahead.

Their optimism encouraged Jorge Pádua and her associates to favor very large protected areas.[56] The formula for deciding how many posseiros or how much private land was tolerable in a protected area was never fully articulated and varied according to local circumstances, but it was almost always ambitious. For example, the presence of an estimated 100 caboclo families in the Jaú area was not considered a serious problem. The several hundred families in the Pico da Neblina area did not deter the IBDF from drawing ambitious boundaries. Jorge Pádua was willing to include areas known or suspected to have Indians in them, even though this was likely to bring the IBDF and FUNAI into eventual conflict. In short, she was willing to gamble that the future would provide solutions to problems caused by defining conservation's stake in Amazonia so ambitiously.

***

By late 1978, Jorge Pádua and her associates at the IBDF had selected eleven areas in Amazonia and three beyond the region to propose for protection (table 3.3, figure 3.2). Scattered throughout Amazonia, the eleven ranged up to 2,321,000 hectares in size. Three were considered scenic enough to be national parks, the rest would be biological reserves. Each was the result of a distinct set of calculations. In some cases, biological qualities were paramount; in others, management considerations or the presence of important allies and special sources of support was an important determinant. Sometimes, the nature of the problems protection would entail were clear; in others, they were only poorly understood. Each was thus a separate pact with the future.

Pico da Neblina

Pico da Neblina was undoubtedly the most prized of the group. Its biological virtues were great: naturalists and scientific teams had been visiting the area since 1908 and had confirmed the presence of many endemic species; Haffer, Prance, and Brown had all identified Pico as a Pleistocene forest fragment. The IUCN's 1968 Bareloche conference had proposed making the area a national park, and Brazilian conservationists had taken up the cause;[57] the IBDF's 1969 conservation study called for the area's protection, and more recently so had RADAM. Venezuela had already established the Serranía de la Neblina National Park on its side of the border, so the combined protected area would be one of the largest in the world. Moreover, Pico was the highest peak in Brazil, appealing to nationalist sentiments, and its dramatic topography gave it potential as an international tourist draw. In keeping with its promise, it was the object of the most thorough field evaluation. The World Wildlife Fund and the New York Zoological Society helped support the expedition, and George Schaller, Keith Brown, and five other scientists took part.[58] The team rated the area as "excellent" on eight of its thirteen evaluation criteria and "good" on the other five, the highest combined rating of all eleven areas.

Pico's drawbacks were as impressive as its virtues, however. The Northern Perimeter Highway was already under construction in the area, and, once completed, the road would transect the park (figure 3.3). A road connecting the upper Amazon region of Brazil to Venezuela was also under construction in the area. Several hundred caboclo families would have to be relocated, and tracts of private land along the Negro River would have to be purchased; Pico's estimated land purchase costs were the highest of the eleven. Gold had already attracted miners to the area and turned the state government of Amazonas, anxious to profit from it, against the idea of a park. Most troubling, perhaps, was that Indians were well established in the area; the proposed park included all of one FUNAI-demarcated indigenous area and much of two others. One had a large Salesian mission with a school, an airfield, and a complement of foreign priests.

Such drawbacks might have caused the IBDF to propose a much smaller area for protection or perhaps entirely lose interest in the area, had not Jorge Pádua sensed that the IBDF had a powerful ally in the National Security Council. The secretive council, which included the president of the republic, all the ministers of state, and the heads of the three branches of the military, was the most powerful of the Brazilian military government's central agencies: it was a virtual government within the government. Its mandate was to insure national security, and its broad interpretation of its mandate drew its attention to Amazonia.[59] The council feared that self-awareness and political mobilization of the tribal Indians of Amazonia would make policing the national frontiers difficult.[60] Concern was especially sharp with regard to the 21,000 Yanomami living along the Venezuelan border, who constituted the largest relatively traditional Indian society left in Amazonia. Few of them spoke Spanish or Portuguese, and although they were found on both sides of the border (approximately 12,000 lived in Brazil), they did not recognize it as applying to them.[61]

The niceties of the constitution and the concerns of FUNAI or the missionaries counted for little in the eyes of the council when placed against the prospect of a politically mobilized Yanomami nation on the Venezuelan border, perhaps the most tense of Brazil's frontiers. Jorge Pádua saw signs that the council would support a national park in the region, probably because it would add another overlay of

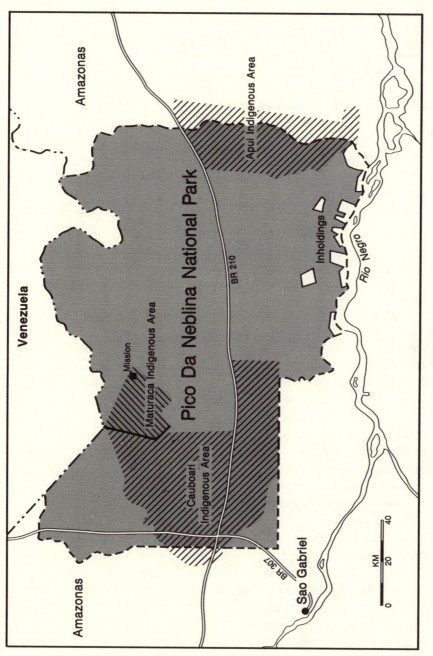

FIGURE 3.3
Pico da Neblina National Park

interest to the area, thereby diluting the Yanomami's territorial claims. The IBDF proposed a two-million–hectare Pico da Neblina National Park.

The decision reflected Jorge Pádua's political acumen and her operating style; she could sense anomalously favorable circumstances and she was willing to play them to full advantage. It also reflected her long-range vision: she knew the military government would not last forever and that the National Security Council's concerns would not always play a deciding role in Amazonia, but she assumed the future would provide park managers with the resources to solve problems as they arose, especially with regard to Indians.[62]

Rio Trombetas Biological Reserve

The proposed Rio Trombetas Biological Reserve also had great biological appeal (figure 3.4). The presence of a number of endangered species had been confirmed, and the area contained five distinct rainforest subtypes, making it a good representative of central Amazonia. It included turtle nesting beaches that had been under the IBDF's protection since 1970,[63] and their incorporation into a biological reserve would make their protection easier. The proposed reserve contained what were thought to be the largest concentrations of brazilnut trees in Amazonia, which allowed the IBDF to stress the compatibility of biological conservation and its forest development mission: the trees might someday be important in improving the stock on which the brazilnut industry depended.

The drawbacks were also formidable. The area had been subjected to considerable disturbance in the past and had received only a "fair" rating from the field evaluation team on "lack of human disturbance." There was considerable private land to be purchased: initial surveys found 103 privately owned parcels (mostly natural brazilnut groves) that totalled 67,000 hectares, or 32 percent of the proposed reserve.[64] Current occupation was heavy: several hundred caboclo families, most of whom made their living collecting brazilnuts, lived along the large shallow lakes in the southern part of the proposed reserve. Although collecting nuts was a relatively benign form of forest exploitation, the inhabitants did exert a constant, destructive hunting pressure on the area's fauna.

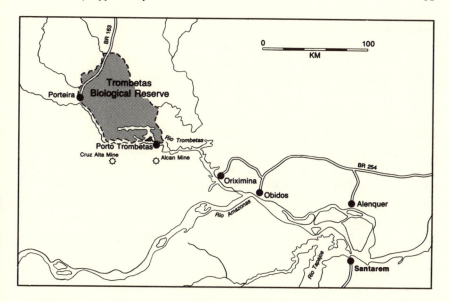

FIGURE 3.4
Lower Trombetas Region

The area's location in a development pole presented the most serious threat. Once the Polamazonia program was underway, the federal government's commitment to it remained strong; it was the main thrust of Amazon development during the 1970s, and the most spectacular projects in the region during this period, including the Serra dos Carajás mines and the Tucuruí dam, were associated with it. New roads already penetrated the lower Trombetas River region in connection with the bauxite mining that would provide the economic base of the Trombetas development pole. Mineração Rio Norte, a company with foreign and Brazilian participation, was scheduled to begin bauxite shipments in mid-1979, and some shipping and processing facilities were already in place on the southern bank of the Trombetas River, across the river from the proposed reserve.

The evaluation team warned that this development would create a number of formidable threats to the area. Poaching, already a problem, was likely to increase, as would illegal timber extraction. As the value of land in the region increased, fraudulent titles to lands within the reserve were likely to appear. The area would become a tempting target for squatters.

The juxtaposition of conservation and development might work to conservation's advantage at Trombetas, however: the Polamazonia program, with its large budget, could afford to underwrite nature protection in its areas of operation. It was already supporting the IBDF's turtle protection along the Trombetas River, and it had helped defray the expenses of the IBDF's expedition to the area.[65] It was therefore likely that a biological reserve along the lower Trombetas River would enjoy greater financial support than the IBDF alone could give it, which would translate into additional personnel, greater funds for land acquisition, and, in general, greater capacity to handle problems as they arose. With this in mind, Jorge Pádua decided to propose protecting the area.

The decision, like so many that informed the IBDF's conservation program for Amazonia, was based on the assumption that conservation and development in the region were inherently compatible, and would be made so in practice by government action. Acting on this assumption made conservation dependent on the long-term capacity and willingness of the Brazilian state to defend nature, so it entailed a risk, but Jorge Pádua, who fully understood the faustian nature of the bargain, thought it a good one nevertheless.

Jaú National Park

Its large size, compact shape, conformity to the local drainage pattern, and mix of forest types made Jaú the very model of the UN's Man and Biosphere Programme's ideal rainforest reserve in the Amazon basin,[66] but it was not biologically exciting. Its vegetation, although largely undisturbed, was typical of the region: closed canopy forest predominated on the upland sites; mixed hardwood and palm forests prevailed in the semi-inundated areas along the watercourses; more open patches of grass, shrub, and woodland were scattered throughout the area. Its fauna included the giant otter, the manatee, and the endangered black caiman, but its overall biological diversity was thought to be low. It appeared to contain no special biological communities nor anything biologically unique.[67] Flat to slightly hilly, the area was scenically unexciting, and the field team gave it low marks for tourist potential.[68]

Jaú had great advantages from an administrator's perspective, however. It was an interest vacuum: no Indians were thought to be present, so FUNAI had no concern for it; the region was an economic backwater and there were no government development plans for it; there were no known gold deposits, and it presented no security concerns. Human occupation was light, even for Amazonia, and there was little private land to be acquired. Roughly a hundred caboclo families lived in the proposed park, most along the lower course of the Jaú River.[69] Aside from itinerant traders and priests, few outsiders ever entered the area. The thirty tracts of private land, mostly brazilnut groves along rivers, comprised only about 1 percent of the park's area.[70]

With such a thin veneer of settlement and interest, the establishment of the national park was likely to involve little monetary or political expense. Moreover, its physical characteristics made it a manager's dream (figure 3.5). The park was roughly diamond shaped, with the three rivers that drained it converging as they approached the Negro River, and providing the only avenues to the park's interior. A guard post at the mouth of the Jaú would control access to more than two-thirds of the area, and another at the mouth of the Unini would control access to the rest. Jaú National Park was a low roll: it neither asked nor needed much of the future.

Neither low endemism nor lack of special biological features counted for much against these advantages in the IBDF's decision to propose the area for protection. Nor, as it turned out, did lack of theoretical pedigree. Wetterberg had assigned top priority status to Jaú because Haffer and Prance had identified the area as a former forest fragment. Later it was discovered that its status was the result of a cartographic error. The large fragment Prance had identified north of the middle course of the Amazon River did not extend west into the Jaú basin; only the slip of a pen made it appear to do so on the IBDF's maps. Given Jaú's other virtues, the discovery of the error—and the area's loss of official priority status—did not dampen the IBDF's enthusiasm. Jorge Pádua said regarding the discovery, "At that point, we were not concerned with theoretical errors."[71]

Rondônia

The IBDF proposed three protected areas in Rondônia Territory: Guaporé and Jaru biological reserves and Pacaás Novos National

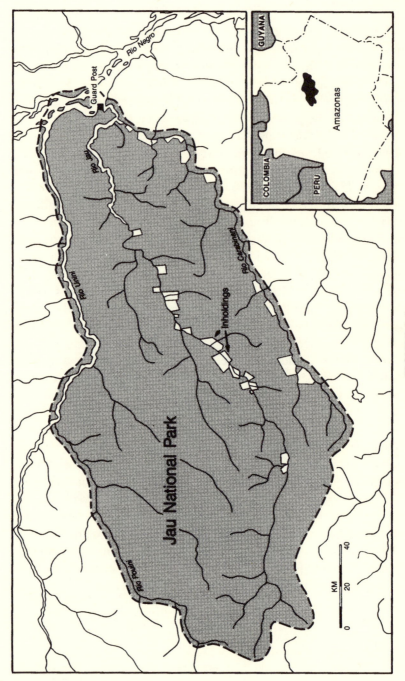

FIGURE 3.5
Jaú National Park

Park. Rondônia had long been a remote, thinly settled region far west of the nation's commercial frontier. Then, in 1960, a road from southern Brazil reached Porto Velho, the territorial capital, and a stream of settlers began to arrive.[72] Rondônia became an area of colonization under the PIN program, and although events there were often overlooked in the excitement of the Transamazon Highway, the large areas of good soil in the territory insured that the colonization would be vigorous. The planned colonies were soon full, and the new arrivals began settling wherever they could.[73] These successes caused Polamazonia's planners to make Rondônia an agricultural development pole, the Polonoroeste. Under the Polamazonia program, INCRA continued to concentrate on small-scale agriculture in Rondônia.

First under PIN and then under Polamazonia, the territory was steadily transformed from a backwater to a booming region of commercial agriculture. Between 1970 and 1975, the number of small farms in Rondônia rose from four thousand to twenty-four thousand.[74] Its rural population, which stood at only fifty thousand in 1970, was growing at the unparalleled annual rate of 17.6 percent during the 1970s.

The biological disruption that accompanied this transformation was enormous; Myers identified the rainforests of the state as among the most threatened in the world,[75] but as was the case at Trombetas, the possibility of outside support for conservation seemed promising. SUDECO, the regional development agency responsible for Rondônia, accepted biological conservation as a part of development, at least in principle, and had helped underwrite the IBDF's expeditions in the territory; it had also expressed a willingness to help support parks or reserves that grew out of those expeditions.[76] The World Bank, then being drawn into the territory's development, had also signaled a willingness to support nature protection and from a Brazilian perspective the resources of the bank appeared limitless. Seizing the opportunity she sensed, Jorge Pádua proposed three protected areas for this relatively small part of Amazonia.

The proposed Guaporé Biological Reserve contained vast, grassy floodplains with the appearance and faunal richness of the more famous Pantanal several hundred kilometers southeast in Mato Grosso state.[77] The evaluation team had found it exceptionally free of human disturbance, thanks largely to its location far south of the territory's main axis of development.

The outstanding feature of the second proposed area, Pacaás Novos National Park, was its highlands: large, tabular massifs bordered by dramatic, dissected escarpments. The massifs were covered with cerrado formations that, unlike similar formations further east in Mato Grosso, had not been grazed or burned, giving them a special importance for research. Forest predominated in the surrounding lowlands. Panthers and jaguars were known to inhabit it, and the presence of many other rainforest species was suspected. Surveys indicated no squatters and very little private land. At its closest point the proposed park was only sixty kilometers from the national highway, BR 364, the main axis of settlement in the territory, and settlement roads were already being cut in its direction from the highway; however, most of the soils were infertile, lessening its appeal to settlers. There had been many confirmed sightings of Indians, but the IBDF held that they were only hunting parties from outside.[78]

The third proposed area, Jaru Biological Reserve, was in the northeast corner of Rondônia, where protecting nature was likely to be difficult. RADAM saw much agricultural potential in that part of the state, and INCRA was already establishing agricultural colonies there. The IBDF had initially considered proposing the old Jaru Forest Reserve as a biological reserve in spite of these drawbacks, but when the National Security Council, for its own reasons, ruled out the IBDF's appropriation of the private holdings on the east bank of the Machado River the forest reserve was dropped from the narrowing list of prospects. Jorge Pádua later changed her mind, reasoning that there might not be another chance to preserve a sample of the region's biota. Working within the narrow limits of the possible, the IBDF drew up a proposal incorporating approximately a quarter of the old forest reserve, an area not much larger than Terborgh's minimum. Because the bank of the Machado River was off limits, the reserve's western boundary would be a long, difficult-to-patrol survey line cutting across the area's drainage pattern. Nowhere else in Amazonia did IBDF conservationists show quite this willingness to take chances in reserve design, or to protect nature in the very teeth of regional development.

Eastern Amazonia

The IBDF also proposed protecting three of the four areas it had evaluated in Amapá. One, the Oiapoque Biological Reserve on the border with French Guiana, was mostly covered by dense rainforest.

The field evaluation team found evidence of considerable human disturbance and saw little tourism potential in the area, but its biological representativeness, the suspected presence of a number of endangered species, and the opportunity to delimit a large yet compact reserve outweighed these deficiencies.[79]

The proposed Cabo Orange National Park along the northernmost stretch of the Amapá coast contained vast tidal flats formed in recent times from sediments carried from the mouth of the Amazon River (figure 3.6). They were covered with plant communities whose character depended on length and frequency of inundation, but that normally included aquatic grasses and burití palms. Mangroves were found along the seaward edge of the flats, and there was rainforest on the higher ground along the western margins of the proposed park. Lago Piratuba, further south, was smaller but similar in most ways.[80]

Cabo Orange and Lago Piratuba had great faunal wealth; the Amapá coast was the last stronghold of many Caribbean birds—flamingos, scarlet ibises, and other birds could be found there in large numbers. (The presence of the birds, whose protection was the responsibility of the DN's Division of Nature Protection, created a built-in bureaucratic constituency for these areas.) Pumas, giant otters, manatees, and several species of sea turtle were found in these areas, and their accessibility from Belém gave them a tourist potential.[81] The human characteristics of both areas were also a plus. There were several small caboclo settlements, an Indian village, and two FUNAI posts close to the proposed Cabo Orange park, and caboclos and Indians undoubtedly hunted and fished in the area, but none were thought to live permanently within it. The field evaluation team discovered no permanent inhabitants, Indians or otherwise, in the Lago Piratuba. The land in both was in the public domain, so the establishment of the two protected areas was likely to be quick and inexpensive, and together they would protect more than half the territory's coast.

Two other areas in eastern Amazonia rounded out the group. One was on Marajó Island, a vast island at the mouth of the Amazon built on fluvial sediments. The island was covered with forests and large stretches of grasslands. At 88,900 hectares, the proposed Marajó Biological Reserve was the smallest of the group, far smaller than the 250,000-hectare minimum for representing the full complexity of a major bioregion. Such was not the aim here, however; Marajó was the only one of the eleven proposed areas belonging to the second class of protected areas Wetterberg recommended, the smaller one designed to preserve a site of special value rather than a

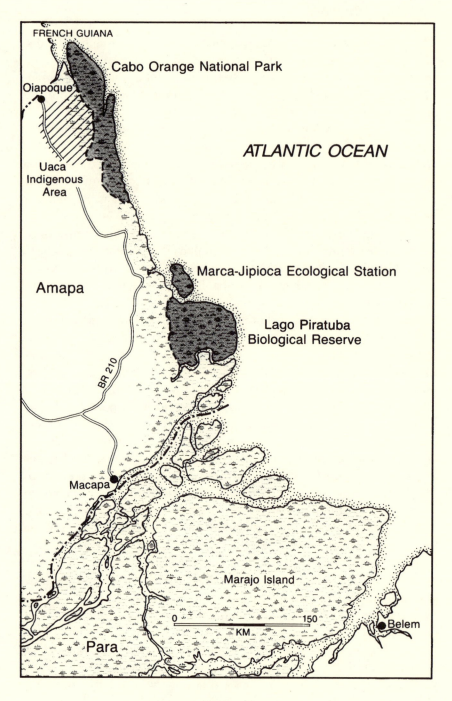

FIGURE 3.6
Protected Areas on the Amapá Coast

whole, representative ecosystem.[82] The area was exceptional among the eleven in its high rating on historical and anthropological value; the island had been the site of a well-documented pre-Columbian culture, and the proposed reserve would protect important archaeological sites.

The area selected for the reserve was little disturbed, but cattle had been raised on the island for more than three hundred years, and planners had made it a development pole, hoping to build a modern livestock industry on the island's traditions of cattle raising. Marajó was thus another of Jorge Pádua's faustian bargains; she was willing to place the reserve in the path of development in hopes that the agencies responsible for that development would fit conservation into their planning.

The final proposal was the Xingu Biological Reserve. The field evaluation team had confirmed that the area on the upper Xingu River was the home of a breeding population of giant otters, could be considered representative of the larger regional ecosystem, and was generally rich in fauna,[83] but some of its discoveries were less promising: there were numerous squatters already in the area, and much of it was in private ownership. These factors, plus the proximity of two Indian reserves and a national highway, meant that managing a biological reserve was likely to be difficult, but because of the high marks it received on biological criteria, the IBDF proposed its protection anyway.

***

Taken together, the proposals revealed much about those who advanced them. One was a loyalty to the original biocentric principles on which Wetterberg's approach was based (table 3.4). The highest ratings for the group as a whole were for representativeness of the natural region, presence of habitat for rare species, ecological diversity, and potential for scientific research. They also revealed a confidence in the IBDF's political and administrative capacity. Half the proposed areas were already the site of activities that conflicted with biological conservation, and only one got top marks for preservation in its natural state. It was assumed that the IBDF could overcome management difficulties, prevent future degradation, and even reverse that which had already occurred.

They revealed a willingness—and capacity—to blend science and pragmatism for maximum advantage. Jorge Pádua and Wetterberg,

TABLE 3.4
IBDF Evaluation of Proposed Protected Areas in Amazonia

Unit	Criterion												
	1	2	3	4	5	6	7	8	9	10	11	12	13
Lago Piratuba	4	4	4	4	4	4	3	4	4	3	1	1	1
Cabo Orange	4	4	4	4	4	3	4	3	3	3	3	2	3
Oiapoque	4	4	4	4	3	3	3	4	1	2	2	3	2
Pacaás Novos	4	4	4	4	3	4	4	4	3	3	1	1	3
Guaporé	4	4	4	4	4	3	3	4	3	4	1	1	1
Jaú	4	4	4	4	4	3	3	4	2	3	2	1	2
Pico da Neblina	4	4	3	4	4	4	4	3	4	3	4	3	3
Rio Trombetas	4	4	4	4	4	3	4	3	3	2	2	1	3
Marajó	4	3	4	4	4	4	3	3	4	3	4	4	1
Xingu	4	4	4	2	4	3	3	2	3	3	1	2	1
Criterion Mean Value	4.0	3.9	3.9	3.8	3.8	3.4	3.4	3.4	3.0	2.9	2.1	2.0	2.0

Criterion

1	Natural region	4.0
2	Habitat for rare species	3.9
3	Potential for scientific research	3.9
4	Physiographic region	3.8
5	Ecological diversity	3.8
6	Unique characteristics	3.4
7	Aesthetic appeal	3.4
8	Absence of conflicting use	3.4
9	Potential for education	3.0
10	Current state of preservation	2.9
11	Value for international tourism	2.1
12	Cultural, anthropological, and historical value	2.0
13	Potential for recreation	2.0

Matrix Values
  4   Excellent
  3   Good
  2   Average
  1   Poor (*Inadequada*)

Source: IBDF/FBCN *Plano do Systema: Primera Etapa.*

aware of the uncertainty still associated with the scientific theories they had embraced, forged a double relationship with these theories. They publicly stressed their importance in shaping the IBDF's program because the theories gave it pedigree and coherence. Yet because they knew future research might undercut them, they were careful not to let the theories dominate the selection process: they selected no area solely, or even primarily, because it had been identified as a

Pleistocene forest fragment,[84] and they were not overly concerned with selecting areas to maximize coverage of Prance's regions.[85] Within the standards of biological value they had established, they let political opportunities determine the regional distribution of conservation energies: Polonoroeste produced favorable conditions in Rondônia, so three proposals were advanced for that small territory; politics in Roraima were unfavorable, so it had no proposals. These steps buffered the IBDF's conservation program against the vicissitudes that accompanied the normal progress of science: should the theories ever be disproved, the IBDF's initiative would not be brought down with them. They also insured that conservation would cut with rather than against the grain of political opportunity.

The glossy 1979 report in which the proposals were set out also reflected a sure political hand. It encouraged its readers to view the proposals as a complementary set rather than a disparate group, thereby allowing the weaker ones to benefit by their association with the stronger.[86] It set out the proposals as "Stage One" of a plan to give Brazil one of the world's best biological conservation programs, one that would eventually include all the types of protected areas that a developed, prosperous nation should have.[87] (The report was named "Plan for the System of Brazilian Conservation Units: Stage One.") This strengthened the associations between Amazon conservation and progress that Brazilian conservationists had always tried to make in the minds of the public and government planners.

In fact, many elements of the report were explicitly designed to appeal to the military men who ran the government:[88] its highly organized structure, its great detail, and its systematic, step-wise implementation phases consciously mimicked planning for a military campaign; its comprehensiveness and ambition, especially its goal of eventually providing the full range of protected areas, complemented the pharaonic development projects of the Polamazonia program.

The appeal of the IBDF's program was further enhanced in 1979, when the World Wildlife Fund, in cooperation with INPA, began its Minimum Critical Size project at a site near Manaus.[89] The project, inspired by Island Biogeography Theory, would isolate rainforest patches by clearing the land around them and then study the changes the patches underwent to produce the kind of precise information needed to refine rainforest conservation policy. Neither Wetterberg nor Jorge Pádua were closely involved with the project, but its initiation added credibility to Island Biogeography Theory and, by extension, to attempts to derive practical conservation guidelines from high-level theory.

＊＊＊

As skillfully drawn up and packaged as the conservation program was, the upper levels of the military government had to be made aware of it. They also had to be persuaded to support it; approving a program of biological conservation in principle had been largely cost free, but setting aside and protecting millions of hectares would not be. The administrative locus of biological conservation was distant from the centers of power, leaving Jorge Pádua and her associates with little formal access to the top levels of government. The IBDF's parent ministry, Agriculture, was a nearly powerless, vestigial ministry. Officially, its task was the important one of increasing food production, but most major programs toward this end were handled by other ministries.[90] Since the IBDF's mission was peripheral to the ministry's agricultural goals, the forest institute was doubly marginal.

Before the "Step One" report was released, Jorge Pádua sidestepped these pinched lines of formal communication by cultivating professional friendships with the senior members of the military government, especially with João Figueiredo, who would replace Ernesto Geisel as president of the republic in March 1979 (while at the same time maintaining her links with the democratic opposition), and used these friendships to promote her program. The military men gradually came to view her as the foremost spokesperson for conservation within the federal government,[91] and once they did, the Ministry of Agriculture's weakness worked to her advantage; it could not restrain her bureaucratic entrepreneurship.

Her lobbying efforts received a strong boost in July 1978, when the Treaty of Amazon Cooperation was signed by all the nations with territory in Amazonia. The treaty, influenced by the previous decade of Latin American conservation work, was strongly conservationist in tone—so much so that the IUCN general assembly passed a vote of praise for the signatory nations—and one of the treaty's provisions pledged the signatory nations to protecting natural areas in their Amazon territories. Most of these nations had established new parks and reserves in Amazonia in the late 1970s (table 3.5), putting pressure on Brazil to take similar action before the reunion of the signatory nations in Belém in 1980.

TABLE 3.5

Protected Areas (10,000 Hectares or Larger) Established in Non-Brazilian Amazonia, 1975–1979

Country	Name of Area	Date Established	Size in Hectares × 1000
Bolivia	Manuripe Wildlife Refuge	1975	1,540
	Huanchaca National Park	1979	541
Colombia	Amacayacu National Park	1976	170
Ecuador	Yasuní National Park	1979	750
	Cuyabeno Faunal Reserve	1979	380
Venezuela	Serranía la Neblina National Park	1978	1,360
	Yapacana National Park	1978	320
	Duida-Marahuaca National Park	1978	210
	Jaua-Sarisarinama National Park	1978	330
Total			5,601

Source: Wetterberg et al., "Conservation Progress," p. 8.

President Figueiredo entered office aware of the IBDF proposal. After testing the political waters and finding no opposition, he incorporated it into his administration's program. On June 5, 1979, World Environment Day, he officially approved the Stage One report as the foundation for the IBDF's conservation program, and signed a decree establishing Pico da Neblina National Park.[92] He authorized Jaru Biological Reserve in July. In September, the Rio Trombetas Biological Reserve and Pacaás Novos National Park were established, and a set of strict, detailed regulations for the management of the new protected areas was signed into law. More protected areas were established by presidential decree the following year: Cabo Orange National Park and Lago Piratuba Biological Reserve in July 1980, Jaú and Pantanal national parks in September.[93] The latter, although beyond Amazonia, protected one of the richest areas of bird life in the world.

The presidential actions of 1979 and 1980 were a triumph for Brazilian conservation. They signaled that conservation was now viewed as a legitimate policy area at the highest levels of the Brazilian government.[94] Jorge Pádua was invited to lecture on ecology and conservation to the alumni of the Superior War College (ESG), the military's key instrument for building elite consensus on national issues. The Brazilian postal service issued stamps honoring the national parks in Amazonia. Jorge Pádua became one of the important conservation figures in South America, and the IBDF gained a reputation as one of the continent's more dedicated and effective conservation agencies.[95]

The gains in Brazilian Amazonia were seen abroad as a great step for international conservation. The new parks and reserves filled the last great gap in the continent's system of representative natural areas and changed the face of Amazon conservation; Brazil accounted for almost half the new natural areas and most of the acreage brought under public protection in Amazonia between 1976 and 1981. The great size of Brazil's new protected areas became the standard to which other South American conservationists now aspired, and the strict regulations for their management set new standards for the entire continent.[96] Finally, there had been a growing fear that science could not, or would not, provide answers to conservation questions, leaving conservationists with little more than intuition in making even their most important decisions,[97] but now a conservation program for one of the world's great bioregions was available to serve as a model of how to infuse science into conservation policy elsewhere.

CHAPTER 4

Conservation Ascendant

While the overriding conservation tasks in Amazonia in the late 1970s were the formulation of a coherent approach and the establishment of a program based on it, the main tasks during the early 1980s were the consolidation of past gains and the expansion of conservation's domain within the extant policy framework. The IBDF's program had to become a routinized, efficiently administered part of the forest agency's mission, and a secure niche in national life had to be carved for the program. A second federal agency, the Secretariat of the Environment (SEMA), became involved in biological conservation and had to mesh its policies with the IBDF's. Conservationists approached these tasks much as they had the earlier ones, balancing sensitivity to their immediate circumstances with a respect for the broader conventions of international conservation.

The IBDF faced three pressing tasks. The first was creating a strong, permanent constituency for conservation. The military government, whose favor provided the IBDF's conservation program with almost all its political support, would not last forever. By the late 1970s, Brazil was increasingly anxious to restore the democratic institutions extinguished with the coup of 1964; even the military had begun talking about a retreat from power. While many of the administrative changes that had worked to conservation's advantage were likely to outlast the military regime, conservationists had to anticipate the more democratic, pluralist political system that would characterize the developed Brazil of the future. To be sure, constituency building began well before the successes of 1979 and 1980, but it was only after those years that it assumed a prominent role.

The second task was consolidating recent legislative successes. The decrees of 1979 and 1980 had created an impressive set of protected areas on paper; now the new protected areas had to be managed. The IBDF's administrative structure had to be adapted to its new conservation program, and general regulations had to be honed into specific, detailed management policies. The gambles Wetterberg and Jorge Pádua had taken in delimiting enormous protected areas and in claiming areas where land-use conflicts were already present—in short, the ambition of the IBDF's conservation program—made this consolidation a pressing task. As with constituency building, providing for the management of the system began well before 1979, but only afterward did it become a pressing task.

The third task was expanding conservation's domain in Amazonia. The successes of 1979 and 1980 had required some tactical retreat: Wetterberg and the IBDF played down the need for general conservation measures in order to concentrate on the more politically attractive protected-area proposals. Moreover, the eleven Stage One proposals were only a small percentage of those areas in Amazonia worthy of protection, and even here there had been tactical retreat: several of the eleven had run into political difficulties and had been temporarily set aside to avoid risking the entire package. This left valuable areas without public protection. If they were not brought into the system, and if effective, basin-wide conservation measures were not instituted, a temporary halt could become the permanent boundary of an incomplete domain.

* * *

Constituency building focused on the scientific community and the public at large. Science had long been linked with the Brazilian national parks; scientific research was one of the rationales for establishing the first national parks in the 1930s, and Itatiaia National Park had became a well-used site of scientific investigation by the 1960s.[1] There was also a congenial tradition of Amazon science for the IBDF to tap: from its early years in the 1950s, INPA had been a center for research on the ecosystems of Amazonia, and in recent years that research had grown steadily. INPA provided a climate conducive to ecological research. Even much of its applied research (in agronomy, for example) was infused with ecological principles.[2]

Building on these traditions seemed important because biological conservation in a world undergoing development found its value underpinnings largely through science: conservation provided science with the undisturbed nature it needed for study, and science led to conservation policies that guaranteed nature would be managed effectively and for maximum benefit.[3] Science and conservation seemed an especially potent political combination in Brazil, whose Positivist intellectual traditions had imbued the nation with a respect for science, and whose commitment to development gave scientists a special role in bringing the nation a more prosperous future; in short, scientists seemed central to progress in Brazil.[4]

Science was always more than a neutral servant of progress, however, and its partisan qualities, expressed by individual scientists or collectively by scientific institutions, strengthened the value of a strong scientific constituency. First, scientists were frequently dedicated conservationists, and scientific institutions were often important elements in conservation networks. Scientists had been important in the conservation movement that emerged in southern Brazil at the beginning of the twentieth century.[5] Alberto Loefgren, director of the Botanical Garden of São Paulo, Alberto José de Sampaio, director of the National Museum in Rio de Janeiro, and Hermann von Ihering, director of the Museum of São Paulo, were all scientists who promoted early conservation measures and put the weight of their institutions behind such causes as the establishment of forest reserves and the promulgation of laws against deforestation.

This partisanship often caused scientists to exempt conservation measures from the full rigor of critical scrutiny. Scientists had been willing to support Wetterberg's proposals publicly and keep their reservations to themselves because they felt that establishing a conservation program for Amazonia while the political climate was favorable was important, and they knew that disagreement among experts was a sure way to drain the momentum from public initiatives.[6] They also knew that the success of the IBDF's conservation program in Amazonia was likely to inspire similar programs throughout the world.

Second, science as a collective, self-regulating enterprise, or what is called the "Invisible College of Science," had its own political interests, and the IBDF's conservation program could advance them. It was widely argued by politicians and public administrators in the 1970s that when left to its own devices, science became hopelessly abstract and neglected the great global concerns. This argument gave rise to demands that science be more closely tethered to social needs.[7] Such demands challenged scientists to show that solutions to real problems emerged when they followed their own interests and instincts. The IBDF's program used recent and sometimes highly theoretical science to settle practical matters: what parts of a biome should be protected? How large should biological reserves be? How many are needed? The program thus boosted even theoretical science's claim to practicality and helped restore confidence in science's capacity to keep Francis Bacon's original promise for it—i.e., "the improvement of man's estate"—when left to follow its own sense of what was important.

Jorge Pádua and Wetterberg had strengthened the operational links between science and conservation in Amazonia by encouraging INPA's participation in many of the evaluation expeditions. Jorge Pádua now went further by arranging for IBDF support for scientists willing to work in Amazonia National Park, the IBDF's one established park in the region before 1979. The response from the scientific community was strong; ten research projects covering a broad range of subjects and managed by scientists affiliated with a number of important scientific institutions were initiated in 1978 (table 4.1). The IBDF intensified its promotion of scientific research after the implementation of Stage One, especially in Amazonia National Park and the Rio Trombetas Biological Reserve. Ten new projects were begun in the former in 1980, and by that year, eleven projects were underway in Trombetas, some having begun even before the reserve had been formally established and most enjoying at least partial IBDF support. Like the research in Amazonia National Park, that undertaken at Trombetas varied widely in subject, linked the reserve with some of the most prominent scientific institutions in the country, and was likely to produce useful management information.

Jorge Pádua hoped to protect the relationship between science and the IBDF's conservation program by setting out formal rules for research. With research in the protected areas expanding rapidly and the legislation of 1979 having only briefly touched the subject, such rules were needed to manage the parks and reserves. Yet the rules would also serve strategic ends. Criticisms were being voiced in the third world of scientists, especially from the developed nations, who had abused research sites or the hospitality of host countries. Perez Olindo, a Kenyan and one of Africa's foremost conservationists, complained of foreign researchers who never made the results of their research available to their host institutions. Geraldo Budowski, a Costa Rican scientist and conservationist, put these real or imagined abuses into a dangerous rhetorical context by denouncing them as "scientific imperialism."[8] The international conservation commu-

TABLE 4.1
Research in Amazonia National Park, 1978–1980

Principal Investigator	Institutional Affiliation	Subject	Year Begun
Aldemar Gomes Bandeira	Goeldi Museum	Termites	1979
Barbara Zimmerman	Department of Zoology University of Guelph Canada	Amphibians	1978
David Conway Oren	INPA	Birds	1979
Gilberto Righi	Department of Zoology, University of São Paulo	Annelids	1980
Helmut Sick	National Museum of Rio de Janeiro	Birds	1979
Inocêncio de Souza Gorayeb	Goeldi Museum	Insects	1980
Jacques Charlwood	INPA	Bats	1979
José Carlos de Oliveira	Zoological Museum University of São Paulo	Fish	1979
José Márcio Ayres	INPA/Department of Anthropology, University of California, Berkeley	Monkeys	1979
Laurence Lacey	INPA	Insects	1979
Lyn Branch	IBDF/U.S. Peace Corps	General fauna	1978
Mário de Vivo	Zoological Museum, University of São Paulo	Primates	1978
Miguel Trefaut Rodrigues	Zoological Museum, University of São Paulo	Reptiles	1979
Nélio Roberto Dos Reis	State University of Londrina, Paraná	Bats	1979
Nelson Fernandes Gomes	Institute of Biosciences, University of São Paulo	Marsupials	1978
Robin Best	INPA	Mammals	n.d.
Ronald Crombie	Smithsonian Institution/ Museum of Zoology, University of São Paulo	Amphibians and reptiles	1978
Roseli Rodrigues	Museum of Zoology, University of São Paulo	Small rodents	1978
Timothy Kurt George	Rural University of Recife/ U.S. Peace Corps	Mammals	1978
Wai Yin Mok	INPA	Pathogenic fungi	1978
William Magnusson	INPA	Crocodiles	1980
William Leslie Overal	INPA/Goeldi Museum	Ants and wasps	1978

Source: IBDF/DPN Research Application Files, Brasília

nity sensed a danger that nationalist sentiment, if aroused by the issue, might force a rupture in the relationship between scientists and conservation managers and responded by promoting vigorous research procedures for protected areas.[9]

TABLE 4.2
State Parks and Biological Reserves

State	Number Established by 1969	Number Established 1970–1977
Minas Gerais	17	4
São Paulo	8	5
Rio Grande do Sul	7	10
Santa Catarina	5	1
Espírito Santo	5	0
Rio de Janeiro	3	3
Paraná	3	1
Totals	48	24

Source: Ludwig, *Brazil: A Handbook,* p. 305.

The IBDF's guidelines, issued in 1982, closely followed international precedent. Jorge Pádua hoped that by conveying a deep seriousness about both research and preservation they would protect the alliance of science and conservation in Amazonia from the criticisms that threatened it elsewhere. The guidelines were rigorous and exact, spelling out detailed research application and reporting procedures. They were exclusionary: parks and reserves were to be research sites of last resort. If suitable sites were available elsewhere, they should be used.[10]

The Brazilian public also had to be cultivated if conservation was to remain politically secure with the return of democracy. Much of the political strength of the American National Park System was based on the satisfaction Americans derived from visits to the parks and from the deep, symbol-based affection they had for the park system as a whole.[11] Jorge Pádua sensed that the potential for similar popular support in Brazil was vast. Life expectancy and literacy rates were increasing, as were levels of material prosperity.[12] Brazil seemed to be transforming itself into the kind of developed society that needed nature reserves to which citizens could occasionally retreat and whose existence was psychologically reassuring. The industrialized and relatively affluent southern states were establishing new state parks and protected areas at a rapid rate in the 1970s, seemingly bearing out this association of development and popular nature appreciation (table 4.2). A developed Brazil would use and support national parks, and if current rates of population growth accompanied that development, demand for national parks would be enormous within a generation or two.[13]

There was little to build on. Opportunities for public recreation had figured heavily in the establishment of Brazil's first national parks in the 1930s: Serra dos Orgãos was created around a group of striking peaks in the hopes that the area, already popular with hikers from nearby Rio de Janeiro, would serve large numbers of citizens of that city; Itatiaia, in the coastal mountains between Rio and São Paulo, was seen by its founders as a future vacation spot for the citizenry of these cities. Yet from its beginning, the Brazilian national park system had failed to live up to its potential for serving the public. Picnic facilities, including cabins and a swimming pool, were built in Serra dos Orgãos, and a museum and gardens were built at Itatiaia in the 1930s and 1940s, but most parks remained without visitor facilities. A visiting American geographer painted a depressing picture of the parks in 1963: inadequate park staffs, meager, run-down visitor facilities, and extensive private inholdings. He ventured to say that most Brazilians did not even know what a national park was.[14] The number of parks and visitors increased over the next decade, but visitors remained relatively few, most parks remained undeveloped, and many had attained only a small percentage of their authorized size (table 4.3). Some of the inholdings were so long-standing they had taken on a quasi-permanence.[15]

Jorge Pádua had begun trying to improve the capacity of the parks to accommodate visitors in the early 1970s, with her greatest early success occurring at Iguaçu National Park at the great falls on the Paraná River. Although the magnificent Hotel of the Cataracts had been constructed in the park in the late 1950s, so many private inholdings—and inholders (over six hundred families)—remained in the park a decade later that it was practically unmanageable. A 1969 IBDF report deemed the inholdings so extensive and well-entrenched that it proposed redrawing the park to exclude most of them; only a small area surrounding the falls would remain a national park.[16] Jorge Pádua refused to accept this dismemberment. She lobbied within the IBDF, found allies, and eventually had her way; the money and political will for the removals was found. Her success at Iguaçu encouraged her to take the same tack elsewhere: using her influence and whatever money became available to remove strategically located inholdings throughout the system, ones that in some cases had been slated for purchase since the 1930s. In all, the IBDF added 2 million hectares to extant national parks between 1974 and 1982.[17]

Parks needed facilities as well as land if they were to develop popular constituencies, so while planning for Amazon conservation was

TABLE 4.3

Authorized and Actual Size of the IBDF Protected Areas (in Hectares), 1972

Area	Year of Establishment	State	Authorized Size*	Actual Size in 1972	Actual Size as a Percentage of Authorized Size
Itatiaia	1937	Rio de Janeiro / São Paulo	12,000	10,000	83
Aparados da Serra	1959	Rio Grande do Sul/Santa Catarina	13,000	3,550	27
Araguaia	1959	Goiás	2,000,000	3,000	<1
Ubajara	1959	Ceará	4,400	64	2
Brasília	1961	Federal District	30,000	28,000	93
Chapada dos Veadeiros	1961	Goiás	625,000	0	0
Monte Pascoal	1961	Bahia	22,500	22,500	100
São Joaquim	1961	Santa Catarina	49,300	0	0
Sete Cidades	1961	Piauí	7,700	5,051	66
Serra da Bocaina	1972	Rio de Janeiro/ Minas Gerais	140,000	0	0
Serra da Canastra	1972	Minas Gerais	200,000	0	0

*No authorized size set for Caparáo, Emas, Iguaçu, Serra dos Orgãos, or Tijuca in the original decrees.
Source: Jorge Pádua, "Brazil's National Parks," p. 461.

underway in the late 1970s, the IBDF built facilities in the extant parks elsewhere in Brazil. A visitor center with a library, interpretive displays, and a large conference room was completed in Brasília National Park in 1978. Rental cabins, picnic shelters, hiking trails, and interpretive displays were built in several parks, and old facilities were refurbished elsewhere. Visitor brochures for the eight most popular parks were prepared and distributed in 1978.

* * *

Wetterberg and Jorge Pádua understood that even a large and appreciative constituency would not secure the program unless the IBDF developed the capacity to manage the areas it brought under its jurisdiction. The task had two distinct components. One involved the direct management of individual protected areas. The other involved program-wide management: a focus of policy making, an administrative hierarchy, and a set of routines for handling program-wide business had to be established. Each management instrument had to be carefully fitted to both the general conservation goals it was expected to advance and the particular circumstances of the IBDF's conservation program. Wetterberg and Jorge Pádua began thinking about system management soon after Wetterberg arrived in Brasília in 1976.

The IBDF called together a widely experienced international team to develop an approach to area management.[18] Biologists from INPA and the U.S. Peace Corps took part. The Polamazonia program lent personnel. A landscape architect supported by the World Wildlife Fund and an architect supported by the FBCN participated. Even Kenton Miller was drawn in, serving as a consultant for a time. Not surprisingly, the approach that evolved was squarely within the mainstream of international practice. Earlier plans prepared by Miller and his associates for other Latin American countries found their way into the IBDF's thinking, as did the model national parks planning manual the FAO had just developed. The ultimate models, however, were the management plans of the U.S. and Canadian national parks, and like them, the Brazilian plans would call for extensive infrastructure and a high level of staffing. In accord with its models, the IBDF's area management plans would have three major elements: visitor service, including interpretation, education, and public relations; environmental management, including scientific research, controlled burning, and wildlife reintroduction; and operations, including park protection and maintenance.

Once the approach had been hammered out, planning for four parks began. In keeping with the strategic considerations that permeated Wetterberg's and Jorge Pádua's thinking, each of the four was given priority because it had a special constituency. Brasília National Park received priority because the IBDF understood what the U.S. National Park Service had discovered decades earlier: a developed national park in the nation's capital would attract an important clientele and would be highly visible to the nation's political elite. Iguaçu had great visitor potential, including foreign visitors who brought foreign exchange with them. Sete Cidades had the support of the Bahian government, anxious to bring tourism to the depressed interior of the state.

The fourth, Amazonia National Park, had a special constituency. Although Wetterberg had never particularly valued the park, Jorge Pádua appreciated the fact that it contained vast areas of rainforest typical of central Amazonia. Nevertheless, she felt planning for it could wait. The 1970s had seen substantial changes in Amazonia—industry outpaced agriculture, per capita income rose, and the region's population became more urban—but it was still a relatively poor, lightly inhabited region at the end of the decade (table 4.4). Jorge Pádua therefore ruled out courting a mass constituency for Amazonia National Park, or any of the parks in Amazonia, for the short term. Because she did, and because she thought immediate threats to the park were minor, she gave a low priority to planning for the park's management.[19] The World Wildlife Fund, however, thought it strategically important to quickly draw up a plan for the park, which until 1979 was the only large protected area in Brazilian Amazonia, and offered to help underwrite the effort. With outside support, the IBDF was willing to give it planning priority.

In 1979, while President Figueiredo was signing most of the Stage One proposals into law, the IBDF published completed management plans for these four areas. Once these were complete and the model was in place, preparing plans became routinized, carried out quickly by smaller teams. Between 1980 and 1982, twelve management plans were completed. Each was published in a glossy, illustrated report laying out zoning and construction plans, and setting personnel requirements. These later plans showed even more ambition and optimism than the first ones (table 4.5). Staffs of over 200 were planned for the larger or more popular national parks like Araguaia, Tijuca, and Iguaçu. Tijuca's management plan, for example, called for 200 park guards and another 160 administrative, interpretive,

TABLE 4.4
Brazil and the Northern Region,* Selected Indicators 1965–1978

Year	Population of the North (in thousands)	Northern Population as a Percentage of National Population	Northern Per Capita Product as a Percentage of National Per Capita Product	Value of Industrial Product/Value of Agricultural Product	
				North	Brazil
1965	3,076	3.80	50.5	77.2	205.4
1966	3,181	3.82	52.0	87.2	251.9
1967	3,290	3.84	49.9	90.7	260.0
1968	3,402	3.86	50.3	94.9	293.2
1969	3,519	3.88	48.7	98.2	321.6
1970	3,651	3.91	50.9	82.1	355.9
1971	3,786	3.94	47.6	96.0	388.3
1972	3,929	3.98	49.9	104.1	358.7
1973	4,108	4.05	48.0	91.0	346.4
1974	4,236	4.07	50.5	100.6	355.4
1975	4,402	4.11	55.1	135.7	375.2
1976	4,577	4.16	59.2	155.7	358.9
1977	4,761	4.21	60.5	183.3	300.8
1978	4,956	4.26	62.7	238.3	325.4

* Includes Pará, Amapá, Roraima, Amazonas, Rondônia, and Acre
Source: SUDAM, *Amazônia: Renda Interna*, pp. 20–22.

TABLE 4.5
Projected Staffing Levels for IBDF Protected Areas

Area	Date of Management Plan	Protection Staff	Other Personnel[1]	Comments
Monte Pascoal	1979	6	9	Small unit, few visitors
Sete Cidades	1979	6	16[2]	Small unit, easy to patrol
Serra dos Orgãos	1980	16	49[3]	Popular but easy to protect
Iguaçu	1981	124	142	Heavily visited unit in populated region
Caparáo	1981	79	102	Much infrastructure
Ubajara	1981	20	91	Small unit with much infrastructure
Sooretama	1981	64	8[2]	Few visitors expected
Poço das Antas	1981	25	10[2]	High level of threat but small and with very limited public access
Tijuca	1981	200	160	Popular park
Araguaia	1981	119	128	High level of threat
Emas	1981	15	14	Open land, easy to patrol
Serra da Canastra	1981	72	73	Large unit in populated region
Itatiaia	1982	80	129	Popular park
Aparados da Serra	1984	42	41[3]	
Amazonia	1979	21	15[2]	Unusually low staffing projection
Rio Trombetas	1982	80	28	Difficult to patrol, few visitors expected
Pacaás Novos[4]	1984	129	38	High level of threat, difficult to patrol
Jaru[4]	1984	30	21	Easy to patrol, small for Amazonia
Guaporé[4]	1984	52	23	Few visitors expected

[1] Administration, maintenance, and visitor service
[2] Plus unspecified number of office personnel
[3] Plus guides and interpreters
[4] Plans not yet officially approved in 1986
Source: Compiled from IBDF/DN management plans, 1979–1984.

and maintenance employees. There would be fewer visitors to the biological reserves so they would have smaller staffs, but plans for most of the reserves were still ambitious. Rio Trombetas, for example, was to have a staff of 108.

Such planning mixed political acumen with ambition. A management plan was a claim on administrative resources and a position from which to begin budgetary and political compromise. The more ambitious the plan, the stronger the opening gambit. Furthermore, since the national parks legislation of 1979 had specified that a management plan be drawn up for each protected area, a plan had some force of law, making it useful in resisting inappropriate uses of the protected areas.[20] Above all, the planning reflected the optimism about conservation's place in the future of Brazil that characterized all aspects of the IBDF's conservation program.

Although planning for the individual protected areas closely followed international practice, circumstances forced system administration away from accepted norms. A centralized administration and a simple line of command were generally preferred for extensive conservation programs like the IBDF's. The concentration of policy-making in one central agency insured against contradictory or discordant policy. A simple line of command, with the directors of each protected area reporting to one chief, allowed efficient policy implementation and monitoring of field operations. Centralized authority and a direct command hierarchy protected conservation goals from subversion by other interests.

There were formidable obstacles to such arrangements in the IBDF, however. First, conservation had no real focus within the institute. The ideal administrative center of the IBDF's conservation program was the Department of National Parks and Equivalent Reserves (DN), already responsible for providing technical services to the protected natural areas and overseeing a miscellany of other conservation responsibilities: maintaining the national list of endangered plants; running manatee, turtle, and migratory bird protection programs; and insuring Brazil's compliance with its international treaty obligations (figure 4.1). The DN was hopelessly understaffed, however; it had only three professionals in 1976, leaving it unable to carry out even its technical tasks. Its expansion was blocked by a civil service rule preventing the IBDF from hiring professionals other than foresters, agronomy engineers, and architects. The DN's small size and inability to discharge even its routine tasks rendered it incapable of acting as a strong center for conservation. In the absence of one, authority for conservation policy was diffused, frequently in an ad hoc fashion, through a number of departments and staff positions at agency headquarters.

Jorge Pádua circumvented the civil service rule by making an arrangement with the FBCN, the private conservation organization,

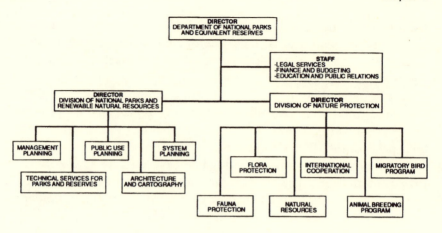

FIGURE 4.1
IBDF Department of National Parks and Equivalent Reserves:
Organization Table

through which the DN took on biologists, wildlife specialists, and park planners who technically became FBCN employees.[21] The FBCN paid them and the IUCN reimbursed it for its "consultation services." With over twenty professionals provided by this arrangement and support personnel provided by the IBDF through regular channels, the DN could carry out the administrative tasks the IBDF's expanded conservation program involved. The DN drew up preliminary budgets for the parks and reserves, designed their facilities, kept their records, supervised research in them, and developed management plans. An ill-defined but generally accepted responsibility for shaping policy went with these tasks, and Jorge Pádua's position as the head of the DN, plus the unit's increasing importance within the forest agency, enabled it to exercise a de facto leadership in conservation.[22]

The second obstacle was the line of command: the IBDF had decentralized authority for its field operations years earlier by appointing *delegados* (representatives) to the states and territories and giving them much power over the institute's activities within their respective jurisdictions (figure 4.2). The budget wishes of the delegados carried great weight at IBDF headquarters;[23] they had wide latitude in spending and could divert money earmarked for one activity to another; and they had considerable flexibility in using the IBDF per-

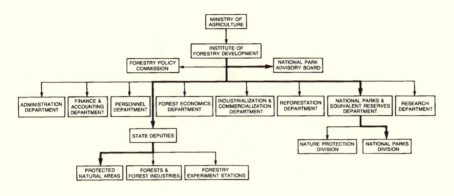

FIGURE 4.2
IBDF Organization Table

sonnel within their jurisdictions. Circumventing the delegados would mean creating a separate line of command for conservation, an expensive undertaking and sure to create confusion. On the other hand, placing conservation within the existing arrangement would bring it under administrators who were not necessarily conservation partisans. Moreover, the delegados were nominated to their positions by the state governments, usually because of past service within the state. The future careers of most of them would be with state rather than federal government, making them sensitive to the wishes of the states, and the states of Amazonia had shown little enthusiasm for conservation.[24]

The IBDF conservationists ultimately had little choice in the matter: expense and potential for confusion ruled out any option other than fitting the management of the protected areas to the existing arrangement. Officially, the delegados would provide the conservation program with "administrative support,"[25] a neutral term that masked the extent of the delegados' control over the protected areas: they would supervise park personnel, have a large say in resource allocations, and make immediate management decisions. While Wetterberg generally favored the more direct system, he thought the arrangement appropriate under the circumstances. It was relatively easy for the delegados, based in the state and territorial capitals, to supervise park management, and because the delegados usually had good political connections with local administrations, they could encourage the states and territories to avoid actions that might run contrary to federal conservation goals.[26] Moreover, the IBDF's conservation program had top-level political support, so the message the delegados received from the IBDF headquarters was clear: advancing the program was an important part of their jobs.

To complement the program's administrative machinery, Jorge Pádua encouraged the IBDF to establish a Parks Advisory Board. Such an organ had been a useful political instrument of American National Park System leadership during the great period of system expansion in the 1930s. Stocked with Rockefellers and the like, the American board had the respect the U.S. Congress normally accorded the privileged, which it used to advance the service's programs and, occasionally, to defend the parks from congressional miscreancy.[27] Jorge Pádua, aware of the precedent, intended the IBDF to use its board similarly, as an instrument for discreet lobbying and as a high-level conduit for information to other sectors of government and society. An active advisory board could also help prevent the centrifugal forces latent in the program's administrative machinery from expressing themselves by reinforcing policy coherence at the center and preventing the diffusion of too much power over the system among the delegados on the periphery.

* * *

Finally, more of Amazonia had to be brought under conservation's sway. The success of the IBDF's Stage One initiative had been bought with compromises and retreats that eventually had to be made good. One was not pressing for region-wide protection measures. Another was concentrating on large, representative natural areas, while leaving the smaller, unique sites for the nonce. A third was shelving a number of promising, biologically attractive proposals.

Political considerations had forced the IBDF to abandon its efforts to protect natural areas in the small northern territory of Roraima. The government of Amapá had objected to three large protected areas within its borders, arguing that withdrawing so much land in the small territory would leave little for economic development. In the face of this objection and the sympathy that greeted it at higher levels of government in Brasília, the IBDF deemed it expedient to shelve the proposal that aroused the most opposition, Oiapoque Biological Reserve. Land conflicts had derailed the Guaporé Biological Reserve in Rondônia at the last moment. SEMA's interest in establishing a reserve of its own on Marajó Island caused the IBDF to put the Marajó Biological Reserve on hold until the environmental agency's intentions could be clarified.

Logistics had forced one promising area, Serra do Divisor on Acre's border with Peru, out of consideration. Several scientists had identified the area as a Pleistocene forest fragment, so Wetterberg had given it his top-priority rating, but mounting an expedition to the remote area proved difficult, and when one finally reached it, logistical problems prevented the collection of sufficient data to justify proposing its protection. These derailed proposals were the most visible shortcomings of the IBDF's conservation program, and Jorge Pádua was anxious to put momentum behind them again, lest the momentum behind the entire program be lost.[28] The IBDF teams continued gathering information from these areas in the years after 1979. Jorge Pádua and her associates worked to overcome objections, redrawing boundaries when necessary, or, in one case, entirely relocating a proposal. The IBDF's second major conservation initiative, Stage Two of the System Plan, unveiled in 1982 and containing eleven proposals for large protected areas in Amazonia, was intended primarily to settle this unfinished business.[29]

Taking care to avoid areas of agricultural potential and mineral worth, the IBDF now proposed five protected areas in Roraima, one of which, Rio Branco National Park, would be the largest protected area in Amazonia. The IBDF and SEMA had reached an accord on their respective areas of interest on Marajó Island, so now the Marajó proposal was back. The Guaporé proposal reappeared, although it was now shifted to an area of less conflict and reduced to less than half its originally proposed size (see figure 7.7 in chapter 7). The Oiapoque Biological Reserve was also back in a reduced form (1,095,000 hectares, down from 1,473,000); a large area already undergoing clearing and certain to cause management problems had been eliminated from the proposal. Finally, a field team had gathered sufficient data to support a Serra do Divisor National Park, so it too was included among the eleven Stage Two proposals.

There was only one wholly new proposal for a major protected area in Amazonia, and only one thwarted Stage One proposal did not reappear in the new initiative. One represented what the IBDF hoped was the future of Amazon conservation; it hoped the other was an exceptional case of permanently unrealized ambitions.

The first, the proposal for Abufari Biological Reserve, originated with the IBDF *delegado* in Manaus, who had heard reports that the low-lying lands and lakes astride the Purus River were rich in wildlife, and, on his own initiative, had commissioned a study that confirmed the reports. The *delegado* promoted the idea of the biological reserve within the state and eventually won the support of the state government. Although Jorge Pádua never understood to her complete satisfaction why the state was so enthusiastic about the reserve, she hoped it was because conservation ideas were taking hold in Amazonia itself.[30] There were other signs that it was: the state of Amazonas had created an environmental council to advise it in 1977, and two years later, Belém established a Municipal Council of Environmental Defense. Shortly thereafter, the Amazonas Board of Education, in cooperation with INPA, began a program to bring the environmental message to school children throughout the state.[31] Jorge Pádua interpreted the state government's enthusiasm for Abufari as the latest expression of this interest, and once it became clear that it was a biologically valuable area, she took advantage of the opportunity. Boundaries for a biological reserve were quickly delineated and Abufari was added to the Stage Two initiative.

The proposed Xingu Biological Reserve showed that even Jorge Pádua's optimism had limits, but it also showed how much it took to exceed those limits. The level of occupation within the proposed reserve was high and much of the land was already in private ownership. Since the area was on the margins of a vigorously expanding agricultural district, squatting and pressure from speculators and large agriculturalists were likely to increase beyond already high levels. Jorge Pádua reluctantly decided it was too late to bring the area under protection and curtailed her efforts on its behalf.[32]

The 1982 initiative took care of unfinished business of another sort in proposing types of protected areas not included in Stage One. The new initiative proposed the first Brazilian wildlife refuges. Smaller than national parks or biological reserves, they would protect unique, discrete biological phenomena rather than whole ecosystems. Such a category had been proposed by Wetterberg in his 1976 report, but Stage One, in accord with its emphasis on representing major bioregions, had focused on larger units. Now sixteen such refuges were proposed along the northeast coast to protect marine manatees. Stage Two also proposed a 360-kilometer parkway through the scenic and biologically rich Pantanal region, a proposal aimed at tightening the links between conservation and the middle class, many of whom already had the autos, leisure time, and discretionary income for driving vacations, and more of whom doubtlessly would in the future.

The old business Stage Two did not address was as important as that which it did, however. By not setting out region-wide conservation measures, it implicitly extended the compromise made earlier. While the need for such measures to complement protected areas was widely recognized among conservationists, Jorge Pádua's decision to concentrate on the latter seemed reasonable, at least for the time being.

The importance of the protected natural area as a conservation instrument was rising as the maintenance of the genetic breadth of species became an important conservation goal: zoos or botanic gardens might suffice for preserving outstanding individuals or small, unique biotic communities over the short term, but they could seldom preserve the genetic variability necessary for long-term species survival.[33] The value of protected areas as part of the future's insulation from the mistakes of the present increased as the sense of how much remained unknown about the natural world, including the full extent of modern civilization's dependence on it, deepened. Natural areas also came to be seen as places where diversity could be produced as well as preserved. The evolutionary opportunities present in protected natural areas might, over the long term, have to compensate for the extinctions in areas where human activity was intensifying.[34]

There were justifications for the concentration growing out of the partition of bureaucratic responsibility. Federal responsibility for Amazonia was highly fragmented among public agencies, each of which had its own legal mandate and area of operation.[35] The Rio Doce Valley Company (CVRD) had its domain at Carajás. Numerous agricultural and industrial development agencies had their own agendas and programs. INCRA was responsible for the disposition of the federal lands, the IBDF for the management of the forest. The Superintendency of Fisheries Development (SUDEPE) developed the fisheries of the region. Given this fragmentation of authority, it seemed wise to stick to a conservation activity for which the IBDF had clear authority, rather than adopt conservation measures for which its authority was questionable.[36] Jorge Pádua also had her own position within the IBDF to consider. She felt that as head of the DN, protecting undisturbed nature was her least disputable responsibility within the pale of Amazon conservation.[37]

Moreover, events beyond her purview appeared to be leading to region-wide conservation measures, making it unnecessary for her to throw much of her own energies, or those of the IBDF, into them. First, other agencies seemed likely to institute programs that would complement the parks and reserves. For example, SUDAM's Natural Resources Division had become a strong advocate of developing Amazonia along environmentally sensitive lines; it advocated only selective cutting of the forest, a cap on the growth of the cities, and limits on intensive agriculture and cattle rearing. Its arguments were making headway within the agency during the late 1970s.[38]

As promising, in May 1979 President Figueiredo had charged representatives of fifteen Brazilian institutions and public agencies (including the Federal University of Amazonas, SUDAM, and the IBDF) with developing a master policy for managing the entire Amazon rainforest region, and in October their "Forest Policy for the Brazilian Amazon" was issued. Strongly conservationist in tone, it recommended concentrating short-cycle commercial agriculture on the flood plains, where it would be least damaging to the rainforest. It proposed limiting agriculture in the upland forest to tree crops, and it recommended zoning all Amazonia according to the natural capacities of the soils. The report appeared to have a strong impact on government thinking: the Third National Development Plan, released in 1980, echoed it, stressing that frontier areas in Amazonia were to be developed in a "non-predatory" fashion.[39]

Finally, Jorge Pádua viewed the new parks and reserves of 1979 and 1980 as her greatest accomplishment, and she sensed that political conditions favored further expansion: a government-sponsored task force had recommended that 60 million hectares of Amazonia be set aside as national forest, a total area many times larger than that already under public protection. Once the Stage Two initiative was unveiled, events seemed to bear out the assumption that there was untapped political potential for preservation. President Figueiredo was as receptive to the Stage Two proposals as he had been to the earlier ones; Abufari and Guaporé biological reserves were created within months of the report's publication.[40] The political momentum behind Amazon conservation appeared strong enough to carry this carefully wrought second phase of the IBDF's program to implementation.

* * *

While the IBDF was establishing its program for Amazonia, the Brazilian Secretariat of the Environment (SEMA) established its own program of biological conservation. SEMA had been established in 1973 amid the international surge of environmental awareness that followed the Stockholm Conference, and Paulo Nogueira-Neto, a biologist and professor at the University of São Paulo, was appointed to head it. Although the agency was established primarily to combat pollution, Nogueira-Neto was already active in biological conservation and decided the new agency would play a major role in that field.[41] Once he made this decision, a whole new set of resources became available to biological conservation. Their successful employ would depend on SEMA's ability to fashion appropriate policies.

SEMA and the IBDF faced similar basic problems in creating their conservation programs. The vast gaps in knowledge of Brazilian flora and fauna, especially in Amazonia, meant both had to rest their programs, to some degree, on uncertain biological assumptions. Both had to find niches for their programs within the broad goals of the federal government and within the vast interest agglomeration that was Brazilian society. Both had to find formulas for integrating biological value and political expedience. Finally, and perhaps most crucially, both had to build the right assumptions about the future of Brazil into their programs. The two agencies also faced some similar tactical challenges in creating their programs: both operated under imperfect or inappropriate basic legislation; both had to compensate for their remoteness from centers of power in the federal bureaucracy.

SEMA's task environment was different from the IBDF's in several crucial ways, however—usually to SEMA's disadvantage. The forest agency was a large, well-established organization; SEMA was a small, autonomous, newly formed agency within the Ministry of the Interior, a ministry with many disparate responsibilities and already the home of some forty autonomous agencies. The Minister of the Interior, officially responsible for SEMA, had little energy to devote to helping his new ward compensate for the disadvantages of its birth. SEMA had no preexisting regional network like the IBDF's delegado system onto which responsibility for running a conservation program could be grafted.

SEMA was more restricted by circumstance in developing its program. The IBDF's 1967 organic legislation gave it undisputable first claims to conservation as its bureaucratic turf. The IBDF was already active in conservation, maintaining turtle protection and bird banding programs and operating a system of parks and reserves in existence since the 1930s. If SEMA's program resembled the IBDF's too closely, it would provoke the latter's hostility. Worse, it would leave

the fledgling agency exposed to the waves of bureaucratic rational-
ization that periodically swept across the federal administrative
machinery, and therefore never free of the threat of the budget axe,
or even extinction.

Finally, Nogueira-Neto's sense of scientific worth and his instinc-
tual estimates of conservation's weight in Brazilian politics differed
from those of Wetterberg and Jorge Pádua. His strong style of leadership permitted his divergent thinking in these areas to strongly
color the decision-making environment of his agency.

These differences were magnified in practice by the absence of a
common font of tradition from which to draw and the lack of a common administrative base on which to build, causing SEMA and the
IBDF's programs for biological conservation to take very different
specific forms in spite of the similarity of their professed general goals.

The first question SEMA faced was what part of the biological
world it should protect. The agency's earliest policy documents
spoke of protecting representative samples of Brazil's major ecosystems, but SEMA decided that, while it would not rule out such areas,
it should focus on smaller areas of unique vegetation instead; it initially foresaw acquiring tracts ranging from minute to approximately
100,000 hectares.[42] The dictates of Island Biogeography Theory
notwithstanding, scientists recognized the virtues of even very small
protected areas. Abele and Connor wrote that a refuge measuring
only a square kilometer might be all that was needed to protect some
life forms that had low mobility and dense populations. Terborgh
observed that thousands of communal birds could be protected by
setting aside rookeries that measured only a few dozen hectares.[43]

Such a focus had several appealing points for an agency in SEMA's
circumstances. It was what Terborgh called "conservation on the
cheap": small financial or managerial outlays would produce great
relative returns, which made it practical for a small, new agency of
unproven financial resources. Equally important, it fit the policy
space left to it by the IBDF. International conservation doctrine
placed preserving the biologically unique on a par with preserving
representative ecosystems. For example, the UN's Man and Biosphere
Program asserted that a complete national program of biological
conservation had to encompass both.[44] By concentrating on such
areas, SEMA could argue it was avoiding the forest agency's turf and
providing an essential complement to the IBDF's programs.

Unlike the IBDF, SEMA declined to incorporate any overarching biogeographic theory into its calculus of value. Nogueira-Neto, a mature scientist, understood that the biological world contained many criteria of worth that could not be captured in any broad theory, or even any combination of them.[45] Many scientists, especially older, more traditional field biologists and others suspicious of the conservation claims of Pleistocene Refuge Theory and Island Biogeography Theory, shared this view.[46]

Strategic considerations reenforced scientific ones here as well. By abjuring theory, Nogueira-Neto created another easily perceived difference between SEMA and the IBDF. Moreover, the forest agency was assembling a package of proposed parks and reserves that it hoped to establish all at once. Making the proposals appear as interlinked pieces of a set was therefore important, and giving them common theoretical referents did this. SEMA, with neither the resources nor the disposition for such an ambitious gambit, did not need the appearance of coherence theory lent policy. Any overarching set of value referents might also restrict SEMA's flexibility in responding to opportunities, while pushing it toward areas that, for a small agency of uncertain prospects, it would be expedient to avoid.

This reluctance to embrace theory had several ramifications. First, Amazonia did not have the same privileged place in SEMA's thinking that it had in the IBDF's. Wetterberg and Jorge Pádua's decision to use Pleistocene Refuge Theory, which dealt only with Amazonia, automatically pulled their attention to the region and made it special. This specialness was reinforced by the importance they placed on saving self-maintaining representatives of major ecosystems: only in Amazonia was preservation on such an ambitious scale still possible. SEMA, with neither guiding principle, viewed the region as biologically important, but not exceptionally so.[47] Second, the reluctance left SEMA more open to outside suggestions for protected areas, and left it with wider latitude in determining what made an area worth protecting.

The latter imparted a certain appearance of casualness to SEMA's procedures for identifying areas of interest. While the IBDF accepted external suggestions, it gave them a lower priority than those derived from its own theory-based guidelines; SEMA, without such internal guides, was fully open to suggestions from any sources: the RADAM project, other agencies, and private conservation organizations. Sometimes suggestions came from scientists familiar with a particular area; for example, a letter from a biologist in Cambridge, England, suggesting the protection of an area at the mouth of the Japura River in western Amazonia prompted SEMA to investigate the area. Sometimes the initial leads came from Nogueira-Neto himself; SEMA's interest in the area at the confluence of the Jutaí and Solimões rivers began when its chief, flying over the area, noted a great concentration of burití palms below him. Whatever its provenance, if an area sounded promising to Nogueira-Neto, he would order the studies he thought appropriate, including overflights, title searches, and ground reconnaissance.

Absence of theory-based guidelines also made SEMA appear unsystematic, even casual, in its determination of an area's biological value. Nogueira-Neto's strong scientific background made him aware of how large the gaps in knowledge of Amazon biota actually were—too large, in his opinion, to permit an exact assessment of the worth of any particular area or an exact determination of how any area would fit into an ideal scheme of Amazon conservation, even after a reconnaissance. For Nogueira-Neto, an area's greatest possible virtue was being "biologically interesting," which was often a matter of initial appearances and intuition.[48] Nogueira-Neto's knowledge and his self-assurance disposed him to trust his own instincts more than any formal evaluation. He pointed with pride to the endangered species discovered in areas that SEMA had decided to protect on little more than his hunch that it contained something of value.

SEMA's seeming casualness in determining biological value did not extend into its evaluation of an area's manageability or the politics of its protection. Here, agency circumstances and the predispositions of its chief prompted caution, occasionally to the point of timorousness. Jorge Pádua was sometimes willing to protect natural areas on arable land because she assumed the IBDF could prevent the incursions of small-time squatters and thwart the schemes of large farmers and speculators. Nogueira-Neto, with a smaller agency and a more limited view of at least the short-term possibilities of Brazilian conservation, assumed that areas with potential for agriculture would be brought under the plough. Therefore, avoiding such areas entirely became agency policy.[49] SEMA's policy with regard to Indians was similar: they were to be avoided entirely. To Nogueira-Neto, the whole of Brazilian frontier history conspired to bring Indians and conservation into conflict. With his lesser faith in conservation's ability to hold its own, he thought it best to avoid having to deal with Indians, whatever the cost in missed short-term opportunities.

SEMA was similarly cautious when delimiting protected areas.

Both the IBDF and SEMA preferred compact areas with boundaries following easy-to-discern natural features. The two agencies also operated with the same general decision calculus with regard to size: delineate an area large enough to accomplish its conservation mission, yet not so large as to be indefensible without straining financial or political budgets.[50] The two agencies differed in their susceptibility to these competing pulls, however. The sense of self-assurance that permeated the IBDF's conservation program, the dictates of Island Biogeography Theory, and what the IBDF saw as the key goal of its nature protection program—i.e., the preservation of whole, self-maintaining ecosystems—all pushed the agency toward delimiting very large, if sometimes problem-filled, protected areas. SEMA, with fewer institutional resources, and without theoretical guidelines pushing it toward vast areas, was more willing to sacrifice size for defensible boundaries and fewer management problems. Like the IBDF, SEMA was willing to include some squatters and private holdings if there seemed no way to avoid them, but it was unwilling to include hundreds of squatters and tens of thousands of acres of private land the way the IBDF had.[51]

Finally, SEMA was hesitant to assume responsibility for an area when not certain it had the resources for its protection. Nogueira-Neto did not think of the protected areas brought under SEMA's management as a system in the biological sense, but he viewed them as such in a psychological sense: he feared that invasion, dismemberment, or extinction of any protected area would engender disrespect for the rest, making assaults on others more likely. Nogueira-Neto eschewed the long-range system planning Jorge Pádua and Wetterberg favored out of much the same fear—i.e., it would commit his agency to "paper parks," areas it was committed to defend but for which it did not have the resources.[52] Nogueira-Neto thought Jorge Pádua put the IBDF's entire conservation program at risk by trying to protect areas like Pico da Neblina and Trombetas, which perhaps conformed to the IBDF's formal value criteria but could not be defended with certainty against whatever the future might bring.

To insure that sufficient care was taken in evaluating and delineating areas, Nogueira-Neto maintained absolute control over all stages of the process and kept the ultimate decision about whether to protect an area for himself. His involvement in the process was so extensive, and he so marked it with his values, that a SEMA administrator referred to the agency's protected areas as "the children of Dr. Paulo."[53]

Another question facing SEMA was which public goals should

predominate in the management of its protected areas. The niche
SEMA would ultimately carve for itself in national life would depend
on how it was answered. Here as well, its choices were circumscribed
by the IBDF's large, extant conservation program. In its early days,
SEMA saw a possible role for itself in tourism and talked of cooperation with EMBRATUR, the national agency for the promotion of
tourism, but little came of the idea.[54] Nogueira-Neto realized that
Iguaçu, Tijuca, Serra dos Orgãos, and the other popular parks of the
South gave the IBDF a constituency among the Brazilian public that
his agency could never match. On the other hand, when the IBDF
established its protected areas as national parks and biological
reserves, it necessarily embraced a set of international norms about
the use of these areas. Argentina's Italo Constantino, vice chairman
of the IUCN's Commission on National Parks, expressed one of the
important norms when he said research that affected the biological
integrity of a park or a reserve was unthinkable.[55] The IBDF therefore had to be careful about the types of research it allowed in its
protected areas, and research had to remain subordinate to preservation as a management goal, even while Jorge Pádua did her utmost to
promote research in the system.

SEMA decided to promote its protected areas primarily as
research sites and defined appropriate research far more broadly
than the IBDF could. In addition to normal biological research,
SEMA saw its protected areas as appropriate control sites for assessing the impacts of development on the surrounding region, as training
grounds for young scientists, as sites for determining the potential
productivity of Brazilian ecosystems, and even as support bases for
social science research in the surrounding region.[56] To encourage
maximum scientific use of SEMA's protected areas, and perhaps to
go where the IBDF could not follow, Nogueira-Neto decided to permit the degradation of up to 10 percent of any SEMA-protected area
for scientific ends. The decision shocked many conservationists in
Brazil, who felt any destruction of nature within a protected area set
a dangerous precedent, but it did unequivocally demonstrate SEMA's
commitment to research.[57]

Nogueira-Neto hoped the emphasis on science would enable
SEMA to cultivate the Brazilian and international scientific communities more effectively than could the IBDF. He also hoped it would
align his agency more closely with the prevailing developmental ethic
of the government; broad scientific programs such as that which

SEMA hoped to establish were what the UN's Economic and Social Council had in mind when it recommended the establishment of experimental field stations as part of regional development programs.[58]

The agency's plans for its protected areas reflected the emphasis on research. New areas would be surveyed for their biological resources, with the results determining which parts could be altered for scientific purposes. A headquarters would be connected to the research areas by a system of trails. The headquarters compound would include laboratories, a scientific library, study areas, and lodging facilities for a dozen or more scientists. The staff would act as guides and assistants for visiting scientists. Staff wives would cook and perform housekeeping chores for the visitors.[59]

Securing SEMA's place in Brazil's public life was a matter of appearances as well as actions. A conservation agency needed the right codes and symbolic referents to gain entry to the ideological universe of public life.[60] It had to give the appearance of good bureaucratic citizenship. Its programs had to appear to be in synchrony with commonly accepted public values. Nogueira-Neto understood this as well as Jorge Pádua did, and was as determined to use image to maximum advantage. SEMA needed a different set of codes and symbols than the IBDF's, however, and had access to different raw material for constructing them.

The IBDF's well-established presence in conservation constricted SEMA's image space as much as its policy space. It placed all the images associated with the national parks out of bounds. The IBDF's role as the overseer of the nation's forests also placed most of the imagery and terminology of forests beyond SEMA's reach. On the other hand, SEMA's decision to emphasize applied science, and, by implication, the immediately beneficial, in the management of its protected areas gave it access to images associated with development and progress.

These considerations and restraints created a vocabulary of preferred and avoided words. SEMA avoided "flora" and "fauna" because they sounded esoteric but not necessarily scientific. It avoided "forest" or its derivatives so as not to raise the IBDF's hackles. "Research" struck a responsive chord, especially among the higher-level technocrats, so SEMA used it whenever possible. For Nogueira-Neto, choosing a name for SEMA's protected areas was an exercise in image building. "Parks" was already too closely identified with the IBDF and would work against the image of serious research

SEMA was trying to project. "Reserves" and "refuges" might imply that resources were being locked up. He thought "station" connoted activity and purpose, and the terms "experimental field station" and "research station" already had secure places in the literature of development. He liked "ecology" because it was scientific but not esoteric, and had positive popular associations. By calling SEMA's protected areas "ecological stations," Nogueira-Neto took advantage of both terms.

It was also largely for image that he settled on 10 percent as the amount of a protected area SEMA would allow to be disturbed for research; he felt that a higher percentage might suggest SEMA was not serious about conservation, and that a lower one could imply that SEMA was not serious about research.

Nogueira-Neto was equally concerned with his own personal image. As the nation's Secretary of the Environment, his visibility was far greater than his real political power, but a positive image could help close the gap. In creating a public image, Nogueira-Neto had several advantages not shared by Jorge Pádua: his credentials as a scientist were strong; he was a distinguished professor rather than a young and still relatively low-ranking professional public administrator; he came from an established family. His agency was relatively free of the political commitments the much larger IBDF had accumulated over the years.

Nogueira-Neto capitalized on these advantages to cultivate several public images, one of which was the detached technocrat-scientist. He tried to stand above the petty squabbles of conventional politics and took pains to keep from being viewed either as a partisan of the military government or a supporter of the opposition[61]—in sharp contrast with Jorge Pádua, who was always in the thick of politics, cultivating the generals while keeping her lines to the opposition open. This image encouraged politicians and his fellow administrators to trust Nogueira-Neto; they assumed he could be taken at face value because he had no political ambitions. According to a SEMA administrator who had extensive dealings with the states, the agency's generally good relations with the state governments was due to this image of selfless public service;[62] here was a federal official with no hidden agenda to be advanced at the state's expense. His membership on the National Research Council (CNPq), a policy-setting body for national science, enhanced his image as a scientist-administrator.

He was also seen as an environmental statesman, a man serving in government out of a sense of responsibility to his country.[63] The image tapped the strains of Latin American civic virtue that Domingo Sarmiento, the nineteenth-century Argentine educator and politician, and Oswaldo Cruz, the early twentieth-century Brazilian scientist and public health crusader, had tapped. Being the independently wealthy scion of an old São Paulo family played to this image, as did the way he returned his salary to his agency's coffers.

Nogueira-Neto's international standing added to his stature at home. His efforts to preserve Brazil's biological endowment automatically made him an important figure in global conservation, and with his patrician manner he moved easily through the corridors of the international conservation movement in the United States and Europe. By the end of the 1970s, he had joined Carvalho as one of the preeminent Brazilian conservationists on the international scene.[64] International conservation groups developed confidence in his judgment and came to see him as central to the success of nature preservation in Brazil. One American conservationist said of him, "Paulo is a major player in international conservation. People trust his advice, his sense of timing and politics."[65] He established a working relationship with the World Wildlife Fund, advising it on projects in Brazil. He became important in the IUCN, and as a member of the American National Academy of Science's Committee on Research Priorities in Tropical Biology, he helped formulate American research policy for the rainforests of the world.

Brazilians respect their fellows who have made their mark in international circles, often to the point of reverence. Ruy Barbosa's role in the World Court in the early twentieth century made him a prominent figure in the Brazil of his time, and he remains a venerated figure today. Nogueira-Neto benefitted from the same national trait; he was a Brazilian bringing credit to his country on the world stage.[66] The image reinforced that of a selfless, disinterested administrator and added to his de facto power at home.

* * *

While defining its policies and feeling its way into Brazilian public life, SEMA gradually brought a group of natural areas under its protection. The first ecological station was Maracá Island, a little-disturbed, 92,000-hectare fluvial island between two branches of the

Uraricoera River in Roraima territory (see figure 8.3 in chapter 8).[67] The territorial government turned the island over to SEMA in 1976. Although Amazonia was not officially a priority region for SEMA, with so much undisturbed nature and so many opportunities for acquisition in the region, it was not surprising that SEMA's first protected area, as well as many subsequent ones, was there.

Later that year, the northeastern state of Piauí gave SEMA the 135,000-hectare Uruçui-Una tract, an area of thorny caatinga (dry scrub vegetation) crossed by gallery forests along the watercourses. In 1977 the federal government acquired the 272-hectare Aracuri-Esmeralda tract in Rio Grande do Sul for the establishment of an ecological station. The tract was the winter roosting site of thousands of parrots, and Nogueira-Neto speculated that bringing it under public protection probably saved them.[68] It was the kind of small but biologically important site Terborgh had in mind when he spoke of conservation on the cheap. The 11,500-hectare Raso da Catarina tract in the interior of Ceará, which SEMA believed to contain the largest remaining undisturbed patch of dry woodland (arboreal caatinga) in the Northeast, came under the agency's control in 1978.

SEMA assumed control of the Anavilhanas Archipelago in the Negro River in 1979 (Figure 4.3). It was the agency's largest acquisition to date, and its history reveals some of the key differences between SEMA and the IBDF's operational values. At one time, both SEMA and the IBDF were interested in protecting the islands. They had a practical appeal to both agencies: there were no Indians and only a few caboclos, and the state and federal governments owned almost all the land, which they were willing to turn over to a conservation agency. The semi-inundated forests of the islands, however, were not typical of those on the surrounding uplands and their species diversity was low, so when the IBDF made species diversity and regional representation its key determinants of biological value, its interest in the islands waned. The archipelago also suffered from its proximity to the Jaú basin, which the IBDF considered the foremost conservation prospect in the Negro River area, and as the IBDF's commitment to Jaú grew, its interest in Anavilhanas further waned.[69]

SEMA's interest in the archipelago grew as the IBDF's diminished. Because the agency had never stressed regional representation or even species diversity as selection criteria, it did not hold the islands' low diversity or atypical biota against them. The islands had several virtues that weighed heavily in SEMA's calculus. First, their preserva-

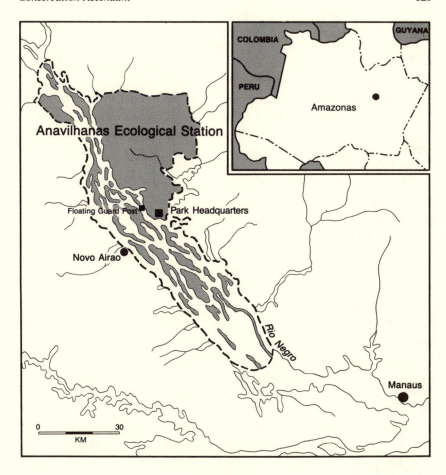

FIGURE 4.3
Anavilhanas Ecological Station

tion might produce immediate returns in regional development. Almost the entire archipelago was inundated during the high-water season, with the water sweeping away fruits and seeds that had fallen from the trees and providing food for fish in the acidic and turbid Negro River. The islands were therefore thought to be important in sustaining the ecosystem of the Negro River and the fishing industry based on it. Second, at its closest point the archipelago was only forty kilometers from Manaus. The city had an international airport and was the headquarters of INPA. The long-established Ducke Research Forest was close to Manaus, and the WWF was setting up its Minimum Critical Size project just north of the city. Manaus was therefore the center of an intensifying circuit of tropical research, and an ecological station comprising the Anavilhanas islands could become an important part of it.[70]

Anavilhanas also showed that when the opportunity presented itself, SEMA was willing to override its normal inclinations and establish very large stations. SEMA eventually acquired not only the islands but a large area of adjoining upland forest that had been under INCRA's jurisdiction. This addition gave the station an area of 350,000 hectares, making it by far the largest tract to come under SEMA's control and larger even than several areas the IBDF was then bringing under its protection.

As more natural areas, including several large ones, came under SEMA's control, its organic legislation became confining. Legislation establishing the agency in 1973 had empowered it to cooperate with other agencies "in the preservation of endangered species of animals and plants, and in the maintenance of genetic material," but it made no mention of a leading or even independent role for SEMA in this field; nor did it authorize the acquisition of natural areas.[71] Nogueira-Neto's decision to concentrate on nature protection was given a wedge of legitimacy when his superior, the Minister of the Interior, gave it his blessing, and the wedge was expanded somewhat in 1977 when the Second National Development Plan was reworded to concede a role for SEMA in the management of natural areas, but the ecological stations remained without strong legal under-pinnings—and the agency remained exposed to the political and administrative uncertainties that sprang from operating outside its clear legal mandate. As the agency's involvement in natural area pro-tection deepened, so did its need to reshape its basic legislation.

SEMA also needed a better administrative niche. It had been set up in 1973 as a "special agency," joining the several dozen such agencies nominally under the Minister of the Interior yet outside the rigid command structure of the federal bureaucracy.[72] Because SEMA's mission was viewed as unique, its connections with its parent min-istry were made especially loose, which gave SEMA freedom of action but also left the Interior Minister with little sense of obligation to his ward. It also left SEMA organizationally distant from the inner circles of power within the Brazilian government.[73]

Nogueira-Neto's success in building his agency's credibility, com-bined with his deft lobbying within the government, enabled him to get the needed legal changes by the early 1980s. A new law explicitly authorized SEMA to establish ecological stations (Lei no. 6.902, April 1981). It set out rules for their management which codified the key decisions Nogueira-Neto had made in previous years. It ratified his stress on applied scientific research by asserting that the stations were to provide "useful information for regional planning and the rational use of natural resources." It also ratified Nogueira-Neto's decision to allow the degradation of 10 percent of an ecological station for scientific ends.

A second law was passed shortly afterward (Lei no. 6.938, August 31, 1981) setting up what it called a National Environmental System, a network of interconnected organizations with considerable formal responsibility for Brazil's environment and centered on SEMA. State and local environmental agencies would be linked to SEMA through the network, as would be what the law called "sectorial organs," administrative units responsible for environmental oversight within public corporations. At the network's head would be a National Environmental Council (CONAMA), which was to advise the president of the republic on environmental matters. (The role was roughly analogous to that of the Council on Environmental Quality in the United States.) As befitted its importance, CONAMA would include representatives of state governments, conservation groups, and the national federations of industry, commerce, and agriculture. SEMA was to be the chief instrument of this council and therefore what the law called the "central organ" of national environmental policy.

These arrangements overcame Nogueira-Neto's isolation within the federal administration. The National Environmental System gave him direct connections to other federal agencies, as well as to agencies at other levels of government. Although SEMA was nominally an instrument of CONAMA, the reverse was really intended: CONAMA would give Nogueira-Neto's decisions an added measure of authority. CONAMA's official role of advisor to the president gave Nogueira-Neto a direct link to the highest levels of the federal government.

The legislation of April and August 1981 did for SEMA what the national park legislation of the 1979–1982 period did for the IBDF's conservation program—i.e., it ratified and consolidated past successes by firmly embedding them in the nation's legal system and provided solid footing for further successes. Jorge Pádua, who first thought Nogueira-Neto overly cautious in grasping opportunities, came to admire his accomplishments as they accumulated and came to see the ecological stations as a valuable complement to the IBDF's program.[74] Nogueira-Neto's accomplishments were viewed similarly abroad; he and Jorge Pádua shared the prestigious Getty Prize for outstanding service to international conservation in 1982. A decade after the Stockholm Conference, biological conservation in Brazilian Amazonia seemed to be well established and to have a bright future.

CHAPTER 5

The Unseen Limits of Amazon Conservation

Even when the IBDF's Amazon conservation initiative appeared most successful, some in Brazil thought the gains were illusory, that the establishment of so many parks, reserves, and ecological stations meant little in itself. They knew Brazilian law had an exasperating indefiniteness to it; it seldom settled things with finality. Laws that contradicted other ones were common and many were totally without enforcement provisions. As one Brazilian observed, "Brazil has many laws, but it does not have one that says all the others have to be enforced."[1]

Some saw the real history of Brazilian conservation not in the laws or regulations but in the nonenforcement and disinterest that nullified them in practice. Conservation measures of the first decades of the twentieth century had produced little of lasting importance because legislation was not enforced and programs were not sustained. The federal Forest Service, whose establishment was hailed as a triumph for conservation, never had more than a minimal budget. The new conservation initiatives of the 1930s also appeared hollow in retrospect, after neglect and nonenforcement overtook them.[2] De Barros wrote that when Brazil established its first national parks it was only trying to prove itself the equal of other civilized nations. In fact, according to Oltremari and Fahrenkrog, there was no authentic tradition of conservation in South America.[3] The fate of the first major conservation measure for Amazonia, the forest reserves of 1961, seemed merely an extension of the old pattern.

Even confirmed doubters were impressed with the initial success of the IBDF's and SEMA's conservation programs, but signs that conservation's successes were not as solid as they appeared accumulated. President Figueiredo never acted on the comprehensive forest policy report, despite the entreaties of scientists and conservation groups. There was speculation that the policy was opposed by agriculture interests to whom the president was beholden, but for whatever reason, the report went into administrative limbo, stalled at the desk of a president who would neither endorse it, denounce it, nor call for modifications. As the months of waiting turned into years, a pessimism about the political limits of conservation spread.[4]

The popular Sete Quedas National Park, centering on a set of falls in the Paraná River, was extinguished by presidential decree in 1981. The government had allowed the construction of a hydroelectric dam downstream even though it would drown the park. A few years earlier, part of the IBDF's regional administration was simply dismantled when it tried to prosecute Volkswagen of Brazil for illegal clearing on its Amazon holdings.[5] The message seemed clear in these cases: when development, or even narrow but powerful economic interests, were in conflict with conservation, the latter had to give way.

Jorge Pádua's appearances at the Superior War College also seemed to offer sobering insights into the depth of conservation sentiment among Brazil's powerful. To guarantee her talks would be well received, she had to stress that the conservation she was advocating fit without friction into the vision of development and progress held by her audience. This meant stressing the immediate economic benefits of conservation and not drifting from the idea that protecting nature was simply an element of good development policy as they understood it. The questions her lectures prompted revealed a disconcertingly low level of understanding of exactly what biological conservation meant. As Jorge Pádua recalled, "I was more likely to get questions about potted plants than ecosystems."[6] Once, legislation drawn up by SEMA was held up on the floor of the national legislature while legislators scrambled to find out what "biota" meant.[7]

The transformation of Amazonia proceeded at a rapid pace in the late 1970s and early 1980s. Ludwig's Jari Project already employed thousands. Construction at Serra dos Carajás was progressing. The cultivation of sugar, coffee, and soybeans was turning large areas along the Belém-Brasília Highway into new agricultural districts. Even larger transformations were on the drawing boards.[8] Plans called for cacao production in Amazonia to go from practically nil to 150,000 tons by 1990. The production of palm oil would triple to 17,000 tons by the same date, and production from rubber plantations would increase from the present 4,000 tons to 105,000. Brazil's share of the world market for tropical sawnwood was projected to rise rapidly, with much of the increase coming from Amazonia. Plans for more hydroelectric dams in Amazonia had already been formulated. With each of these projects the domain of nature was whittled away.

A pessimistic reading of Brazilian conservation history, when combined with these plans, suggested that perhaps the whole edifice of conservation in the 1970s and early 1980s had been built of weak material: a positive public image, the largess of foreign conservation organizations, and the willingness of powerful public agencies to cooperate with conservationists if no real costs were involved. Perhaps the president's willingness to establish so many parks and reserves and support so much conservation legislation was based on a cynical realization that conservation decrees and regulations had great symbolic value but little cost.[9] Jorge Pádua, Nogueira-Neto, and their associates had skillfully worked the political system for conservation's benefit. Perhaps the reverse was also true: those who held real power in Brazil had skillfully used the symbols of conservation for their own ends. Perhaps symbolic and superficial conservation was all that was possible, and more substantial measures involving even short-term economic opportunity costs or restraints on profit were beyond reach of even the most skilled and prescient conservationists.

Some interpreted the IBDF's concentration on the formal establishment of protected natural areas as a tacit admission of this weakness; As Harroy had observed, setting aside areas for protection was a far simpler task than actually protecting them.[10] In fact, some felt that the IBDF's program hurt conservation's long-term prospects in Amazonia because placing so many natural areas under the scant protection afforded by legislation produced only the dangerous illusion of progress.

Jorge Pádua conceded the literal truth of many of these points. She understood the deeply political nature of Brazilian public administration, and how it produced opportunities for conservation as incidental by-products of the pursuit of other goals. She understood how politics caused conservation opportunities to appear suddenly, seemingly out of nowhere.

She admitted that her program had a carefully crafted political dimension and that its success was due in large measure to skillful administrative entrepreneurship—much of it her own. She even conceded that the program was something of a gossamer and tenuous edifice. But she discounted the deeper doubts to which this gave rise because she assumed conservation's gains took place against a broad backdrop of progress. The particular opportunities on which she capitalized might close and there might be temporary reverses, but the future would allow for the consolidation of today's tenuous successes.[11]

Jorge Pádua's faith was based on two key assumptions: first, the transformation of Amazonia would take place under the direction of a federal government committed to rational development and biological conservation; second, the social transformations that accompanied the emergence of a modern Brazil would create a secure political constituency for conservation over the long term.

Both assumptions were widely held. International observers and prominent Brazilian conservationists believed that the Stockholm Conference and international attention given Amazonia in the following years had prompted a fundamental change in attitudes at the top of the Brazilian government. Robert Skillings, the head of the World Bank's Brazil section, argued that the Forest Policy report of 1979 signaled an environmental maturity on the part of the federal government. Carvalho concluded from the Third National Plan that the federal government now had "a high degree of concern" for the biological resources of the nation.[12] The establishment of an internal environmental advising group by the powerful Rio Doce Valley Company (CVRD) in 1981 to guide it with the Carajás iron extraction project seemed further confirmation of this.

The increasing sensitivity to the environment exhibited by the agencies of international development would reinforce Brazil's commitment. The United States amended its Foreign Assistance Act in 1979 to make its aid agencies more sensitive to the impact of their policies on the rainforest.[13] The Economic Commission for Latin America (ECLA), one of the last of the UN organs to embrace environmentalism, began showing more concern for the natural world. The World Bank also showed increasing concern for the environment, especially in Brazil: it insisted that the Polonoroeste project be environmentally responsible, and when it agreed to underwrite the Carajás project, it touted its determination to see that the project was carried out in an environmentally sensitive fashion.[14]

Given the assumption of Amazon development under state control and within a climate favorable to conservation, Brazilian conservation measures of the 1970s and early 1980s appeared sensible. Getting the outline of biological protection sketched onto the landscape of Amazonia was the most pressing task, even if the outline was initially rough and largely on paper. Conservationists had to get there first with natural areas, zoning patterns, and environmental guidelines.[15] No amount of support for conservation could be turned into effective action after the region's biological endowment had been degraded.

The argument for concentrating on legislation and formal decrees was also buttressed by history. Most of the world's early protected areas had been formally established before the capacity to manage them existed.[16] As dangers to the protected areas arose in the normal course of regional development, so did their protection. Wetterberg's earlier experience in Chile convinced him this was a valid general rule of conservation.[17] He was confident the same thing would happen in Brazil in due course. Writing with Prance and Lovejoy, he asserted that for many of the new protected areas in Amazonia, "the lack of staffing does not constitute a threat at this stage of development."[18]

While Jorge Pádua was at the crest of her success, an issue arose to test the assumptions on which Amazon conservation policy rested. A region of commercial agriculture had developed west of Bananal Island during the 1970s, but the region's access to markets depended on unpaved and seasonally impassable roads to the south (figure 5.1). The Belém-Brasília Highway was just east of Bananal Island, so a proposal to build a connector road across the island was advanced. The only feasible route for the road, however, was through Araguaia National Park on the northern end of the island.

The road would be a direct violation of the park codes of 1979, so Jorge Pádua and the FBCN campaigned hard to kill the proposal. The international conservation community came to the park's defense: the head of the IUCN's Commission on National Parks and foreign scientists implored President Figueiredo to disapprove the road. Jorge Pádua felt this was such an important issue she threatened to resign if Figueiredo authorized it. In October 1982, while she was abroad representing Brazil at an international conference, the president authorized the road. When she returned, Jorge Pádua carried through on her threat, perhaps hoping her resignation would cause the president to change his mind. It did not; road construction began.[19]

* * *

The ideal of development seemed like the logical conceptual foundation for the new doctrines of conservation practice that evolved in the 1960s. Like development, biological conservation was increas-

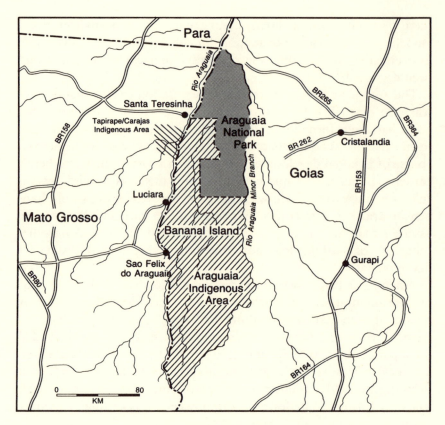

FIGURE 5.1
Araguaia National Park and Environs

ingly scientific and professional in its values and, thanks to the rise of the ecological critique, increasingly ambitious in its view of its own capacity to advance the universal commonweal. The rational cast of development would lead its practitioners to appreciate conservation's capacity to maintain conditions for further improvement in human well-being. Conservation measures would act as guides to development, channeling it into the most naturally productive areas. They would insure that economies did not erode the land base on which their prosperity was based. They would insure genetic stock for future well-being and would allow citizens of newly developed countries to enjoy direct contact with nature. Development would in turn create the unobstructed policy space and the social bases of support that conservation needed.

Development theorists viewed the politics of development primarily as instrumental politics; the key role of the political system in the modernizing state was creating the conditions of progress. They also saw the role of politics in the modernization process as a minor one, and they expected it to diminish over time. As Lundberg wrote in 1963, "the initiative in forcing the pace of change lies with science, education, and technology." He added that "politics can be no more than the handmaiden of change, and will be so increasingly in the future."[20] While most of those who formulated postwar development theory understood that politics was not exactly a selfless process, they assumed that politics would henceforth take its values from development, and once development got underway, a nation's political life would be determined by it.

This was seen as a good thing; development theory's respect for professionalism in the service of the public was matched by a contempt for traditional interest politics and the politicians who served the old system. The norms of development practice included policies to undercut social groups seen standing in the way of progress and to strip power from tradition-bound politicians unwilling to serve development goals.[21] Politicians and state bureaucrats would be rewarded to the degree to which they were faithful to development's ideals and effective in putting them into practice. Politics defined by the ideals of development was most suitable for ambitious conservation programs that promised to advance the goals of universal human betterment in a professional, systematic fashion.

As nations developed under the guidance of professional planners and their political servants, many strong bases of support for conservation would emerge within their societies, further tilting the political system toward conservation. One was the working class. The informal sector of the economy would shrink as its members were absorbed into the more productive and remunerative salary and wage sectors. Income distribution would become more equitable, rapidly transforming the lowest rungs of society from peasants and marginalized urban workers into a prosperous, stable working class. This North American–style working class would visit the national parks by the millions and form an important political constituency for protected nature. Much of Jorge Pádua's energies had gone into preparing the national parks for such a constituency.

Another base of support was the middle class. Middle-class enthusiasm had made environmentalism a strong force in the United States.

With middle-class backing, the environmental movement became large and powerful enough to hold the attention of the media and adopt mass-participation tactics. Its middle-class base also gave the environmental movement the financial resources to develop a cadre of professionals necessary for cohesion and continuity: administrators, lobbyists, public relations specialists, etc.

There was a precedent for such support from the Brazilian middle class. Urbanization in the Brazilian South in the 1930s created a larger, more self-assured middle class, and like the middle class elsewhere, some of its political activity and restless concern for the commonweal focused on conservation issues. The Touring Club of Brazil and the Brazilian Federation of Feminine Progress both included conservation among the issues that concerned them.[22] Groups that focused wholly on conservation, such as the Society of Friends of Alberto Torres (an essayist who wrote extensively on the conservation of Brazil's forests), also found their niche among the middle-class organizations. These organizations waxed, waned, and succeeded each other over the following decades, but conservation remained a fixed part of the agenda of the middle class. With increasing development, those conservation traditions were likely to blossom and become politically powerful, as they had elsewhere.

There was also the socioeconomic elite. As the United States matured into an industrial state, big capital so completely triumphed and society was so molded by the imperatives of industrialism that by the 1920s the nation's socioeconomic elite no longer felt embattled. It could take a detached, almost seigniorial view of the rest of society. This view, which initially expressed itself in individual, sometimes quixotic acts of philanthropy, was soon institutionalized in foundations run off the great fortunes of Ford, Rockefeller, and others.[23] These foundations, sponsoring social research and committed to the public good as they saw it, became the most detached expression of elite self-interest in the United States; they insured that the rational and the self-serving were joined in forms that appeared seamless.

The elite and its institutions attached themselves to conservation issues early on. The Rockefellers and their foundations were early supporters of the American national park system and espoused vigilant management of the public lands. Even when the ideal of unfettered economic development reigned, there was a current of concern for conservation issues among the elite and its institutions: Laurance Rockefeller provided financial support for the establishment of the Conservation Foundation in 1947; the Ford Foundation underwrote the establishment of Resources for the Future in 1952; John D. Rockefeller III underwrote the founding of The Population Council in 1953 and served as its first president. Once environmental disruption became an issue, this elite network quickly embraced it.[24] The secure and prosperous elite of a developed Brazil might be expected to behave similarly.

Finally, there was the scientific community. Collectively and individually, scientists in developed nations were important in the political process; they raised broad questions of public interest that found their way to the center of the political agendas of their nations. Their role in the emergence of environmentalism was typical. As Brazil developed, scientists could be expected to play a similar role in Brazilian society and become the important social force for conservation they were in the developed world.

Development in practice, however, was inevitably narrower, less far-sighted, and less revolutionary than it was in theory. Development was as much an instrument of interest politics, albeit a new instrument, as it was the creator of a new, more enlightened form of politics. Development in practice was always restrained by extant societal and political interests; without heeding these interests, development could not advance. Developmental theorists may have seen their constructs as apolitical prescriptions for promoting general welfare, but in practice they never were. Those who forged conservation doctrine seemed only dimly aware of the persistent, probably inevitable gap between development theory and practice. Conservationists linked their doctrines to the former, but conservation programs had to make their way in a world defined by the latter.

Even in the early twentieth century, the vision of progress, on which the ideal of development ultimately rested, drew much of its vigor from the services it rendered powerful interests in the industrialized societies of the West.[25] Domesticated and adapted to the era of mass production, it promoted consumerism and thereby helped solve one of the challenges of industrial capitalism: creating new demand to match the increasingly productive industrial plant. A future that promised ever-increasing prosperity legitimized the rule of those who promised to bring it about. Its promotion served as a point of agreement for the diffused elites of the complex developed societies. The popularized belief in material progress was thus a powerful binding agent in industrialized societies, binding consumers to producers, the governed to the governors, and the elites to each other.

The transformation of the vision of progress into the universal ideal of development after the Second World War had a similar base in self-interest.[26] The United States and her postwar allies would have to procure raw materials from the undeveloped world and would need foreign outlets for their manufactured goods; therefore, an integrated global economy would be essential. Isaiah Bowman, who advised the State Department on postwar territorial arrangements, stressed the need to avoid conventional forms of imperialism, which would leave the world divided into competing empires and inhibit the growth of the global economy. They might also preclude U.S. access to European colonial holdings and crimp U.S. economic growth.

The task, as Bowman and others saw it, was to create a new international order of independent states out of the remnants of the old colonial world. Universal progress toward development would have to be one of the central features of this new order. Only the development of former colonies and of states with colony-like economies would insure markets for the goods of the industrialized world, provide new investment outlets, and undercut the appeal of international communism. Thus, the surface of development was scientific and benevolent, tinted perhaps by a Wilsonian idealism, but not far beneath this was the self-interest of the powerful and established. One element gave the vision its appeal, the other its direction and power.

Development efforts in Brazil, like international efforts, were shaped by powerful economic and political self-interest from the beginning. The real history of development in Brazil was as much in the shifting interests it served as in the rising figures of production. Like most of Latin America, Brazil occupied an ambiguous position in the international order of the prewar world; its economy was colonial in its main features, but the nation was politically independent, giving Brazilian politicians the freedom to tap the vision of progress for their own ends even before it was transformed into the ideal of international development.[27] In the 1930s and early 1940s, the authoritarian president, Getúlio Vargas, took steps to create a modern industrial economy in Brazil: a five-year plan of directed industrialization was introduced; state-owned companies were formed to mine iron ore and to produce aircraft; and a national steel company was established to build Brazil's first major steel plant.[28]

These steps had broad sociopolitical consequences. They created an important investment outlet for local investors, who had seen their traditional investment opportunities in export agriculture destroyed by the high tariffs and collapsing international markets of the depression era. They attracted foreign capital to Brazil and created a broker role for the local business classes. They minimized tensions and competition among the nation's many economic elites by expanding the economic pie in which they could share. The steps also had a more narrowly political dimension. Vargas had destroyed the old republic, which had relied on an elaborate network of feudal-like obligations stretching across traditional class lines, and in its place he created a corporatist state modeled after the new fascist states of Europe. Having dispensed with the old network of obligations for support, Vargas had to rely heavily on direct popular appeal through the mass media. Progress, and the promise of a better life for all, became a key element of Vargas's demagoguery.[29]

When Vargas fell shortly after the war, his successors restored the republican political institutions dormant during his regime, but the restoration was not complete; there could be no full return to the old politics after the experiment with mass appeal. The republican politicians of the post-war era relied on mobilizing voters through promises of good jobs, economic reforms, and a better life as much as Vargas had. Thus the promotion of progress became as important in political equations of the postwar democratic system as it had been in the corporatist state it replaced.[30] Now, however, Brazil's promotion of progress through industrial development went with the grain of the international order; it now derived a large measure of legitimacy from its confluence with international ideals, and it could tap the international sources of developmental expertise and capital now available.

The growth that took place in the late 1950s under President Kubitschek placed the captains of industry at the apex of the nation's economic elite; it expanded the middle class and brought it self-confidence and prosperity; it brought a measure of material well-being and security to the more privileged sectors of the working class. Yet despite Kubitschek's rhetoric of change and the actual accomplishments of his presidency, he respected powerful elements of the old order.[31] He did not threaten the privileges of the more established groups, even when development theory called for it. He was hesitant, for example, to go against the interests of the rural landowners by promoting serious land reform or the political enpowerment of the peasantry. He introduced a new professionalism into the bureaucracy, but he allowed the modernizing technocrats to be constrained by a conservative bureaucratic environment, and he allowed interests committed to the sociopolitical status quo a veto over their plans. Under Kubitschek, development remained at its core a political device, in part a banner around which a powerful coalition of established interests could rally, in part a dream of a better life for those who did not share at prosperity's table.

The changes that took place under the banner of development did destabilize the existing order, however. With industrialization, the working class became larger and more militant. In the countryside, modernization eroded the old seigniorial system, leaving the peasants with neither its benefits nor its restraints.[32] Rural unrest spread and highly militant peasant unions filled the vacuum. After the short term of Jânio Quadros in 1960 and 1961, João Goulart came to power. Goulart, who did not share Kubitschek's commitment to the sociopolitical status quo, tried to give more power to the peasantry and the working class, causing social tension to rise.[33] Foreign investment slowed in the early 1960s, inflation rose, economic paralysis set in, and fear spread through the privileged sectors of society. The military staged a coup in 1964 to staunch the spreading chaos and counter the threat to the established order that it posed.

The military used the ideology and practice of development in many, sometimes subtle, ways. At first the military assumed it could quickly set the nation right through selective disenfranchisements and limited changes in the representative system, and then turn power back to civilians. Elections in 1965, however, showed that the populists against whom the coup had been directed still retained considerable popular support and caused the military men to revise their thinking.[34] They came to believe the aims of the coup could only be achieved with the destruction of the bases of leftist power, and this would take years of authoritarian rule.

The prospect created a two-part dilemma. First, the military would wear out its welcome long before it could achieve its goal. The coup enjoyed the support of a broad coalition of interests: the middle class, which feared losing what it had recently gained; landowners, who feared expropriation; industrialists, who feared loss of economic privileges; and the military's own officer corps, which feared insubordination in the ranks. This made for a broad base of support, but little more than fear held it together.[35] Under normal conditions, military rule was not the preferred form of government for any element of the alliance, so while the leaders of the coup might be hailed as saviors at the moment, their support was likely to evaporate as the immediate sense of danger receded.

Second, it threw the military into a crisis of values. The military had long viewed itself as a key institution in Brazil's future. The Positivism of Auguste Comte, which envisioned a utopian society based on science, social planning, and a benevolent authoritarian government, had a strong impact on the Brazilian military in the late nineteenth century.[36] When military men looked at the corrupt First Republic and its self-serving politicians, they concluded that only they could lead the nation to the bright, rational future that Positivism promised. While the popularity of Positivism declined in the early twentieth century, the military continued to view itself as the core institution of national life. Colonel Nery da Fonseca in 1940 wrote in his widely read *Geopolítica* that Brazil could become a great power in a matter of decades, but only under the direction of an efficient and determined central government.[37] The military saw itself as the only institution on which such a government could be based and, by extension, the only institution capable of leading the country toward the greatness that Brazil's location, size, and resource base permitted.

Yet the military's view of its place in national life contained contradictory elements. The military was not the conservative, oligarchical institution of the Latin American stereotype. The army, especially, had long been a predominantly middle-class institution.[38] Like the middle class in general, the military set great store by political legitimacy. (Shortly before the coup, officers circulated memos in which they tried to convince themselves that a coup would be legitimate because Goulart had overstepped his constitutional mandate.)[39] The military also subscribed to the ideal of democracy. Many of its senior officers had fought in Italy in the Second World War and had been imbued with Allied political values during the experience. The military had overthrown Vargas and helped restore democracy after the Second World War. It still saw itself as a defender of Brazilian democracy, and remaining in power, although seemingly necessary under the circumstances, would affront the military's own democratic and legitimist values.

Adopting the promotion of development as the key rationale for remaining in power offered a way out. It would allow the military to give expression to its view of itself as a key institution in national life while at the same time assuaging its democratic conscience; it was remaining in power to create those conditions modern democracy demanded. A development orientation would also link the military government to a tradition of promoting modernization that stretched back to Vargas, and it would derive legitimacy from the connection. Like preceding postwar governments, it would derive a measure of international legitimacy from its embracement of a key international ideal. Moreover, in the early 1960s development theorists had begun promoting the idea that modern militaries could be key institutions in promoting development, adding further respectability to its rationale for remaining in power.[40]

Policies that promoted development would find instant favor with the middle class, and if the military government could deliver on its promises of greater stability and material prosperity, the middle class would likely put its questions about legitimacy and its preference for representative government on hold. The promotion of development would also allow the military to favor a key group of allies, the industrialists, with state action.[41] Finally, economic expansion might, as Evans put it, act as "a solvent for social tensions"[42] and thereby take the edge off the class conflict that had sharpened in the preceding years.

At the same time, development theory justified many of the steps the Brazilian military felt necessary to restructure national politics. Its characterization of traditional Latin American politicians as self-serving obstacles to progress sanctioned the military's evisceration of those political institutions it considered a threat to its aims and power. Development literature's portrait of organized labor as demagogic and aggressive, a social force that, in the words of one developmental economist, "does not respond to the realities of economic development,"[43] justified the military's repression of unions in its efforts to atomize and depoliticize the working class. Development literature's insistence that institutions such as the village, the church, and the school had to be revamped to create a complex of values and motives more favorable to development sanctioned policies that undermined institutions around which popular discontent could form. Its insistence that universities be brought under the public organs of development justified the repression of opposition within the nation's educational and intellectual elites.[44]

The breadth of development prescriptions also allowed the military to pick those that served its political ends, yet still maintain the facade of professionalism.[45] Celso Furtado, who called for the immediate creation of a broad base of prosperity through the development of lagging regions and programs to meet the needs of the poor, was forced into exile. Roberto Campos, whose ideas of development through massive state-directed projects and the infusion of foreign capital conformed more with the inclinations of the military, became the most powerful civilian in the government.[46]

Simply embracing national development could not solve all the military's political problems, however. First, the range of specific development prescriptions available was a two-edged sword. While it allowed the military to choose the most politically attractive development options, it also forced it to make choices, thereby opening divisions within the military itself. Thus while the pursuit of development was a way of uniting a consensus behind the military, maintaining internal equilibrium demanded constant compromise and negotiation in deciding exactly which vision of development should guide policy.

Second, the military government's power to effect its will with regard to development had limits. Although the coup revamped the national bureaucracy to make it a more efficient instrument of the military's wishes, parts of the bureaucracy remained beholden to special interests. The government's command over the bureaucracy was further subverted by the pervasiveness of *panelinhas,* informal groups of administrators, professionals, and businessmen bound together by personal ties and the potential for mutual advancement that grew out of their complementary positions. Thus, the Brazilian power structure remained in good measure a vast aggregation of interests, many with the capacity to subvert and limit the effectiveness of public programs.[47]

Finally, while development theorists tended to see the development process as a cornucopia of benefits sufficient to sustain governments that promoted it, no Brazilian government, including a military regime, could afford to rely exclusively on some master policy for its support, even assuming it could extract maximum benefits from it. Brazilian society was too complex, with too many centers of economic and latent political power.[48] There was always a need for ad hoc side payments, concessions, and de facto concords to satisfy particular interests or to arrive at compromises that allowed a fundamental policy thrust to achieve some broader political objective.

Thus while the general goal of development was a powerful, multipurpose political instrument in the hands of the military government, or any national government, its inherent limits in building consensus and maintaining the political equilibrium meant that, in practice, development policy always had to be shaped by political considerations and supplemented by ancillary actions.

***

Amazonia's role in national life under the generals (and under their predecessors, for that matter) has to be seen in light of development's political uses and limitations. The military government viewed Amazonia as a region with some contributions to make to national development, but since it was far from the nation's southern heartland and the real engines of the Brazilian economy found there, its future was not of great importance from the strict perspective of economic development. Remoteness and lack of consequence, however, made Amazonia a good place to make the compromises and side payments necessary for maintaining the sociopolitical equilibrium. Accordingly, the military's Amazon planning initiatives were heavily shaped by political considerations.

The Program of National Integration (PIN), the military's most ambitious program for Amazonia to date, never made sense if viewed purely as an agricultural development project. By the time it was undertaken, ample experience in Latin America had shown that opening new lands was more expensive and far riskier than increasing production in established agricultural districts.[49] PIN's cost-benefit projections never showed a net benefit; the program's advocates casually argued that it would create the conditions of its success as it went along.[50]

It did, however, illustrate the complexity of the political equation into which Amazonia figured under the generals. PIN would sweep one of the loose ends of economic expansion under the rug. The government projected GNP growth rates of 9 percent from 1970–1973, but by its own estimates, employment would grow at only 3.1 percent per annum, lower even than the projected population increase.[51] Unless something was done to absorb the labor excess that capital-intensive economic expansion was creating, unemployment could become dangerous and destabilizing. The government's Institute of Economic and Social Planning estimated that agricultural colonization of Amazonia was the least expensive way of creating a large number of new livelihoods quickly.

PIN would also heal the rifts that the government's fundamental development policy choices had created. The dominant strategy of the military during the first few years following the coup was to rely heavily on foreign capital to finance modernization and to emphasize Southern industrial development, but opposition to this approach coalesced in the late 1960s around General Afonso de Albuquerque Lima, a senior military officer and the Minister of the Interior.[52] He argued that the concentration of development efforts on the South exacerbated regional differences and destabilized the nation. He saw foreign investments, which were being welcomed by the government, as a serious threat to national independence. By 1969 there was a serious split within the armed forces on the interrelated issues Albuquerque Lima raised: foreign capital versus domestic resources, strong versus weak compensatory regional policies.

The technocratic establishment feared that the policies Albuquerque Lima advocated would divert resources from the southern industrial heartland. Technocrats also feared his rhetoric would undermine the positive investment climate that they had worked hard to create; a recent left-wing military coup in Peru had already made foreigners skittish about further investments in South America. But Albuquerque Lima had support among the officer corps, especially among the junior officers. The Minister of Transportation and the Minister of Commerce and Industry were sympathetic with his view.

Eventually, the opposition prevailed and Albuquerque Lima was forced from power. But because his argument was consonant with a strong thread of thinking within the military and society, some sort of accommodation seemed prudent. PIN was that accommodation: unlike the main thrust of the government's development policies, it would be strictly national in financing and direction; it would be an explicitly compensatory regional program.

PIN would also symbolically confront paranoia over Amazonian sovereignty, which was long-standing but which had recently taken new, sharp forms. Throughout the early twentieth century, Brazilians thought they discerned designs on the region by the great world powers.[53] After the Second World War, the national press fed the public a steady diet of foreign threats to the region. An off-hand proposal by Julian Huxley that Amazonia should become an international scientific reserve received front-page coverage in the Brazilian press, as did Harrison Brown's passing suggestion that India's surplus populations might best be shipped to Amazonia. After a book distilling Brazilian paranoia over the region appeared in 1957 and became a best seller,[54] fears of losing Amazonia multiplied and took truly baroque forms. The Americans were suspected of wanting to flood the region for a vast submarine base, of wanting to colonize it in case of a nuclear war, and, most farfetched, of wanting to use it as a tropical Siberia for their black militants.[55]

Albuquerque Lima gave this paranoia a new form. He objected to the flow of foreign capital into the resource extraction projects, which he felt weakened Brazil's grip on Amazonia, just as it weakened the nation's control over its own economy. He objected to policies that had promoted urbanization in the region; much of Belém and Manaus's recent growth took place at the expense of smaller towns and the backlands of the region. He feared this rural stagnation undercut Brazil's grip on the region just as surely as did massive foreign investment.[56] To secure Amazonia, Albuquerque Lima wanted it more fully integrated into the national ecumene, and he wanted this done with national, not foreign, capital. "Integrate or lose" ("Integrar para não entregar") was his slogan.

Whatever its personal beliefs about the foreign threat to Amazonia, the military had to respond now that Albuquerque Lima had given this threat a powerful new symbolic context. With its emphasis on small farmer settlement and the creation of a prosperous and totally Brazilian agrarian landscape, PIN met one of the more fatuous strains of Brazilian nationalism, yet one that had always demanded a response.[57]

To the extent that PIN referenced development theory, it was as much an effort to avoid its dictates as to follow them. Mainstream theory deemed agricultural modernization crucial to national development; the capacity of the countryside to feed the expanding industrial cities and absorb the output of new industries had to be raised. It also favored land reform to free economic and social forces held in check by archaic land ownership patterns. It held that in very backward regions, aggressive land reform, including expropriation of the seigniorial class, might be the only way to make agriculture play its role in development.[58]

No area was a better candidate for vigorous land reform than Northeastern Brazil. Much of the overworked, overpopulated land was concentrated in the hands of a renter-oligarchy that saw little need to increase productivity, while most farmers worked parcels too small to provide an adequate living. The military government was reluctant to tamper with the socioeconomic order, however. The oligarchs were an important part of its support base. Moreover, the peasants of the Northeast had become very militant and left-leaning during the years before the coup; their threat to the established order helped bring the generals to power. Since the coup, the seigniorial class of the Northeast had kept the peasants under control, an important service in the eyes of the military.[59] "Land without men for men without land," one of the PIN program's slogans, implicitly expressed the hope that it might drain enough excess population from the Northeast to avoid the need for reform there.

PIN's abandonment was as politically laden as its initiation. It was undercut by SUDAM, which viewed INCRA as a rival and feared the power PIN gave it.[60] It was opposed by large capital interests that saw public colonization schemes as competitors for development incentives and long-term threats to the region's investment climate. In this atmosphere of hostility, PIN was slowly ground down as much by funding shortfalls, corruption, and bureaucratic ineptitude as by Amazonia's inherent shortcomings for commercial agriculture. It was finally abandoned when the value of the program's political dividends declined. The need to appease the nationalists was diminished by the new international standing and prestige that economic growth was creating. As a means of dealing with dissent, co-optation and the promise of a better life were being eclipsed by the increasingly direct repression of the Médici presidency.

The succession of development programs in Amazonia was thus due less to the triumph of planning rationality than to a number of shifts in the political equation that diminished PIN's usefulness. The Polamazonia program that replaced PIN conformed more to the physical reality of Amazonia's economic potential, giving rise to the impression that a greater rationality had come in to play, but the conformity was largely incidental; political circumstances allowed it—no inexorable march toward progress demanded it. This meant that while the Polamazonia program, with its concentration on selected areas, did open opportunities for conservation in Amazonia, the opportunities were political to their core. They were also ephemeral. They were random openings in the unceasing play of national and regional politics, not broad, firm niches that evolved as developmental rationality took increasing control of the region's future.

***

Biological conservation, like Amazonia, was far from the center of the military government's concern. Maintaining the profits of its business allies, keeping its regional supporters in power, keeping the middle class prosperous, and keeping those below the middle class docile were important intermediate goals on its road toward the creation of a stable, conservative body politic. Development defined as immediate economic expansion would deliver a wealth of material goods to distribute in the pursuit of these goals. What conservation promised—i.e., insurance that development remained in long-term harmony with the natural world—was not particularly useful in the pursuit of any of them and therefore had little intrinsic value within this political universe. In fact, to the degree to which conservation restrained the delivery of politically useful economic goods, it had negative value.

Nevertheless, conservation programs, like development programs, could help keep political equations in balance. But because conservation did not serve any fundamental goals, the political equations into which it fit tended to be superficial and ever changing, with conservation advancing a mix of transitory ends. While some of these ends were important to the government, conservation itself was never more than an instrument or a minor consideration in the affairs of state.

The problem that first prompted government support for Amazon conservation was Brazil's image abroad. When environmentalism became an international issue in the early 1970s, Brazilian leadership sensed danger. Its international standing might be damaged if foreign media attention focused on the environmental costs of its economic miracle. Multinational environmental accords might restrain its ability to accept polluting industries or might force it to divert capital to pollution control. Brazilian economists staked out anti-environmental positions; Mário Henrique Simenson, a future minister of finance, asserted that "future generations will have the right to criticize us severely if we sacrifice per capita income growth for other priorities," i.e., environmental protection.[61] The Brazilian ambassador to the United States protested that the implementation of any world-wide environmental policy would perpetuate the economic gap between developed and underdeveloped countries.[62]

Brazil also sensed opportunity in the rise of environmentalism. The two pillars of traditional Brazilian foreign policy were its almost exclusive concern with South America and its close alliance with the United States, but during the late 1960s and early 1970s, these seemed progressively less appropriate. America's dominant position in Brazil's trading economy declined and American foreign policy neglected Brazil, wounding national pride. As the generals viewed it, its traditional relationship with the United States no longer fit Brazil's new world status.[63] Nor did a foreign policy that extended only a short way beyond its borders. Brazil's economic growth had given it wide-ranging economic interests: Petrobrás, the national oil company, had acquired interests in Middle East petroleum; Brazilian banks were investing in West African cacao. Brazil aspired to the leadership in the developing world that it felt it had earned.

Accordingly, Brazil began to assert a new, independent, and global foreign policy with an African initiative in the early 1970s.[64] Brazil's foreign minister visited nine sub-Saharan countries, and Brazil staked out a neutralist African policy conspicuously at variance with that of the United States.

Now, with the rise of environmentalism, Brazil saw another chance to assert third-world leadership. Nothing in the development prescriptions they had received from the West prepared third-world leaders for the environmental message.[65] Most third-world governments had based their claims to legitimacy on their commitment to development, and state administrative machinery had been organized around such a commitment. Environmentalism questioned established ways of doing things in such vital areas as public health, agriculture, industrialization, and natural resource management, and it threw past progress in these areas into question. The result was disorientation throughout the third world.

Brazilian officials played on this disorientation by denouncing plans for the Stockholm Conference, claiming environmentalism was a ploy by the developed nations, who, having achieved high levels of prosperity, wanted to prevent the less developed nations from doing the same.[66] The Brazilian delegation to the conference, led by Antônio Delfim Neto, the Minister of Finance and the most important civilian in the government, adopted a highly combative stance, hoping to rally third-world opinion behind Brazil's anti-environmental position.

There was more receptivity to environmentalism in the third world than the Brazilians had anticipated. The socialist bloc saw environmental disruption as something it could blame on international capitalism and, intended or not, its arguments to this effect added to environmentalism's credibility. International conservationists had previously convinced African leaders of the value of protecting wildlife, so when the broader environmental message arrived, many in Africa were prepared to consider it. Moreover, the conference organizers, anticipating criticism such as Brazil's, took measures to blunt it. They agreed that development would be treated as a cure rather than a cause of environmental problems in underdeveloped nations. They set up special sessions on the environmental problems of the third world. They endorsed the position that the cost of environmental protection should be added to the budgets of foreign assistance programs, not shifted from other areas within them.[67]

The careful preparations brought pro-environmental sentiments to the fore at the conference. Several delegates argued for economic growth even at the expense of the environment,[68] but they were the exception; consensus rather than conflict prevailed. The U.S. delegation reported widespread agreement on most substantive issues and noted the "excellent atmosphere" and the "high level of amity" that characterized the conference.[69]

The success of the conference made it a disaster for Brazil. It was now in a highly visible position with little backing in the international community, even among the third-world nations to whom it was supposed to appeal. The international press widely and negatively reported the behavior of the Brazilian delegation at Stockholm, and as the full effect of the conference sank in around the world, Brazil's environmental performance came under critical scrutiny.[70] The rash of environmental actions taken by the Brazilian government in the period after the Stockholm Conference—establishing SEMA, rewriting national planning documents to include environmental objectives, passing antipollution legislation—were concessions to the international climate and attempts to repair the damage.

The creation of Amazonia National Park, the infusion of conservation rhetoric into planning documents for Amazonia at the point of shift from PIN to Polamazonia, and the institution of the PRODEPEF wildlands survey were due largely to the realization that Amazonia was a good place for expressions of concern for the environment, just as it was a good place to satisfy so many other political side demands. There was a natural affinity between Amazonia and conservation from the government's perspective: an off-center region was the ideal place to give expression to an off-center policy demand.

The military government was never particularly interested in what conservation promised most insistently in Amazonia, a more rational approach to the region's landscape and its future. The government had insisted that conservation plans for Amazonia be scientific and rational, but this was largely to maintain the facade of planning rationality it wanted of all policy initiatives; it had also insisted that plans for PIN appear rational. Indeed, a conservation program that acted as a true agent of such rationality would have reduced the government's freedom to use Amazonia in working out solutions to other problems that arose from the play of politics.

New, supplementary reasons for supporting Amazon conservation arose in the years following the Stockholm Conference to reinforce the original one. In 1974, in another major foreign policy shift, Brazil refocused on South America.[71] It wanted to insure access to its neighbors' markets (Latin America accounted for only 7 percent of Brazil's foreign trade in 1960, but the percentage would more than double by the end of the 1970s) and lead them as a unified block in global politics. To these ends, Brazilian diplomacy concentrated on negotiating a series of bilateral and regional treaties.[72] The centerpiece would be an Amazon treaty in which all nations with territory in Amazonia would pledge themselves to cooperate in the region's management. Since all the Andean Pact nations had territory in Amazonia, such a treaty could serve as a counterweight to that older regional pact that excluded Brazil.

There were formidable obstacles to such a treaty, however. Brazil's relationship with its Spanish-speaking neighbors had long been characterized by mutual distrust, and its relations with the Andean countries were clouded by conflicting claims and ambitions in Amazonia.[73] Brazilian writers associated with the military had contributed to the atmosphere of distrust. Colonel Mário Travassos, considered the founder of Brazilian geopolitics, argued in the 1930s that Brazil was in competition with its neighbors for control of the continent's interior and that the winner would dominate South America. Child observed that writers who followed Travassos "frequently present[ed] an almost Darwinian vision of a cruel and competitive international environment."[74]

Younger Brazilian geopolitical analysts realigned their thinking during the boom years of the late 1960s and 1970s to reflect Brazil's new self-assurance and importance in the world order; they now proposed that Amazon development be an international rather than a strictly Brazilian undertaking. Meira Mattos envisioned vast developing regions spanning Brazil's international boundaries with Colombia, Peru, Bolivia, and the Guianas (figure 5.2).[75] Far from calming Brazil's neighbors, this was viewed as a new and pernicious manifestation of Brazilian territorial ambition, and it made them suspicious of improvements in communication and transportation in Brazilian Amazonia. Plans for the Transamazon Highway were greeted with a conspicuous lack of enthusiasm in Spanish America.[76] In fact, feelings against Brazil were running so high among its neighbors that when Brazilian president Geisel and Bolivian president Suarez signed an economic cooperation pact in 1974, Bolivia's opposition politicians denounced it as a sell-out to Brazilian imperialism

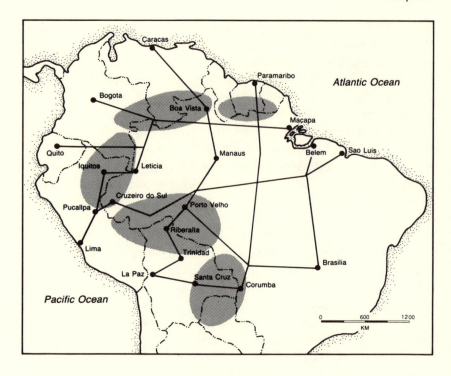

FIGURE 5.2
Amazon Frontier Interchange Areas. Adapted from Meira Mattos,
Brasil: Geopolítica e Destino, p. 76

and students rioted in La Paz. The Brazilian president was forced to strongly deny his country had ambitions of continental domination.[77]

Intense diplomatic efforts persuaded Brazil's neighbors to consider the idea of an Amazon treaty, but the draft Brazil prepared raised the old fears. The frequent passages referring to collective security, regional economic integration, and joint resource exploitation sounded like Brazilian imperialism speaking the new language of development.

If Brazil was to have its Amazon treaty, a different pretext for it would have to be found. The Intergovernmental Technical Committee for the Defense of Amazon Flora and Fauna (CIT), founded at the urging of international conservationists by the six Amazon Basin countries in 1975, had worked well because the protection of nature was not an issue on which international ambitions or fears could easily settle. The plans for conservation in Brazilian Amazonia then being drawn up by Wetterberg and Jorge Pádua had won the respect of the other nations of the basin and had been adopted as a model for other regional conservation programs. In light of this, Brazilian diplomats thought conservation might serve more ambitious national ends.

The redraft of the treaty played down collective security and regional development while emphasizing the protection of Amazon nature, which it held to be the "collective and exclusive" responsibility of the Amazon nations. Nature protection was so prominent in the revised text that one observer complained that from reading it, it would be difficult to discern that the region had a human population.[78] With this new emphasis on nature protection, Brazil set its continental ambitions in a benign context while projecting an image of maturity and responsibility. The approach worked; the other Amazon nations signed the Treaty of Amazon Cooperation in Brasília in July 1978.

Once the treaty was in effect, Brazil came under pressure to show that it took the treaty seriously. The recent establishment of several large protected areas in Amazonia by other signatory nations sharpened the pressure. Implementing Stage One of Jorge Pádua's conservation plan, approved in principle by the CIT and by then already almost fully formulated, was ideal.[79] With its ambitions, firm grounding in science, and widespread approval among conservationists, the plan would allow Brazil to leap to the forefront of Amazon conservation and derive all the immediate foreign policy benefits.

Finally, there were domestic considerations. The military government appealed continually to the self-interest of the middle class and the nation's economic elite during its first decade in power. It claimed to be a bulwark against the communism and anarchy that had threatened the middle and upper classes in the early 1960s, and it continually reminded them that its economic programs were bringing unprecedented prosperity. The appeal was successful; the military government was perceived by the middle class as responsible for the good times of the early 1970s, and the government enjoyed broad, if sometimes grudging, support among the middle reaches of Brazilian society.[80]

The boom showed signs of strain as early as 1974. Foreign debt began to mount and the steep rise in the price of petroleum imports threw Brazil's balance of payments off kilter. The profits on investment by foreigners were increasingly repatriated as the 1970s progressed, creating a greater need for foreign loans to maintain economic expansion.[81] The world recession at the end of the 1970s constricted markets for Brazil's exports. As these problems forced up inflation and unemployment, the middle class saw its previous gains erode and its future cloud over, causing it to lose faith in the military regime. Industrialists and other businessmen saw their profits decline, and their previous buoyancy was replaced by caution. As Linz observed, since the authoritarian regime's claims to legitimacy had to be based on performance, once the economy over which it presided turned sour, it had few props of support left.[82] By the end of Geisel's presidency in early 1979, support for the military was deeply eroded in all sectors of society; most Brazilians wanted the generals to go.

When Figueiredo entered office in March 1979, he enacted a number of measures to shore up support for the government.[83] Although he had built a reputation for sinister competence as the head of the Military Intelligence Service, he promoted himself as a personable, accessible leader once he became president; he instituted a call-in radio show on which he answered selected questions with avuncular common sense. He opened the political system by releasing political prisoners, allowing exiles to return, and permitting new political parties. He lifted press censorship, albeit slowly and unevenly.

The government hoped a highly visible conservation program would help it maintain the support of the middle class. Conservation and access to nature had been an issue for the professional middle class for most of the twentieth century.[84] Parks were places where the Latin American middle class could enjoy the good life based on North American and European models and were therefore potent symbols of modernity and progress for it. The Vargas government, sensitive to the symbolism, had established Brazil's first national parks and national conservation programs as part of its effort to keep middle-class support.[85] The parks and reserves established by Kubitschek were part of his strategy of appealing to the urban middle class. Now, with the economy faltering, the new national parks and biological reserves of the 1970s and early 1980s, like political liberalization, were portrayed as the fruits of development. They were a gambit to shift the attention of the middle class beyond the present shortcomings of its life to the more prosperous future that the government still promised, one in which the benefits of past economic successes would be fully reaped.

Brazil's political and economic problems deepened between 1979 and 1982. The nation's universities were shut by strikes in 1980, and a militantly nationalist faction was growing within the officer corps, destabilizing it and threatening its consensus.[86] Further oil price increases depleted Brazil's foreign reserves, and the deepening world recession further constricted markets for its exports. The state became the captive of its own institutions, the publicly owned corporations, whose 1981 deficit was 5.8 percent of the gross domestic product (GDP).[87] Industrial production and real income declined; unemployment and inflation rose.

The implementation of the IBDF's conservation program took place against the backdrop of this crisis, and as the crisis deepened, the knot of political circumstances that sustained Amazon conservation unraveled. Managing the debt replaced continental ambitions as the driving force of Brazil's foreign policy.[88] Considerations of international image and aspirations to third world leadership were put on hold. The need to impress the middle class with the baubles and bangles of progress paled before the task of holding the economy together. Jorge Pádua's success in keeping the IBDF's conservation program on track for so long against this darkening background was a credit to her skills.

It seems logical in retrospect that the road through Araguaia National Park would be the issue to pierce the illusions. By mid-1982, the international debt crisis was causing Brazil's sources of credit to dry up, and its external debt was becoming unmanageable. Brazil entered debt relief negotiations with the International Monetary Fund, and as a condition for extended credit, the fund insisted that Brazil generate large balance-of-payments surpluses.[89] The road across Araguaia National Park would violate the 1979 national park legislation, but linking the developing trans-Bananal agricultural district to the Belém-Brasília Highway would increase the region's capacity to export its products.

* * *

Not only did the commitment to development fail to create a secure political niche for biological conservation, but Brazil's development policies, so heavily conditioned by political considerations, failed to prompt the societal transformations on which Brazilian conservationists had counted.

The belief that advanced countries showed less developed ones the image of their own social future was common in South America during the 1960s and 1970s. ECLA subscribed to it, as did Brazil's business and government elites. The belief was held by conservationists

around the world: Clawson wrote that the great social transformations caused by economic development would shape opportunities
for conservationists everywhere.[90] This assumption was explicit in
Miller's work and was an important supporting prop of conservation
strategy for Brazilian Amazonia in the 1970s; the Amazonia of the
future would be a modern, developed region in a modern, developed
Brazil.[91] This belief encouraged Jorge Pádua to overreach her immediate political opportunities; she trusted the future to secure what
conservation could grasp only tenuously today.

It was clear by the early 1980s that social change in Brazil had not
followed North American or Western European models, in spite of
the economic gains of the two preceding decades. Free of the need to
satisfy the disenfranchised working class, the military government
insured maximum international competitiveness by keeping wages
down and skimping on programs to raise the standards of living of
the working class. Its encouragement of technology- and capital-
intensive production limited the capacity of the modern sector to
absorb labor from the informal sectors. As a percentage of the work
force, the informal sector had dropped only slightly over the previous thirty years.[92] The government's unwillingness to undertake land
reform left vast regions of rural poverty and peonage. Income distribution became more, not less skewed: the poorer half of Brazilian
society received 17.4 percent of the national income in 1960, but
only 12.6 percent in 1980. Brazilian economic expansion in the
1960s and 1970s did raise real incomes for many of the poor, but the
rise was modest and was wiped out in the hard times of the 1980s.[93]

The changes in society that did take place could hardly be called
modernization and they did not create firm social bases of conservation support. The tens of thousands of urban workers who remained
outside the formal sector built squatter settlements on the periphery
of Brazil's major cities. Unlike similar settlements in nineteenth-century North America, these grew to form vast districts encircling and
sometimes overlooking the cities.[94] In these settlements and in the
center-city slums that complemented them, the insecurity, marginal-
ity, and poverty of the working class took on a permanence that set it
apart from other elements of Brazilian society and made it unable to
discharge the political role that conservationists had envisioned for
it. It was too poor and immobile to use the national parks, too concerned with its immediate welfare to express much interest in remote
conservation issues.

The middle class grew and prospered during the years of economic expansion.[95] By the end of the 1970s, it had taken on the appearance of the middle classes of developed countries, with autos, appliances, suburban houses, and attractive apartments now within its purchasing range. But as the boom played itself out, real incomes fell and the prospect of good jobs became less certain. The material accouterments of the good life, only recently come within grasp, slipped away, and the middle class exchanged its sense of confidence for desperation.[96] The middle class became too embattled, too fearful of falling into the vast pool of poverty just below it, to organize itself around broad issues of general welfare as it had in North America and Europe. The organization that did take place was usually local, ad hoc, and directed at immediate issues.[97]

Thus while middle-class traditions of civic responsibility gave the Brazilian environmental movement of the 1980s its form, the harsh reality of current middle-class conditions determined its scale and substance. The Brazilian environmental movement was similar to the movement in the United States and the developed countries of Europe in the types of organizations in which it expressed itself. The organizations that were found in the major Brazilian cities and many smaller ones as well would have been recognizable to a member of the Sierra Club. The movement used many of the same tactics and represented a similarly broad range of the middle-class political spectrum, from conservative, older bird watchers who advocated quiet persuasion to young, Marx-quoting environmentalists who favored confrontation and direct action.[98]

The scale and effectiveness was less, however. The largest of the Brazilian conservation organizations were orders of magnitude smaller than their counterparts in the United States. The Brazilian Foundation for the Conservation of Nature (FBCN), the oldest, best-known, and most respected national organization, had approximately 10,000 members in the mid-1980s. The Associação Mineira da Defensa do Meio Ambiente, the major conservation organization in Belo Horizonte, Brazil's third-largest city, had approximately 160 active members.[99] The environmental groups outside the more developed areas of the South were sometimes merely fronts for one or two active individuals. This left the Brazilian movement too small and financially weak to support the cadre of professionals or the sustained programs so important in the United States.[100] The FBCN had to rely on foreign support to maintain even its modest environmental education and public relations programs.

The weakness of the movement was exacerbated by a lack of political skills among its membership. A politically active and knowledge-able populace was supposed to be a concomitant of economic development, but the years of dictatorial rule that had left most Brazilians outside the circles of power also left them with a limited understanding of micropolitics and a limited repertoire of political skills.[101] The more conservative wing of the movement showed some political sophistication—it knew how to persuade government officials and quietly support conservation administrators—but much of the movement had less sophistication or skill. Environmentalists often denounced environmentally harmful policies, yet they were incapable of sustained action. Often their discontent over the environment was subsumed into a broader discontent, rather than being parsed into manageable problems that could be tackled one by one.[102] The organized conservation movement thus entered the democratizing politics of the 1980s with a political skill base no stronger than that of the middle class in general.

During the "Brazilian miracle," the nation's economic elite prospered as never before, but a network of elite institutions did not arise to support conservation. There were important industrial families in Brazil whose rise dated back to the early twentieth century, but the prominence of industrial capitalism in Brazil was more recent. As late as the 1950s, the traditional landed oligarchs held sway in much of the country, and industrial capitalism was by no means secure in its dominance of the Brazilian political system.[103] Even in the South, it was challenged by fortunes based on trade, and industrialists seldom thought of themselves as a coherent class. The chaos of the early 1960s heightened their feelings of insecurity.

The industrial elite's prosperity under the military did not give it a strong sense of class-identity; it was too wedded to state-directed economic expansion to have any sense of detachment from it. Nor did its prosperity produce much of a seigniorial sense of self-confidence. There was too much dissent beneath the surface, too much of Brazil left out.[104] The concords with other sectors of society—labor, farmers, the middle class—on which so much of the security of American industrial capitalism rested had never been reached in Brazil. Without this sense of identity and self-confidence, it could not develop a broad sense of public responsibility.

This left the task of defining the commonweal at a few loci within the government itself: the president and his chief advisors, the ministries of planning and finance, the National Security Council, and the Superior War College (ESG). All were committed to unimpeded economic expansion as the keystone of the commonweal.[105] The ministries of planning and finance were creatures of it. The ESG, the National Security Council, and the senior military cadre were committed to it by strong traditions dating back to nineteenth-century Positivism, and by the logic of their position. Under the military, entry into the circles of power required agreement with standing national goals, including maximum development, and with the basic prescriptions for achieving them. There was no purchase in Brazil's power structure for elite institutions that might question the principles of development as they were expressed in official policy.

As democratic politics returned to Brazil in the mid-1980s, the elite was as fragmented and insecure as it had been before the military came to power. To the extent that it had any introspective vision, it saw itself less as a dominant class and more as a player in a game of interest politics made volatile and desperate by the failed social transformations of the 1970s and the economic reverses of the 1980s. Incapable of the detachment necessary to define its own interests in broad terms, it remained uninterested in creating the kind of network of elite, public-minded institutions from which the conservation movement in the United States derived so much of its power and direction.

Finally, in the 1980s neither Brazilian scientists nor scientific institutions could offer the strong support on which the conservationists had counted. While Brazil's traditions of Positivism seemed to confer great respect on the scientist, they actually devalued him. The respect for science they engendered was narrow and extended little beyond applied science.[106] The scientist's job was solving problems given him by others: government officials, industrialists, or society in general. This role allowed respect for leading scientists—as noted earlier, Brazilians still venerate Oswaldo Cruz—but there was little place for the scientist as worldly philosopher, political participant, or even shaper of the problems that science should address.[107] Science might have been central to progress within the Positivist world view, but it was still just a trade.

The sociology of Brazilian science reinforced this view. The profession was low-paying and involved working with one's hands. These factors made scientific careers unattractive to those from the reaches of society where public questions were normally defined; Paulo Nogueira-Neto was an often-noted exception. Scientists instead were drawn from the middle classes, and frequently from immigrant stock.[108] People from such backgrounds might help solve Brazil's public problems, but they were seldom allowed to define them.

Developmentalism also undercut the sociopolitical role of the scientist. Because of its extraordinary intellectual hegemony during the first two postwar decades, development theory was allowed to define the world on its own terms. Nature became a stock of natural resources to be brought to the task of global progress. Culture was defined within development's prism: Meier and Baldwin defined traditional cultures as those that had "struck a balance with nature at an elementary level" and, as a consequence, were "unsuccessful in [the] conquest of [the] material environment."[109] With the world so defined, the imperatives of development could set the values and define the tasks of social and natural sciences. Sociologists were set to creating modernizing bureaucracies. Psychologists were to smooth the adjustment of traditional peoples to modern lives. Anthropologists were to figure out how to replace traditional, collective values with individual initiative and the work ethic. The natural and physical sciences were to turn nature into progress.[110]

The Brazilian government, already predisposed toward an instrumentalist view of science by the military's Positivist intellectual traditions and the social roots of Brazilian science, adopted and sharpened development's perspective on science. Because it wanted all the benefits that development theory insisted science and technology could produce, it allowed planning and economic development organs to become the most important sponsors of research.[111] Under their aegis, institutes dedicated to very specific development-related problems—increasing cacao or sugar production, for example—became the best-funded bastions of science in the nation. Development planning agencies had a large say in graduate science training through their influence on higher education budgets, and the training they promoted focused on narrow, usually production-related problems.

Fields not promising immediate, tangible yields were seen by science bureaucrats as luxuries Brazil could not afford, and they were viewed with the contempt Positivists of an earlier era had heaped on metaphysics. The National Research Council (CNPq), the most important scientific organ of the Brazilian government, was placed under the Ministry of Planning, the nation's premier agency of economic development in 1975, which further subjugated science to development-oriented administrators.[112]

Ecological science suffered acutely from this subjugation because it seemed better at identifying problems caused by human action than at serving those who wished to alter nature in the name of progress. Ecology as a scientific culture also placed higher values on activities that did not disrupt the natural world than on those that did. Ecology, like conservation itself, was therefore permeated with fundamentally different values than those that undergirded Brazil's development planning, in spite of Jorge Pádua's and Nogueira-Neto's frequent protestations to the contrary. Ecology was also too value-laden for either the Brazilian scientific tradition or the prevailing view of science as merely a neutral instrument in the hands of planners. While ecology and environmental science did find a measure of government support during the boom years, even then there was only a minor and never wholly comfortable place for them in the pantheon of Brazilian science.

Politically exposed in the best of times, environmental sciences suffered disproportionately as the fiscal crisis of the 1980s deepened. Research money from the National Research Council and most other national sources for INPA's ecological projects had dried up by the mid-1980s.[113] INPA came under pressure to become self-supporting, which forced it to accept contract work on development projects and to assign highest priority to studies with immediate, easily measurable paybacks.[114] Its aquatic biology was reoriented toward the short-term commercial productivity of the region's rivers. It inaugurated a large, expensive wood-products laboratory intended to strengthen the commercial wood industry in the region, but only staff ecologists with their own foreign sources of support had the resources to do field research.[115]

The redemocratization of the early 1980s reduced the constraints on scientists as participants in the national political process, but the institutional ties of science to the organs of development, its tradition of narrow focus, and its financial straits left Brazilian science, and environmental sciences in particular, in a poor position from which to advance conservation in the political arena.

* * *

In summary, when the instruments of public administration were revamped to promote national development after the coup of 1964, the conventional development perspective became entrenched throughout the federal government;[116] adherence to it was the road to success for agencies and ambitious administrators. The support of the producing sectors in Amazonia—ranching, commercial farming, mining, etc.—reinforced this dominance among agencies active in the region. Thus in large measure the conservation gains made by the IBDF in Amazonia ran contrary to basic administrative values, although those involved did not fully realize it. Jorge Pádua and her associates exploited the personalist side of Brazilian politics to implement a politically attractive conservation program during what, in retrospect, was a period of anomalously favorable circumstances, but their success did not overcome the fundamental political weakness of biological conservation: roots that never penetrated beyond transitory expedience.

Those who would direct the IBDF and SEMA's conservation programs in the 1980s therefore found themselves in a far more arid environment than their predecessors had expected—or planned for; they would have to work without a deep or enduring government commitment to conservation and without broad, powerful bases of social support for conservation goals.

CHAPTER 6

The Lees of Success:
The IBDF in the Eighties

The erosion of political support for biological conservation in the 1980s undercut the IBDF's conservation program in several ways. One was through its impact on the IBDF's organizational culture. Economic development regained its full former importance to the IBDF, a process reinforced now by Brazil's debt crisis. The forest institute intensified its commitment to commercial forestry and the generation of revenues through licenses, cutting permits, and fines for forestry code infractions. Its personnel rolls in the mid-1980s reflected this commitment: most of its more than six hundred professionals were forest or agricultural engineers, and most of the balance were lawyers, professional administrators, or economists.[1] This gave the agency a culture dominated by production-oriented professionals; Brazilian forest engineers, like those elsewhere, saw trees as products and forests as timber stands rather than habitats.

IBDF conservationists were unable to count on their allies elsewhere in the federal government to compensate for their isolation within their own agency; the power of their allies was undercut by the same emphasis on production that had undercut them. For example, by the mid-1980s, SUDAM was no longer receptive to its Natural Resources Division's advocacy of developing Amazonia according to the region's "natural calling" which left the division isolated and without a base of power.[2]

The weakness of conservation factions within individual agencies also left them unable to force their agencies to cooperate with each other on conservation-related issues. SUDAM's Natural Resources Division thought it important to maintain the forests of Amazonia by directing cattle projects to the natural campos and other areas of nonforest vegetation. But while SUDAM frequently dealt with the

IBDF with regard to revenues and exports it had no contact with the forest agency on the allocation of incentives for new cattle ranches in the region. There was little cooperation between INCRA and the IBDF on the environmental aspects of settlement colonies.[3] Neither IBDF conservationists nor those in INCRA concerned with the environmental consequences of its actions were powerful enough to force their agencies to forge links of cooperation on conservation issues. One DN administrator said, "IBDF has many environmental interests in common with other agencies, including INCRA, but, regrettably, it does not have environmental links with them."[4]

The Park Advisory Board might have compensated for the weakness and isolation of the IBDF conservationists, but it never became the effective instrument Jorge Pádua envisioned. With no tradition of upper-class public responsibility in Brazil, the key ingredient of a powerful, benevolent advisory body was missing.[5] The disinterest of Brazil's social elite allowed the board to be dominated by its government members, most of whom represented agencies with regular contact with the park system: FUNAI, SEMA, INCRA, and the armed forces.[6] With no political reason to support the IBDF's conservation programs, its government members gave the board a low priority, making it difficult even to get a quorum at meetings. The board was practically moribund by the mid-1980s, and to the extent that it still functioned, it did so only in a limited, technical way, giving other agencies a chance to review plans for the park system.

Administrative weakness left conservation exposed to the full brunt of government fiscal retrenchment that followed Brazil's debt restructuring negotiations.[7] IBDF leadership viewed conservation as marginal to its main mission and saw the parks and reserves as agency resource sinks, so the DN was a prime target. As the waves of budget reductions became more severe in the 1980s, the DN's morale sank and its sense of isolation grew. One DN official complained that "no one higher up in IBDF is especially interested in us or looks out for our welfare."[8] Low morale and cuts in real income sent many of the DN's best people elsewhere for employment. Prohibited from replacing many of them, the staff shrank by attrition. The DN's park planning unit, for example, with six or seven staff members under Jorge Pádua, had been reduced to two by the mid-1980s. The staff shrinkage eroded the DN's capacity to carry out even routine technical tasks.

Ideological isolation, loss of favor, and reduced operating capacity had two related effects on the IBDF's conservation program. First, centrifugal tendencies latent in the machinery of policy were unleashed, allowing decision making authority to seep outward. This permitted a large number of random impulses to enter conservation decisions, inevitably to the detriment of conservation itself. Second, the power remaining with those officially responsible for the conservation program was often expressed in narrow, involuted forms inappropriate for the tasks that the program faced in the 1980s.

In spite of the latent centrifugal tendencies always present in the administrative structure of the IBDF's conservation program, official favor had acted as a cement, holding the program together and allowing coherent, proactive policies in the 1970s and early 1980s. Under Jorge Pádua, the DN, although without direct authority over the system, did provide leadership on budget, personnel, and policy matters, and many of the major operational decisions regarding the protected areas were made within the DN or were strongly influenced by its advice. When favor was replaced by indifference, major decisions about the parks and reserves moved upward to higher levels within the IBDF and outward to the states themselves.

When decision making moved upward, it entered the domain of administrators who usually had little commitment to biological conservation and who were inclined to factor other, more pressing agency concerns into their decisions.[9] The DN's advice was seldom solicited, or if solicited, it was usually confined to narrow technical matters.

There were several practical consequences of this upward movement. First, it decapitated the conservation program, cutting the field off from the DN, its natural source of leadership, while preventing the DN, the one IBDF unit with a strong sense of responsibility for the program, from exercising that responsibility. Second, by marginalizing the IBDF unit that was, in effect, the repository of agency conservation experience and memory, it made consistent policy making impossible.

Third, it made even the technical, routine side of the DN's job more difficult. The IBDF central administration decided what data it wanted from its field units, including the parks and reserves. It changed its reporting requirements frequently and seldom enforced them, especially with regard to little-valued conservation data. The DN had no say in the type of information it received from the field, and what little it did receive was often inconsistent and incomplete. This, plus the normal problems of data collecting and record keeping in third-world bureaucracies, made it difficult for the DN—or anyone else—to evaluate performances, spot emerging problems, or even get an accurate picture of conditions in the field. As a DN official related, "The delegado's staff in Amazonas knows more about what's going on in the parks in the state than we do. If we want to find something out, we have to call Manaus."[10]

It became difficult for DN professionals in Brasília to gain needed field experience. Because the DN and the field units were organizationally distant, with layers of indifferent bureaucracy between them, a transfer from the headquarters to the field would involve much uncertainty and paper work, and once in the field, eventual transfer back to Brasília was not certain. Knowledge of this tended to keep DN professionals frozen in place in Brasília. For example, a DN specialist had developed interpretive plans for several national parks, but because no one in the parks had any experience with such plans—nor, apparently, any interest in them—none of them had been implemented.[11] The logical step would have been for him to transfer to a park and take charge of the implementation himself, but he would not consider it. Even assuming it could have been arranged, it probably would have put him under the authority of someone with no interest in interpretation anyway. He feared that once out from under the protective wing of the DN, his effectiveness would have been even more limited by isolation in a hostile administrative environment.

Given the general disinterest of higher levels of IBDF administration in conservation, it was natural that some power over agency conservation decisions would diffuse to the states along the ligaments of the agency's field organization, but the process was further encouraged by changes in federal-state politics that accompanied the revival of democratic institutions in the early 1980s. In the years before the military came to power, the states of Amazonia looked to the federal government to provide for their welfare through the federal agencies, and the states, in return, loyally supported the regime in the national capital. The symbiotic arrangement went into abeyance during the more authoritarian days of the military regime because support articulated through the emptied representative political structures meant little to the federal government. As party politics revived in the 1980s, and particularly after the direct election of governors in 1982, this support again became a valued political commodity in Brasília, and the IBDF came under more pressure from above to do the bidding of the state governments.[12]

The diffusion of power to the states, like the upward drift to higher levels in the IBDF, worked against conservation: previously the message the delegados received from agency leadership was "listen to the states while looking out for the conservation program;" now it was simply "listen to the states." The states' message to the delegados was universally clear: promote activities that stimulate economic growth—tree plantations, commercial logging, and spin-off industries.[13] Such economic growth enhanced state revenues, provided opportunities for investment, and, in general, lubricated local politics. The population growth that attended it increased a state's representation in the national legislature, an important consideration as democratic institutions were revitalized.

On the other hand, attitudes toward biological conservation varied from state to state.[14] Sometimes conservation initiatives were opposed as inhibiting economic growth. Sometimes a place was conceded for conservation, and sometimes total indifference reigned. Occasionally sudden changes in attitudes took place. The early 1980s saw the government of Amazonas encouraging the establishment of the Abufari Biological Reserve, but after the government changed, a more hostile attitude toward conservation emerged. No matter how positively they felt about conservation, however, the state governments of Amazonia gave it a relatively low priority because it produced little of immediate benefit to them.

The pressure from the states to expand forest production, when added to that emanating from agency headquarters, translated into a daunting number of production-oriented responsibilities for the delegados. The delegado to Pará had to oversee reforestation projects and the operation of over two thousand enterprises registered with the IBDF: cacao and brazilnut plantations, saw mills, logging operations, and wood product factories. He also had to maintain experimental forests and a wood products laboratory. Like the other delegados, he had few administrative resources left for conservation.

The relationship of the delegados to the IBDF conservation program in the late 1980s was thus the reverse of what it had been in the late 1970s and early 1980s. During the earlier years, delegados were encouraged to respect the conservation side of their charge, whatever their personal inclinations. During the latter years, whatever their personal sentiments, there was little they could do to advance conservation. This produced a range of situations in the states of Amazonia, running from bad to worse. The delegado in Pará seemed genuinely interested in conservation and the state government was not hostile to it, but he had little time and fewer resources left over from high-priority matters to assign to it. Nevertheless, he did what little he could.[15] In Amapá, where the IBDF delegado and the government of the territory appeared totally uninterested in conservation, less was done.[16] A local man had been hired to live in the Lago Piratuba reserve and act as a watchman, but apart from this, the IBDF could not mount an active management regime for either Lago Piratuba or Cabo Orange. Even efforts to get the delegado to conduct surveillance overflights and occasional patrols of the two areas were unsuccessful.

The second consequence of conservation's loss of political advantage was an involution of policy and vision. One might compare the process to the explosion of a supernova; once most of the decision making authority had moved beyond the ambit of conservation administrators, that which remained collapsed inward under the weight of indifference and resource limitations.

Involution was evident in leadership style. Bureaucratic entrepreneurship and imagination were needed to search out political resources still available to conservation in the 1980s. The IBDF's conservation program had been built on entrepreneurial leadership. Indeed, it was overbuilt for routine—or even excellent—management skills; maintaining it would have required entrepreneurship and vision even had the 1980s been as favorable to conservation as had been hoped. Conservation did not attract appropriate leadership, however.

Jorge Pádua's successors fell into two categories. Some were professional administrators who had spent most of their careers elsewhere in the agency and who neither identified with conservation nor were experienced in conservation management. To them, the DN was a step on the career ladder, rather than a repository of special values. Acting to advance conservation the way Jorge Pádua had would have been foolish. The IBDF's conservation program during the 1970s was a good outlet for entrepreneurial, risk-taking leadership. While political support for conservation was building, going outside official channels the way Jorge Pádua had done seemed likely to pay off in attained goals and enhanced careers. During the 1980s, the IBDF's conservation programs, with neither external political support nor the likelihood of rapid growth, did not offer an attractive field for administrative entrepreneurship: in an organization that no longer highly valued its conservation mission, such action would have only reduced chances of further personal advancement.

Jorge Pádua's other successors were more closely identified with conservation: usually they had spent much of their previous careers in the DN, and some had long associations with Jorge Pádua. However, they tended to be bureaucrats and technicians rather than visionaries or entrepreneurs: Jorge Pádua had counterbalanced her own entrepreneurial tendencies by attracting solid administrators and planners to the DN. They had made their mark through the competent discharge of technical tasks or as good staff people. When they reached positions of authority, they tended to see their jobs largely in technical or narrowly professional terms.

Angela Bernardes Quintão, who became the head of the DN in 1986, is illustrative of this second, conservation-oriented group. An architect by training, she was involved in drawing up the Sete Cidades management plan and Stage Two of the system plan. Thanks to the competence she displayed in performing these tasks, she acquired a reputation as one of the most promising of the young conservation administrators who received their training under Jorge Pádua.[17] When she became head of the DN, she set about increasing productivity, clearing lines of authority, and, in general, increasing the unit's professionalism. Less dynamic than Jorge Pádua, Bernardes Quintão saw her job as largely administrative, and she viewed the entrepreneurship that Jorge Pádua had practiced as a luxury rather than an essential. She speculated that someday, when the unit's administrative problems were brought under control, she might become more involved in politics to further conservation goals.[18]

* * *

The DN leadership tried to hold to the literal course set for it by Jorge Pádua and Wetterberg in all areas of policy, but powerlessness, manifesting itself as centrifugation of authority, involution of vision, or both, really determined the substance of the IBDF's conservation actions in the mid- and late 1980s. Relations with foreign conservationists and enforcement of regulations were two areas where involution of vision dominated.

Their largely technical and managerial interpretation of their jobs was natural, given their predispositions and the immediate administrative tasks they faced, but it prevented Jorge Pádua's successors from taking advantage of those potential sources of extra-agency support that remained, especially foreign conservation organizations, which were increasingly concerned for rainforests. Although there were many formal links of cooperation between Latin American conservation agencies and their foreign counterparts, the important connections were personal ones, based on friendship, mutual respect, and an understanding of what each party could do for the other. Foreigners depended on Brazilians to interpret what seemed like the Byzantine complexities of Brazilian politics and to guide their involvement in Brazilian conservation. For their part, Brazilian conservationists counted on foreign conservationists for financial support, technical advice, and the prima facie credibility they derived from foreign connections.[19]

The links between the IBDF's conservation program and the international conservation network, built in large measure on Jorge Pádua and Wetterberg's friendship, were ruptured when the two left the scene. The links were never fully rebuilt by their successors. Foreign conservationists had difficulty figuring out the IBDF after Jorge Pádua left. Some of her successors were unknown to them, and while some were known, and even admired, they were shifted around within the IBDF too rapidly for stable relationships to develop. Foreign conservationists therefore tended to look outside the IBDF for their Brazilian contacts. For its part, the IBDF saw putting the DN's house in order as more important than reconstructing links with sources of support abroad. By the mid-1980s, speculation rather than communication characterized the relationship between the conservationists within the IBDF and possible sources of foreign support, depriving the IBDF's program of the advantages it had formerly gained from its more intimate relationship, as well as any further advantages derived from increased interest in rainforest conservation abroad.[20]

Their contracted sense of responsibility sometimes prevented DN administrators from seeing the political dimension of their tasks. As with so many of Jorge Pádua's actions, the vigorous tone of the regulations covering research in the protected areas was at least partly for effect; they were to show the IBDF's seriousness about protecting nature and to prevent always-prickly Brazilian national pride from making an issue of "scientific imperialism." Ideally, political considerations and administrative responsibilities would play off against each other: the regulations would increase the IBDF's stature as a responsible preservation agency and insure against sacrifices of park integrity, but political sensitivity would prevent excessive bureaucratic zeal in enforcement.

Under Jorge Pádua's successors, the DN saw its role with regard to research as enforcing the 1981 regulations to the letter.[21] Application procedures were to be followed precisely and rejections were common.[22] The DN rejected a 1983 request from the Institute of Biophysics of the Federal University of Rio de Janeiro to collect marsupials to study their reproduction because it was felt that the collecting could be done elsewhere. Even several collecting requests from the Rio de Janeiro Botanical Garden, itself part of the IBDF, were turned down in 1985. Some of the botanical garden's requests were not accompanied by what the DN considered sufficient justification. In other cases, the DN felt the garden's herbaria already included sufficient material in the plant families to be collected.

DN officials held that the early flush of research in Amazonia National Park and the Trombetas Biological Reserve had produced little of value in managing them; sometimes researchers had merely provided species lists to the IBDF. Sometimes the scientists concluded their research and were never heard from again, presumably publishing their results in inaccessible foreign journals.[23] The DN's response was a more restrictive attitude; it preferred to admit only scientists it knew from experience or those who had already built reputations for solid work. Such scientists were thought most likely to obey the regulations once they got out to the field, where no one was watching them. When there was doubt, the DN preferred to err on the side of caution and say no.

The DN zealously ferreted out illegal research. Normally, the cumbersome regulations simply caused scientists to look elsewhere for field sites, but occasionally they circumvented the process through informal arrangements with the park director or the state IBDF delegado, or by surreptitiously conducting their work without any approval. The DN suspected that scientists in Rio de Janeiro regarded Tijuca National Park, the closest large natural area to Rio, as their own teaching and research preserve. It even suspected that scientists attached to the Rio Botanical Gardens illegally collected plants in the park and falsely identified the collecting sites. A DN investigation in 1985 uncovered several unauthorized projects in the park. It tracked down those involved and made it clear that such research would not be tolerated in the future.

As might have been expected given the view of their task taken by Jorge Pádua's successors, Stage Two of the system plan remained the chief guide for departmental decisions,[24] and indeed, as called for in Stage Two, management plans continued to be produced and implemented and new areas continued to be brought under the IBDF's protection. Yet initial appearances were deceiving; little remained of the policy coherence that had made the program so effective in its earlier years.

The management plans developed in the late 1970s and early 1980s were to be fully implemented within five years, but tight budgets and low priorities made postponement of capital expenditures the norm. This made progress dependent on external pressure and support, over which the DN had no control. In some cases, the impetus for progress came from a state government hoping to promote tourism. The government of the northeastern state of Piauí, for example, hoping to make Sete Cidades National Park a tourist attraction, pressed the IBDF to make it fully operational, and even paid some of the costs of its development. Moreover, Sete Cidades was small, with modest infrastructure demands, and could be fully serviced with a small staff.[25] In other cases, impetus came from a delegado's personal interest. The delegado to Minas Gerais, for example, was genuinely concerned about the Caparaó and Serra da Canastra areas and gave their management plans a higher priority in his budget requests than warranted by any detached political calculus. The same anomaly prevailed in Goiás: although it was still a frontier state characterized by a frontier mentality, a succession of IBDF delegados had shown a special interest in parks and year after year had pressed the IBDF to push ahead with its plans for Araguaia National Park in the northern part of the state.[26]

The Poço das Antas Biological Reserve illustrated the degree to which fortuitous circumstances had to converge for consistent progress to be possible. The reserve was a refuge for the golden lion tamarin, a small, spectacular, and very endangered primate that had taken on a great symbolic value to Brazilian and international conservationists, and its protection had become a public issue in Brazil. Moreover, the FBCN and foreign conservation groups, most notably the National Zoo in Washington, D.C. offered to support the implementation of the relatively straightforward and inexpensive management plan.[27] As a consequence, Poço das Antas was the one area whose management plan was almost fully implemented by the mid-1980s.

Preparing the parks for visitors required a combination of planning, implementation, and ongoing management largely beyond the capacities of the IBDF's conservation program in the 1980s, as Brasília National Park illustrated. An imposing visitor center had been built in the late 1970s, but funds to furnish or staff it could not be found in the 1980s. The building had deteriorated to such a degree that it needed extensive repairs by 1984. Somehow, money for the repairs was found, probably because of the symbolic import of the national park in the nation's capital, but even after the work was completed, the IBDF was unable to furnish it, so it remained empty, and by 1986 deterioration was well underway again. Popular use of the park was limited to a small day-use area of natural springs and lakes, while most of the park, including the visitor center, remained off limits, as it had for nearly a decade.[28]

Field staffs had also suffered from budget retrenchments, making the management of visitor programs difficult. In most cases, actual staffing was much less than what the DN saw as minimal for the protected areas in their present state (table 6.1).[29] The more popular southern parks—Iguaçu, Tijuca, and Serra dos Orgãos—had the largest staffs, although only Iguaçu was staffed at half the DN's estimated necessary minimum. The gap was growing in the 1980s; staffs were smaller in 1985 than they had been in 1982 in most areas for which comparable figures were available, and by 1986 hiring freezes had caused further reductions in some.

Jorge Pádua's cultivation of a popular constituency for the parks through facilities development had begun to show returns in the late 1970s, when visitor use of most parks increased substantially (table 6.2), but the inability to expand or even staff visitor facilities in the 1980s appeared to have affected park use: the quality of information on park attendance deteriorated in the 1980s, as did most conservation information from the field, but it did indicate that the trend of increasing popular use of the parks in the 1970s stalled in the 1980s. Only urban Tijuca and Brasília national parks saw increases in visitors. No parks become newly popular, and most declined in visits.

* * *

The capacity of the IBDF's conservation program to hold to a fixed course of system expansion, or even to respond to evolving conservation doctrine, was reduced by conservation's loss of political weight. Because the conservation program was no longer highly valued by

TABLE 6.1
Protection Staff in IBDF Protected Areas, 1979–1985

Unit	IBDF Estimate of Adequate Protection Staff	Actual Size of Protection Staff			Actual 1985 Staff as a percentage of Adequacy Estimate
		1979	1982	1985	
Aparados de Serra	—	2	—	—	
Araguaia	20	10	7	11	55
Brasília	—	20	19	19	
Caparáo	—	13	—	—	
Chapada dos Veadeiros	—	6	—	—	
Emas	20	5	5	4	20
Iguaçu	70	58	61	56	80
Itatiaia	—	21	—	—	
Lençõis Maranhenses	—	—	—	—	
Monte Pascoal	8	10	4	7	88
Serra da Bocaina	25	10	2	2	8
Serra da Canastra	—	10	—	—	
Serra dos Orgãos	55	15	12	9	16
Sete Cidades	15	9	8	5	33
Tijuca	100	67	61	48	48
Ubajara	15	5	7	5	33
Pantanal	—	—	6	9	
Córrego do Veado	8	—	3	4	50
Nova Lombardia	10	—	6	5	50
Sooretama	30	—	18	11	37
Una	9	—	—	6	67
Amazonia	20	9	9	5	25
Cabo Orange	—	—	—	—	
Jaú	5	—	—	2	40
Poço das Antas	—	—	—	1	
Pacaás Novas	12	—	—	6	50
Lago Piratuba	—	—	—	1	
Rio Trombetas	—	—	6*	5	
Jaru	—	—	—	2	
Guaporé	3	—	—	1	33

* 1981
— Indicates unit not established at the time or data not available
Source: IBDF/DN internal records, 1979–1986.

top IBDF administrators, they were less inclined to listen to the DN and more inclined to listen to other voices on how the program should be run.

One of the cornerstones of Wetterberg's success in Brazil, and one of his contributions to international conservation, was the answers he offered to long-standing questions of proper reserve size, number, and selection criteria, but while his answers derived substance from

TABLE 6.2

Visits to National Parks and Biological Reserves, Selected Years 1937–1984

	1937	1958	1975	1979	1982[1]	1984
Itatiaia	5,000	51,000	63,143	54,576	No Data	
Iguaçu		14,600	386,496	712,317		420,778[2]
Serra dos Orgãos			73,669	96,975	93,658	
Ubajara			14,716	39,059		28,618
Araguaia			30	47		57
Emas			0	43		30
Caparáo			1,808	5,514	5,674	
Sete Quedas			133,040	163,710	Decommissioned	
Sete Cidades			3,813	16,565	18,773	
Tijuca			1,460,379	1,015,389[2]		1,141,501
Brasília			196,861	312,130	651,232[3]	
Serra de Bocaina			No Data	2,422	2,321	
Serra da Canastra			No Data	3,296	1,304	
Amazonia			No Data	No Data	15	

[1] No visitors reported to other units in system 1982–1984
[2] More restrictive counting introduced
[3] More liberal counting introduced
Source: Bernades Quintão and Lima Beserta, "Análise da Situação," and IBDF annual reports 1982–1984.

their scientific referents, the science of the time was tentative.[30] Estimates of how large a species population was necessary for long-term viability increased in the 1980s; Wilcox, for example, wrote in the early 1980s that two hundred and fifty was the approximate size threshold for maintaining genetic variability in a population of a wildlife species whose sex ratio was even, whose age cohorts were in phase, and whose individuals of reproductive age were all reproducing.[31] Since few populations in the wild met even one of these conditions, the true minimum viable size was even larger. This and similar work implied that top rainforest predators and other rainforest species with large ranges needed areas many times larger than those the IBDF had set aside.

The longer perspective that conservationists adopted with the entry of distant posterity into the pale of concern also caused estimates of "how much is enough" to rise. The length of concern Wetterberg had assumed in the mid-1970s when he applied the dictates of Island Biogeography Theory to reserve size soon appeared improvidently short. Shaffer, writing in 1981, lengthened Wetterberg's span of concern by an order of magnitude. For him, conservation should aim at allowing the smallest isolated population of a species a 99 percent

chance of remaining extant for 1,000 years.[32] Wilcox also suggested
that conservationists need be concerned about the species attrition
likely to take place over the next thousand years. Lovejoy argued
that conservationists had to keep in mind that "the ultimate goal is
to protect ecosystems at as close as possible to their original and
characteristic diversity, both today and a millennium hence." Myers,
assessing past conservation achievements in the light of this thinking,
wrote that "the Ark...is far too small."[33] While the new conservation dicta were not qualitatively different from those on which
Wetterberg's proposal was built, they did demand a larger cut for
conservation than even Jorge Pádua had thought necessary.[34]

The Amazon part of the ark also seemed to have been designed
with inadequate blueprints. The science on which the IBDF's plan
had been based was a mix of general theory and specific data, but
there seldom had been a thorough knowledge of any area when protection decisions were made. Now the scientific map of Amazonia
was gradually being filled in, which offered the possibilities of a new
precision in selecting protected natural areas. Moreover, as research
produced a better knowledge of the distribution of Amazon species,
the specific shortcomings of the IBDF's system became apparent. For
example, Rylands and Mittermeier determined that the IBDF's system inadequately protected Amazonia's primates.[35]

With the IBDF conservationists now reactive players, as they had
been under Magnanini a decade before, they were no longer in a
position to advance their own proposals or shape policy to conservation dicta through their own initiatives. The DN evaluated outside
proposals, but its evaluations counted for little when placed against
the exigencies of federal-state politics, or even against the IBDF's
own administrative convenience. This allowed system expansion,
like park development, to become the sum of disparate impulses
strong enough to force action from an agency now largely indifferent
to biological conservation. The situation discriminated against the
continuity that the DN held so dear: none of the areas added after
1982 had figured in the IBDF's system plan. It militated against large
protected areas, scientifically informed selection, and even against
Amazonia itself (table 6.3).

In most cases, large areas would mean more political and economic problems than smaller ones. They always had, but now there
were no powerful players who, like Jorge Pádua, were willing to
accept such problems for the sake of conservation. The states were

TABLE 6.3
IBDF Protected Areas Established Beyond Amazonia, 1976–1986

	State or Territory	Year Established	Area in Hectares[1]
Atol das Rocas	Rio Grande do Norte	1979	36,200
Serra da Capivara	Piauí	1979	100,000
Una	Bahia	1980	11,400
Lençõis Maranhenses	Maranhão	1981	155,000
Patanal Matogrossense	Mato Grosso	1981	135,000
Córrego do Veado	Espírito Santo	1982	2,400
Nova Lombardia	Espírito Santo	1982	4,400
Abrolhos[2]	Bahia	1983	91,300
Saltinho	Pernambuco	1983	500
Serra do Cipó	Minas Gerais	1984	33,800
Comboios	Espírito Santo	1984	800
Chapada Diamantina	Bahia	1985	153,000

[1] To the nearest 100 hectares
[2] Maritime national park; area given is ocean surface
Source: "Parques Nacionais e Reservas Biológicas Nacionais," addendum sheet to IBDF, *Código Florestal.*

not willing to set aside vast areas that might be useful for development. The IBDF was not willing to accept expensive management responsibilities.

Science was seldom a serious consideration because it did not figure into the calculations of states when they asked the IBDF to bring an area under its protection, or into the IBDF's decision to accept it. The establishment of the Serra do Cipó unit was typically unscientific. It had been a state park in Minas Gerais, but it contained large private inholdings whose purchase would be expensive, so the state proposed making it a national park, thereby transferring the expense of the land purchases, as well as park management, to the federal government. The DN official who evaluated Serra do Cipó for its biological attributes wrote that "the technical criteria were against it, it was not of national park quality," but higher IBDF administrators ignored the DN's evaluation and made it a national park, a decision the DN interpreted as a "strictly political" concession to one of the most powerful states in Brazil.

To the extent that science did enter the process, it was usually in an incidental, reactive way, as the Comboios and Saltinho biological reserves illustrated. Comboios was a turtle nesting site on the coast of Espírito Santo. The small, southeastern state owned the area but wanted to shift the expense of managing it to the federal government, so it offered it to the IBDF. The agency had been monitoring the turtle nesting site, so it reluctantly assumed responsibility for the area rather than risk its loss. The even smaller Saltinho Biological Reserve in the northeastern state of Pernambuco had been an IBDF forest experiment station, but it was no longer needed as such. Rather than wholly abandon the area, the IBDF reclassified it as a biological reserve, a step it took with little input from the DN.[36]

Chapada Diamantina National Park illustrated how natural area selection now worked and the best that could be expected from it. A North American botanist noticed the presence of several rare orchids in the Chapada Diamantina region of Bahia's arid interior, and, concerned about the threat commercial orchid collectors posed, he suggested making the area a national park.[37] The DN determined that Chapada Diamantina had merit. It had aesthetic appeal in addition to its rare species: its high ridges received enough rainfall to make them islands of lush vegetation looming dramatically above the semi-desert. Yet the DN did not judge the area more worthy of action than any of a score of similar proposals from the states. A new road from Brasília to Salvador, the capital of Bahia, passed through the Chapada Diamantina region, however, making it accessible to tourists, so the state seized on the idea of the national park as a way to stimulate the economy in this depressed and neglected region. The Bahian government lobbied the federal government for the park, and the state's newspapers promoted the idea. The chance to please the powerful northeastern state greatly enhanced the proposal in the IBDF's eyes, and when Bahia offered to defray part of the park's costs, the IBDF's last objections vanished.[38]

None of the new areas added in the mid-1980s were in Amazonia: the outward diffusion of power over natural area selection worked against Amazonia as surely as it did against scientific criteria or large size. State governments supported natural area initiatives for three reasons: tourism, recreation for their citizens, and a genuine concern for nature. The states of the Northeast were most interested in using parks as tourist magnets; the more urbanized states of the South were interested in recreation for their citizens and in protecting nature for its own sake.[39] None of these motives was strong in Amazonia in the 1980s, making the region a political vacuum from a conservation perspective and allowing the IBDF's attention to be pulled away from it by the politically attractive opportunities for parks and reserves arising elsewhere.

Some in the IBDF held that new areas should not be established in Amazonia, even if the opportunities arose somehow. Given the emphasis the states and the IBDF were putting on revenue-generating activities, the additional resources needed to protect new areas were not likely to found: they would have to be taken from existing parks and reserves. While protected areas throughout Brazil were inadequately staffed, those of Amazonia were especially so: no area in the region had a staff of more than ten, and some had no personnel at all. Originally, the low staffing reflected Jorge Pádua's view that the protected areas in the South, where threats were usually greater and more immediate, had more pressing staff needs, but once the hard times of the 1980s arrived, the product of conscious policy became fixed by lack of power. IBDF conservation officials argued that attempting to spread such modest field resources even thinner would endanger conservation's past gains in the region.[40] The delegado in Pará concurred: "I would like to see more parks, but under current conditions, they would cause more problems than they would be worth."

There was one important exception to this forced abandonment of Amazonia, but more than anything it illustrated how the IBDF conservation program's capacity for coherent, scientifically informed action had dissolved. The Inter-American Development Bank was underwriting the improvement of the federal highway between Rondônia and the state of Acre further west, but aware of the criticism directed at the World Bank for its participation in the environmentally destructive Polonoroeste project, it insisted that steps be taken to protect Indians and nature before the road opened Acre and adjacent sections of Amazonas state to a flood of settlers. The DN, assigned to identify the natural areas to be protected, turned to Stage Two of the system plan, but the report contained only one proposal for the region, Serra do Divisor. Moreover, the RADAM recommendations in the region were too ill defined to be useful.[41] The DN therefore faced a task similar to Wetterberg's and Jorge Pádua's original one: developing a set of proposed protected areas for an entire region practically ex nihilo.

The restraints were now far greater, however. The DN had to take FUNAI's wishes more seriously than Jorge Pádua had to: if it picked any area FUNAI thought contained Indians, it would probably lose to FUNAI in inter-agency negotiations.[42] Although under no explicit orders, the DN also had to be more careful to avoid good agricultural land; it knew proposals containing large fertile areas would not be viewed favorably at higher levels. The DN knew it should avoid areas where there was much squatting or private land: even with the international banks involved, it sensed that large financial commitments to conservation were unlikely to be kept.

Because the DN was now far from the centers of power and its administrators were not politically attuned, its sense of the possible was vague. It knew what was outrageous: a request for half the area, for example. It also knew what was safe: it could probably ask for three "substantial" areas if they contained few squatters and no Indians. It did not have a feel for the large middle ground between the clearly reasonable and the out-of-bounds, however,[43] which rendered it incapable of acting as Jorge Pádua had, probing the limits of the possible and then pushing conservation's case to those limits.

The Acre project also showed how political weakness and depleted resources had rendered the DN incapable of making scientifically satisfying rather than merely expedient decisions. Because upper levels of government still demanded the appearance of rationality from the federal bureaucracy, scientific justification had to accompany any proposals the IBDF advanced. But, anxious to get on with the road construction, higher officials insisted that the IBDF make its selections quickly. This double message put the DN in a bind. Only Serra do Divisor, explored under Jorge Pádua, was relatively well known. Elsewhere, inhabitants, travelers, or a scientist had noted the presence of a rare species or had listed the local flora and fauna. These few spots were surrounded by large areas about which little more was known than could be deduced from remote sensing—i.e., the general character of the vegetation and perhaps whether it had been disturbed.

The DN did what it could. It gathered information from likely sources: INPA, the Goeldi Museum in Belém, the Rio Botanical Garden, and various universities, and it planned to supplement this with information gathered from the field. It had neither the time nor the resources for a thorough expedition, however; one small team—two or three people—would spend several weeks in the vast region, and only a fraction of that actually in the field. It was only enough time to deepen knowledge of those areas about which something was already known, not to fill the interstices.

Once back in Brasília, the team would have only a few weeks to sift through its information and make its recommendations. It was a foregone conclusion that Serra do Divisor would be among the recommended areas; it was already relatively well known, and its status as a left-over proposal from an earlier era gave it special standing. The DN wished to make its other selections on a broad mix of scientific criteria, including level of endemism, species diversity, the presence of endangered species, and general uniqueness, but it would not have sufficient information; all the DN was likely to know with any confidence about the areas it had examined was their general representativeness of the wider region, and perhaps whether they contained a rare species or two. Selections would therefore have to be made on these criteria.

DN officials were unhappy with the process. They saw the restraints under which they were forced to operate as reflecting the way conservation was an afterthought, something squeezed into wider plans for the region, rather than an integral, value-giving part of the development process. Agency officials felt that the entire selection exercise was strictly pro forma, and they had no faith in their ability to select the best areas under the circumstances: the young DN official upon whom much of the responsibility for the selection would fall said, "In a hundred years, no one will know if the right areas were preserved or...how much was lost when we made our choices."[44]

***

Lack of favor combined with a lack of synchrony with the dominant political forces in Amazonia to prevent the IBDF's conservation program from responding to far-reaching changes in conservation doctrine. Even as the importance of natural areas in biological conservation continued to be revised upward, it was becoming apparent that by themselves, protected areas could not prevent biotic impoverishment, even if they were perfectly planned and managed.[45] Miller and Wetterberg understood the importance of conservation measures for the entire landscape of Amazonia, but Wetterberg, sensitive to the lay of opportunity, had been willing to concentrate on protected natural areas and settled for making general pleas for the respect of nature outside them.

The need to extend conservation measures to the entire landscape of Amazonia appeared so pressing by the 1980s that it could no longer be ignored. First, given the extreme patchiness of Amazon species, any system of protected natural areas, even one several times larger than that Jorge Pádua or Wetterberg had in mind, would still leave much Amazon nature unprotected. In fact, conservation measures would have to be applied almost everywhere if the loss of thousands of species was to be prevented. As the region's population increased and more forest was cut, this became an immediate concern.

Second, by the mid-1980s it appeared likely that the greenhouse effect would rearrange global climates. When great climate changes had taken place in the past, corresponding changes in the earth's biogeography occurred as plants and animals altered their ranges. Species had faced only natural barriers, such as oceans and mountain ranges, to range adjustments in the past, but future shifts would take place on a landscape dominated by human activity. If Amazonia was not managed to permit range adjustment, species confined to protected areas would be trapped as the climate changed.[46]

Finally, scientists found convincing evidence that much of the rainfall in Amazonia was secondary precipitation. Air from the Atlantic moved westward over the Amazon basin, where its moisture was released as rain. Much of this water was reabsorbed into the atmosphere, where it condensed and fell again. It appeared that more than fifty percent of the rainfall resulted from reabsorption in some areas of Amazonia.[47]

If the forest were cut, more water would be lost to the system through runoff, reducing evapo-transpiration and secondary precipitation. The implications were ominous: in those large parts of Amazonia where even a slight dip below normal precipitation caused drought stress, large reductions in precipitation would lead to extensive species loss, and perhaps even wholesale forest replacement with more xeric formations. Even an ideal system of protected areas would be threatened by a large drop in precipitation. Sioli wrote, "It is doubtful whether the remaining forest islands... [would] be able to stand such a climatic alteration."[48]

While conservation needed a larger cut, it did not need an exclusive one: much of the landscape could be altered for human use and still serve conservation ends. Areas in which hunting was allowed would maintain most of their diversity, and so would areas open to wood gathering and selective cutting. Some commercial timber extraction would be compatible with the preservation of genetic diversity, as would collecting forest products such as rubber, brazil-nuts, and medicinal plants. Stands of commercially valuable timber species or plantations of cacao, palm oil, rubber, or cashew trees, while of little use in preserving species diversity, would maintain some of the original forest's evapo-transpiration potential. Traditional swidden agriculture could be practiced in much of the upland forest, since at low population densities only a small percentage of the rainforest was in use at any time, and small disturbed areas easily grew back. Cash-crop monocultures could even be practiced on the few patches of fertile terra firma soil.[49] The semi-inundated lands along the rivers were lower in species diversity and endemism than the terra firma forests, so some of them could be given over to intensive use with little risk of species loss.[50]

Such a landscape of mixed uses would, in theory, benefit a number of groups. Past development had meant extermination or deculturation of the tribal Indians but a landscape managed with conservation goals in mind would retain sufficient biological richness for them to practice their traditional lifeways,[51] and their reserves would be useful parts of the landscape rather than nonproductive set-asides. Conventional rural development also displaced caboclos while failing to provide a secure niche for small farmers. On a landscape of small clearings and limited monoculture, these groups would be less subject to displacement, more secure in the land they occupied.

This range of benefits produced a theoretical commonality of agency interest. Conventional rural development aimed at providing a better life for small farmers, INCRA's clients, had an almost unblemished record of failure in the rainforest. As early as 1973, Nelson wrote that "few spheres of economic development have a history of...failure to match that of government-sponsored colonization in humid tropical zones," and subsequent experience, including the Transamazon colonization schemes, had done little to alter this assessment.[52] FUNAI had an interest in such a landscape: the agency acknowledged that the most important thing it could do for its Indian charges was protect their land which it conceded was impossible under the conditions created by conventional development.[53]

Promoting such a mixed landscape through cooperation with a wide variety of social groups had become a part of international conservation doctrine by the 1980s.[54] The integrated approach to conservation and human settlement was now seen as more moral, practical, and politically suitable in the third world. It also brought conservation doctrine in line with the international human rights movement, which had made native peoples a prime object of its concern, and conservation derived an added measure of respectability from the alignment.[55]

In practice, however, the common weakness of conservationists,

Indians, and the poor on an Amazon landscape of alien values and powerful interests inimical to their welfare set these groups against each other. Because Amazon development made little provision for the poor or the landless, they were forced to fit in where they could. Squatters probed Indian lands.[56] There they occasionally faced hostile Indians, but Indians were less feared than gangs of pistoleiros in the employ of a local landlord. Protected natural areas were also attractive targets for squatters. The areas were weakly defended, and the law of posse applied to parks and reserves as it did to the rest of the public domain. There squatters need not worry about Indians or private owners resorting to extra-legal means to remove them. Indians were also relatively secure in the protected natural areas, where their legal rights were not nullified by the fire-power of private interests or by development agencies powerful enough to ignore the law.

The agencies that represented the small farmer, the Indian, and conservation were set against each other by the logic of their circumstances. Each was on the margins of bureaucratic power in Amazonia,[57] and each could discharge its responsibilities to its clients only in areas where private capital and the more powerful public agencies had few intentions. Each agency therefore perceived the other's turf as a soft spot on a difficult landscape, as a place where it could be true to its obligations. INCRA sold out peasants when they were in conflict with cattle ranchers or speculators, but it did defend squatters at the expense of Indians. If enough landless peasants became established in an indigenous area, INCRA would attempt to secure titles for them and move the Indians elsewhere. It also defended the rights of squatters in protected natural areas, as it did in the Cuniã Ecological Station in Rondônia (see Chapter 8).

FUNAI's inability to defend Indian lands was a national scandal in the 1980s. It steadily lost administrative autonomy. The legal system tilted against FUNAI's charges: a law was passed permitting the compensation of non-Indians removed from Indian lands, which encouraged invasion by those who hoped for compensatory payments. FUNAI had to stand by helplessly while the Minister of the Interior sanctioned gold mining in indigenous areas. When invasion pressures from the unprincipled were added to those of the merely desperate, defending the Indian lands became a hopelessly outsized task for FUNAI; an estimated 90 percent of Brazil's indigenous areas had been invaded by the mid-1980s.[58]

Nevertheless, the agency zealously protected Indian rights in protected natural areas; it could do so without risking reprisals or the subversion of its agents. It showed its zeal at Araguaia National Park. When Indians in the park established links with pelt traders and began hunting out the commercially valuable fauna, the IBDF asked FUNAI to cooperate with it in suppressing the hunting. FUNAI declined, arguing that while the activity was distasteful, the Indians were on their customary lands, so they were within their constitutional rights to hunt, even commercially, within the park.[59]

For its part, the IBDF had viewed areas occupied by Indians and caboclos as weak spots on the political landscape. It was willing to establish parks and reserves even when it meant forcing the removal of hundreds of caboclos. When it had the political strength to do so, it had ignored the presence of Indians in areas it wanted to protect. At Pico da Neblina, it had even been willing to play along with the National Security Council's fears of the Yanomami for conservation's advantage. By doing so, the IBDF had created additional areas of conflict and tensions between itself and its would-be allies.

This intrinsic competitiveness, exacerbated by past opportunism, made the alliances necessary for an integrated program impossible. DN administrators felt that nature, poor settlers, and tribal peoples were perhaps compatible with protected nature elsewhere, where harmony and reason prevailed, but life in Amazonia on the margins of power was raw, uncertain, and selfish, and no amount of rhetoric or wishful thinking could change that. Opposed groups struggled among themselves for dominance, with higher-level public decisions merely ratifying the results of those struggles.[60] Moreover, IBDF conservationists feared that, even if such alliances were attempted, their now-reduced power would leave them unable to prevent conservation goals from being subverted in the normal give-and-take among allies. Thus, Wetterberg and Jorge Pádua's tactical decision to emphasize protected natural areas at the expense of broader conservation measures was turned into rigid necessity in the 1980s by conservation's lack of allies or political power.

If anything, the IBDF's conservation policies became even more involuted over time. DN administrators were aware of the recent research on secondary precipitation in Amazonia, and they understood its implication: the future of their parks and reserves was linked to the fate of the forest in general.[61] However, they preferred to define their responsibilities in accord with their resources rather than conservation needs; they concentrated on tasks they thought they could handle, like getting the right size uniforms to the guards in the field. The DN shifted responsibility for more general matters upward, arguing that concern for the forests of Amazonia as a whole belonged at the highest levels of the IBDF administration.

Top IBDF administrators also knew about recent research on secondary precipitation in Amazonia and they understood its implications for the forest. They recognized that they had overall administrative responsibility for Brazil's forests; the agency's organic legislation of 1967 made that clear. There was a strong consensus among them that extant laws pertaining to forest clearing should be enforced and policies that encouraged clearing—subsidies for establishing cattle ranches in forest areas, for example—should be ended.

Nevertheless, they too were reluctant to take firm steps on forest clearing. They knew from experience that vigorous enforcement of general conservation measures was likely to generate powerful opposition. Rather than follow the agency's mandate into areas where few friends and many potential enemies waited, they diffused responsibility outward and passed it upward. The IBDF let primary responsibility for enforcing forest clearing laws devolve to its delegados in the states and territories. The delegados, sensitive to the local political climate, taking the devolution as a sign that top IBDF administrators did not want to become involved in the issue, and lacking administrative resources, seldom enforced the rules.[62]

IBDF leadership also held that responding to the new findings about Amazon precipitation and other scientific discoveries with broad conservation implications was beyond the agency's purview; and that fashioning a response should be, in the words of one administrator, "a matter for national debate."[63] Given the powerful mix of economic and political interests propelling forest clearing in Amazonia, and the absence of any strong voice for environmentally sensitive policies, a real national debate was impossible, but the position did strike a safe pose of administrative humility and allowed the IBDF to avoid setting a difficult and politically unwise course.

This reluctance to accept responsibility for the biological resources of the entire landscape was complemented by an exclusionary stance on protected area management. The competitiveness of so many forces in Amazonia meant that if other interests were given even a toehold of legitimacy in the natural areas, conservation would no longer be secure even in its bastions. Under the rhetoric of goal compatibility, desperate peasants and corrupted Indians would destroy the nature that conservationists had worked so hard to protect. As it was, the presence of Indians and caboclos in the protected areas was viewed as a time bomb that would become more difficult to defuse with passing time.[64] DN officials were appalled by suggestions that parks and reserves be opened up to human habitation or exploitation.

Outside observers were split on the appropriateness of this response. Brown condemned it and attributed it to the backwardness of Brazilian conservation administrators: they simply had not caught up to international thinking.[65] Much of the Brazilian conservation community saw the logic of it, however, and defended it against the tide of international doctrine. Some Brazilian conservationists became outspoken opponents of the emphasis the IUCN's World Conservation Strategy had placed on integrating conservation, native lifeways, and material production for fear of undoing Brazil's past conservation gains. In response to suggestions that limited hunting be allowed in some of Brazil's protected natural areas, FBCN's director, Ibsen de Gusmão Camara, replied, "Not one alligator!"[66]

Both positions seemed right and wrong, which perhaps offers a key insight into the limits of the IBDF's conservation policies after political favor and power were withdrawn from them. Lacking allies or outside support, the IBDF conservationists were probably correct in not taking an aggressive, visible role on the general issue of rainforest clearing and in not venturing beyond the narrow pale of natural area protection into a world where rivals and powerful interests lurked and where the danger of appearing ineffectual and foolish was a serious matter. But to the extent that it did not take the full, known scope of the problem of Amazon conservation into account, it was a desperate and ultimately self-defeating kind of correctness, one that left the IBDF unable to either expand conservation's domain or protect past successes.[67]

CHAPTER 7

Defending the Natural Areas in the Eighties

The IBDF's parks and reserves in Amazonia were the core of its conservation turf. Most of its conservation energy had been spent on their establishment; other conservation goals had been sacrificed or put on hold for their benefit. Now the political weakness of conservation affected the natural areas profoundly. They had become relics of another, more optimistic era; they had been founded when conservation's importance in Brazil seemed to be increasing. They had been delineated before the political limits of Brazilian conservation had revealed themselves to be so narrow—indeed, before they had become so narrow. The relict system became increasingly outsized for conservation's political resources in the 1980s.

The most obvious consequence was a lack of material resources. The IBDF was not able—or willing—to give the natural areas ample budgets. Protected areas under the wing of special development projects faced the same problem: conservation was a poor competitor when matched against revenue-generating activities. Infrastructure and staffing were therefore always far less than envisioned when the areas had been established or their management plans drawn up.

Other problems compounded that of insufficient material resources. Conservation's marginal status within the IBDF placed field managers under superiors who lacked experience in conservation management and who were not led by circumstance to pay attention to conservation problems. This left field personnel without consistent guidelines, or even a clear idea of whom they should turn to for guidance. Without guidance, and often without training, they had to fall back on their own untutored instincts in protecting their parks and reserves.

The inability of conservationists to influence the direction of regional change, or even to fit their goals into that change, made protected areas enclaves on hostile landscapes. They were little valued by those who directed regional development and seldom understood by those caught up in it. The alien quality of the protected areas made their staffs seem like foreign officials performing absurd tasks to the local inhabitants. This forced field staffs to concentrate on defending their areas from regional development, rather than on making positive contributions to it. It also forced nature protection to begin at reserve boundaries and molded it into literal forms: patrolling boundaries, expelling invaders, and interdicting contraband. Even these tasks were made more difficult by the inability of conservationists to forge alliances with others at the margins of power in Amazonia.

Management weakness decoupled the fate of the system. In spite of the prominence publicly accorded overarching theory in its natural area selection, the IBDF's actual criteria were nearly as complex as the biological and political geography of Amazonia itself: each protected area was the result of a separate equation factoring in biological worth, inherent manageability, competing interests, and opportunities for outside funding. Therefore, while each protected area faced many of the forces transforming the region, no two faced the same mix. The result was a very diverse set of management tasks for IBDF field staffs. Strong management would have tended toward equal results, overcoming whatever disparate problems arose and holding all the parks and reserves to the same goals of nature protection. Because the resources to meet all problems were not available, the fate of natural areas was exposed to these varied local circumstances. Each protected area was thus the stage for its own drama. Each added to the picture of the system's fate.

***

Amazonia National Park, thanks largely to two special characteristics of its history, provides perhaps the clearest contrast between the early hopes of IBDF conservationists and subsequent reality. The first was the date of its founding: it was the only IBDF-protected area in Amazonia antedating Wetterberg's and Jorge Pádua's system plan; consequently it was the only one not informed by their values and strategic considerations. The park was delineated by PIN planners in the early 1970s as part of wider PIN plans for the lower Tapajós

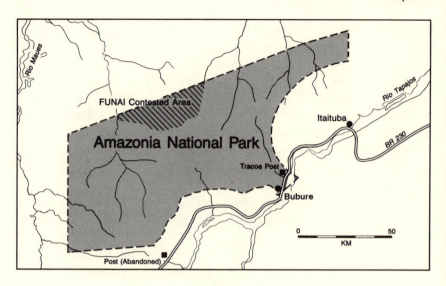

FIGURE 7.1
Amazonia National Park: Boundaries as Originally Established

River region. Because they had little idea of what made a good protected area and were under little pressure to learn, their chief considerations seemed to be getting the job done quickly and insuring that the park did not interfere with the economic goals of the Tapajós planning initiative.[1] This showed in the boundaries they drew. Most were straight lines, easy to draw but not ecologically sensible (figure 7.1). Others were placed with no thought for visitor appeal or efficient park management. The southeastern boundary of the park, for example, was placed well north of the Transamazon Highway—this was convenient for road managers, perhaps, but it cut the park off from the Tapajós River and made most of the park inaccessible to managers or visitors. The park did not come under the IBDF's authority until 1974, after the key decisions had been made.

The second special characteristic was the nature of the park's management plan: it was the only plan of the initial four not prompted by a looming threat or the need to accommodate an extant constituency. This detachment allowed planners to make the plan into a visionary document, perhaps the clearest statement of what IBDF conservationists and the international team that assisted them saw as the role of national parks in the Amazonia of the future. The plan envisioned the park as part of a developed, affluent region in a developed, affluent

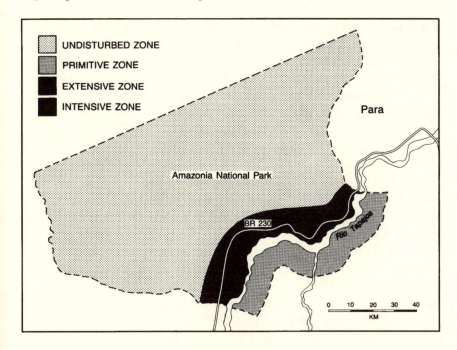

FIGURE 7.2

Amazonia National Park: Proposed Zoning and Boundary Changes. Adapted
from IBDF, *Parque Nacional da Amazonia: Plano de Manejo*

Brazil. It would accommodate a large clientele similar to that of the
great national parks of the North American West, one comprised of
people from the immediate region, the nation, and foreign countries.

Preparing for such a future demanded that the park's flawed legacy
be corrected: first, the plan proposed redrawing the eastern and western boundaries along two streams draining into the Tapajós; second,
it proposed expanding the park southward to include the Transamazon Highway, a section of the Tapajós River, and a strip of land
on the opposite bank (figure 7.2).

The park would be developed as the region around it developed.
The plan divided the park into four management zones. The park's
vast interior would be an unaltered zone; no tampering with nature
would be permitted. South of the Tapajós River would be what the
plan called a primitive zone. Scientific work and some recreation
would be permitted, but no permanent structures. The inhabitants of
Pimental, a town on the south bank, would be relocated out of the

park, and the site would return to its natural state. Facilities for education, research, and recreation would be constructed in a zone that ran along the Transamazon Highway, but these facilities would not substantially alter the natural environment. Finally, there would be a zone of intensive use where the Transamazon Highway entered the park from the east. Park headquarters, administrative offices, staff lodging, a visitor center, and a museum would be located here. The IBDF hoped to refit a large building erected in connection with the construction of the Transamazon Highway as the park headquarters.

The high level of management the plan called for would be supported directly through visitor fees and indirectly through money spent in the region by the large, affluent clientele the park would attract. This clientele would also give the park a popular political constituency and create strong local interest in its perpetuation.[2] The planning formula was similar to that devised for the first national parks of the North American West, and its success, due largely to national and regional development in the following years, was undeniable. Everything, however, turned on such development.

The Lower Tapajós region had grown rapidly in the 1970s and 1980s, as planners had foreseen, but it was chaotic growth that resulted from primitive, unrestrained expression of powerful economic forces, not the ordered growth foreseen by the regional planners or the park's management plan. The settlement schemes along the Transamazon Highway had failed and been abandoned, leaving a scattered, stranded population of semi-commercial farmers, their fields unkempt and filling with second growth.[3] Itaituba, fifty-five kilometers from the park, was an unruly boom town, not the modern capital of a modernizing region.[4] The city had become the rear base of a gold rush further south; its main industries were provisioning prospectors, buying gold, and, apparently, prostitution. Uncontrolled forest clearing for cattle was taking place around the city. Such growth had made the park an alien enclave on the regional landscape. It was of little use to those drawn to the region in hope of finding wealth, nor to those who had actually found wealth and power in the region's chaotic growth; they saw no reason for it, and they attributed its presence to unfathomable administrators far off in Brasília.[5]

Original plans called for the park to be fully operational by 1984, but the absence of local support for it combined with conservation's financial and political straits at the national level to prevent much progress. Repeated efforts in the early 1980s to effect the boundary changes had come to nothing, and by the mid-1980s the IBDF, knowing further efforts would be futile and might even expose the park to dismemberment, had stopped trying.[6] Past, non-park uses of the area continued. In the mid-1980s, a bar and hotel remained in the park on an inholding called Porto Buburé. On the banks of the Tapajós just above unnavigable rapids, the establishment was an embarkation point for miners heading to their claims; they traveled from Itaituba in trucks and congregated at the establishment, where they waited for boats to take them up river. The management plan had called for the quick removal of the inholding, but although the owner was willing to sell, funds for the purchase had never become available.

Some rudiments of the park's infrastructure had been built, but by the mid-1980s, decay was more obvious than progress. Guard cabins had been built where the Transamazon Highway entered the park, but one had been vandalized and abandoned. The park headquarters had never been established. The highway contractor who owned the building intended for the headquarters wanted a high price for it, and as negotiations dragged on, the era of fiscal austerity set in, dimming hopes of getting it for park use. The empty building gradually deteriorated beyond hope of restoration. There was no permanent management presence in the park; it was considered too primitive to be the seat of its own administration, so it was run from IBDF facilities in Itaituba.[7]

The park director was typical of many IBDF field managers in that he was inexperienced and untrained in conservation; he had been on the job only a year and had previously managed a commercial sawmill. He was also typical in his lack of a clear understanding of what his agency expected of him.[8] He had never met the IBDF state delegado. He had never talked to the director of the DN, and he knew little about what the unit did or what it could do for him. The indirect chain of command left him with little support at the regional level and cut him off from what should have been an important source of direction and advice: the DN.

It also left the director on his own to define his responsibilities toward the park. The era of Wetterberg and Jorge Pádua was prehistory to him, and the management plan was one of its more fabulous artifacts. He could not imagine where the money or will to implement it would come from, nor did he see much sense in trying to do so under the circumstances. He saw his mission as a narrower, more defensive one: protecting the patch of nature entrusted to his care.

He had a staff of nine, large for a protected area in Amazonia, but only a small fraction of what the management plan called for or

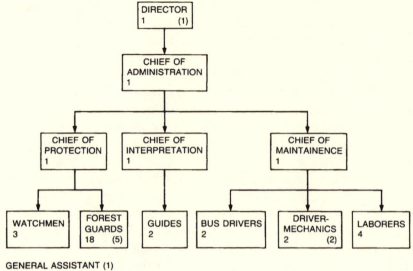

FIGURE 7.3

Amazonia National Park: Staffing Chart. Adapted from IBDF, *Parque Nacional da Amazónia: Plano de Manejo.* Numbers in parentheses indicate incumbents in mid-1986.

what the defense of a million hectares required (figure 7.3). His staff was also relatively untrained. The IBDF trained park guards, but because it did not consider the task important enough to develop a specialized training course, it offered them the same generic training given to all forest guards. It concentrated on supervising forestry operations and protecting plantations, but offered nothing on the problems guards most frequently faced in natural areas: squatting, illegal clearing, and poaching.[9]

Given his limited resources, the director focused on the manageable problems and tried not to worry about the others. He put most of the staff's energies into patrolling the 100-kilometer stretch of the Transamazon Highway, the most accessible part of the park.[10] Using the small staff cabin at the eastern end of the park as a base, guard teams patrolled the eastern part of highway several times a week in their small truck, and occasionally patrolled all the way to the western end of the park. During the wet season, when even the four-wheel-drive truck had a hard time in the deep mud of the highway, patrolling to the western end had to be suspended.[11]

The staff's capacity to keep areas distant from the road under surveillance was more limited. It did not have the boats or personnel to patrol along the Tapajós River. The director suspected that inhabitants of the south bank crossed to poach and cut wood in the park, but he could do nothing about it. The vast interior of the park north of the Transamazon Highway was even less accessible. Posseiros had lived along some of the little watercourses in the interior of the park when it was founded, and the director assumed they were still there. He also suspected that gold miners were working in the interior, but he was not certain. He could have patrolled the interior in at least a minimal fashion with a helicopter, but he did not have access to one. The army and INCRA operated helicopters in the vicinity, but arranging for a loan of their service was impossible at the local level: neither the INCRA office nor the army post in Itaituba had the necessary authority. The park director speculated that perhaps officials in Belém had the authority, but he knew his request would lack the political edge to cut through the red tape.

Nevertheless, the management regime was successfully meeting the immediate threats to the park. Patrolling along the highway, while difficult and irregular, had made an obvious difference; whereas no forest remained along the Transamazon Highway between Itaituba and the park, rainforest closed in on the road as soon as it entered the park. The level of depredation along the Tapajós was low and did not extend much past the shoreline. The inaccessibility of the park's interior made serious degradation unlikely. The director was confident that even with the modest resources at his disposal, he could continue to defend the park against the poachers, squatters, and miscellaneous trespassers who posed day-to-day threats to it. The balance of defense and threat was an uneasy one, however, as long as the park's regional alienation and lack of apparent purpose remained.

An active scientific program and a large number of visitors would have made the park's purposes and benefits obvious and, as originally envisioned, would have provided a counterweight to regional interests that opposed the park. The deteriorating status of ecology in Brazil and the difficulties of working in Amazonia precluded the former, however. Research in the system as a whole held its own during the early 1980s, but research in Amazonia ground to a halt (table 7.1). By the mid-1980s, the cabins near the Tapajós River built to accommodate scientific teams stood empty.

Visitors were few. Most of the people entering the park in the mid-

TABLE 7.1

Research in the National Parks and Biological Reserves, 1978–1985

				Number of Projects Authorized						Comments
	Pre-1978	1978	1979	1980	1981	1982	1983	1984	1985	
Amazonia		10	10							See table 4.1
Aparados da Serra		3		1		2			2	
Atol das Rocas								1	1	
Brasília	1		2	3	2		1		1	
Caparaó				1		2				
Chapada dos Veadeiros										
Corrego do Veado	1						1		1	
Emas			1	2						
Iguaçu				1	1				1	
Itatiaia*			1	2		3	1	2	3	Several long-running projects
Marinho dos Abrolhos								1	1	
Monte Pascoal					1			1		
Nova Lombardia										
Poço das Antas				3	1	1	1	2	2	Includes ongoing projects sponsored by the Rio Botanical Gardens
São Joaquin				1					1	
Serra da Bocaina		1		1						
Serra da Canastra		2	1	3					1	
Serra da Capiara	3							2		One project authorized to begin in 1986
Serra do Cipó	1								2	
Serra dos Orgãos			1	1	1	1		2	1	Research primarily in connection with ongoing Franco-Brazilian archaeological project
Sete Cidades	1									
Sooretama				1	1				2	
Tijuca*	3			1		1	1	5	2	Does not include regularized projects (see p. 71).
Rio Trombetas		3	6	2						
Una										One undated project

*Underreported due to unauthorized research.

1980s were miners heading for the embarkation point at Porto Buburé. The park received only 425 bona fide visitors in 1985, and most of these were local youths who drove out from Itaituba, spent a few hours there, and drove back to the city. Few non-local Brazilians and only 49 foreigners visited the park that year, and most of the latter were Americans who came in small commercial tour groups and stayed for only two or three days. The capacity of the staff—or the IBDF—to increase the number of visitors, especially foreign visitors, was limited by the primitive conditions in the park and the difficulty of arranging transportation within it. The few foreign tour operators who understood local conditions and could plan for them ultimately determined how many foreign visitors came to the park. There was little the park staff could do to counter their park's obscurity beyond cooperating with these operators and trying to accommodate the occasional tourist who made his way to the park on his own.[12]

The failure of the park to develop a scientific or tourist constituency exposed it to more serious threats than the occasional poacher. For one, it remained vulnerable to the uncertainty that surrounded land ownership in Amazonia. A private citizen had brought forth a claim dating from the nineteenth century for an enormous tract of land along the Tapajós River, 600,000 hectares of which were within the park. Neither the director nor DN administrators in Brasília knew what would happen if the claim was upheld in the courts. They feared that efforts to extinguish the claim through negotiations were likely to get little support within the region. In private hands, the land could be fitted into the regional economy; as protected nature it remained alien and unexploitable.

Lack of a scientific or tourist constituency also left the park exposed to administrative machinations. The forest within the park became an increasingly attractive timber source as other sources disappeared, and the National Highway Department (DNER) had already tried to gain access to it. Every rainy season many of the wooden bridges along the Transamazon Highway washed out, and every dry season the DNER rebuilt them. As wood became scarcer, the DNER asked the IBDF for permission to cut in the park. The IBDF refused, but in time the problem of finding wood outside the park would increase the pressure on the IBDF to give in, or on INCRA, which still held title to the land along the highway, to reassert its authority and permit the cutting. Once cutting began for road work, it would probably be allowed for other public purposes, and eventually for private ends as well.

Finally, lack of a constituency left the park vulnerable to political intrigues. President Figueiredo had removed a 6,000-hectare area on the park's eastern flank in early 1985, just as he was about to leave office; the area contained a limestone deposit to which a local cement manufacturer wanted access, and the president made it available to him, ostensibly for the benefit of the region. Neither the park director nor the DN knew anything was afoot, so they had no chance to protest, and they had no recourse afterward.[13] While land deals that smacked of cronyism were frequent under civilian and military governments alike, this one seemed to say the park was up for grabs.

* * *

The equation for the Rio Trombetas Biological Reserve was a tense one balancing high risks against the prospect of ample management resources. It was clear from the beginning that any reserve in the area would face serious management problems. The Trombetas River, the reserve's southern boundary, was the main artery of regional commerce and the axis of regional development. Many caboclos lived in the proposed reserve, and others just outside hunted and fished within it. Bauxite processing and shipping facilities were being built near the reserve, bringing increased population, economic activity, and pollution to the environs.[14] Yet the problems were counterbalanced in the minds of those who proposed the reserve by two key assumptions: that the IDBF would throw its political and financial weight behind the defense of the reserve, and that the politically powerful, well-financed government agencies involved in the development would become the reserve's patrons, subsidizing its management and mitigating the harmful effects of their operations on it.[15]

The Trombetas reserve was thus an expression of the willingness of Jorge Pádua and her associates to overreach their own confirmed resources and a reflection of the optimism that had shaped the entire IBDF conservation program. The reserve's success depended on history justifying that willingness, but it did not: unlike Amazonia National Park, there was no balance—not even a precarious one—between threat and defense at Trombetas.

The management plan, which the IBDF had given high priority and had completed in 1982, met substantial threats with the straightforward approach the IBDF would use elsewhere: concentrating staff and facilities at likely points of serious incursion. The reserve's head-quarters would be built on the east bank of the Trombetas River near the turtle nesting beaches, and from it the beaches could be kept under thorough surveillance. Ten guard posts, most outfitted to accommodate small guard and research teams, would be placed at strategic points in the reserve (figure 7.4). The plan would require a large and specialized staff: eighty guards and a total staff of 110 (figure 7.5).

As the IBDF had hoped, the Trombetas reserve received financial support from the Polamazonia program, enabling most of the caboc-los to be removed and most of the private land to be purchased.[16] The implementation of the management plan also began. Three guard posts were placed in the reserve, a small staff was hired, and a patrolling regime was instituted.[17] A temporary reserve headquarters was established in the nearest large town, Oriximiná, some 100 kilo-meters down river, and a large boat was bought to ply between the town and the reserve. Research facilities capable of accommodating twenty scientists were constructed near the site of the future head-quarters, and an active research program was begun.

Then implementation stalled. The Polamazonia program, under increasing pressure in the mid-1980s to produce exportable products while also facing trimmed budgets, reduced spending that did not contribute directly to bauxite operations, including spending on the reserve. The IBDF, facing its own budget cuts, could not cover the shortfall.

The Trombetas reserve had a staff of ten in 1986, large by Amazon standards, but essentially a skeleton staff. The large boat was out of commission. Oriximiná remained the seat of the reserve's management, but there was no money to maintain the headquarters, a small building on the town's outskirts, so it sat empty; the director ran the reserve from a makeshift office in his living room. Management resources at Trombetas were roughly similar to those at Amazonia National Park, but there was a difference in the scale of the problems they faced. The settlement schemes along the Transamazon Highway had been gradu-ally abandoned in the mid- and late 1970s, leaving Amazonia National Park out of the main path of development, and leaving modest threats and modest management resources in at least a fragile, temporary equi-librium. The development of the Trombetas pole had accelerated in the late 1970s, with new mines and new processing units, an influx of workers, and an expanding informal economy. The city of Porto

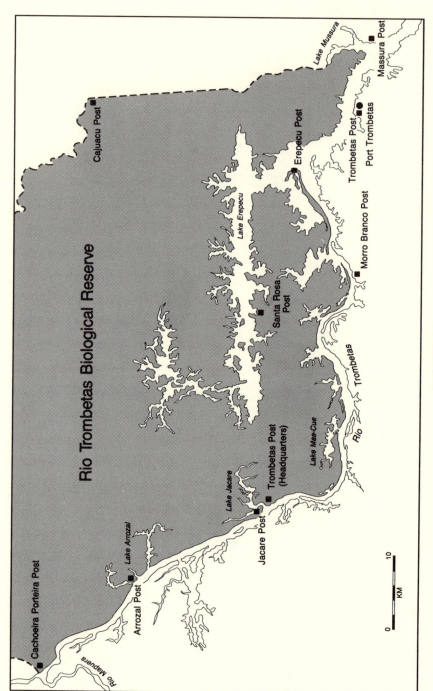

FIGURE 7.4
Rio Trombetas Biological Reserve: Southern Sector

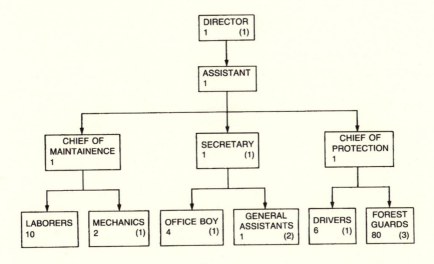

FIGURE 7.5

Rio Trombetas Biological Reserve: Staffing Chart. Adapted from IBDF, *Reserva Biológica do Rio Trombetas: Plan de Manejo.* Number in paretheses indicates number of incumbents in mid-1986.

Trombetas across the river from the reserve had seven thousand inhabitants by 1982 and was growing steadily.

The impact of all this on the reserve was tangible. Smoke from bauxite processing deposited a thick mantle of residue well into the reserve and was defoliating areas of the forest. Effluent from bauxite processing and sewage from the town were dumped untreated into the river.[18] As the increased economic activity drew migrants and created markets, the reserve became a tempting destination for those seeking a small plot to grow crops for subsistence or sale.[19] Squatters invaded the reserve in the early 1980s, mostly along the margins of the Trombetas River. Some caboclos who had previously been moved out of the reserve reinvaded it.

Released from the need to respect the environment and pressed to show profits, the development agencies became threats to the reserve in their own right. Electronorte, the public power company in Amazonia, decided to build a dam at Porteira Falls, where the Trombetas River entered the reserve. Electronorte did not even inform the IBDF that it was planning the dam; the forest agency only learned about it when reserve guards encountered an Electronorte survey team in the reserve.[20] Even the early stages of dam construction caused damage. A large construction camp at the dam site spilled into the reserve. Electronorte cut a service road through the reserve to get around the falls, and squatters were clearing land along it. When completed, the dam would change the water levels of the Trombetas River downstream, with unknown consequences for the river's turtles and other aquatic life.

Unlike the director at Amazonia National Park, the director at Trombetas had been in his job a long time, ever since the reserve was established in 1979. The administrative distance between the protected areas and the DN left little opportunity for conservation field personnel to advance into administrative positions in conservation.[21] Since protected areas in different states and territories were organizationally distant from each other as well as from the DN, even lateral movement within the system was difficult. Those committed to conservation often felt condemned to dead-end careers by an administrative arrangement that so devalued what they did and restricted their mobility. Some were willing to accept this as the price of their commitment, but acceptance was usually tinged with resignation and, among some of the older field personnel, with regret. The director at Trombetas had seen scientific research bloom in the late 1970s and early 1980s, and then wilt to nothing. He had seen press coverage of the reserve peak and fall off. Jorge Pádua, who had visited the reserve in 1981, was the last head of the DN to have done so. The current delegado in Belém had not visited the reserve.

His long experience notwithstanding, the director at Trombetas adopted essentially the same strategy as had the director at Amazonia National Park: concentrate on the tractable problems and ignore the others, no matter how serious. The dam at Porteira Falls was an example of the dilemma he faced regarding the development agencies: he reasoned that since his job was defending the park against illegal incursions, and since the dam was illegal, he should protest. On the other hand, mild protests would be ignored and loud ones might lead to the elimination of the entire area from the reserve. Given his options and their likely consequences, he quietly accepted the dam.

Instead, he concentrated on defending the reserve from hunters, caboclos, and other small-time invaders. As was the case at Amazonia National Park, there was no permanent staff in the reserve, so guards went out in teams from Oriximiná and, using the guard posts as bases, patrolled in motorized canoes. Guards checked boats coming out of Lake Erepecu for lumber, fish, or pelts; only brazilnuts taken from the groves remaining in private hands were allowed to pass.

The director made monthly trips up the Trombetas River to check conditions personally. A special task arose during turtle nesting season. Even before the reserve had been established, IBDF personnel had camped at the turtle beaches during nesting time to prevent caboclos from capturing the turtles while they were concentrated there.[22] After the reserve was established, this policy continued, with the reserve staff, supplemented by IBDF personnel from elsewhere, patrolling the beaches from temporary encampments.

This kind of immediate, limited defense proved insufficient. Half a dozen guards could not expel all the squatters in the reserve or prevent new squatters from establishing themselves, nor could they prevent all poaching. Their efforts did, however, cause resentment among the region's caboclos, who threatened violence. This created an undercurrent of fear among the guards; they knew that at an isolated post they would have little chance against a group of armed and angry men. Only one of the three posts had a working radio, increasing the feeling of isolation and exposure among the guards. Fear had led one to quit in early 1986 and made replacing him difficult.

The lack of political resources left the director unable to control the turtle beaches. In past years, the IBDF had found it impossible to keep all the turtle nesting beaches, which were spread out over ten kilometers along the river, under constant surveillance. The forest agency was satisfied to keep poaching to a small fraction of the stock, which it did until 1984. That year the poaching got out of hand, and the director estimated that a third of the population was lost. The following nesting season, IBDF forest guards swept the area in a military-style operation, arresting more than thirty caboclos and confiscating their weapons.

Under the military government, the sweep merely would have increased the inchoate resentment of the reserve, but the reintroduction of democracy in that year had changed the political climate. The caboclos protested that the action threatened their livelihood,[23] and they gained the support of the local Catholic church and the Partido Trabalhista, the left-wing workers' party. The latter argued that since the owners of remaining brazilnut groves in the reserve were allowed to harvest them for profit, the caboclos, who depended on hunting and fishing for their subsistence, also had a right to the reserve's resources. Leaflets were distributed in Oriximiná demanding unrestricted access to the reserve.[24]

The IBDF's central administration knew that a few seasons of open turtle poaching would be disastrous for the turtles, but it wavered, fearing that continued vigorous policing of the nesting beaches might be dangerous in the unsettled political climate of the nation. It felt no countervailing pressure from the region to defend the reserve. Not only did the caboclos resent it, but so did many of the local entrepreneurs. Loss of access to many groves in the reserve had cut into the business of the local brazilnut exporters. By resorting to subterfuge, they had regained some access to the groves, but the existence of the reserve complicated their lives.[25] After determining which way the political winds blew, the IBDF decided against any more sweeps by forest guards; the reserve's staff would be on its own in defending the turtles in the future. Only last-minute protests by international conservation groups got the beaches adequately protected during the 1986 and subsequent nesting seasons.

Faced with an array of problems he could not manage, the director made his psychological adjustments. He drew up imaginative plans that required just a few more men and a little more money. He envisioned a guard post at Porteira Falls, where the river entered the reserve, and another downstream, where the river left it. At the former, bills of lading would be issued for cargos entering the reserve, and only cargos accompanied by these documents would be allowed to pass the second post. Such a system, he reasoned, would control the commercial exploitation of the reserve. He also searched for the bright side of the setbacks. He held that the location of the now-vacant IBDF building on the edge of town had discouraged people from reporting infractions in the reserve: his own house was closer to the port and therefore a better location for his office. He also reasoned that, with the reserve's own boat out of commission, getting to the reserve would be difficult for his staff were it not for the Electronorte supply boats going to the dam construction site at Porteira Falls.

Yet his sense of abandonment beneath the optimism, his sense of being stranded in a remote Amazon town after the conservation tide had ebbed, seemed to more accurately reflect the state of affairs at Trombetas. It was obvious that the gamble—establishing a nature reserve in the face of development—had not paid off. Conservation did not have the political weight to command the necessary respect, so instead of becoming an important factor in regional development, the reserve had become nearly weightless in the political calculus of that development. At worst, it was an obstacle to those who would determine the region's future. At best it was an object of their casual charity, the kind that rides for the reserve's staff on Electronorte's supply boats represented.

Casual charity would not prevent the reserve from continuing to fade into the region's history. The reserve's turtles were living under a temporary reprieve. A one- or two-year failure of political will would be sufficient to drastically reduce and perhaps destroy the population. Indeed the entire reserve had only a temporary lease on life. In time, the new squatters would become legally protected, entitled to compensation if removed. The difficulty and expense of their removal would mount in the coming years, and sooner or later it would no longer seem worthwhile to those who allocated public funds.

* * *

The IBDF's three protected areas in Rondônia—Guaporé and Jaru biological reserves and Pacaás Novos National Park—were also in the eye of Amazon development. Rondônia, like the lower Trombetas region, was one of the Polamazonia development poles, the Polonoroeste. New settlers flowed into the region in the 1970s and 1980s, transforming it from a backwater into a vigorous agriculture frontier. There were key differences between the Trombetas reserve and the IBDF's protected areas in Rondônia, however: the latter had high levels of financial backing, a powerful foreign patron, and an important official place within the wider regional development program.

All of these advantages, which made the Rondônia areas unique among Amazon protected areas, could be traced to the World Bank. The bank, which saw the expansion of commercial agriculture in western Brazil as a means of increasing Brazil's agricultural exports, agreed to underwrite the Polonoroeste program in the early 1980s.[26] The bank's financial support for Polonoroeste, totaling over half a billion dollars (the largest commitment it had ever made in Brazil), was funneled into a wide variety of projects. It funded the paving of BR 364, the main highway to southern Brazil. It underwrote agricultural credit programs and more colonization schemes. It paid for infrastructure in the rapidly growing towns and for a mix of social services.

The bank, politically susceptible to popular opinion in the developed world, insisted that Brazil's development plans for Rondônia make provisions for nature, and it earmarked funds for nature reserves.[27] This commitment made an unusual amount of money available for the IBDF's protected areas in the state. The DN's planning staff was by now too small to draw up management plans for the three areas, so the bank, through the Polonoroeste project, paid for the expensive recourse of outside consultants. Once the plans were completed, several million dollars were earmarked for the infrastructure they called for. Headquarters compounds for the three areas were completed in 1985. Electrified throughout, they contained administrative offices, research facilities, and accommodations for staffs of at least twenty. Staffs were quickly hired, vehicles and patrol boats were acquired, and management regimes were instituted.

The World Bank's commitment also meant political protection for the parks and reserves. Soon after Pacaás Novos National Park was established, the Rondônia state government began constructing a highway from Ji-Paraná, on BR 364, to the town of Costa Marques on the Guaporé River. The most direct route was through the park, so that was the one the state engineers intended to follow. The bank, however, insisted the route be changed, and the road, already cleared from Ji-Paraná into the park, was rerouted around its eastern flank (figure 7.6).[28]

While the three protected areas in Rondônia shared the advantage of the bank's patronage, they shared little else. Pacaás Novos, the largest of the three and the only one designated a national park (thanks to the imposing tabular mountains in its interior), was clearly in the path of settlement. Before 1980, the nearest large area of forest clearing was approximately sixty kilometers northeast of the park.[29] Between 1980 and 1983, penetration roads pushed southwest from the highway, in some cases right up to the park's boundaries. Discontinuous patches of forest clearing appeared along these roads where new ranches and farms were being established. The cleared areas grew, coalesced, and spilled over the park's eastern border.

With World Bank support, the park was prepared to meet the first threats posed by advancing settlement. The headquarters was constructed on the northeastern boundary of the park, where the abandoned road to Costa Marques entered it. From it the guards could patrol the park's exposed eastern boundary, part of which was the Urupá River. Although not very large, the river formed a distinct and defensible boundary. Further east, where the boundary was just a survey line, the park director planned to cut a trail and have his men patrol it on foot or horseback, a simple and probably effective measure.[30]

The Guaporé Biological Reserve, southwest of Pacaás Novos on the Guaporé River, was less directly in the path of development

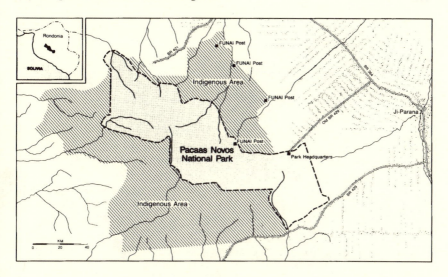

FIGURE 7.6
Pacaás Novos National Park and Surrounding Indigenous Area

(figure 7.7). The river had been the main axis of settlement in Rondônia in the past, but it was far from BR 364, which had replaced it in that role. Life in the area remained largely traditional. Families along the Guaporé and its tributaries still collected rubber and brazilnuts, fished, and practiced subsistence agriculture. Ranches were scattered on the lowlands.[31]

The Guaporé reserve, nevertheless, did present some serious management problems. At approximately 600,000 hectares, it was not one of the largest reserves, but it lacked the physiographic unity that often characterized the smaller ones; it spanned the basins of several tributaries of the Guaporé River, but it did not include the entire drainage area of any of them. Jorge Pádua had wanted to include the lower courses of these rivers in the reserve, but several large water buffalo ranches were already well established there. The state argued that their expropriation would hamper economic development, so a survey line through the grasslands north of the ranches became the reserve's boundary.[32] At FUNAI's insistence, an area along the upper Branco River inhabited by Indians was also deleted from the proposal, leaving a boundary that cut across the drainage pattern in a remote, difficult-to-patrol part of the reserve.

The management plan took these awkward boundaries into account

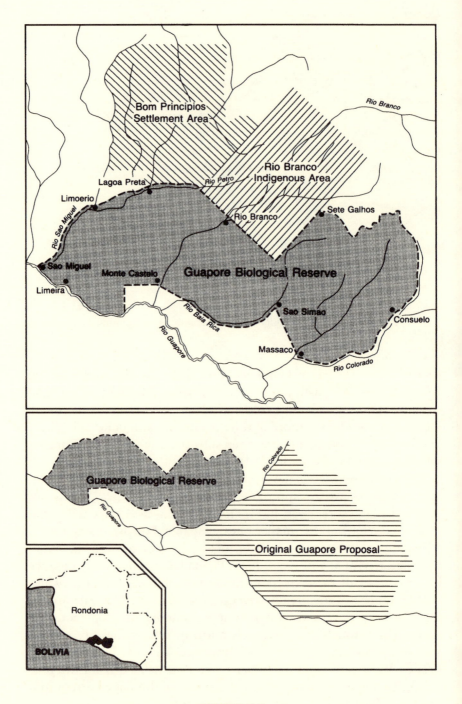

FIGURE 7.7
Guaporé Biological Reserve: As Established and Originally Proposed

TABLE 7.2
Planned Management Facilities in Guaporé Biological Reserve

Site	Activities	Facilities
Limeira (Headquarters)	Administration Research support Patrolling	Administrative offices Airfield and hangar Boat docks Lodging for researchers Laboratory and herbarium Staff lodging and mess
São Miguel	River surveillance	Floating guard post
Monte Castelo	Patrolling Research support	Floating guard post
São Simão	Patrolling Research support	Floating guard post
Massaco	Patrolling Research support	Floating guard post
Consuelo	Patrolling Research support	Terra firma guard post
Sete Galhos	Patrolling	Terra firma guard post Landing strip
Rio Branco	Patrolling Research support	Terra firma guard post
Limoeiro	Patrolling	Terra firma guard post Landing strip
Lagoa Preta	Patrolling Research support	Terra firma guard post

Source: IBDF, *Reserva Biológica de Guaporé; Plano de Manejo* (draft).

when it called for a staff of seventy-seven, two-thirds of whom would be guards, and for the construction of nine guard posts on the perimeter of the reserve, mostly on the Guaporé's tributaries (table 7.2).[33] The headquarters was located on the Guaporé River and became the seat of an active management regime shortly after it was completed.

Jaru Biological Reserve was the most inherently manageable of the three. Logistical support would be easy: during the high-water season it was only three hours by boat from Ji-Paraná, the largest town in the region and the IBDF's regional headquarters. At 268,000 hectares, Jaru was only slightly larger than Wetterberg's minimum size and was one of the smallest of the IBDF's protected areas in Amazonia (figure 7.8). The few squatters in the area had been removed, and the little private property purchased. The reserve was compact and no roads approached it. It was roughly coextensive with the drainage basin of the Igarapé (small river) São Pedro, whose mouth was the only natural passage to the interior. Finally, the Lourdes indigenous area was just south of it. Its Indians, who had made national headlines in 1984 when they captured some settlers on their land, acted as a buffer to invasion. And while the Indians occasionally crossed into the reserve to hunt, they made no claims on it.

The reserve's only obvious shortcoming was its western boundary, a survey line that imperfectly divided the São Pedro basin from the Machado River and left a narrow strip of land between the park and the river. Jorge Pádua had wanted to include this strip in the reserve but the National Security Council would not permit it.[34] In the short term, this did little to compromise the reserve because the strip was lightly settled.

As was the case at Pacaás Novos, the headquarters, which was in the southwest corner of the reserve on the banks of the Machado River, was placed to meet the first threat large-scale regional settlement was likely to present. New roads and accompanying forest clearing were approaching from the southwest and had already come within fifteen kilometers of the reserve by the mid-1980s. Once settlement reached the west bank of the Machado River, which would happen in a few years, the river would have to be intensively patrolled, and the headquarters was ideally located for this. Anticipated ease of management was reflected in the personnel the reserve's management plan called for. While plans for Guaporé called for a staff of 75 and those for Pacaás Novos 167, planners thought a staff of 51 would be sufficient for Jaru.

The patronage of the World Bank thus improved the management capacities of each of the natural areas. Idiosyncratic local circumstances, however, exerted such a powerful influence on any natural area in Amazonia that even short-term management success in Rondônia was largely determined by such circumstances. The World Bank's support might tip the balance in favor of an area's defense, but only slightly.

The headquarters site at Jaru, like many riverine areas of Amazonia where settlement had penetrated, was malarial.[35] Although the dormitories, offices, and dining hall were screened, and the staff avoided the river at dawn and dusk, the incidence of malaria among the reserve staff was high. There had been times when all the guards were in Ji-Paraná recovering from the disease. The director in the mid-1980s was a young forest engineer who had already been struck twice. Staff resignations were high due to the malaria, and finding replacements was difficult. The staff, which had numbered more than half a dozen in the past, was down to the director and two guards.

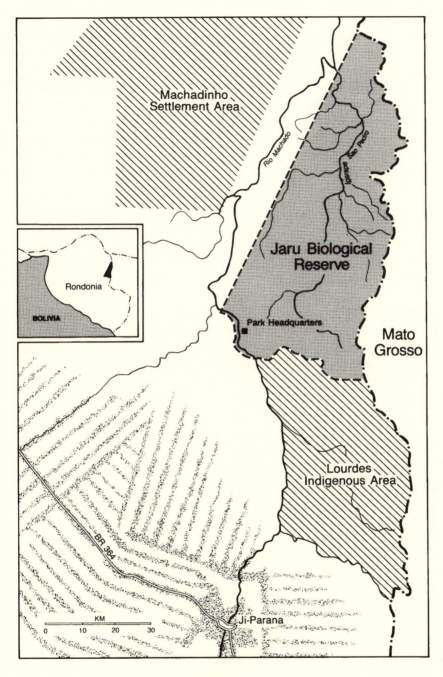

FIGURE 7.8
Jaru Biological Reserve and Environs

This made surveillance of more than a small part of the reserve impossible. The guards regularly patrolled the Machado River in front of the headquarters and along the Igarapé Água Azul, the reserve's southern boundary, but there was no guard post at the mouth of the Igarapé São Pedro. The director did not have the staff to man a post there, much less patrol the interior beyond it. Yet such was the intrinsic manageability of the reserve that it could practically defend itself. Squatters might stray into the reserve, or Indians might enter it to hunt, but with transportation in the region river based, the reserve's boundaries along watershed divisions protected it effectively.

The near-term prospects for the Guaporé reserve were likewise almost entirely determined by regional circumstances, which for the moment posed only minor management problems. Many caboclos remained in the reserve along the São Miguel River in the mid-1980s, including the hundred or so inhabitants of the village of Limoeiro (INCRA had promised to relocate these caboclos to one of its settlement schemes, but had not yet done so). While the director wanted the caboclos compensated and removed eventually, he was not concerned about them in the short term. He felt similarly about the several dozen Indians who lived in the reserve along the Branco River. They were remote and too few to do much damage.

More advanced economic activities posed only two minor threats to the reserve. One was commercial fishing along the section of the Guaporé River included within the reserve. The commercial fishermen used nets, and the director felt they were real intruders. The headquarters was ideally placed to patrol the river, however, and the staff had new patrol boats and ample gasoline.[36] (The staff did not bother caboclos fishing for their own consumption; the director knew fish were an important part of their diets, and he reasoned that their take, caught with hooks rather than nets, was small.)

The other threat was in the far eastern part of the reserve. It contained patches of good soil, and speculators, taking advantage of the undefended boundary, had cut roads into the reserve and were clearing land in hopes of getting title or rights to it. All the clearing was the work of a few speculators, so the director was confident the problem was small enough to be managed by expulsion. FUNAI, the IBDF, and the state of Rondônia planned a combined sweep of the area to this end.

The more distant prospects for the IBDF's protected areas in Rondônia were darker, however. The World Bank did not alter conservation's basic position in either Rondônia or Brazil as a whole. Conservation remained politically weak in a state and nation committed to rapid economic growth. It remained in competition with small settlers and Indians, and areas of protected nature remained without functional links to the landscapes in which they were set. The bank's patronage thus only shored up conservation's inherently weak position. But the bank's participation in the developmental aspects of Polonoroeste—the agricultural districts, the booming cities, the increased circulation of investment capital—also reinforced the dominant Brazilian political and economic trends.

The World Bank's eventual withdrawal from Rondônia would have different impacts on conservation programs and the economic transformation under way there. The latter would continue of its own momentum, and as it did, Rondônia would become an increasingly difficult place to preserve nature. The ability of conservationists to discharge their responsibilities would deteriorate as conservation subsided to the low level of importance its own political resources were capable of earning for it. The long-term prospects of the three protected areas in Rondônia were already becoming clear in the late 1980s.

Jaru's natural defenses were strong as long as rivers were the main arteries of transportation, but it had weak defenses against the roads that were the real vectors of settlement in Rondônia. Long, straight penetration roads that ignored natural drainage and respected none but the largest rivers were opening one part of northeastern Rondônia after another to settlement.[37] Mato Grosso was a rapidly growing state, and eventually the reserve would face roads from the east as well.

The Machado River would deter the advance of settlement on its western flank in the short term, especially if the river was diligently patrolled and the strip of land between the river and the reserve remained only lightly inhabited, but the long-term prospects were poor. The massive Machadinho agricultural settlement west of the Machado River was likely to be fully occupied by the early 1990s. When this occurred, spontaneous invasion or planned colonization would be likely on the eastern bank. Since the percentage of good soils in the Machadinho project was the lowest of all such colonization projects in Rondônia,[38] a stream of failed settlers from the project could threaten the reserve even sooner. The government of Rondônia, anticipating such an eastward thrust of settlement and probably wishing to encourage it, planned a road across the Machado River and through the reserve.[39] Once settlement jumped the river, with or without the state road, the reserve would have no natural defenses on its western flank.

Defending the reserve in the face of future regional development therefore will require much larger protection budgets than the current ones. While the World Bank remains involved in Rondônia, increasing budgets to meet the increasing level of threat might be possible, but when that involvement ends, so will any prospects of defending the reserve against the settlement approaching it.

The picture at Pacaás Novos was similar. Pacaás Novos was prepared to face the first wave of settlement, which would break on its eastern flank, but time would expose progressively less defensible segments of its perimeter. Getting from park headquarters to the boundary in the southeast, the next area likely to come under pressure from settlers, involved a circuitous trip of hundreds of kilometers on roads that were not always passable. As areas farther to the west came under pressure, patrolling would become increasingly difficult and expensive. The area south of the park had already been penetrated by new settlement roads in the mid-1980s, and clearings were beginning along them.

The picture at Pacaás Novos was darkened by the failure of conservationists and indigenists to reach a modus operandi in Amazonia. The Pacaás Novos region had a long history of Indian-white conflict (one small area had been the scene of seven or eight armed and sometimes deadly confrontations since 1960)[40] but when the park was proposed, little was known about the Indians of the region beyond their obvious bellicosity. Neither the IBDF nor FUNAI knew how many Indians lived in the proposed park. Jorge Pádua thought the Indians sighted in the area only used it as a hunting ground,[41] which perhaps was wishful thinking, but none could dispute it. In the years after the park's establishment, FUNAI, with World Bank support, systematically surveyed central Rondônia for its Indian census, and when it found a considerable permanent population, it declared its intention of setting aside the entire region, including the park, as an indigenous area.[42]

The IBDF objected, and under pressure from the World Bank, the two agencies negotiated a compromise in 1985. A large area almost totally surrounding the national park would become an indigenous area, but the park itself would not. FUNAI felt this was an important concession, but it made little difference in practice; the Indian agency placed a post in the park and operated at will throughout the area, treating the park as theirs. The park's staff had the resources to operate only in the eastern end of the park, so the IBDF had no corresponding management presence in the interior. IBDF administrators differed on the long-term implications of this. Some felt the IBDF and FUNAI would eventually work out in the field the accommodation they had been forced to work out on paper, but most were more pessimistic. As IBDF conservationists lost their earlier optimism, their view became similar to SEMA's: Indians and protected nature could not be made to mix. The park's director held that the arrangement reduced him and his staff to FUNAI auxiliaries, protecting the Indians but not necessarily nature.[43]

Jorge Pádua, now an outside observer, feared that settlement in the region would combine lethally with the Indian problem.[44] The indigenous area south of the park, which contained good soil, had already been penetrated by settlement roads, and clearing was already taking place. As settlement became consolidated, this area would become increasingly attractive to speculators, ranchers, and large farmers. Such groups had influence with the state government so political pressure to open the Indian lands would increase. Perhaps it would be resisted while the World Bank was funding the Polonoroeste project, but the bank's political leverage was not likely to outlive its financial involvement. Once the land was fully opened to settlement, its Indians would retreat northward into the park. And once they settled in, Jorge Pádua thought it likely the park would be transformed into an indigenous area exclusively, first in fact and then in name. Not everyone in the IBDF agreed with this fatal scenario, but they did agree with one of its assumptions: the need to accommodate the Indians would combine with the inexorable advance of the settlement frontier to place the park under daunting and probably irresistible pressure.

Guaporé's long-term prospects were not very different. Although Guaporé's environs were as yet little developed,[45] INCRA had plans for an agricultural settlement west of the Rio Branco indigenous area and just north of the reserve. The state already planned to connect the settlement to central Rondônia with a road running right to the reserve's boundary.[46] FUNAI, which routinely entered the reserve to contact the Indians living along the Branco River, wanted to transfer this part of the reserve to the indigenous area. These threats—from

Indians, the press of settlement, and the state's designs—were less pressing than comparable ones at Pacaás Novos or Jaru, but they would grow while the resources to meet them would likely not. As this occurred, the reserve's managers would become like King Canute telling the waves to desist.

***

The management equations for the three protected areas in Amazonas State—Jaú and Pico da Neblina national parks and Abufari Biological Reserve—lacked the two counterbalancing elements that defined the equations for the Rondônia areas (figure 7.9). They were not in the eye of regional development. Except for its capital, Manaus, the state had been relatively unaffected by the changes that were transforming many parts of Amazonia in the 1980s. Amazonas was still remote from the national core, and the populations of most areas of the state showed little recent growth.[47] Except around Manaus, there was no real settlement frontier, and caboclo culture still held sway along most of the state's waterways. On the other hand, the protected areas in Amazonas did not have access to the financial support that regional development agencies made available to protected areas in their ambit.

Given how this bargain worked out at Trombetas and in Rondônia, one might conclude that the protected areas in Amazonas were better off for the lack of such support, but this was not necessarily the case. Without it, the IBDF was unable to establish protection regimes in any of its natural areas in the state: all three were under a parks supervisor in the IBDF office in Manaus, and none had supervisory personnel permanently posted to them in the mid-1980s. This left them even more subject to the vicissitudes of local circumstance than other protected areas in Amazonia, and it produced what was probably the IBDF's most serious failure.

Pico da Neblina National Park was the biggest gamble among the IBDF's initial proposals. Although not in an area targeted for regional development, Pico was rife with competing interests: Indians, prospectors, and the military. Jorge Pádua had been willing to capitalize on temporary political advantage in creating the park, but she was aware of how far she was overreaching the IBDF's political resources. She knew that other interests in the region would have to be accommodated. She hoped when the time came, the IBDF would be strong

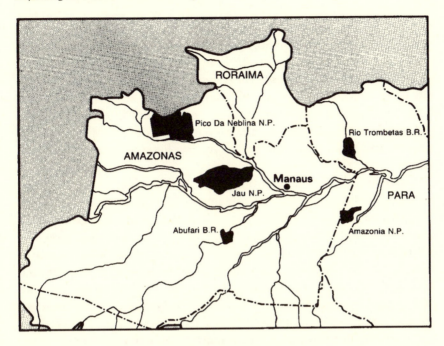

FIGURE 7.9
IBDF Protected Areas in Pará and Amazonas

and resolute enough to reach a settlement that would keep the park undiminished and manageable.[48]

Two components of the calculation were off the mark. First, in such a remote area, pronouncements made in Brasília often counted for little unless they could be backed up by local administrative instruments, so the IBDF needed a strong presence at Pico if it was to have a strong hand in determining its future. The IBDF never managed it. The region was far from the IBDF delegado in Manaus and was, in fact, one of the least accessible areas of Amazonia. This meant that active management would involve difficult logistics and greater expenses than the IBDF could afford without special funding sources. As of the mid-1980s, there were still no guards in the park, nor even a permanent IBDF presence. An IBDF administrator based in the near-by town of São Gabriel da Cachoeira looked after the park as best he could, and the parks supervisor in Manaus made occasional visits.[49]

The second component was the initial catalogue of the park's management drawbacks; while imposing, it was incomplete. The first surveys of title records had revealed relatively little private land in the park, but a later, more thorough survey of the Negro River area revealed that 80 percent of the land along the river was privately held.[50] The IBDF feared that thorough surveys elsewhere would turn up more private holdings. Gold mining in the area had increased since the park's establishment, and the powerful interests vested in the continued flow of gold made it politically difficult for the IBDF to remove the miners from the park, even if it had the physical means to do so.[51]

Most important, while Jorge Pádua had predicted that the presence of Indians would cause problems for the park, she did not foresee how serious they would be. The 1967 Brazilian constitution guaranteed Indians unrestricted use of the lands they occupied "by custom," but national park legislation neither prohibited establishing parks (or reserves) where Indians were present nor exempted Indians from park regulations. This placed indigenous rights and biological conservation (and, by extension, FUNAI and the IBDF) in potential conflict in many parts of Amazonia, but at Pico da Neblina the presence of so many Indians made the potential especially great.

Such contradictions were common in Brazilian law, and the conflicts they caused were normally resolved by raw political or economic power.[52] In the late 1970s, when conservation enjoyed official favor, the IBDF sometimes had managed to override FUNAI's objections to the establishment of a particular park or reserve. This was the case at Pico.[53] Jorge Pádua knew this would cause conflicts, but she assumed once the park was operating, the IBDF would be in a strong negotiating position with regard to the Indian agency. This seemed reasonable in the late 1970s, when FUNAI was weak and Amazon conservation was enjoying official favor, and as things went from bad to worse for the Indian agency it seemed even more reasonable.

FUNAI in the mid-1980s was demoralized and in turmoil: it had four heads between September 1985 and May 1986; it failed to make provisions for the 2,000 Indians whose lands were to be flooded by the Balbina Dam. Nevertheless, FUNAI's position relative to the IBDF had steadily improved because, first, the political power of its charges rose. A national organization for indigenous peoples was formed and established links to the international human rights network. Indians developed a new militancy and political savvy: with national press coverage, Indians made hostages of settlers who invaded their lands; Indian groups occupied FUNAI regional offices

and staged demonstrations in Brasília. International indigenist organizations took up their cause and publicized their struggles abroad.
This increased the pressure on FUNAI to represent the Indians with
more than its customary zeal and increased the pressure on the federal government to allow the agency to do so.

Second, FUNAI's knowledge of the whereabouts of Brazil's
Indians steadily increased. Many of the areas the IBDF had selected
in the late 1970s for protection had not yet been thoroughly surveyed by FUNAI, so even when the Indian agency suspected a sizable
Indian presence, it could seldom prove it; according to a FUNAI
administrator, "The IBDF moved too fast for us." Through the chaos
and the setbacks of the 1980s, FUNAI continued to identify Indian
lands,[54] and its survey teams confirmed the presence of Indians in
many IBDF-protected areas. Whereas the IBDF could allow its
actions with regard to Indians to be guided by wishful thinking during the 1970s, a decade later, FUNAI could counter the IBDF with
solid data.

When it had the data, FUNAI had the stronger legal position
because Indian rights were more deeply rooted in law than the inviolability of the IBDF's protected areas: the right of Indians to unrestricted use of their lands was guaranteed by the constitution, while
the parks were protected only by legislation. The IBDF's conservation
program had previously taken advantage of the fact that legal niceties
normally meant little in Amazonia, but now FUNAI's strong legal
position, when buttressed by its new knowledge of the distribution
of Indians in Amazonia and the new visibility of Brazilian Indians,
gave the Indian agency a strong hand in its conflicts with the IBDF.

The two agencies established a joint working group to settle
conflicts, but FUNAI, aware of its stronger position and under little
pressure to make hasty settlements, treated the working group lightly.
Different FUNAI representatives appeared at successive meetings,
making sustained negotiations difficult. FUNAI representatives also
arrived with little authority; they had to refer everything to their
superiors for ratification, and given the chaos that had enveloped the
Indian agency, ratification was seldom forthcoming. The lack of
conflict resolution was a source of ongoing frustration for the IBDF,
but with no high cards, there was little it could do to force the pace.

The IBDF's position with regard to the Indians at Pico da Neblina
was especially weak. Long contact with the Salesian mission had
given the Indians of the Maturacá Indigenous Area a strong sense of

their own identity and a willingness to assert their rights.[55] As important, FUNAI had a physical presence in the area, while the IBDF did not. Thus, while much of the area was legally both a national park and an indigenous area, it was more the former in reality. Indian agents expelled visitors from the part of the park that overlapped with the Cauaboari Indigenous Area. They added insult to injury by expelling even IBDF officials.[56]

The parks supervisor in Manaus believed that with some radical surgery to remove unmanageable areas, the park could be saved and eventually managed, essentially what Jorge Pádua had hoped would happen, although the parks supervisor conceded that the IBDF was not in a position to dictate terms to others, a key part of Jorge Pádua's scenario. On the other hand, Nogueira-Neto felt the IBDF had waited too long to establish a management regime and to deal squarely with the Indian problem, and this had already cost it the park in everything but name.[57] Whatever their prognoses, however, no one thought the park in its present form was a success, or that it could be made into the one Jorge Pádua had envisioned.

At Jaú National Park, the absence of the kind of bargain the IBDF had struck in Rondônia and at Trombetas worked to conservation's advantage. While management resources were slight, the lack of regional development meant that the inherent management virtues that had so impressed the IBDF in the late 1970s remained undiminished. No new roads bypassed the natural checkpoint at the mouth of the Jaú River; no settlers spilled into the thinly populated basin; no surge of speculation complicated its simple land ownership picture.

The IBDF adopted an economical and pragmatic management strategy for Jaú: it would control the mouth of the river rather than try to impose direct controls over the entire basin.[58] A floating guard post was placed where the Jaú River flowed into the Negro River and a small guard team hired on contract from INPA was posted there. The team allowed only rubber and brazilnuts out of the park. Trade in these products was not viewed as a threat to the park, even though it was clear that not all the products came from the few private inholdings or the small tracts the caboclos were entitled by law to exploit. The IBDF was not so casual with regard to pelts and meat of wild animals; neither was allowed out. Federal law prohibited hunting in the national parks, and since little game could be taken on the small private tracts or the squatter homesteads, the IBDF assumed that any wild animals had been taken on park lands. IBDF officials knew the caboclos hunted on the public lands for their consumption, but this did not concern them much; limited subsistence hunting was viewed as tolerable. The IBDF had much the same attitude toward fish. National park statutes prohibited fishing, but the IBDF aimed only at keeping fish from getting to markets outside the basin.

The IBDF was equally concerned with who entered the basin. The owners of private tracts and established posseiros were allowed in, but the guards denied entrance to caboclos whom they did not know, fearing they might settle in the basin. Commercial fishermen and those looking for aquarium fish were likewise kept out, as were sports fishermen who came upriver from Manaus. Itinerant traders were excluded; the IBDF did not want the caboclos to develop a taste for the commercial goods the traders sold, fearing it would prod them into more intensive exploitation of their surroundings. Caboclos and traders complained, but the IBDF stuck to its policy. The guards also denied entrance to priests. The parks supervisor in Manaus was adamant about the need for this; he viewed priests as agitators bent on stirring up discontent among the caboclos, who were currently willing to accept the restraints put on their lives by park management.

The management regime was a success. The park was gradually being depopulated, with people staying or leaving according to whether they could live with restrictions confining them to traditional caboclo lifeways. The older ones, who were set in their ways and on whom the restrictions imposed little hardship, usually stayed. The younger ones, who were often ambitious or who had developed a taste for commercial products, usually left. The number of caboclo families in the park was down to approximately sixty by 1986, and according to IBDF officials in Manaus, the reduction had already had an effect; the increasing abundance of birds and other animals was apparent even to casual observers.[59]

Jaú, more than any other IBDF-protected area, should have been an unqualified success. After all, the IBDF chose to protect the area because Jorge Pádua and her associates assumed it could be defended against anything the future might bring. But the future now held threats that exceeded the IBDF's ability to meet them. One was the possibility of regional development initiatives. IBDF officials had heard rumors that Electronorte was considering a dam at the mouth of the Jaú. Whereas the dam at Porteira Falls might cause considerable damage to the aquatic life of the Trombetas reserve, a dam at the mouth of the Jaú would destroy the park by flooding its heart.

Although such a dam seemed unlikely in light of the low head it would produce and the problems Electronorte had encountered at Balbina Dam, the power company's decisions were not always what reason would dictate. And the IBDF would have no more influence on a decision regarding a dam at Jaú than it had at Trombetas.

The other threat was the possibility that the IBDF might not be able to enforce the rules on which its management strategy was based. Under the military regime, which had destroyed most instruments of lower-class political power, the IBDF could take measures of questionable legality, like interdicting access to traders and priests, without fear of the consequences. As events at the Trombetas River turtle beaches showed, however, the rules of the game were changing with the return of democracy. Areas of ambiguity or conflicting rights would no longer be decided automatically against the caboclos. And as events at Trombetas had also shown, the IBDF's top administrators were now less likely to stand fast against the protests of caboclos and their allies, even if capitulating meant abandoning a protected area to depredation.[60]

* * *

The outcomes of the IBDF's efforts to protect its natural areas in Amazonia thus varied widely, as the institute's management weaknesses were exacerbated or mitigated by immediate circumstances. Yet one overriding conclusion emerges: failure needed only predictable circumstances. When the thrust of regional development engulfed protected areas, it began to erase them. When there was interest conflict, which was nearly universal in Amazonia, the protected areas suffered invasion, dismemberment, and sometimes extinction in everything but name.

Conversely even modest success depended on anomaly. The entry of the World Bank into the Polonoroeste project had a deus ex machina quality to it. The absence of conflict at Jaú combined with the area's physical characteristics to give it an unusual degree of manageability. The IBDF's ability to impose its will on the neighbors and residents of its protected areas depended on special political circumstances. In almost all cases, the favorable anomalies seemed likely to be replaced by more normal, less favorable circumstances: development would advance; temporary political advantages would evaporate; interest conflicts would emerge or sharpen. This play of norm and anomaly gave failure an air of permanence and success a temporary appearance. Some protected areas—Trombetas, for example—seemed to be inexorably shifting from the region's landscape into its history. But for even the more successfully protected ones—Jaú, Guaporé, Jaru—the future was more an enemy than a friend. The IBDF's natural areas thus reflected the fate of the forest institute's conservation program in general: success came when, in Jorge Pádua's words, "everything came together," and it ended when the knot of favorable circumstances that sustained it unraveled.

CHAPTER 8

Hobson's Choice—SEMA in the Eighties

The first half of the 1980s was kinder to the Secretariat of the Environment's (SEMA) conservation program than to the IBDF's. In a sense, SEMA's program was preadapted to the hard times of the 1980s by the agency's modest circumstances in the previous decade and by Nogueira-Neto's inherently pessimistic view of conservation's political potential. SEMA's greater initial caution in selecting protected areas meant less conflict with Indians, settlers, and caboclos, and it left SEMA in a better position when the power of these interests became greater than that of conservation. Most of SEMA's ecological stations in Amazonia were smaller than the IBDF's parks and reserves. They were more compact and relied more on natural, easy-to-defend boundaries. Maracá de Roraima was a fluvial island. The Maracá-Jipioca station consisted of two islands off the Atlantic coast of Amapá. SEMA's two stations in western Amazonia were at the confluence of major rivers and had water along much of their perimeters.[1]

SEMA's administrative structure now conferred advantages that conservationists in the IBDF envied. Whereas the IBDF's juxtaposed production and conservation mandates had worked to conservation's advantage in the 1970s, when the latter had top-level support, the juxtaposition insured that the parks and reserves were only a minor concern to the forest agency in the 1980s, once that support was withdrawn. The ecological stations, on the other hand, remained a central concern to SEMA: the Ecological Division, responsible for overseeing the stations, was the largest and most important of SEMA's major divisions.[2] Administrators in the division had direct access to Nogueira-Neto. He charged it with a special sense of purpose and its administrators with confidence in his ability to make things come out right.[3] When a problem arose, a frequent response in the division's ranks was "Dr. Paulo is working on it," a phrase that conveyed at least optimism and normally absolute faith.

SEMA's centralized management, established in part because SEMA did not have the resources for a decentralized administration like the IBDF's, also seemed better suited to the 1980s.[4] SEMA's Ecological Division did much of what the DN did: it conducted station feasibility studies, oversaw research and management policy, and kept records,[5] but it also oversaw day-to-day field operations. This kept the lines of authority between headquarters and those in the field short and unambiguous. SEMA had no delegados beholden to the state governments or with questionable loyalty to conservation setting priorities or attenuating communications between headquarters and the field. Although SEMA had representatives in the capitals of about a third of the states and territories, they were expediters rather than administrators and had no independent say in station management. Communication between the stations and Brasília sometimes bypassed them.

SEMA's centralized arrangement allowed agency headquarters to prescribe day-to-day station operations in detail. An administrator in Brasília who was personally acquainted with each station had drawn up management programs for them prescribing patrolling routines, vehicle use, and even the number of hours a day a station's generator should run. The programs were translated into estimates of fuel and lubricant needed, wear on tires and engines, and even repair work necessary to keep equipment serviceable. These estimates then became the basis of a station's annual budget and allowed SEMA to spoon out its modest funds with a knowledge of exactly where each cruzado was going. Agency headquarters stayed in frequent radio contact with the stations, demanding news of any problems and giving instructions for day-to-day management.

SEMA also benefitted from Nogueira-Neto's continued leadership. He remained at the head of SEMA until late 1986, setting its policy and controlling all phases of its operation. His presence remained so commanding that the agency and its director often seemed indistinguishable; as Jorge Pádua put it, "Paulo was SEMA and vice versa." Whereas the IBDF's conservation program suffered from unimaginative leadership after Jorge Pádua's departure, SEMA under Nogueira-Neto showed much imagination in meeting the challenges of the 1980s.

Nogueira-Neto maintained SEMA's strong contacts with Brazilian development agencies and international sources of support, and aid from these sources allowed SEMA to establish management regimes at many of its stations. Facilities in the Acre River station were underwritten by the World Bank and the Inter-American Development Bank. SEMA's ecological station near the Jari Project received support from its managing consortium.[6] By the mid-1980s, several ecological stations in Amazonia had completed headquarters compounds and guard posts, and most had personnel assigned to them. At Maracá de Roraima, for example, a mix of external funding sources had allowed SEMA to build a large, fully electrified headquarters compound. It had two large houses for the station staff, accommodations for several dozen visitors, and two well-equipped laboratories.

The savvy of SEMA leadership in the 1980s was reflected in how it handled scientific research. The prominence SEMA had accorded research was a two-edged sword; it brought SEMA's conservation program into alignment with the development ideology pervasive within the federal government, but it also brought pressure to actually establish vigorous research programs. It became apparent in the 1980s that the Brazilian scientific establishment was neither large enough nor sufficiently well funded to make full use of SEMA's stations, however. This was especially the case in Amazonia, a place of difficult logistics and a long, expensive journey for most Brazilian scientists, who usually had tropical ecosystems much closer to home.

SEMA responded by aggressively promoting research in its stations. It made agreements with Brazilian universities: the latter would direct research to the ecological stations in return for SEMA's accommodation of their needs. Twelve such agreements were in effect by 1984. SEMA also made research funding agreements with a number of public entities, including the National Research Council (CNPq), the Federal Research Financing Agency, the Ministry of Education, and the Polonoroeste project. The regional development agencies, SUDAM in Amazonia and the Superintendency for Northeastern Development (SUDENE) in the Northeast, provided additional funds for station research. Funding SEMA's research allowed these agencies to farm out their own ecological responsibility. Together, these sources had provided over 120 grants for scientific work in the stations by 1985.[7] Sometimes the donors determined the nature of the research; in other cases, they let SEMA support projects it deemed worthy. Occasionally SEMA dipped into its own operating funds to support research in the stations.

SEMA also showed less regulatory zeal than the IBDF in dealing with scientists. SEMA in the 1980s had no general suspicion of scientists. To the contrary, it held that scientists were SEMA's best friends. Scientists did noble work and it ennobled them; they could be trusted to work unsupervised in the stations. SEMA's review process was similar to the IBDF's, but its application procedure was simpler. SEMA was also willing to negotiate on research design; if it deemed an initial proposal unacceptable, it tried to reach a compromise with the researcher.[8]

By dint of its agreements and hospitable attitudes, SEMA built solid research programs in many stations, especially in the South. By 1984, the Juréia ecological station in São Paulo State had been the site of thirty-six research projects, with most of the researchers affiliated with the University of São Paulo, Brazil's best university. The Taim station, on the coast of Rio Grande do Sul and accessible to the universities of the southern states, had been the site of thirty-two projects by the same year. INPA regularly used the Anavilhanas station; by 1984 it had seen fourteen projects.[9]

SEMA, faced with much the same strategic problem as the IBDF with regard to region-wide conservation measures, showed considerable skill in limiting its responsibility for them. SEMA administrators were generally aware of Salati's findings regarding secondary precipitation and understood their implications for Amazon nature, but they also knew what IBDF administrators knew: acting aggressively on those findings could lead into political quicksand. SEMA placed responsibility for general conservation on the IBDF, arguing that since the forest agency had overall responsibility for Brazil's forests, it was responsible for dealing with the implications of Salati's work.[10]

SEMA was not free to leave it at that, however. The forest code of 1965 had supplemented the older 50 percent clearing limit with prohibitions against cutting forests along the margins of water bodies, near springs, on mountaintops, and on steep slopes.[11] Logically, enforcement responsibility should have fallen to the IBDF when the agency was established in 1967, but its founding legislation was ambiguous on this point and the forest agency made no attempts at enforcement.[12] Then, in the same spate of legislation establishing the National Environmental Council (CONAMA), responsibility for these categories of protected lands, now called "ecological reserves," was assigned to SEMA. The assignment was viewed within the agency as a hot potato;[13] the prohibitions implied that every bridge constructed in Amazonia in the last 15 years was illegal, as were many of the new port facilities and, probably, most of the houses along the rivers of the region. SEMA did not wish to be identified with an absurd law, nor did it relish the possibility of being cornered into enforcing it someday; the prohibited categories included an enormous amount of land, so SEMA could be dragged into conflicts with development interests almost anywhere.

SEMA responded by first operationalizing the regulations. The regulations of 1967 did not precisely define mountaintops, steep slopes, river banks, or other categories of prohibited areas, so a 1985 CONAMA resolution provided clear definitions.[14] It differentiated between urban and rural areas and developed more flexible regulations for the former. SEMA also drew up a list of exemptions, which included clearing for the normal infrastructure of economic development (bridges, dams, roads) and for the structures of traditional Amazon life (caboclo housing, cattle pens, small docks, etc.). It then proposed cooperative agreements with the states, which left to the states the identification of legally protected areas within their borders, as well as law enforcement.[15] To encourage state cooperation, SEMA would allow the states to fine offenders and keep the proceeds; in effect, SEMA was offering them a lucrative operation, what a SEMA administrator called "an industry of fines," in return for their assuming the visible role in enforcing the law. SEMA would remain in the background, training state personnel in delineating ecological reserves and enforcing the law. By the mid-1980s, agreements had been signed with Roraima and Pará and were under negotiation with Rondônia and Acre, and SEMA was relieving itself of an awkward responsibility.

Finally, the progress of Amazon science in the 1980s added luster to SEMA's conservation program and to Nogueira-Neto's image as a prescient administrator. Island Biogeography Theory came under increasing attack.[16] It was argued that the relaxation rates calculated by Diamond, Terborgh, and their associates for newly isolated areas were much too high—the result, it was charged, of faulty procedures and insufficient data. Critics also argued that field tests had placed too much stress on birds and mammals in estimating species loss from isolated habitats, and that if proper attention had been give to smaller, less mobile life forms, a more stable view of the ecology of small, isolated places would have emerged.

A convincing pattern of Pleistocene forest fragments failed to emerge. The credibility of Prance's postulated forest islands was undercut when ten species of the Bugnoniaceae family, thought to be endemic to the Manaus area and used by Prance to argue for a Pleistocene fragment centered on Manaus, were collected elsewhere in the basin. Further work added to the confusion.[17] With continued failure to find convincing traces of the fragments, the view that the distributional shadows of the Pleistocene forest had been erased by time gained wider currency.[18]

Prance's phytogeography came to appear oversimplified at best. With more field work, earlier impressions of regional homogeneity gave way to a view of Amazonia as a mosaic of infinitely varied biological communities. While several scientists forwarded regional systems for Amazon flora, there was seldom agreement among them, and a new tentativeness replaced the convergence of opinion that had accompanied the publication of Prance's scheme.[19]

These developments had strong implications for Amazon conservation. If the critics of Island Biogeography Theory were correct, smaller areas might not lose their species—or their conservation value—as rapidly as previously suspected; Boecklen and Gotelli wrote that the species-area relationship was at best a "weak conservation principle."[20] For Pleistocene Refuge Theory to be a useful guide to conservation, being merely correct was not enough; if time had erased the impress of the Pleistocene from the distribution of Amazon biota, the sites of Pleistocene forest fragments were not likely to be biologically richer than other areas. If Prance's phytogeographic regions did not reflect the reality of plant distribution, protected natural areas representing these regions were no more likely to preserve a balanced sampling of Amazon biota than areas selected on the basis of other criteria. In fact, there was a general disillusionment with grand theory as a practical guide to conservation. Mares, assessing the state of biological conservation in South America in the mid-1980s, concluded that "theory offers no panacea or any alternative to...field biology."[21] Jorge Pádua and Wetterberg had known these theories might be tarnished in time, and their pragmatism in the actual selection of parks and reserves was intended to protect their program against that eventuality. Yet for strategic ends they had so identified their program with the theories that the accumulating doubt reflected poorly on the IBDF.

Erosion of confidence in the IBDF's value referents worked to SEMA's advantage in two ways. First, SEMA's approach now appeared perspicacious rather than merely opportunistic. It had the flexibility to deal with the complexity of Amazon biology that new knowledge was revealing. Second, the theories on which the IBDF had relied implied that the forest institute was performing the important conservation task—protecting the big representative areas—while SEMA was gathering the leavings, the smaller, atypical areas that, while perhaps deserving of public protection, could wait for the time being.[22] Now it was becoming clear that geographical gradients and patchy, localized distributions, especially of fauna, were very common, and therefore a few very large protected areas would protect a smaller percentage of Amazon biota than had been previously thought. If the endangered species, unique floral assemblages, and sites of exceptional biological richness discovered over the last decade were to be protected, many smaller areas aimed at very specific conservation tasks had to be created.[23] Thus, SEMA's program now appeared to be less a minor complement to the IBDF's and more a highly credible alternative.

Fortuitous circumstances and skillful leadership allowed SEMA to maintain the momentum of system expansion well into the 1980s: normally it added several stations a year during the first half of the decade, and by 1986 it had established twenty-four throughout Brazil, with eleven in Amazonia (figure 8.1). The future looked even more promising: another ten stations were slated for establishment, seven more areas were under study, and an additional five areas were being held by other government agencies for eventual transfer to SEMA.[24]

* * *

Nevertheless, like the IBDF, SEMA in the 1980s was acting on a set made ever starker by Brazil's fiscal crisis and the political uncertainty that accompanied the onset of redemocratization. To be sure, SEMA was preadapted to the 1980s and showed much skill in meeting the challenges of the decade, but beyond a certain point, this was no longer sufficient to counter hostile basic trends. Nogueira-Neto managed to blunt numerous threats to his agency and even make progress in some areas, but in the long run, he could not prevent the general deterioration of his agency's ability to carry out a credible program.

Scarce resources turned past successes into problems for SEMA, as they had for the IBDF. Nogueira-Neto's success in bringing so many areas under SEMA's protection created a formidable management

FIGURE 8.1
SEMA's Ecological Stations

task. The agency had never operated with ample funding, but the situation had worsened considerably by the mid-1980s. Serious budget shortfalls in station operations became the norm, and capital budgets were increasingly constricted.[25] In SEMA's early days, money had been available through the agency's budget or special appropriations to purchase land, but by the mid-1980s, the government's fiscal crisis made that impossible, with rare and minor exceptions. General appropriations for station infrastructure had also shrunk greatly, leaving many stations with inadequate, partly completed facilities. None of the stations in Amazonia had full staffs or fully implemented management plans in the late 1980s.[26] Initial surveys (to identify research opportunities and decide which areas could be sacrificed for science) had been conducted in most of the stations, but

TABLE 8.1
SEMA Ecological Stations in Amazonia, 1986

Station	State or Territory	Size in Hectares	Staff Size	Status	Special Funding Source
Jari	Pará	227,000	2	Operational	Jari Project
Maracá-Jipioca	Amapá	72,000	3	Operational	
Cuniã	Rondônia	100,000	5	Operational	Polonoroeste
Rio Acre	Acre	77,500	0	Implementation phase	World Bank
Cara Cara[1]	Roraima	386,000	0	Implementation phase	
Niquiá[1]	Roraima	288,000	0	Implementation phase	
Anavilhanas	Amazonas	350,000	3	Operational	
Maracá	Roraima	101,000	2	Operational	
Jutai-Solimões	Amazonas	288,000	0	Land held in reserve	WWF-US
Juami-Japurá	Amazonas	572,000	0	Implementation phase	WWF-US
Mamiraua	Amazonas	200,000	0	Under study	WWF-US
Carajás[2]	Pará	26,000	0	Under study	CVRD
Median Size		214,000			

[1] Cara Cara and Niquiá to be jointly administered
[2] To be staffed by CVRD
Source: SEMA records and interviews.

detailed resource surveys had not been completed in any of them (table 8.1).

The constricting of finances took its toll on SEMA's staff, in spite of generally high morale at headquarters. Real income for SEMA personnel declined seriously in the 1980s, as it did for most public employees.[27] Staff members sought better-paying jobs in more favored areas of government service or in the private sector. Low pay and hiring freezes made it difficult to replace those who left, let alone replace them with persons of equal ability. Almost the entire technical and professional cadre at headquarters had turned over between the early and mid-1980s, deeply depleting the agency's pool of skills and experience. Turnover rates in the field, where poor pay was often compounded by isolation, danger, and poor living conditions, were higher, and replacement with competent personnel was more difficult. The administrator in charge of station operations estimated that by the mid-1980s, 75 percent of management problems at the stations were due to depleted staffs or the lack of experience and competence among those who remained.

Nogueira-Neto was forced back on other public agencies and his international connections to compensate for the darkening financial picture, but the potential of these sources was limited, especially in covering routine station management. INCRA and the state governments were willing to turn unneeded tracts over to SEMA, since it relieved them of an unwanted responsibility, but they seldom took an interest in the management of these areas, especially once conservation lost its high priority. International conservation groups were also reluctant to involve themselves in management.[28] Assistance with land purchases or the construction of station infrastructure were discrete, sometimes even dramatic steps, but supporting the management tasks of a foreign government agency was mundane, possibly corrupting, and not likely to produce clear returns.

The research support Nogueira-Neto had cobbled together out of commitments from various Brazilian institutions also came undone. These institutions, caught in their own budget squeezes, protected their core operations by eliminating funding for peripheral activities—like supporting SEMA's research program. By mid-1986, SEMA had accumulated a backlog of twenty-two projects that it had promised to support, but for which it had not received funds.

The bleak funding picture of the mid-1980s forced Nogueira-Neto to pursue any new leads for support. In one case, an American scholar asked the National Geographic Society in Washington, D.C., to fund a study of conservation policy-making in Brazil, and the society sent the proposal to Nogueira-Neto for evaluation. The scholar had previously received Nogueira-Neto's assurances of cooperation, but when the proposal arrived from the society, Nogueira-Neto belittled it and closed his response by suggesting that if the society was really interested in Brazilian conservation, it should fund his agency's own projects instead of such research.[29]

Nogueira-Neto also developed a plan to reconstitute much of SEMA as a private foundation.[30] This would put him in a better position to seek funds from foreign conservation foundations reluctant to directly fund government operations, and it would release the agency from the government's hiring and spending restrictions. Privatization would likely lessen the government's sense of obligation to the agency, but by now the benefits derived from that sense were so modest that risking their loss seemed worthwhile.

While SEMA continued to add natural areas to its system in the 1980s, it was unable to take full advantage of the credibility scientific advances conferred on its preferred approach to area selection—i.e., one based on the unique biological characteristics of an area. Instead, financial and administrative considerations intruded ever more forcefully into SEMA's calculus. Thus SEMA, in spite of the fact that it, unlike the DN, retained final authority over selection decisions, also lost the capacity to keep a high level of biological integrity in the process.

SEMA's reluctance to accept areas that did not come with a patron grew, even though it meant that areas of biological value might be permanently lost. For example, the state of Goiás was willing to give SEMA the 37,000 hectare Coco-Javaes tract. SEMA thought the area should be protected, but it was on the agricultural frontier of northern Goiás, and although Coco-Javaes itself did not contain much arable land,[31] the possibility of encroachment loomed larger every year. SEMA felt protecting it would cost more than it could afford, and until outside assistance could be found, it preferred to leave it in state hands, even if it meant risking losing it altogether.[32]

Such reluctance made SEMA's choices increasingly hobsonian; it was limited to those few areas where outside agencies were willing to turn over land and support management regimes. SEMA's involvement in area evaluation or even management planning was a luxury it was willing to forego. By 1986, Nogueira-Neto could write with candor that "sometimes we protect an area simply because it is available."[33]

The establishment of the Carajás Ecological Station illustrates the degree to which SEMA had lost de facto control of the expansion of its own protected-area system. The Rio Doce Valley Company (CVRD), the government-controlled corporation developing the Carajás iron mining complex, decided to set aside some nature reserves[34] and asked the Goeldi Museum in Belém to identify appropriate areas. The museum's scientists came up with three tracts, and after determining that their preservation would not reduce iron production or increase costs, the CVRD offered them to SEMA as an ecological station. The CVRD would develop the management plans, build the facilities, and pay for the guards. SEMA, which could not afford to send its own personnel to assess the areas, accepted; it was in such straits that it was willing to accept an area sight unseen, selected and managed for it by another agency, if it did not have to foot the bill.

The desire to keep up the momentum of system expansion, coupled with now-limited choices, sometimes turned SEMA's selection criteria into post hoc rationales for taking what was offered.[35] In one instance, an electrical power authority in Minas Gerais offered the IBDF an island that had formed when a dam was built, flooding the land behind it. The island had been severely degraded by years of overgrazing, so the forest institute declined, saying, in effect, that there was nothing left on the island to preserve. The authority offered the island to SEMA, which accepted, arguing that it could be used to work out restoration programs for similarly degraded areas.[36]

SEMA's constricted options now also led it into the same kind of chancy dependence on the future that Jorge Pádua, in her optimism, had imparted to the IBDF's conservation program. The Polonoroeste program was willing to support an ecological station in Rondônia, and INCRA was willing to turn over the Cuniã area in the northwest corner of the state to SEMA.[37] The area had considerable biological value: while not particularly diverse in species, the presence of inundated lands made it rich in wildlife.[38] Furthermore, the Cuniã River, which ran through the station, was the spawning grounds for fish that later found their way into the Madeira River, so protecting the area would contribute to the regional economy.

The tract INCRA offered SEMA was seriously flawed from a management perspective, however. It was only 60 kilometers from Porto Velho, Rondônia's rapidly growing capital (figure 8.2). Its boundaries and immediate regional setting were far from ideal: the Madeira River was the logical southeastern boundary of the station, but since most of the riverbank was already occupied, it was excluded from the station; to the northwest, INCRA planned to settle colonists along highway BR 319, so the station would begin four kilometers in from the highway. Forty or so caboclo families lived on a lake in the interior of the tract. They had been there at least twenty-five years, so there was no question about their squatters' rights. Some willingly moved to nearby agricultural colonies, but others refused to leave, and INCRA declined to remove them.

SEMA accepted the area, nevertheless, and would manage it as best it could with Polonoroeste support. It constructed a guard post at the mouth of the Cuniã River and planned another at the southern tip of the station on the bank of the Madeira River. A third guard post would be built along the northwestern boundary once settlement began along BR 319, and eventually a swath around the station's entire perimeter would be cleared and patrolled. The agency planned a post in the interior, close to the caboclo settlements.[39] The caboclos would be prevented from using any resources except those

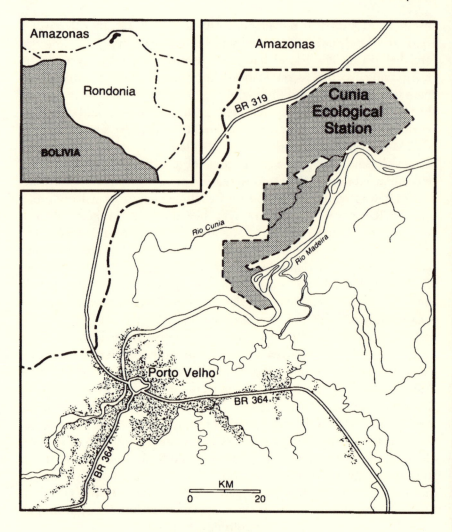

FIGURE 8.2
Cuniã Ecological Station

of the small tracts they were entitled to occupy.[40] This, SEMA hoped, would force the caboclos to leave the station.

Thanks to Polonoroeste funding, there were five guards at the station by 1986, and SEMA expected authorization to hire at least five more. But those in Brasília who developed the management plan for Cuniã knew that even a large guard complement could not defend the station. Settlement along the Madeira River and BR 319 would give it too many neighbors along too much of its perimeter. SEMA planned to educate the station's neighbors about the benefits protected nature conferred on them and to appeal to their sense of responsibility, but SEMA administrators knew how thin such defenses were; Amazon history showed that whenever there were large numbers of people close to the forest, the forest suffered.[41]

* * *

While SEMA's greater initial caution and centralized administration worked to its advantage in the 1980s in managing its natural areas, factors arose to overwhelm these advantages. First, unseen problems emerged at the stations despite all caution. For example, as hard as Nogueira-Neto tried to avoid Indians, ones bellicose enough to paralyze management appeared in the Íque station in Mato Grosso.[42] Second, the failure of Brazilian conservationists to make the overall landscape of Amazonia more hospitable to conservation meant the defense of nature had to begin at the boundaries of SEMA's protected areas, as it did at the IBDF's. Finally, SEMA could seldom place more than a token staff in its stations or give them more than token operating budgets; it was never free to staff the stations according to the level of threat they faced. SEMA's frequent dependence on the largess of other agencies meant it was not always in control of station protection.

Thus the ecological stations were, like the IBDF's protected areas, outsized for the resources available for their defense, which made them passive entities whose fortunes could be modified only slightly by their managers. SEMA might be able to capitalize on extrinsic circumstances, if positive, or blunt them, if negative, but it had little real control over them. The Maracá de Roraima and Anavilhanas stations illustrate many of the challenges SEMA faced in an era of extreme resource scarcity, as well as the extremes of the agency's success and failure in meeting them.

Fortunate circumstances, capitalized on by skillful management, made the Maracá station in northern Roraima one of the more secure natural areas in Amazonia. It was a compact fluvial island (figure 8.3). The journey from Boa Vista, the territorial capital and the station's support base, was not a long one: 150 kilometers by road, which could be covered in two and a half hours during the dry

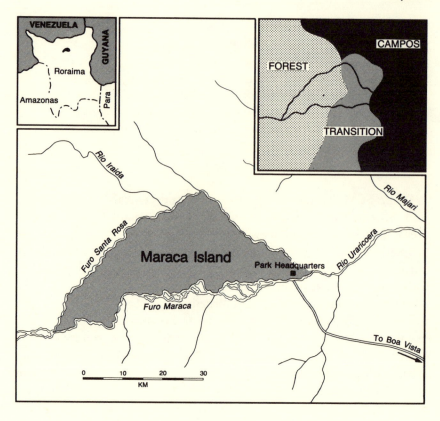

FIGURE 8.3
Maracá de Roraima Ecological Station

season, and perhaps twice that during the rains. External threats were minor. To the east of the station were prairies dotted with clumps of shrubby vegetation and crossed by files of palm trees along the watercourses.[43] Large, not very prosperous ranches and small Indian villages gave the prairies only a thin patina of habitation. To the west, where the rainfall was heavier, forest stretched for hundreds of kilometers, and although occupied by Indians and penetrated by gold miners, it was little known or disturbed. Miners traveling upriver in small boats camped and hunted on the island but since the gold fields were further west, they were more of a nuisance than a threat.

The station had a staff of only two, a manager and a guard, but both were dedicated. The manager had been on the job since the late 1970s and had a reputation as one of SEMA's best field men.[44] He knew how to deal with the territorial government. He had learned how to deal with his own agency; he could present his needs so as to get the response he wanted. The manager spent most of his time in Boa Vista, convenient for making purchases, seeing to the repair of equipment, and dealing with the territorial government. He had made many informal credit arrangements in Boa Vista, which enabled him to make a necessary purchase or repair a vital piece of equipment during the financial droughts. He stayed in daily radio contact with the station and made regular trips to it to assess its condition and bring supplies, spare parts, and repaired equipment. The station was accessible enough to permit weekly visits during the dry season, although during the rains he made the trip less frequently.

Day-to-day responsibility for the station fell to the guard, who lived at headquarters with his family. Like the manager, the guard had been on the job a long time by SEMA standards: six years—long enough to learn what the job entailed. Yet he could not patrol more than a small fraction of the reserve. The station had a perimeter of approximately 200 kilometers, and while the watercourses surrounding the station made for distinct boundaries, they were full of rapids, so patrolling their full length would have been impossible for one man. There were no trails or roads beyond the eastern tip of the island, so overland travel in the station was equally difficult. Routine patrolling was limited to the waterways surrounding the eastern tip.[45]

The manager compensated for the limited patrolling through carefully cultivated relationships with the neighboring ranchers. They had become proud of the station and protective of it, preventing trespass from their lands and reporting suspicious events to the guard. On the other hand the ranchers knew the hunting was good in the station, so they turned a blind eye to forays into it by their own men. The manager did not make an issue of it; he thought the forays a small price for the services these neighbors rendered.

While the combination of fortunate circumstance and skillful management made Maracá one of the more physically secure natural areas in Amazonia, it had been dangerously exposed politically. The island had much to offer as a research site. It was biologically varied: the eastern end was a mix of forest, prairie, and wet grasslands, while to the west the forest became denser and the clearings smaller and less frequent. The island had never been heavily occupied (at the time of the station's establishment there had been four small farms near the eastern tip), and its fauna reflected the lack of past depredation: pumas, giant otters, several species of monkeys, and the whole range of smaller rainforest species had been sighted.[46] The research facilities at the headquarters were impressive and well maintained.

Yet the research facilities had been used at less than 5 percent of capacity during the mid-1980s.[47] Occasionally a scientist from the south or from abroad would briefly visit the station, and groups of college students sometimes used it for field training, but only one researcher, an INPA scientist based in Boa Vista, was using it regularly. The facilities had an air of abandonment. The laboratories lacked the feel of places used by scientists on a sustained basis. It was a testimony to the inability of the ecological stations to deliver what had been promised for them—substantial contributions to the scientific base of national development.

The problem was suddenly and spectacularly solved when the Royal Geographical Society of Great Britain announced what its press release called an "expedition to help save the Amazon rainforest." The endeavor, officially called the Maracá Rainforest Project, brought forty British and Brazilian scientists to the Maracá station over a twelve-month period beginning in late 1986. The scientists used the station as a base for research on rainforest regeneration, soil formation and erosion, and entomology. They also reached far afield to study settlement around Maracá.[48] The expedition-like format and the surfeit of publicity surrounding the project gave it an aura of naïveté and earned it some suspicion among scientists already working in Amazonia, but it was a boon to Maracá. It brought international attention to the station and produced a body of scientific work that increased the station's appeal to future researchers.

Maracá's success, no matter how impressive, was based on anomalous and nonreplicable circumstances. First its physical characteristics were exceptionally favorable for protection. Second, the station had kept its small but dedicated staff because it offered advantages that were seldom the lot of nature protection personnel in Amazonia. The manager could live in a city that he found pleasant. He also enjoyed the frequent excursions to the station, whose natural beauty he appreciated. The manager got along well with the guard, whom he considered as much a friend as a subordinate; during his visits to the station, the two men took the patrol boat out for a few hours of fishing. He also derived great satisfaction from his job, and from the high regard in which he was held in Brasília.

Maracá allowed the guard and his family a life they valued. Their house was comfortable, and the site healthy. They appreciated the tranquility of the station and the bounty of the site; mango and guava trees remained from the old farm where the headquarters now stood. While the job meant isolation and no opportunity for the daughter to attend school, the family considered these drawbacks a small price for the advantages of the site. Since the station was close to Boa Vista, the guard and his family could break the isolation with monthly shopping trips to the city.

The degree to which the manager and the guard's circumstances were unusually favorable was illustrated by the fate of the second guard, who, until early 1986, had lived with his family in a cabin along the Santa Rosa branch several miles from the headquarters. His living conditions were more typical for guards in Amazonia; the cabin was small, without electricity, and insecure, and he and his family were not happy there. After the cabin was vandalized, probably by miners traveling along the Santa Rosa, the guard asked to move into the unoccupied house at headquarters, which would give the family electricity, security, and the company of another family. When the manager told him he was not needed at headquarters, he quit rather than return to the former site.

Finally, the royal expedition, which made the station a focus of Amazon research, had a deus ex machina quality to it. It was a unique event that Nogueira-Neto had confected through his international connections. It did not change the fact that, taken together, SEMA's ecological stations were an outsized research facility; neither the Brazilian nor the international research network was large enough to make good use of it and thereby give substance to one of Nogueira-Neto's strongest rationales for the system.

***

No anomalous combination of fortune and management skill came between the Anavilhanas station and the reality of Amazonia in the 1980s. SEMA invested heavily in the station, as befitted the agency's high regard for the Anavilhanas Islands and its ambitions for them. It built an elaborate headquarters near the middle of the archipelago (see figure 4.3, p. 125). It also built three floating guard posts and transported them to a site near the headquarters for eventual deployment to strategic locations.[49] An agency representative was hired and established in an office on INPA's campus in Manaus.

Guards were hired. Three small boats were purchased to patrol the islands as were two larger ones to ply between Manaus and the station, transporting supplies and personnel and enabling the representative to make supervisory trips to the station.

The station was more difficult to manage than SEMA had envisioned.[50] It was not easy to patrol: the river flowing through the archipelago was a major tributary of the Amazon, and most of the region's commerce flowed along it; professional fisherman used it; settlers who lived along the river hunted and fished in the archipelago, and the dry-land part of the station was inaccessible and lacked distinct boundaries in several places. The agency was hesitant to disperse the floating guard posts. The life of the guards and their families was difficult enough while the posts they occupied were together near headquarters; they made minimum wages, their housing was cramped and damp, and they subsisted largely on manioc and fish, but at least they had each other for company and, being near Novo Airão, their children could attend school. They feared that their dispersal to remote sites in the islands would leave them and their families isolated and surrounded by caboclos hostile to them and the reserve. Rather than risk losing the guards, SEMA left the posts where they were.

Proximity to Manaus was of little benefit because access to the station was exclusively by river; moving bulk supplies, heavy equipment, and scientific parties was more complicated by boat than by truck. The crew had to be assembled, and arrangements had to be made to get cargos and scientists to the docks. SEMA depended on INPA's river pilots, so trips to the station had to be planned around the pilots' availability.

Moreover, SEMA's big boats proved difficult to repair and expensive to run; they consumed ten times as much fuel per mile as SEMA's light trucks.[51] The latter drawbacks became increasingly serious concerns as SEMA's financial problems grew.

SEMA could not meet the management challenges presented by Anavilhanas. It devised a fall-back patrolling routine that consisted of three infrequent patrols: one northward from headquarters along the Apuaú River, the station's northeastern boundary; another down the Negro River through the lower islands, and a third up the Negro River, following one of the main channels on the outward leg and the other on the return.[52] Although administrators in Brasília would have liked more frequent patrolling, they were unwilling to spend more on fuel or risk more repair bills. They consoled themselves with the argument that the infrequent patrols would at least "show the flag" and remind people that the islands and the surrounding waters were officially protected.

The SEMA representative in Manaus could not maintain even this limited patrolling routine. Brasília's fuel consumption estimates were too low, but agency headquarters was reluctant to acknowledge that a problem existed. This placed him in a dilemma: maintain the patrolling routine and over-spend his fuel allocation or reduce patrolling and stay within budget.

He thought headquarters' interest in showing the flag demonstrated an ignorance of local circumstances. Infrequent patrolling, he reasoned, was more likely to cause contempt than respect for the station. He felt the caboclos who lived along the western bank of the Negro River would not change old habits without a heavy management presence.[53] The motors of SEMA boats on their infrequent patrols could be heard across the water for miles, long before visual contact was made, giving trespassers in small boats time to duck into a convenient inlet or, during high water, to simply slip into the flooded forest. He also felt that commercial fishing was undeterred by SEMA's slight presence; on one trip, the SEMA supply boat encountered more than a dozen illegal fishing nets in the waters of the station. On the other hand, he knew how greatly SEMA valued staying in budget, so he reduced the range of the patrols; only the central area of the station saw a patrol boat with any frequency. The northern islands, as well as the terrestrial part of the station, were left beyond the range of routine patrolling.

The representative could no longer carry out other important parts of his job by 1986: maintaining contact with the station, making sure it received necessary supplies, and personally supervising its operations. The radios were broken and there was no money to fix them. SEMA's two large boats were out of action; one had been written off, and the other was undergoing engine repairs with no completion date in sight. The representative was supposed to make two trips a month to the station, but April 1986 was the third month in a row he had not been able to get there. Equipment, supplies, and spare parts for the station had accumulated in his office in Manaus, and with the radio out of order, he had little idea of what was happening in the islands; he had to rely on hearsay and messages brought by third parties. Much of the representative's time was spent trying to hurry along the engine repairs and, failing that, trying with little success to borrow a boat, pilot, and crew from INPA. For all intents and purposes, station management had ground to a halt.

So had the scientific programs. The need to move everything by water made working there expensive and inconvenient under the best of circumstances, but when SEMA's boats started to fail, the problems associated with research became daunting. One scientist had to rely on regular river transport to get to the town of Novo Airão. Once there, she would flash a prearranged light signal across the river and hope one of the guards in the station would see it and come for her in a patrol boat. Discouraged, she eventually discontinued her research.[54] By 1986 there was no active research there whatsoever.

Logistical problems turned what had been one of Anavilhanas's strongest points in SEMA's eyes—its location near a major center of Amazon research—into a disadvantage. Had no other sites been available, scientists might have put up with the obstacles to working there, but the WWF's Minimum Critical Size project and INPA's Ducke Forest were both a short distance from Manaus and easily accessible by road. Both areas were in part undisturbed, and a formidable body of scientific knowledge about them had accumulated by the mid-1980s. Therefore, unless a scientist needed to work in the várzea forest found on the Anavilhanas Islands, either alternative research site was more attractive.[55]

The breakdown of station management and research led to mutual recrimination. Brasília placed most of the blame on SEMA's representative in Manaus; his inability to keep the boats running or maintain the patrolling routine were cited as proof he was not up to the job, which SEMA considered rather simple. According to administrators in Brasília, "He couldn't do the job, and all he had to do was follow our plan."[56] For his part, the SEMA representative complained that administrators in Brasília were insensitive to the problems he faced; they saddled him with an unworkable management plan and an inadequate budget. He saw the underestimation of fuel consumption rates, which he thought typical of Brasília, as leading to unrealistic expectations of field personnel such as himself. Although it was not clear where the balance of the blame lay, the question was ultimately moot; the scarcity of management resources, when coupled with the geography of the station, gave competence little to work with.

* * *

SEMA's troubles in the field were minor compared to those it faced in Brasília, however—especially those stemming from its early decision to concentrate on biological conservation. The decision seemed reasonable (perhaps "shrewd" is more accurate) when it was made. SEMA was not a powerful agency at its founding. With only modest financial and administrative resources, and located within a ministry indifferent to its welfare, SEMA had to move cautiously in finding a niche in Brazilian public life.[57] The protection of natural areas in the face of other pressing environmental tasks was viewed by many environmentalists as a soft option, but Nogueira-Neto saw the soft option as his best, and perhaps only choice.[58]

Emphasis on biological conservation gave SEMA leeway to act without offending powerful interests; the nation was vast, and enough of it was lightly settled that, with care, natural areas could be selected to avoid conflict with those who could harm the agency. By helping development agencies discharge their environmental responsibilities in a convenient, inexpensive fashion—i.e., by setting aside areas for which they had little use—Nogueira-Neto could gain them as a constituency. The destruction of Brazilian life-forms was viewed by foreigners as a matter of serious global consequence, and international aid for nature preservation was already flowing into South America. By focusing on biological conservation, SEMA could gain foreign support.

The decision's most obvious drawback was that it involved the invasion of another agency's turf, and despite Nogueira-Neto's efforts to put functional distance between his program and the IBDF's, many in the forest agency saw SEMA's program as an usurpation of their responsibilities and a needless duplication of effort. Wetterberg criticized SEMA's involvement in biological conservation in his 1975 and 1976 reports and recommended that SEMA direct full its attention to pollution.[59]

Nogueira-Neto argued that as long as nature was being protected, it did not matter who was doing it. He also argued that SEMA's decision advanced the IBDF's goals: having two agencies involved increased the total resources available.[60] These arguments were lost on many in the IBDF, as they were on Wetterberg, but the turf problem seemed manageable. Relations between the two agencies were cordial during Jorge Pádua's tenure because she and Nogueira-Neto were friends. She turned to him, the more experienced scientist, for advice on scientific matters.[61] She gave Nogueira-Neto a seat on the IBDF's Parks Advisory Board and encouraged SEMA's participation in the IBDF's area evaluation expeditions. Moreover, there seemed to be enough conservation resources to go around in the 1970s, and with each agency in control of its own conservation program, they could steer them out of each other's way. While the friendship between Nogueira-Neto and Jorge Pádua and the potential complementarity of the two programs did not lead to ongoing technical cooperation or policy coordination, it did prevent the inherent competition Nogueira-Neto's decision had created from souring interagency relations.

The real benefits of SEMA's decision, however, stemmed from deemphasizing pollution. The legislation establishing SEMA made it clear that its primary goal was bringing Brazil's pollution under control, especially water pollution. This made sense; the need for such control in Brazil was pressing.[62] Industrial districts like Cubatão, the petrochemical complex near São Paulo, were among the most polluted urban areas in the world. Unregulated use of pesticides and herbicides had become a serious threat to rural populations. But after some early rhetoric about tough environmental standards, SEMA quietly moved away from the pollution issue and left others, primarily state governments, to deal with it as best they could.[63] SEMA, during the early and mid-1980s, continued to involve itself only incidentally with pollution. It offered advice and technical support to state environmental agencies, but it avoided taking salient positions on the environmental disruption caused by major development projects, arguing that it could most effectively work quietly behind the scenes to mitigate the damage of such projects.[64]

Unlike protecting nature, fighting pollution had serious strategic disadvantages. It would have earned SEMA the enmity of those who viewed pollution abatement as an irksome and expensive task—i.e., Brazil's politically privileged industrialists and powerful state planners, who saw unfettered industrialism as the main avenue to a developed Brazil. The forest agency, even if incensed, was a less formidable foe than these groups.

Fighting pollution offered few advantages in way of compensation. International condemnation of Brazil's attitudes toward pollution did not translate into material support for anti-pollution measures because, except perhaps for the bad example Brazil might set for other developing nations, its failure to mitigate pollution was seen as hurting only itself.[65] Furthermore, those most affected carried little weight in the political equations of the military regime. The workers of the southern cities were most exposed to industrial pollution, but their votes had been emptied by the suspension of democracy and the repression of their unions. Farm workers were increasingly exposed to toxic chemicals, but their organizations had been destroyed with the coup of 1964. Pollution was an issue for the urban middle class, but the suspension of representative government and the shunting aside of its civic organizations meant that it, too, was politically disenfranchised. Thus, while controlling pollution would have been a service appreciated by many segments of Brazilian society, it would not have given the agency much of a political return.

Moreover, emphasizing biological protection over pollution control could be placed in a favorable rhetorical light. Nogueira-Neto framed SEMA's choice thus: "Tight budgets did force an early decision on SEMA: should it spend all available money protecting the lives of people badly affected by heavy pollution, or should it instead expend its funds primarily on genetic banks for the benefit of untold future generations?"[66] So framed, the decision fit into the rhetoric of sacrifice that the Brazilian military had adopted to justify the costs of its modernization programs. It also played to a major theme of national self-criticism: Brazilians' view of themselves as a nation more interested in quick rewards than long-term benefits, a trait they called "immediatismo" and that they saw as the root cause of many of Brazil's problems. By choosing to provide for the future rather than the present, SEMA appeared to be striking a blow against a major national flaw. Nogueira-Neto's image as a scientist-administrator rather than a politician helped him carry off the argument.

While the decision to deemphasize pollution was shrewd and perhaps necessary for SEMA's survival (it was certainly a precondition for the agency's extensive conservation program), the political equation beneath it was not robust; rather, it depended on several impermanent conditions: Jorge Pádua's ability to dampen the IBDF's structural antagonism toward SEMA, SEMA's ability to clearly complement the IBDF's conservation program, and a political environment that allowed SEMA to deemphasize pollution control with little political cost. During the 1980s these conditions evaporated, and the decision came back to haunt SEMA like an avenging ghost.

Once Jorge Pádua left the IBDF, the major counter to the structural antagonism between the two agencies was removed. Once the two became dependent on the happenstance of external funding and political impetus for the progress of their conservation programs, they could no longer maintain the distinctions that had separated them; their programs converged on the diminishing core of opportunity that remained to conservation. The two agencies responded by attempting to ignore each other: it was hard to find mention of the IBDF in SEMA's reports and vice versa, even when those reports claimed to summarize the state of nature preservation in Brazil.[67] SEMA discouraged routine contacts with the forest agency, and by the mid-1980s the patterns of avoidance had become deep behavioral ruts, even though the headquarters of SEMA and the IBDF were only a few kilometers away from each other in Brasília.[68]

Absence of contact allowed mutual ignorance and contempt to become rooted in the cultures of the two agencies. An experienced SEMA administrator closely involved with the ecological stations thought that recreation and tourism were the sole objects of the IBDF's protected areas. He did not know that the IBDF managed biological reserves, much less that the IBDF stressed preservation as the system's primary goal.[69] SEMA officials held that the IBDF's reliance on unproved theory was foolhardy: it had led to reserves that were too large and too poorly located to be defended. SEMA pointed with pride to its success in avoiding entanglements with Indians and took pains to compare that success with the IBDF's failure.[70]

For their part, IBDF administrators viewed SEMA's system as the product of opportunism unconstrained by standards of biological worth. An IBDF administrator held up the Carajás station as an example: "Imagine! Establishing a reserve on top of an iron mine just because someone offered you the land."[71] He added that the CVRD had offered the IBDF a similar deal, but his agency had the integrity to turn it down. IBDF personnel held that SEMA lacked scruples when it came to scientific research. Unlike the IBDF, whose standards they viewed as demanding but correct, they argued that SEMA would allow anything to take place in its stations if it could be called science. They were especially contemptuous of SEMA's policy of allowing its stations to be degraded if research called for it. One said, "As if enough destruction isn't going on in Amazonia, SEMA has to encourage even more in the areas it's supposed to be protecting!"[72]

By the mid-1980s, its competition with the IBDF had cost SEMA an ally whose aid could have made the difference between success and failure in many of its endeavors in Amazonia. Asking the IBDF delegado in Manaus for help was a seemingly obvious solution to SEMA's logistics problem at Anavilhanas. With a staff of 110 in the state, the IBDF could keep its river boats in order, and one of them made routine trips upriver to Jaú National Park, passing through the Anavilhanas archipelago on the way. The SEMA representative did not ask for assistance; doing so would violate agency policy, he explained.[73] The IBDF delegado knew of SEMA's problems with Anavilhanas but did not offer assistance. One his assistants explained that while there was no overt animosity between the two agencies in the state, it was wise to respect the long tradition of non-interaction.[74]

The rivalry and mutual distrust were too deep to allow the agencies to turn to each other for support in developing more expansive conservation programs. SEMA personnel held that the IBDF had no real interest in the overall state of the forest, only in its short-term commercial exploitation. For their part, IBDF administrators viewed SEMA as an unreliable partner in any forest-wide initiative because they saw SEMA's interest in biological conservation as disingenuous, an incidental product of its reluctance to assume its real mission, controlling pollution.

The reverse side of SEMA's decision, deemphasizing pollution, had even more serious consequences in the 1980s. Perhaps Nogueira-Neto originally intended for SEMA to take a leading role in pollution control once it became a secure agency, but the 1980s brought poverty and restricted options, not security. His international supporters were patient with his reluctance to take on pollution aggressively, which they attributed to his political acumen and preference for pursuing his goals quietly. If anything, his reluctance added to their respect for him, and since they were interested in biological conservation themselves, they were not inclined to prod him into actions that might endanger his efforts in this area.

Many Brazilian environmentalists were less understanding. Those from the badly polluted urban areas of the South were seldom moved by Nogueira-Neto's arguments about protecting genetic resources for future generations, or by his argument that responsibility for pollution control should be left to the states and those industries that had caused it. To them, SEMA was ducking its proper task and abandoning those most in need of its protection. They held that SEMA's decision to downplay its own pollution responsibility left the states with all the political problems attending the issue but without the benefit of federal leadership. According to an American environmentalist with extensive South American contacts, environmental groups in São Paulo felt that "SEMA simply wasn't a presence there. It never went after the tough issues. São Paulo was on its own when it came to pollution."[75] As government tolerance of industrial pollution and the massive, botched use of defoliants during the construction of the

Tucuruí Dam in Amazonia emerged as major environmental scandals, SEMA came under fire for not taking early, vigorous action.

Similar criticisms of SEMA had been voiced in the 1970s, but as questions of public welfare became more prominent with redemocratization, pollution became a popular issue in Brazil's big cities, and criticism of SEMA's policies grew louder.[76] SEMA's protected natural areas seemed very remote to the newly enfranchised voters of the noisy and dirty cities of the South and to the politicians who had to listen to voters for the first time in a generation. The balance of political opportunity thus shifted toward pollution issues.

A new Ministry of Urban Development and the Environment was created in 1985 to make the federal bureaucracy more sensitive to the demands that the return to democracy were placing on it. SEMA was transferred from the Ministry of the Interior, where it had enjoyed much autonomy, to this new ministry, of which it was a more integral part. The new ministry's orientation was urban, with responsibility for urban housing, urban infrastructure such as water and sewer systems, and urban services such as garbage removal and public transportation. SEMA found itself in a ministerial portfolio into which pollution abatement easily fit but biological conservation did not.

SEMA increased its pollution-related activities in an effort to adjust to its new circumstances; a SEMA administrator estimated that by 1986, approximately 30 percent of the agency's resources were going into pollution, and he expected the balance to shift to pollution within the next year or so.[77] It was too late: rumors of Nogueira-Neto's imminent departure were widespread by this time, even within SEMA itself. It was said that top administrators saw him as insensitive to urban problems and therefore no longer the man to lead SEMA. It was also said that in spite of his statesmanlike pose, he had become too closely identified with the generals by dint of his many years in office, and that the new democratic politicians neither liked nor trusted him. Clearly, his priorities were no longer in keeping with the spirit of the times. In late 1986, Nogueira-Neto, increasingly hemmed in by the changing political currents, resigned. His replacement had a background in pollution issues and saw those, rather than biological conservation, as SEMA's proper focus.

Nogueira-Neto's departure from SEMA marked the end of an era for Amazon conservation: the old political universe of the military dictatorship was gone; the scientific and pragmatic considerations on which conservation planning had been based had been superseded; the heroic days of the mid-1970s were memories; the conservation tide had come in and gone out. This is the place to ask what, in the end, was accomplished. And beyond that: what lessons does the era hold for the future of biological conservation in Amazonia and elsewhere?

CHAPTER 9

Discerning the Limits of Providence in the Nineties and Beyond

The recently closed era of Amazon conservation was impressive in many ways. Perhaps never before had science been given so great a role in conservation policy, nor had respect for biological resources been such a constant presence in decision making, at least during the earlier years. The IBDF's and SEMA's programs were models of pragmatism, of how to fit conservation into highly politicized environments without losing sight of basic goals. The programs brought millions of hectares of rainforest and other tropical ecosystems under public protection.

Yet there was an impermanence to these successes: the conservation gains of the era now seem as much a part of the past as do the programs responsible for them. In some cases—Rio Trombetas, for example—conservation's gains faded into history as the region took on a new identity. Other protected areas like Pacaás Novos, and even the most successful ones like Jaú, became passive entities, waiting for the future—in the form of expanded Indian rights, new development initiatives, shifting sociopolitical power, or the ebb of international support—to overtake and erase them.

This failure to post more than temporary gains was the greatest shortcoming of Amazon conservation during the era examined here. To be sure, nature was not so reduced as to make future conservation efforts impossible, which conservationists of the 1960s and 1970s feared would be the cost of their generation's failure, but the institutional defenses of Amazon biota were no stronger at the end of the era than at the beginning. This meant more was lost than gained. Future conservation programs will protect a region whose natural defenses of remoteness and size are less formidable; they will face more advanced technologies and an international economy more capable of turning nature into commodities; they will face larger, more mobile populations—more fishermen with nylon rather than cotton nets, more settlers with chainsaws rather than axes.

What is to blame for this? The individuals involved most centrally in the events described here had some mistaken notions about their task environment. Miller mistook developmental rhetoric for political reality, which led him to overestimate the degree to which rationality and dedication to the commonweal drove regional development. The conservation doctrines he promulgated, the ones on which conservation policy for Brazilian Amazonia ultimately rested, were therefore based on a flawed premise. Jorge Pádua and Wetterberg overestimated the Brazilian military government's commitment to planning rationality, which led them to overreach the limits of their resources in establishing the IBDF's conservation program. They also had an incorrect vision of Brazil's future, which led them to miscalculate the amount of political support for conservation in coming years.

It is clear in retrospect that mistakes were made in shaping the instruments of policy: responsibility for the IBDF's conservation program was never sufficiently centralized; the IBDF's Parks Advisory Board did not work well; the structural antagonism at the heart of SEMA and the IBDF's relationship was never overcome. There were some serious miscalculations: the IBDF's faulty land ownership surveys caused trouble in several places; Nogueira-Neto overestimated the inherent fit of SEMA's program to the prevailing developmental norms of the federal government, and therefore his ability to derive support from the agencies of development; SEMA overestimated the accessibility of the Anavilhanas station, which was a chief cause of its later troubles there.

One should not make too much of these shortcomings, however. The incorrect notions about the future of Brazilian society and the rationality underlying development were mistakes only in an intellectual sense: they did not lead to inappropriate actions. Miller's doctrines and Wetterberg's plans, while based on a belief in the eventual triumph of the rational, were also eminently suited for the political universe in which they were launched. Jorge Pádua's faith in the future of Brazil as a modern developed nation did not blind her to the need to craft the IBDF program to immediate political circumstances. Nogueira-Neto's overreliance on the agencies of development was based as much on need as faith.

In fact, there was a consistent, contextual intelligence to most of the actions that shaped Amazon conservation during those years. Wetterberg and Jorge Pádua understood their immediate political environment and skillfully shaped conservation policy to fit it. With his independent approach, Paulo Nogueira-Neto adapted conservation to the logic of his agency's circumstances, even turning bureaucratic realpolitik and manipulation of national insecurities into useful instruments of biological conservation. Those who directed Amazon conservation during those years squeezed the most out of their political resources and filled most of the policy space open to them. By diverting resources from pollution control, Nogueira-Neto even extended biological conservation's domain at the expense of another environmental issue. It was not until later that conservation leadership became unimaginative and bureaucratic, but this was more a product of conservation's diminishing circumstances than a producer of them.

Nor did the administrative or management shortcomings matter much while Amazon conservation was politically favored. Such favor gave the DN administrative weight and allowed it to act as the center of the IBDF's conservation program, in spite of the DN's ambiguous formal authority. This political favor made the delegados mindful of their conservation responsibilities; it even turned the IBDF's decentralized line of command to conservation's advantage. The ample resources flowing from political favor allowed SEMA and the IBDF to carve separate conservation niches for themselves and complement each other's programs, in spite of their basically competitive positions.

It was only when conservation lost favor that its political space became crabbed and the imperfections of its administrative instruments became serious impediments. Conservation's reduced priority was ultimately responsible for the diffusion of decision making away from the DN. The reduction turned the role of the delegados from an advantage into a drawback. It was lack of elite favor that incapacitated the Park Advisory Board, not the inherent relationship of the board to the program. Lack of favor forced the IBDF's and SEMA's policies to converge in search of scarce resources and brought the latent competition between the two agencies to the fore in such a destructive fashion.

Thus the blame for Amazon conservation's shortfall does not lie with those who made and executed policy: their mistakes were few in comparison with their correct decisions. Nor can the blame be placed on the administrative instruments: they worked well in spite of their imperfections when conservation was politically favored.

The root cause of the shortfall was conservation's lack of a committed political constituency, which was because none of the powerful players in the Amazon political arena had more than an abstract interest in what conservation promised most insistently: a more sensible future and a more vigorous commonweal. Development also promised broad human betterment and a more sensible future, and it, too, was valued primarily as the solution to political equations. But development prescriptions expanded the material base of society and thereby offered a cornucopia of political rewards, so there were reasons for a deep, if always colored, commitment to development by the powerful. The political virtues of conservation, however, never extended beyond appearances. In fact, to the extent that conservation interfered with the production of the material goods on which the Brazilian political system ultimately depended, there were strong disincentives to putting conservation prescriptions into practice.

This made conservation's political space inherently unstable. The need for the appearance of a commitment to conservation could arise from many parts of the political system. It could arise suddenly and could disappear just as suddenly. Conservation's political space was inherently shallow because the need for appearances carried only so much weight in political equations. Conservation policies always had to be fitted into the shifting cracks and crevices of political opportunity; yet without the power that comes from advancing the deep interests of the powerful, conservationists were never able to shape their own political space in more than marginal ways.

When large opportunities opened temporarily, as they did in the late 1970s, conservation policy might take on a coherent appearance, but the need to adapt to unpredictable and marginal political space guaranteed that policy would eventually become dysfunctional: political shrewdness and adaptability would be more valued than a commitment to consistency; the capacity to project the correct image would be more rewarded than the ability to deliver solid conservation gains; political survival would take precedence over fealty to long-term goals. Above all, conservationists would be unable to act with continuity or for a longer-term posterity, since the actions of one era, shaped to the political spaces of that era, become inappropriate for the next. Eventually, conservationists would lose the capacity to act even with shrewdness, or to prevent history from pulverizing their past successes. This, of course, was exactly what happened to the Amazon conservation initiatives once they ran out of fortuitous political circumstances.

* * *

A new, promising era of conservation was beginning in Brazilian Amazonia as the 1990s opened. International attention was again fixed on Brazil's environmental record, especially with regard to Amazon rainforest clearing. International development agencies were increasing the environmental components of their projects in Amazonia. Conservation's star was on the rise in Brazilian public life: a strong environmental plank had been written into the new constitution; President Fernando Collor was declaring himself an environmentalist; a reorganization of the federal bureaucracy had centralized responsibility for nature protection; and there was talk of a cabinet-level Ministry of the Environment.

Long-standing impediments to conservation were overcome in the late 1980s: subsidies for cattle ranches in Amazonia were ended, something conservationists had been unable to do even at the height of their successes in the late 1970s and early 1980s; many of the recommendations of the Amazon Forest Policy were signed into law after a decade in limbo.[1] More resources were flowing into the field. Whereas the director of Amazonia National Park could not get a helicopter for aerial surveillance in the mid-1980s, three helicopters were assigned full time to policing Amazon deforestation in 1990, with more promised.

The political environment in which this surge of conservation interest plays itself out in the 1990s is bound to be different from that of the 1970s and 1980s. Brazil now has a democratic rather than an authoritarian government. Brazil's foreign policy has few of the same goals it had twenty years ago. The development theory from which conservation doctrine took its compass readings has changed. Yet will the political environment of Brazil in the 1990s be different in ways that most fundamentally define conservation's opportunities? Will the political environment be more stable and predictable? Will conservation be less marginal to powerful interests? Will its promise of a more sensible, provident future have more intrinsic political appeal than it did during the 1970s and 1980s?

Probably not. The return to democracy was not a revolutionary event: it dislodged few of the social groups that supported the military or its commitment to uninhibited economic expansion. In fact, these groups' belief that the military government no longer served them was what, at least in part, drove the officers back to their barracks.[2] These powerful groups are no more likely to have an interest in conservation under a democracy than they did under military rule. The sense of elite public-mindedness, which might somewhat offset the narrow self-interest of the powerful, does not flourish in the economic stagnation and political uncertainty that will undoubtedly form a large part of the background against which politics will be played out in the 1990s. Nor is the middle-class vision of an environmentally benign Brazil likely to carry much weight under such circumstances. Working-class environmentalism is likely to focus on immediate, quality-of-life issues rather than remote biological conservation, thus allowing these issues to continue to take back the political energy that conservation had appropriated from them.

Moreover, democratic government brings its own threats to the rainforest. Now that the rural landless have been given back their political voice, the government is even more likely to support the law of posse, which has been enshrined in the new constitution, and to turn a blind eye to its abuse, even in protected areas. The government will find itself under pressure to provide land for the rural landless,[3] and vast, still lightly populated Amazonia is one of the few regions of the nation where ambitious settlement programs are possible. The democratic government has to keep the military out of politics; sending it to occupy Amazonia's underpopulated frontiers is an ideal way to do this.[4] Finally, Amazonia has always been a good place to pay off political debts of all sorts: to individuals with get-rich-quick schemes; to whole groups, like cattle ranchers in search of subsidies; or to regional politicians with a need for lucrative contracts to hand out to their supporters. Democratically elected politicians, with even more political debts than the generals had, are going to be even more attracted to Amazonia for this purpose.

Will international pressure force the Brazilian government to be mindful of Amazon nature in spite of itself? There is cause to believe it will: external pressure was in large part responsible for the conservation cycle examined in this book; Brazil's enormous debt will make it even more sensitive to demands articulated through the international financial system in the 1990s. The tightened environmental guidelines that have accompanied recent World Bank and Inter-

American Development Bank loans are certain to have some impact on Brazil's environmental behavior.

On the other hand, the environmental critique, as an international political force, is bound by its own historical circumstances. At first glance, the rise of the development ideal and then environmentalism appear as similar processes. As an ordering principle for the international system and a blueprint for the future, universal development replaced older colonial ideals when it became obvious that the latter would not provide a workable frame for the postwar world. The environmental critique arose when it became apparent that the norms of conventional development would sow the seeds of its own destruction. Once the critique became coherent and convincing, it engaged most of the institutions of the international order.

But there was a key difference: the rise of environmentalism, and with it the importance of biological conservation, was not accompanied by any great historical trauma that shook established interests to their foundations. There was no disorganized world for it to reorder, no new coalition of interests for it to bind and serve. Instead, it had to be grafted onto an entrenched international system. As the community of international conservation evolved, it became linked to the main elements of the postwar order in many sustaining ways. International businessmen sat on its boards of directors. Much of its funding came from foundations fueled by the profits of international business. Much of organized conservation's power came from its access to the instruments of international finance and development. As might be expected, to the extent that there was a coherent world view within the international conservation community, it was a profoundly conservative one; conservation had only to persuade those in power that respecting the biological world offered a more reasonable path to what they valued. The view made conservation's task appear manageable within the confines of the established order, and it discouraged organized conservation from trying to alter the order in any but superficial ways.

Environmentalism derived some independent power from the fact that it could engage the public of the developed world and international scientific networks. Yet those were themselves limited political forces: public opinion is fickle and often ill-informed or shallow. The capacity of scientists to shape policy is always restrained by science's dependence on other political forces to pick up both its tab and its message.

Conservation's lack of deep political roots meant that when conservation issues arose, neither environmental thought nor organized conservation action could affect the international system's basic modes of operation. For example, even as the future came to appear more fragile and the present's pale of responsibility to it lengthened, the principal instrument of temporal mediation remained the discount rate. As long as it did, the need to cover the costs of money pressed hard on the world's natural environment, even as knowledge of the consequences of that pressure increased. Profits everywhere continued to be built on the environmental externalities that the discount rate ignored.

Conservation's lack of deep political roots also meant that the commitment of the more powerful elements of the international system to ameliorating conservation problems did not have to extend beyond the theater of public opinion. This practically guaranteed that gestures would outweigh substantive action, that pronouncements would outweigh commitments; that high-level environmental planning sponsored by the international development agencies and events along the long-penetration roads they financed would have little connection to each other. It produced an unwritten, perhaps unconscious alliance between the institutions of international development and the Brazilian government. They would cooperate in producing the images of conservation progress, and they would jointly ignore the reality beneath the images.

The recent changes in conservation's niche in the international development and finance network have thus likely been ones of appearance and degree, not essence. The increased public pressure on the network as a result of the emergence of the rainforest clearing issue has caused it to increase its outlays on conservation programs, expand in-house conservation expertise, and increase its loan oversight, but this pressure has not altered the core values or the basic goals of the system. It is too transitory; there are too many reasons why it is shrewder to simply hunker down or ride out the current wave of environmental concern with superficial and reversible responses.

Therefore, while Amazon conservation will take place in a very different-appearing political environment in the 1990s, the environment is not likely to be different in essentials. Conservation policy will still have to be fitted to a shifting, unpredictable field of opportunity. The opportunities may be quite large in the near future and allow for impressive accomplishments, but because conservation is still not valued for what it promises, those opportunities will open against an indifferent background. And once they close, as they must, the conservation accomplishments shaped to them will erode. Even with intelligent leadership and efficient instruments, conservation programs for Amazonia will likely be condemned to yet another cycle of ultimately ineffectual action played out against a diminishing biological patrimony. Conservation's future successes in such an environment will be like past ones: tactical, local, and temporary. The main line of Amazon nature's future is likely to be in the broad losses that these successes occasionally punctuate.

To make it otherwise, conservation has to be made to transcend the immediate play of politics and political interests. Miller understood this; it was his great insight. It is what he attempted to do by attaching conservation to a new history he thought was unfolding before him, one in which development was replacing the old, narrow political institutions with a way of managing human affairs inherently more respectful of the commonweal and the future. He, along with Wetterberg and Jorge Pádua, was wrong in believing that the institutions of this new history were in place. It was the rhetoric, not the institutions, that was in place. Conservation therefore became attached to the rhetoric, but not to deeper processes, and it was in the fissure between the rhetoric and the reality of modern development, both on the international stage and within Brazil, that conservation got lost.

Brazilian and foreign conservationists are now trying to devise new strategies to take advantage of the new openings for Amazon conservation that seem to lie immediately ahead. But the same fundamental task Miller faced—attaching conservation to a history that does not lead to failure, in spite of all the intelligence and energy committed to the cause—faces those concerned with Amazon nature today.

* * *

What courses of action might make Amazonia's biological endowment more secure in the future? One is to promote the formation of a landscape that mixes conservation goals and environmentally benign human activity—in other words, the landscape of sustainable development so popular within the international conservation network. Ideally, a landscape that mixed conservation and human activity would be the best one for both: conservation would protect the base of material life; the selective use of Amazonia for production would reduce overall pressure on the region's biological resources.

A planning template for Amazonia in which productive and conservation ends are mixed in a complementary fashion has been taking shape, thanks to work by Goodland, Fearnside, Goulding, and others.[5] The mix would be fine-grained, often finding expression in close proximity, as in a farmer's field and the undisturbed median separating it from his neighbor's. Sometimes the two interests would be intertwined, as in natural areas that would serve as sources of rubber, game, and building material and yet also would protect endangered species. Sometimes they would be expressed in the same act: the establishment of a tree plantation that would provide incomes while maintaining some of the evapotranspiration potential of the forest. Modest efforts are already underway to create such a landscape. For example, extractive reserves, areas that would provide livelihoods for rubber tappers but also preserve the forest, have been established in Amapá and Acre.[6]

The dangers of this approach should be pointed out, however. First, it does not, in and of itself, change the configuration of Amazon politics; maintaining the proper relationship between human activity and nature on such a landscape ultimately depends on institutions and politics that have shown themselves incapable of taking full account of conservation values in the past. By promoting such a landscape, conservationists risk becoming the unwitting allies of those very forces that shaped Amazon development into such unsatisfactory forms in the past. They risk making conservation a disadvantaged player in a regional free-for-all once again.

Could a landscape characterized by intimate yet mutually beneficial contact between nature and human activity in Amazonia be maintained if accompanied by political institutions sensitive to the voice of local constituents? Probably not. All human landscapes have political constituencies. They have to deliver enough benefits to their constituents to prevent defection to another vision of the proper landscape. It is unlikely that a fine-grained, mixed landscape could do this: freedom of action would be too restricted.

Finally, mixing development and conservation in a fine-grained pattern would make it difficult ever to know if a development initiative was ultimately protecting or menacing nature. Most would likely have both advantages and disadvantages from a conservation perspective, but it would be impossible to determine if the net result was positive. For example, would the establishment of new plantations of tree crops create enough evapotranspiration potential to offset the hunting pressure their workers would place on the surrounding forest? The same question would have to be asked of extractive reserves, and there would never be a conclusive answer, which would, of course, leave the field open to politics, or even just wishful thinking.

Another approach might be to encourage the replacement of short-term political expedience with a more detached, economic calculus in guiding the region's future, and thereby establish the kind of developmental regime on which Miller's conservation formulas were predicated. It has a certain appeal. An Amazonia subjected to more rational economic policies during the past two decades would be a less disturbed region than it is now.[7] Ranching and agricultural subsidies caused the clearing of millions of hectares of forest that would not have been disturbed without them. Many—perhaps most—of the roads and dams constructed over the last two decades would not be there if rigorous cost-benefit analysis had been undertaken early in the planning. The cities of Amazonia would be smaller had they not been subsidized in so many ways. Perhaps letting economic rationality determine the future of Amazonia would bring development and nature into an equilibrium that would be satisfactory from both perspectives.

Even assuming that the political will could be found to let the region's development be guided by accepted principles of economic rationality, satisfactory results from a conservation perspective would not be likely. The interest and discount rates, two related rates based on capital rents, are at the center of operationalized economic rationality. They are essential components of cost-benefit analysis, optimal allocation modeling, and other determinants of rational behavior. Yet neither they nor calculations of economic rationality based on them can escape political distortions.

Returns to capital are increased by its investment in areas where the accounting boundaries are favorable, i.e., where the greater share of the benefits are retained by the investor while the costs are externalized, or fall on others. An industry that makes large profits because it does not have to pay to clean up the pollution it causes is an example of one enjoying favorable accounting boundaries. Because accounting boundaries are subject to law and public policy, their placement is an inherently political issue. Their exact location cannot be forecast with certainty in any single case because of the complexity of micropolitics, but in the aggregate, the boundaries are likely to favor those with capital to invest, be they individuals or institutions, because their financial resources will give them disproportionate power in the political arena. Furthermore, externalities often fail to become political issues for those who bear their costs because externalities are frequently diffuse, and fall on groups that crosscut self-conscious political groupings.

Discount and interest rates are thus in part built on externalities. They are also, at least in part, summarizing expressions of the political status quo, perhaps the most comprehensive ones there are. Much of their usefulness is derived from the political information they convey, but useful does not mean rational in any deep sense.

Calculations of economic rationality will discriminate with special severity against posterity, because posterity, which cannot vote or riot, is incapable of speaking for itself in the political arena. It is also a constituency that can give no support to those who provide for it; as one politician cleverly put it, "What has posterity ever done for me?" Posterity therefore will never be able to set the rules of cost and benefit accounting so as to protect itself from today's earth-transforming activities.

Given this, long-term conservation goals and economically rational development are unlikely ever to converge in practice. Economic calculations are likely to overvalue immediate development simply as a function of the persistent bias against the environment and the future built into calibrations of the rational. Each new road and production facility, each new use for tropical hardwoods will expand the base on which a new round of biased calculations will be made, just as, under current circumstances, they expand the base for short-sighted and opportunistic politics. Therefore application of the calculus of economic rationality is likely to slowly but inexorably destroy the biological endowment of the region, rather than lead to some equilibrium between nature and development.

Amazon nature is thus threatened most seriously by those very instruments to which mediation with the future has been entrusted: the political and economic system, writ large. The way the relationship between present and future values is calculated cannot be trusted, nor can the way value is assigned within the political process. Amazonia has to be protected most vigilantly against those very instruments thought capable of protecting it. The thought is depressing because it makes mounting an effective defense of the natural world appear far too difficult; sufficient biological conservation measures, certainly in Amazonia, appear beyond the limits of providential behavior.

Yet human collectives do seem capable of developing a sense of concern for the future that is more than the sum of the short term interests of their members. Part of our problem with regard to the future might lie in the simple fact that, as Talbot Page observes, society is not used to making conscious choices on intertemporal criteria.[8] Moreover, as Caldwell points out, the primary impetus for acting with conscious regard to the future is the realization that the likely one is not the preferred one,[9] and only recently has science made the future appear likely to suffer from our actions. Thus we have only recently been brought into the moral shadow of our prosperity, and only recently has this given rise to what McNeill has called the "noisy concern for the future."[10]

Embedding such concern in the institutions of human governance will be a slow process, however; it cuts against many grains of self-interest. It will also be an uneven one. Until this embedding occurs, concern for the future will be only a modest political force, like that which propelled Amazon conservation in the recent past. Conservationists should therefore pursue a strategy that accounts for both the likely failure of conventional political and economic instruments of providence and the modest but real resources that concern for the future will make available for conservation in the immediate future. Under the circumstances, what we might call a coarse-grained approach seems appropriate.

Several years ago, Page wrote a monograph on rational and just mineral-consumption policy in which he wrestled with the problem of the chronic political underrepresentation of posterity, and with calculations of economic rationality likely to cause what he called "the drift into unlivable futures."[11] Page concluded that the surest way of guaranteeing that the future would have the resources it needed was to establish generational "exit requirements." Any period of time would be responsible for handing over to the next period an essentially undiminished resource base. Given that these exit requirements were met, intratemporal resource allocations could follow any formula devised by that generation. Page was unclear on many of the details of his scheme—for one, exactly what an undiminished resource base meant in practice—but his primary intent was not to present a complete plan but rather a general approach to provisioning prosperity that would not subject the future to the present's inevitably self-serving calculations of its obligations toward it.

Because we face essentially the same problem with regard to Amazon nature, a strategy in the same spirit ought to be considered. Perhaps large parts of the region—ideally, all that remains undisturbed—should be off limits to alteration, even in those cases where conservation and the goals of development appear compatible at first glance. Such a policy would leave nature less subject to the exigencies of politics and the miscalculations of rationality because it would reduce the ecotone between nature and human intent. The approach calls for a straightforward protection strategy; no complex calculations, manipulation of property regimes, or management of political systems would be necessary. Success or failure would not be ambiguous. The approach would even be confluent with economic rationality to a point; Amazon nondevelopment would have produced more net economic returns than many Amazon development projects undertaken over the last two decades. The legal foundation for such an approach in Amazonia is already in place: the 1978 Treaty of Amazon Cooperation, with its strong emphasis on conservation.

There are obvious drawbacks to such an approach, especially when compared to those that take the compatibility of development and conservation as a premise. It will encounter opposition in Brazil because it will eliminate Amazonia's role as the playground of Brazilian politics. It runs counter to the momentum of development and to all the interests with a stake in it. It is out of alignment with the lingering myth of Amazon empires and the traditions of settling questions of Amazon sovereignty through occupation. The approach leaves a vast number of details to be worked out: How should "undisturbed" be defined? How do indigenous cultures fit into the scheme? The bluntness, prohibitive quality, and conceptual isolation of the approach mean that it would be difficult to build coalitions around it—although if such coalitions are destructive to Amazon nature in the long run, this is not a disservice to conservation.

Yet the problems with this approach are surmountable. The cost of the deferred benefits springing from setting aside the undisturbed parts of Amazonia, even given the inherently skewed calculations of economic costs and benefits, would be an infinitesimal part of the world's annual product. Therefore, putting the costs of such an approach on the global tab would not appear to be an inherently unrealistic goal. Furthermore, the approach need not, and should not, be thought of as exclusively applicable to Amazonia. Large areas of the earth's surface should probably be placed beyond the pale of modern economic development: short-grass prairies, Arctic tundra and taiga, mountain environments, and other rainforests. They produce little of economic value while rendering considerable environmental services. Their transformation is likely to take place under political systems and institutions every bit as short-sighted as those under which parts of Amazonia have been transformed in the recent past. Including Amazonia in a global program to protect such areas would avoid singling out Brazil or the other Amazon nations to pay for global environmental health.

In closing, let me suggest that perhaps the most fundamental judgment of an era should be based on its capacity to act congruently with its own understanding of the future. An era that can do so has a strong claim to an underlying rationality and morality; one that cannot is profoundly wanting. Our era is especially challenged by this criterion: the future has only recently become so clear, so extensive, and so sensitive-appearing to our actions; yet our mechanisms of providence, as embodied in political and economic institutions, are not now capable of dealing with the implications of this. Perhaps nowhere is the gap between what needs to be done and the institutional means so great as it is with regard to Amazonia's biological endowment. Perhaps our success in closing the gap—by setting that endowment out of the reach of current mechanisms of providence and by ultimately fashioning new ones—will be the criterion on which posterity will judge our underlying rationality and morality.

APPENDIX 1

Acronyms

CIT - Comité Intergovernamental Técnico para a Proteção e Manejo da Flora e Fauna Amazônica/Intergovernment Technical Committee for the Protection and Management of Amazon Flora and Fauna. A working group of government officials from Brazil, Bolivia, Colombia, Equador, Peru, and Venezuela responsible for coordinating the Amazon nature protection policies of the six nations.

CITES - Convention on International Commerce of Endangered Plant and Animal Species. Ratified by Brazil in 1975.

CNPq - Conselho Nacional de Desenvolvimento Científico e Tecnológico/National Council for the Development of Science and Technology. Government body with considerable budgetary and policy-setting authority for Brazilian science.

CONAMA - Conselho Nacional do Meio Ambiente/National Environmental Council. Body established in 1981 to oversee the national environment. Has wide membership among government agencies and civil organizations. The Secretary of the Environment is its executive officer.

CVRD - Companhia Vale do Rio Doce/ The Rio Doce Valley Company. The national mining corporation responsible for the development of the Carajás mining complex. Has shown considerable initiative in establishing environmental programs in its areas of operation.

DN - Departamento de Parques Nacionais e Reservas Equivalentes/Department of National Parks and Equivalent Reserves. IBDF department responsible for oversight and planning of IBDF's protected natural areas.

DNER - Departamento Nacional de Estradas de Rodagem/National Highways Department.

DPN - Divisão de Parques Nacionais e Recursos Naturais Renovavais/Division of National Parks and Renewable Natural Resources. Division of the DN with specific responsibility for the protected natural areas. Sister division of the Divisão de Proteção da Natureza/Division of Nature Protection, responsible for various flora and fauna conservation programs and for carrying out Brazilian conservation obligations under international treaties.

ECLA - The UN's Economic Commission for Latin America (later ECLAC, Economic Commission for Latin America and the Caribbean). Body responsible for formulating and promulgating development strategies for Latin America. Under the influence of the Argentine economist Raul Prebisch, became an important source of development doctrine in the 1950s and 1960s.

ESG - Escola Superior da Guerra/Superior War College. Chief instrument for the formation of elite consensus on the government's major policies during the military regime.

FAO - UN Food and Agriculture Organization. Long active in forest management in South America, and from the late 1960s, an important sponsor of
conservation initiatives on the continent.

FBCN - Fundação Brasiliera para a Conservação da Natureza/Brazilian
Foundation for the Conservation of Nature. The most important private
conservation organization in Brazil and a key player in the establishment of a
system of protected natural areas in Amazonia.

FUNAI - Fundação Nacional do Índio/National Indian Foundation (Ministry of
the Interior). Federal agency responsible for the welfare of Brazilian Indians.

IBDF - Instituto Braziliero de Desenvolvimento Florestal/Brazilian Institute for
Forest Development (Ministry of Agriculture). Federal agency with prime
responsibility for the management of the nation's forests, including those in
Amazonia, and the agency with the primary responsibility for biological
conservation.

IICA - Inter-American Institute of Agricultural Sciences. Institute of the
Organization of American States that sponsored conservation research and
training at its campus in Torrialba, Costa Rica. In 1973, the campus became
the Center for Research and Training in Tropical Agriculture (CATIE).

INCRA - Instituto Nacional de Colonização e Reforma Agrária/National
Institute for Colonization and Agrarian Reform. Agency responsible for
federal settlement schemes in Amazonia and manager of most federal land in
the region.

INPA - Instituto Nacional de Pesquisas da Amazôna/National Institute for
Amazon Research (under CNPq). Carried out much of the scientific research
incorporated into Amazon conservation planning.

IUCN - International Union for the Conservation of Nature and Natural
Resources. Swiss-based international conservation organization that has long
supported conservation work in South America.

PDAM - Plano de Desenvolvimento da Amazônia/Development plan for
Amazonia. Keyed to PND, the National Development Plan. Three PDAMs
figured in the events described in this book. The first, I PDAM, ran from
1972–1974, the second, II PDAM, from 1975–1979, and the third, III
PDAM, from 1980–1985.

PIC - Projecto Integrado de Colonização/Integrated Colonization Project.
Large, government-sponsored settlement schemes established in Amazonia
under the PIN plan. Primarily agricultural, although usually including some
industry.

PIN - Plano Nacional de Integração/National Integration Plan. Plan to use the
Transamazon Highway as the spine of an ambitious settlement initiative for
Amazonia. Unveiled in 1970, all but abandoned in 1974.

PND - Plano Nacional de Desenvolvimento/National Development Plan. The
second one, II PDN, accorded protected nature a place in national development planning.

POLAMAZONIA - Programa de Polos Agropecuários e Agromineração da
Amazônia/Program for Amazon Agro-livestock and Agro-mineral Poles. The
planning initiative that focused development efforts in Amazonia on selected
areas of high growth potential. The successor to PIN and the key component
of II PDAM.

PRODEPEF - Projecto de Desenvolvimento e Pesquisa Florestal. UN-sponsored
program to upgrade Brazil's forestry industry in the early and mid-1970s.
Wetterberg conducted his study under the wildlife management section of the
program.

RADAM - Radar Amazonas do Brazil/ Amazon Radar Survey Project (Ministry of Mines and Energy). Produced detailed maps of Amazon soils, vegetation, mineral deposits, and land-use potential, largely from information derived from an extensive radar survey of the region.

SEMA - Secretaria Especial do Meio-Ambiente/Secretariat of the Environment (Ministry of the Interior, then Ministry of Urban and Environmental Affairs). One of the two federal agencies involved centrally in biological conservation in Amazonia. Created and maintained a system of ecological stations.

SUDAM - Superintendência do Desenvolvimento da Amazônia/ Superintendency for Amazon Development. Belém-based regional development agency for Amazonia. SPVEA (Superintedência de Valorização Econômica da Amazônia) (Superintendency of Amazon Economic Expansion) was its predecessor. SUDENE (Superintendência de Desenvolvimento do Nordeste) is the comparable agency for the Northeast and SUDECO (Superintendência de Desenvolvimento do Centro-Oeste) for the Center-West, including Rondônia.

UNDP - United Nations Development Programme. Financially supported conservation planning in the developing world, especially from the late 1960s onward.

UNESCO - United Nations Educational, Scientific, and Cultural Organization. Important sponsor of international conservation research, action, and organizations following the Second World War.

WWF - World Wildlife Fund. Swiss-based international conservation organization active in funding and directing much conservation work in Brazil. The semi-independent U.S. branch of the organization, WWF-US, was most active in Brazil.

APPENDIX 2

Interviews

Araujo, Vivaldo C. de. Supervisor of Amazonas National Parks. April 30, 1986. Manaus.

Barragana, Márcio Luiz. Director, Guaporé Biological Reserve. May 2, 1986. Porto Velho.

Bernardes Quintão, Angela Tresinari. Director, DN. March 19, May 16, 1986. Brasília.

Blake, Robert. Senior associate, International Institute for Environment and Development. November 1, 1985. Washington, D.C.

Bramble, Barbara. International program director, National Wildlife Federation. October 24 (phone, 1986). Washington, D.C.

Brown, Keith. Entomologist and professor, University of São Paulo at Campinas. May 9, 1986. São Paulo.

Burley, William. Senior associate, World Resource Institute. October 28, 1985. Washington, D.C.

Camara, Ibsen de Gusmão. President, FBCN. July 4, 1984. Rio de Janeiro.

Cantarelli, Victor Hugo. Wildlife management specialist, DN. May 22 and 23, 1986. Brasília.

Carvalho, Alberto Guerreiro do. Director, Rio Trombetas Biological Reserve. April 26, 1986. Oriximiná.

Costa, Joaldo Bezerra. Adjunct secretary for ecosystems, SEMA. March 19, 1986. Brasília.

Falleiros, Auro. IBDF liason officer, FUNAI. May 28 and 30, 1986. Brasília.

Fearnside, Philip. Ecologist and research professor, INPA. April 3 and 15, 1986. Manaus.

Ferreira, Lordes Maria. Management planning coordinator, DN. March 18, May 30, 1986. Brasília.

Ferreira, Raimondo Egídio de Castro. Director, Amazonia National Park. April 24, 1986. Amazonia National Park.

Figueiredo, Heloiso Bueno. Supervisor of station management, SEMA. March 6 and 19, May 20 and 22, 1986. Brasília.

Freitas, Maria de Lourdes. Environmental director, CVRD. November 13, 1986. Knoxville.

Goodland, Robert. Ecologist, Office of Environmental Affairs, World Bank. May 17, 1984 [phone]. Washington, D.C.

Goulding, Michael. Aquatic ecologist, Museu Goeldi. July 5 and 6, 1984. Belém.

Guimarães, Antonio José Costa de Freitas. IBDF delegado - Pará. April 22, 1986. Belém.

Horwith, Bruce. Office of Technology Assessment, U.S. Congress. January 6, 1986 [phone]. Washington, D.C.

Jesus, Fábio de. Interpretation specialist, DN. March 14, 1986. Brasília.

Joels, Luiz Carlos de Miranda. Assistant field director, Minimum Critical Size Project. April 7, 1986. Manaus.

Jorge Pádua, Maria Tereza. Former director, DN. April 19, 1984. Washington, D.C.; July 23, 1984, São Paulo; March 26, May 13 and 26, 1986. Brasília.

Klever, Edgar Henrique. Secretary for ecosystems, SEMA. February 21, 1986. Brasília.

Kramer, Peter. Director of conservation, WWF-International. August 29, 1986. Gland, Switzerland.

Lima, Augusto A. de Araújo. Cartographic engineer, DN. March 14, May 29, 1986. Brasília.

Little, Henry P. Deputy director, The Nature Conservancy International Program. January 22, 1986. Washington, D.C.

Lovejoy, Thomas. Program director and vice-president for science, WWF-US. November 26, 1985. Washington, D.C.

Maia, Amauri da Silva. IBDF delegado - Amazonas. April 30, 1986. Manaus.

Meira Mattos, Carlos de. Geopolitical writer and retired Brazilian army general. July 2, 1984. Rio de Janeiro.

Milano, Raquel. Director, Division of National Parks and Nature Protection, DN. February 21, 25, and 28, March 7 and 21, May 12, 1986. Brasília.

Miller, Kenton. Director general, IUCN. August 26 and 27, 1986. Gland, Switzerland.

Monteiro, Sérgio Arraes. Director, Pacaás Novos National Park. May 2 and 3 1986. Ji-Paraná.

Moore, Alan. National parks consultant for Latin America, IUCN. March 19, 1986. Brasília.

Nogueira de Sá, Luis Fernando. Architect, DN. May 27, 1986. Brasília.

Nogueira-Neto, Paulo. Brazilian secretary of the environment. July 20, 1984; February 21 and 22, 1986. Brasília.

Paula, Alberto Costa de. Research coordinator, DN. March 13 and 18, 1986. Brasília.

Pittman, Howard H. Political scientist and geopolitical analyst. December 18, 1985 [phone]. Washington, D.C.

Pandolfo, Clara. General director, Department of Natural Resources, SUDAM. July 9, 1984. Belém.

Rankin, Judy McKean. Forest ecologist, INPA. July 13, 1984; April 14, 1986. Manaus.

Ribeiro, João Carlos. SEMA representative in Amazonas. April 7 and 8, 1986. Manaus.

Rocha, Sérgio Brant. New-area evaluation specialist, DN. February 24, March 6, May 29, 1986. Brasília.

Santiago, Eurico. Director, Jari Biological Reserve. May 3 and 4, 1989. Ji-Paraná and Jari Biological Reserve.

Schubart, Herbert. Associate director, INPA. July 13, 1984. Manaus.

Silva, Guttemberg Moreno de. Superintendent, Maracá de Roraima Ecological Station. April 19, 20, and 21, 1986. Boa Vista and Maracá de Roraima Ecological Station.

Simões, Nairo Serpa. Coordinator of ecosystem management, SEMA. March 6, 1986. Brasília.

Skillings, Robert. Chief of Brazil Programs Division, World Bank. April 23, 1984. Washington, D.C.

Taylor, Kenneth. Executive director, Survival International–U.S.A. December 13, 1985. Washington, D.C.

Trent, Douglas. Environmentalist. April 1, 1986. Belo Horizonte.

Viera, Roberto. Former director, INPA. April 3, 1986. Manaus.

Wendt, William. Director of Latin American Programs, U.S. National Park Service. October 1 and 25, December 9, 1985. Washington, D.C.

Wetterberg, Gary B. Former FAO consultant to PRODEPEF. April 25, 1984; December 20, 1985; January 24, October 29, 1986. Washington, D.C.

Wright, Michael. Vice-president, WWF-U.S. January 3, 14, and 27, 1986. Washington, D.C.

NOTES

Introduction

1. Wilson, *Biological Diversity Crisis,* p. 703.

2. Wilson and Willis ("Applied Biogeography," p. 522) wrote, "For an indefinite period of time man must add as little as possible to the rate of worldwide extinctions and where possible he should lower it." In a similar vein, Terborgh ("Preservation of Natural Diversity," p. 715) wrote, "Our goal as conservationists . . . is to prevent, over the period of transition to a steady state society, the process of species loss from running too far ahead of species gain."

3. Sternberg ("Development and Conservation," p. 255) wrote that "no period has witnessed a more extensive and rapid transformation of the planet's vegetation cover than that under way in the tropical lowlands of Latin America."

4. See U.S. Interagency Task Force on Tropical Forests, *World's Tropical Forests,* p. 11; and Guppy, "Tropical Deforestation," p. 930, for the extent of tropical rainforest in each country.

Chapter 1

1. Quoted in Cornish, *Study of the Future,* p. 70. See Van Doren, *Idea of Progress,* p. 186.

2. Adler, "World Bank's Concept," p. 32.

3. Ardnt, "Development Economics," pp. 24–29; Adler, "World Bank's Concept," pp. 32–33; Domhoff, *Policy-Formation Process,* pp. 101–108.

4. Bryant and White, *Managing Development,* pp. 4–7; Dickson, *Politics of Alternative Technology,* p. 23; Adler, "World Bank's Concept," pp. 30–42. For a classic exposition of this view, see Meier and Baldwin, *Economic Development.*

5. Structural shifts in the economies of developed nations toward services and high-value goods had steadily diminished the value of raw materials relative to other factors of production. In fact, Urquidi (*Challenge of Development,* pp. 63–64) saw raw materials as likely to be so abundant and low-valued that he was concerned about the threat to modernizing economies posed by the diminishing capacity of such materials to earn foreign exchange.

   Bryant and White (*Managing Development,* p. 5) wrote that "Most economists in the 1950s assumed that industrialization was essential for growth and hence concentrated on what needed to happen for industrialization to proceed." Anderson ("Politics and Development Policy," p. 261) wrote that "The goals of development policies are increased productivity through inputs of technology and scientific technique, capital, and investment in basic public services." Beyond these basic axioms, agreement broke down somewhat. For example, the World Bank was a strong advocate of export-oriented growth strategy, while ECLA (the Economic Commission for Latin America), some more left-oriented developmentalists, and some of the major third world nations—India, for example—preferred a heavier reliance on import substitution and state capitalism. There were also differences of opinion on the importance of agriculture, with some feeling that industrial development had to be accompanied by modernization in the countryside, and others holding that agricultural development could wait until industrialization forced the modernization of the agrarian sector. Finally, there was disagreement on the need to manage population growth. Some held that greater populations simply meant greater potential market demand and labor reserves, but others saw them as a threat to development potential. Most development theorists seemed to take a neutral position, holding that it was a fact of life that had to be accepted as part of any development situation.

6. Coleman, "Resurrection of Political Economy," p. 34; Anderson, "Politics and Development Policy," p. 261; Bryant and White, *Managing Development,* p. 158. The early postwar ascendance of Keynesian economics, with its stress on public intervention in national economies, encouraged this view.

7. UN, ECLA, *Economic Development,* p. 1. Nash wrote that the state had to "confront the social and cultural system head on" (quoted in Coleman, "Resurrection of Political Economy," p. 34).

8. Meier, *Science and Economic Development,* p. 234, 361.

9. Roett, *Brazil: Politics,* p. 165. See Ludwig, *Brazil, A Handbook,* Chapter XIX, "Economic Development Planning," for a concise summary of development planning during this period and the Kubitschek era.

10. Burns, *History of Brazil,* pp. 454–466.

11. Roett, *Brazil: Politics,* p. 118.

12. Daland, *Exploring Brazilian Bureaucracy,* p. 121; Roett, *Brazil: Politics,* p. 121.

13. These men were part of a generation of Brazilian economists that had been especially influenced by the ideas of the UN's Economic Commission for Latin America. Roett (*Brazil: Politics,* p. 166) writes that "Contacts with ECLA in the mid-1950s exposed [Brazilian] planners and economists to the then-prevailing doctrines of the commission. Of highest priority was rapid economic growth with a substantial role for the state as the engine of growth." For an analysis of the structure and socio-economic dynamics of the modernizing Brazilian economy during this period, see Evans, *Dependent Development.*

14. For data on the performance of the Brazilian economy during this period, see Ludwig, *Brazil: A Handbook,* Chapters IX–XII, XIV–XVI. For a more compact summary, see Roett, *Brazil: Politics,* pp. 167–168.

15. Roett, *Brazil: Politics,* p. 196.

16. In 1922, Forbes concluded from the accumulated work on man–environ-
    ment interactions that "the ecological system of the twentieth-century
    world must include the twentieth-century man as its dominant species"
    (Forbes, "Humanizing of Ecology," p. 89). For an extensive discussion of
    the perspective of nineteenth- and early twentieth-century scientists on
    man's impact on the natural world, see Duncan, "Social Organization."
    Also see Worthington, "Ecological Century."

17. Worthington, "Ecological Century," p. 66.

18. Sauer, "Agency of Man," p. 66. For earlier expressions of this view, see
    Glacken, "Changing Ideas." Sauer's perspective was compatible with the
    new, critical examinations of modern technology undertaken after mid-
    century. Far from seeing technology as the instrument of universal
    progress, Ellul, who published his groundbreaking *La Technique* in 1954,
    saw it as a societal force with a momentum of its own and dangerously
    unmindful of its social and environmental impacts. Others expressed con-
    cern for technology's tendency to produce unintended negative conse-
    quences, what Brooks later called its non-linear effects. Dubos worried that
    modern technology was leading civilization into a dangerous dependence
    on a frail, overarticulated production system from which it could not
    retreat if someday it had to. See Dickson, *Politics of Alternative
    Technology,* pp. 36–37; Brooks, "Knowledge and Action," p. 126; Dubos,
    Man Adapting, p. 527.

19. As late as 1962, Bates (quoted in Egler, "Pesticides," p. 246) could write
    that "Ecology may well be the most important of the sciences from the
    viewpoint of long-term human survival, but it is among the least under-
    stood by the general public, and the least supported by research." The fol-
    lowing year, Harroy (quoted in Caldwell, *In Defense of Earth*, p. 89) wrote
    that "it is strange to find how little public opinion and national or interna-
    tional authorities seem to be aware of or even worried about [the natural
    environment]."

20. Holdgate et al., "World Environmental Trends," p. 25.

21. Smut's term "holism," coined in the 1920s, was brought into disrepute by
    plant ecologists who, in its name, applied the characteristics of individual
    organisms to plant communities (Egler, "Pesticides," p. 242). The use of
    ecological concepts by sociologists to describe the behavior of human soci-
    eties debased them and eroded their usefulness (Ellen, *Environment,
    Subsistence, and System,* p. 67). The term "biosphere," given its meaning
    as the domain of life by Vernadsky in 1929, remained freighted with mys-
    tical overtones (Caldwell, *In Defense of Earth,* p. 45). Caldwell (p. 81)
    noted how the environmental impact of development was the subject of
    many individual papers presented at the UN's 1963 Geneva conference on
    the problems of less developed nations, but the critical points they raised
    never fused into a general critique—or even came into much of a focus.

22. Caldwell, "Changing Structures," p. 154.

23. Ellen, *Environment, Subsistence, and System,* pp. 75–79. During those
    years, the term "environment" in its modern meaning first came into use

and was so quickly adopted that its recent origin would often be forgotten (Grant, *Thinking Ahead,* p. 60).

24. This paragraph follows Holdgate et al., "World Environmental Trends," especially pp. 24–25.

25. Farvar, "Interaction of Ecological and Social Systems."

26. Many early twentieth-century anthropologists were aware of the tight links between human cultures and their natural environment. They also understood how fragile those links were when subjected to modern influences. In 1927, McKenzie ("Concept of Dominance," p. 32) wrote about the way modern life and the international economy "penetrate[d] new parts of the world in catastrophic fashion." This strain of anthropological thought moved to the periphery of the discipline during the first postwar decade as the drive for development rearranged the priorities of the social sciences. Ellen (*Environment, Subsistence, and System,* p. 69) writes that "the social and cultural anthropology of the two decades beginning in 1945 was dominated by theories which were either openly hostile to the ecological perspective or accommodated it only awkwardly." See Ellen, pp. 69–73, for a discussion of the reemergence of the ecological perspective.

27. Bryant and White, *Managing Development,* pp. 14–40; Mishan, "The Wages of Growth."

28. Mishan ("The Wages of Growth," p. 75) echoed an increasingly prevalent view when he wrote that "it is hard to think of any broad class of economic activity that does not generate spillover effects that are worth thinking about."

29. Boulding, "Legitimacy of Economics," p. 28. Most postwar economists treated externalities—i.e., the unaccounted costs (or benefits) of production—as minor, local issues (Sachs, "Approaches to a Political Economy," p. 294). Mason ("Resources in the Past," p. 20) writes that "Milton Friedman lumps the whole problem of externalities under the innocuous phrase 'neighborhood effects'." Others accepted the pervasiveness of externalities but wrote them off as a subject of serious inquiry because they were difficult to accurately measure, and were likely to come in mixed packages of benefits and costs that neutralized each other anyway.

30. Childe, *Man Makes Himself,* p. 180. For a like perspective, see Morgan, *Ancient Society,* p. 12.

31. Roberts, "On Reforming Economic Growth," p. 122; Baumol, in U.S. Congress, *Analysis and Evaluation,* p. 500. As Tucker (*Progress and Privilege,* p. 217) later stated the argument, "Each generation does not simply use up resources and impoverish things for the next. If it acts wisely, it builds up a capital plant that makes it even easier for the next generation to utilize what resources remain."

32. Page, *Conservation and Economic Efficiency,* p. 158; Tullock quoted in Dasmann, *Ecological Principles,* p. 24; Baumol, in U.S. Congress, *Analysis and Evaluation,* p. 500.

33. Van Doren, *Idea of Progress,* p. 192, wrote that whatever doubts existed

focused on the capacity of "social engineering to keep pace with mechanical engineering."

34. Van Doren, *Idea of Progress,* p. 185.

35. Duncan, "Social Organization," p. 57; Ellen, *Environment, Subsistence, and System,* p. 68. As early as 1954, Clark (*Study of Prehistory,* p. 22) wrote that "a more fruitful conception, and one increasingly shared by prehistorians and natural scientists, is to regard men and human societies as elements in specific ecosystems, the pattern of culture... being viewed as the product of adjustment and interaction between specific social needs and aspirations and the possibilities of relevant climate, soil and animal and plant life."

36. Forrester, *World Dynamics;* Meadows et al., *Limits to Growth.*

37. Page, *Conservation and Economic Efficiency,* p. 204. See Attfield, *Ethics of Environmental Concern,* Chapter 6, "Future Generations."

38. Meier and Baldwin, *Economic Development,* p. 125. Such an assumption could be seen in the planning exercises of the 1950s and the 1960s, which often picked a point in the future considered the farthest limit of reliable prediction, planned up to that point, and ignored what was beyond, even if trends of population growth, congestion, and resource demand seemed to point to grave problems just over the time horizon. Landsberg et al.'s influential 1963 study, *Resources in America's Future,* for example, took the year 2035 as the horizon and paid no more than passing attention to the period after that date, even though the presented data clearly pointed to serious scarcity problems after it.

39. Mishan ("Wages of Growth," p. 77), using synthetic substances as an illustration of this point, observed that while the risk of serious genetic or ecological consequences from any one synthetic substance is small, as the number of such substances multiplies over time the aggregate risk of some calamity grows until it becomes inevitable. The issue of nuclear wastes reinforced this new configuration of the future. By producing substances that would remain harmful for hundreds of millions of years, the present was imposing a clear burden on distant posterity.

40. McNeill, "Historical Perspective," p. 59. The number of articles on environmental topics in the *New York Times,* for example, went from 153 in 1960 to 1,704 a decade later. Caldwell (*In Defense of Earth,* p. 80) writes that, "[in] the late 1960s... concern of the informed minority became sufficiently pervasive and intense to arouse a wider public and, more importantly, to give power to an emotionally committed political movement."

41. Kay and Jacobson, (eds.) introduction to their *Environmental Protection,* p. 6; Sills, "Environmental Movement," p. 2. The concern of the international development community increased slowly in the decade before the Stockholm conference. The FAO began promoting conservation programs in Africa, Asia and South America in the 1960s, and in 1970, it set up a Conservation and Wildlife Branch in its Division of Forest Resources.

42. There were eleven such agencies in the world at the time of the conference; a decade later there were over a hundred (Caldwell, *International Environmental Policy,* p. 278).

43. Flynn (*Brazil: A Political Analysis,* p. 445) writes of that period: "Brazil basked most warmly in the sun of international financial and business approval as a stable system,...providing sure profits in its fast-expanding, efficiently run economy."

44. Quoted in Dasmann, *Ecological Principles,* p. 16. See Caldwell, *In Defense of Earth,* p. 121.

45. Guimarães, "Bureaucracy and Ecopolitics," p. 15.

46. Sternberg, "Development and Conservation," p. 262.

47. Quoted in Wetterberg et al., "Analysis of Nature Conservation," p. 1.

48. Boardman, *International Organization,* p. 36 and elsewhere.

49. Quoted in Nash, *Wilderness and the American Mind,* p. 371.

50. McConnell, "Conservation Movement."

51. Leopold, *Sand County Almanac,* p. 274.

52. Odum, "The Strategy of Ecosystem Development," p. 269. Systems modeling added credibility to the argument by demonstrating that the best way to protect complex systems, be they economies, organisms, or ecosystems, against sudden, unpredictable state changes was to build buffers into the systems and insure that sufficient slack resources were available to ride out the consequences of such state changes. See Cyert and March, *Behavioral Theory.* For a later synthesis of this and like work, see Day, "Adaptive Economic Theory," p. 12.

53. See Page, *Conservation and Economic Efficiency,* pp. 9–12, 146, and elsewhere.

54. Moore, personal communication, March 19, 1986.

55. Di Castri, "Biosphere Reserve Concept," p. 2. Also see Lowenthal, "American Scene."

56. Boardman, *International Organization,* p. 60; Caldwell, *International Environmental Policy,* p. 187; Curry-Lindahl, "Background and Development," p. 164.

57. Caldwell, *International Environmental Policy,* p. 187; Curry-Lindahl, "Background and Development," p. 164; Boardman, *International Organization,* p. 62.

58. Miller, interview, August 26, 1986. Miller mentioned the following as having a profound impact on his thinking, either during his graduate training or afterward: Thomas (ed.), *Man's Role in Changing the Face of the Earth;* Dasmann, Milton, and Freeman, *Ecological Principles for Economic Development;* Farvar and Milton, *The Careless Technology.*

59. Although Miller was a prolific writer on conservation topics from the mid-1960s onward, the most complete expression of his views appears in his later (1978) *Planning National Parks,* which was intended primarily as an instruction manual and guide for Latin American park managers and natu-

ral resource planners. Unless otherwise noted, the discussion of Miller's approach follows this work. Miller's approach to conservation planning, which he instilled in numerous students at the Interamerican Agricultural Institute in Costa Rica (IICA) was called a "school" by Armondo Sampere, an FAO official in Latin America and, for a while, Miller's superior (Miller, interview, August 26, 1986). Perhaps out of modesty, Miller himself disowned the term.

60. Bryant and White, *Managing Development,* pp. 230–231.

61. Stillwell ("National Parks in Brazil," p. 393) attributed the lack of conservation tradition to the absence of colonial connections with Europe or North America during the late imperial era.

62. Miller, *Planning National Parks,* pp. 241–247, 413.

63. Miller, interview, August 26, 1986.

64. Miller, *Planning National Parks,* p. 550. On p. 564, Miller argued thus: "When parks are planned as elements of development, there is no need to feel awkward about the value of birds, ecological diversity, or vanishing species, if the combined values attributed to water, tourism, recreation, education, and rural employment are sufficient to carry the cost of the park and make it the 'most economic use of the land.'"

65. Miller, *Planning National Parks,* p. 501.

66. Marx and Lenin detested the destruction of nature that they attributed to capitalism, so conservation enjoyed what one scholar called "impeccable Marxist-Leninist credentials." Appreciation of nature also found favor with affluent conservatives; it fit into their nostalgia about the simpler, more manageable past, and they often saw their appreciation of nature as setting them off from the vulgar masses. Progressive liberals saw preserved nature as part of the landscape on which the middle-class good life was lived, and it therefore enjoyed a large place in their visions of the future. See Boardman, *International Organization,* p. 17.

67. Miller, *Planning National Parks,* p. 564.

68. Miller, *Planning National Parks,* pp. 67–68.

69. It adopted a set of standard categories that it hoped would become universally recognized at its 1969 general assembly (Dasmann, "Development of a Classification System," p. 389).

70. Miller, *Planning National Parks,* pp. 16–17. Here as well, Miller was attempting to bring conservation in line with mainstream development planning. For example, the UN's Department of Economic and Social Affairs (*National Resources,* p. 42) was willing to accept the idea of protected natural reserves as long as they were managed for well-defined, practical ends.

71. Miller, *Planning National Parks,* p. 240.

72. Brower, "New Decade," p. 3; Udall, "Nature Islands," p. 3.

73. Miller, interview, August 26, 1986. Holdridge, "Determination of World Plant Formations"; Holdridge, *Life Zone Ecology;* Tosi, "Zonas de Vida Natural en el Peru"; Di Castri, "Esquisse Ecologique du Chili."

74. Through their sponsorship of research and experimental programs, the Rockefellers had been promoting international development since the Second World War. John D. Rockefeller, Jr., Nelson's father, had been involved with the U.S. National Park System for much of his life; he was instrumental in establishing the Great Smokey Mountains and the Grand Teton national parks, and two of the National Park Service's early directors, Horace Albright and Newton Drury, were members of the Rockefellers' "outer circle" of advisors and clients. That interest in national parks was continued in the next generation of Rockefellers, and in the 1960s "the brothers" lent their support to African wildlife preservation, most notably through their involvement with the school of wildlife management at Mweka. The Rockefellers had oil holdings and land in Latin America, and Nelson's early political career at the U.S. State Department had been in the Latin American section. Laurance had made a grand tour of Latin American national parks in 1967, which was featured prominently in *National Geographic*. The incident with Miller was strikingly similar to one that occurred in 1924, when John D. Rockefeller, Jr., invited Horace Albright, then superintendent of Yellowstone National Park, to come to New York to present a proposal to acquire the Jackson Hole area just south of the park and thereby save it from commercial development. For this episode and other examples of Rockefeller involvement in the U.S. National Park System, see Collier and Horowitz, *The Rockefellers*, pp. 147–149.

75. Miller, interview, August 26, 1986. Miller's program appeared at an opportune moment for UN backing; UNESCO was about to launch its Man and Biosphere Program, one of whose aims was developing an international network of protected areas for scientific research.

76. Miller gathered a team of seven experts to assist him. While they worked with individual countries participating in the program, Miller travelled throughout Latin America from FAO headquarters in Rome, and later from the project's base in Santiago, Chile, meeting with government officials, setting up training workshops, and supervising the work of his team. For the work carried out during this period, see Miller, *Planning National Parks*, appendix VI–B, "Summary of Systems Planning Experience in Latin America," pp. 412–446. Also see Wetterberg, "Decade of Progress."

77. Miller, interview, August 26, 1986.

78. The chief of Brazil's national parks, Alceo Magnanini, had told the 1968 IUCN regional meeting at Bariloche that Brazil did not favor any joint South American conservation efforts, presumably for this reason. (IUCN, *Latin American Conference*, p. 416.)

79. Meyers, "Problem of Disappearing Species," p. 231. In 1970, the UN's Man and Biosphere Program named the tropical rainforest as one of the seven major biomes on which it would concentrate its research, and by making the conservation of genetic resources one of its major program goals, MAB further increased the importance of the tropical rainforests within the program. Richards (*Tropical Rain Forest*, p. 405) had suggested

as early as 1957 that the rainforests of the world ought to be viewed as vast reservoirs of future evolutionary potential because of their species diversity.

80. UNESCO, "Task Force," p. 27. The point was dramatically highlighted in 1972, when the IUCN compared Raymond Dasmann's recent map of the world's biomes to the UN List of National Parks and Reserves; all the new protected areas in other biomes, especially on the African savannas and grasslands, heightened the sense that tropical rainforests were inadequately protected.

81. Miller, interview, August 26, 1986. The U.S. Interagency Task Force on Tropical Forests (*The World's Tropical Forests,* figure 2) estimated in 1980 that of the 590 million hectares of open and closed tropical forest in South America in the mid-1970s, 30 million were in Bolivia, 35 million in Venezuela, 36 million in Colombia, 65 million in Peru, and 300 million, more than half the entire forest acreage in South America, in Brazil. The vast majority of the Brazilian rainforest was in Amazonia.

82. Katzmann, "Paradoxes of Amazon Development," pp. 447–448.

83. Sawyer, "Frontier Expansion," pp. 185–186; Pompermayer, "Strategies of Private Capital," pp. 420–422.

84. Ludwig, *Brazil: A Handbook,* pp. 374–376; Mahar, *Frontier Development,* pp. 6–13, 115–116, and elsewhere. The measures of 1966 and 1967 were known collectively as Operation Amazonia.

85. For detailed discussions of PIN planning, see Mahar, *Frontier Development;* Moran, "Government Directed Settlement"; Kleinpenning, "Evaluation of the Brazilian Policy."

86. Mahar, *Frontier Development.* p. 18. Mahar is the source for the material in this paragraph.

87. Foweraker, *Struggle for Land,* p. 137. For detailed discussions of the PIN's failure, see Mahar, *Frontier Development;* Bunker, "Power Structures"; Stone, *Dreams of Amazonia;* Moran, *Developing the Amazon.*

88. Meier and Baldwin, *Economic Development,* pp. 375–383; Bryant and White, *Managing Development,* pp. 275–294; UN, ECLA, *Economic Development,* pp. 24–29.

89. For example, Urquidi (*Challenge of Development,* p. 62) wrote that "today it would be inconceivable to leave agricultural activities to chance and the free play of supply and demand."

90. Urquidi (*Challenge of Development,* p. 115) wrote that "nothing can be gained by postponing [programs] because of incomplete or inexact data." ECLA economists wrote that "only by launching [agricultural] reform wholesale can we learn to carry it out" (UN, ECLA, *Economic Development,* p. 40).

91. For a precise and recent expression of this idea, see Meira Mattos, *Geopolítica Pan-Amazônica,* pp. 146–147, and elsewhere.

92. Wetterberg, interview, January 24, 1986.

93. Stark, "Nutrient Cycling Pathways and Litter." Nicholaides et al., "Continuous Cropping Potential," pp. 340–341. On closer inspection, the "terra roxa" soils on which PIN planners had built their hopes for Amazon settlement proved to be a variety of soils of varying agricultural potential. On this point, see Moran, "Government Directed Settlement," pp. 313-314.

94. PIN planners had written that "only the continuous terrestrial access to [the] higher lands [of Amazonia] will stimulate man's penetration and settlement in the hinterland" (Ministry of Transportation, "Amazonian Highways," p. 11).

95. Stone, *Dreams of Amazonia,* p. 90. For Brazilian attitudes toward the development of Amazonia, see McDonough, *Power and Ideology.*

96. Kleinpenning, "Further Evaluation," p.81.

97. Decreto no. 74.607, September 25, 1974, Art. 5.

Chapter 2

1. Miller, *Planning National Parks,* p. 495, called Wetterberg's environmental codes "perhaps the most ambitious and exciting" legal innovation in Latin American conservation.

2. Wetterberg (interview, November 29, 1986) said, "I understood my marching orders to be fill the gaps in wildlands conservation. The Amazon was the big gap in Brazil and South America." Wetterberg's own doctoral dissertation, "The History and Status of South American National Parks," was important in pointing out the degree to which Amazonia was a missing link in biological conservation on the continent.

3. Shortly after Wetterberg's arrival in Manaus, a conservationist suggested that he concentrate on getting the federal government to agree to give over a fixed percentage of Amazonia to biological conservation, with the selection of the particular areas to preserve coming later. Although conceding the approach had the virtue of simplicity, Wetterberg dismissed it as tactically unwise (Wetterberg, interview, July 25, 1984). In "Preservação da Natureza," section 3.9, Wetterberg and Jorge Pádua dismissed the approach as "inappropriate and arbitrary."

4. Pandolfo, interview, July 9, 1984. Quadros was known for his strange enthusiasms and impulsive behavior; he had once, without warning, banned bikinis on the beaches of Rio. As Jorge Pádua (interview, May 13, 1986) remembered him, "Jânio [Quadros] was a bit crazy, but fortunately, parks and conservation were two things he was crazy about." Pandolfo described Quadros' creation of the forest reserves as "an impulse."

5. Wetterberg, interview, April 25, 1984.

6. Wetterberg et al., "Analysis of Nature Conservation," p. ii.

7. Wetterberg, interview, April 25, 1984. Daland, *Exploring Brazilian Bureaucracy,* p. 407, writes "The military expects...decisions to be made according to the rational model of decision making by experts versed in the technology of the matter at hand."

8. Jorge Pádua and Bernardes Quintão, "Parks and Biological Reserves," p. 310. In fact, one of Wetterberg's tasks was to examine what little was known about Amazon biota for its conservation implications. Miller (*Planning National Parks*, p. 439) wrote that Wetterberg was to "synthesize the published work of various Amazon specialists into a common format from which biologically significant nature conservation priorities can be tentatively identified."

9. Lovejoy, "The Science of Amazon Conservation," p. 2. Miller, *Planning National Parks*, p. 440.

10. Wetterberg et al., "Analysis of Nature Conservation," p. 3. This view of Amazonia as a sea of homogeneous jungle, which Prance ("Phytogeographic Subdivisions," p. 195) suspected was common among South American politicians, was also politically dangerous because it encouraged a belief that one preserved area anywhere in Amazonia would adequately represent the entire rainforest.

11. Udvardy, "Classification of the Biogeographical Provinces"; IUCN, "Biotic Provinces of the World"; Holdridge, *Life Zone Ecology;* Ducke and Black, "Phytogeographic Notes"; Rizzini, "Nota Prévia."

12. Prance, "Phytogeographic Subdivisions."

13. Wetterberg and Jorge Pádua ("Preservação da Natureza") wrote that Prance's phytogeographic regions were the "spine" of the conservation plan.

14. Prance, "Conservation Problems," pp. 192–195.

15. Wetterberg, interview, December 20, 1985. He made essentially the same point in his "Case Study," p. 3.

16. Lovejoy, "Designing Refugia," p. 674.

17. Flenley, *Equatorial Rain Forest,* p. 127. Such an explanation, however, did not square with the great importance of allopatry in evolution—i.e., speciation caused by the physical isolation of two parts of a breeding population. The shortcoming seemed especially severe in Amazonia, where physical barriers to movement within the vast rainforest were few and minor. See Haffer, "General Aspects," p. 7.

18. Haffer, "Speciation in Amazonian Forest Birds." The assumption that tropical regions were long unchanged had been questioned as early as 1949, when Gentilli wrote that the distribution of Australian biota held evidence of large-scale climate change during geologically recent times. Scientists working in Africa in the early 1960s began to infer from the distribution of the continent's flora that its climate had been different in the Pleistocene. See Gentilli, "Foundation of Australian Bird Geography"; Moreau, "Vicissitudes of the African Biomes"; Carcasson, "Preliminary Survey."

19. Vanzolini, "Zoológica Sistemática"; Vanzolini and Williams, "South American Anoles"; Prance, "Phytogeographic Support." Direct pollen evidence for refuge theory was based on two cores taken from currently forested areas of Rondônia, which indicated the areas were covered by savanna vegetation during much of the late Pleistocene. Flenley, however (*Equatorial Rain Forests,* p. 71), judged this evidence "ridiculously slight."

20. Haffer, "Speciation in Amazonian Forest Birds."

21. Myers, "Islands of Conservation," p. 600.

22. Talbot, "International Role," pp. 302–303.

23. UNESCO, "Task Force," p. 20; Lovejoy and Oren, "Minimum Critical Size"; Sternberg, "Development and Conservation," p. 221.

24. Lovejoy, "Discontinuous Wilderness," p. 13.

25. Richards, "National Parks," p. 225.

26. It was also a special concern to conservationists; islands were usually places of high endemism, so the destruction of island habitats would more likely extirpate unique flora and fauna than would the destruction of comparable continental areas. The large number of island plants threatened with habitat loss was discussed at the 1949 Lake Success conference establishing the IUCN. An inventory of the world's insular flora was proposed, although not acted on, at the IUCN's 1956 general assembly in Edinburgh (Boardman, *International Organization,* pp. 60–62).

27. MacArthur and Wilson, "Equilibrium Theory"; MacArthur and Wilson, *Theory of Island Biogeography.*

28. For example, assuming a like degree of isolation, the number of species to be found on an island in an archipelago of islands of like habitat could be computed thus: $S = S_o A^z$, where A is the area of the island and S is the number of species on the island. S_o is a constant for a given species group. The exponential modifier, z, assumes a value between .18 and .35. After Diamond, "Island Dilemma."

29. MacArthur and Wilson, *Theory of Island Biogeography,* pp. 3–4.

30. For reviews of this work, see Wilson and Willis, "Applied Biogeography"; Diamond, "Island Dilemma"; Terborgh, "Preservation of Natural Diversity."

31. MacArthur and Wilson and many of their successors, including May, who extended their theoretical work, and Cody, Diamond, and Terborgh, who tested the theory in the field, were aware of and wrote extensively about the conservation implications of Island Biogeography. See Wilson and Willis, "Applied Biogeography"; May, "Island Biogeography and the Design of Wildlife Reserves"; Diamond and May, "Island Biogeography and the Design of Natural Reserves"; Diamond et al., "Island Biogeography and Conservation"; and Terborgh, "Faunal Equilibrium."

32. Terborgh, "Preservation of Natural Diversity," p. 718.

33. Wetterberg, interview, December 20, 1985.

34. Endler, "Pleistocene Forest Refuges."

35. Wetterberg, interview, December 20, 1985; Nash, *Nature of Natural Sciences,* pp. 278–279.

36. FAO, "General Programme," pp. 38–39.

37. Projeto RADAM Brasil, *Levantamento de Recursos Naturais,* Vol. 16, pp. 581–589.

38. Simberloff, "Models in Biogeography"; Simberloff and Abele, "Island Biogeography Theory"; Abele and Patton, "Size of Coral Heads."

39. Abele and Connor, "Application of Island Biogeography," p. 89.

40. Simberloff, "Models in Biogeography"; Lynch and Johnson, "Turnover and Equilibria."

41. Abele and Connor, "Application of Island Biogeography," p. 93.

42. Wetterberg et al. ("Analysis of Nature Conservation," p. 6) write that "Controversy occasionally arises over certain aspects of island biogeography's relationship to conservation practices . . . but these arguments continue to be refuted." They cite Witcomb et al. ("Island Biogeography and Conservation: the Limitations of Small Preserves") as an example of such refutation.

43. Richards, "Some Problems"; Fittkau and Klinge, "On Biomass and Trophic Structure."

44. See Terborgh, "Preservation of Natural Diversity," and Lovejoy, "Designing Refugia."

45. Terborgh, "Faunal Equilibria," cited by Wetterberg in FAO, "General Programme," p. 26.

46. Sullivan and Shaffer, "Biogeography of the Megazoo," cited by Wetterberg in FAO, "General Programme," p. 26.

47. Wetterberg, interview, January 24, 1986. Such a tack had its dangers. As Schiff ("Outdoor Recreation," pp. 546–547) observed, "The value of flexibility in uncertain environments is much too precious to surrender to the unbending tyranny of formulas." Nevertheless, given the policy environment created by the generals and their top administrators, the immediate need for firm numbers outweighed whatever costs in lost future flexibility might be incurred.

48. Terborgh ("Preservation of Natural Diversity," p. 719) writes that "Protection only in parks is not sufficient because an appreciable segment of any contained population will forage beyond park boundaries." See also Costantino, "Present Trends," pp. 69–70.

49. FAO, "General Programme," p. 27.

50. See UNESCO, "Task Force," pp. 18–19.

51. UNESCO ("Task Force," p. 18) recognized the problem in its efforts to establish an international system of biosphere reserves: "It is recognized that only rarely will it be possible to characterize a biome by means of a single reserve owing to the many ecological gradients which....produce geographical variants within a single biome." But lacking any firm grip on the problem, it fell back on general prescription: "This type of variability will determine the number of biosphere reserves necessary to provide adequate representation of any one biome, and should be considered during the first phase of the selection procedure."

52. FAO, "General Programme," p. 27; Wetterberg, interview, January 24, 1986.

53. Terborgh, "Preservation of Natural Diversity." In fact, Wetterberg decided that protecting just such an area, the Pantanal Matogrossense, the vast, seasonally inundated headwater area of the Paraguay River, was the most important habitat preservation task facing Brazil (FAO, "General Programme," p. 66).

54. Wetterberg, letter to Pieter Oyens, WWF-US Program Officer for Brazil, July 3, 1986.

55. Jorge Pádua, interview, March 26, 1986.

56. Jorge Pádua, interview, March 26, 1986.

57. Wetterberg wrote in FAO, "General Programme," p. 50, that "The designation of second or third priority should not be construed as meaning a lack of importance but rather should be taken as an indication that these areas are not suspected of a high endemism potential according to the forest refuge criteria used here."

58. Miller (*Planning National Parks,* p. 408) wrote that "the park team will have to recognize those cases where the battle for a first-priority site may...be a losing battle; they may save scarce resources by selecting the second-level priority site immediately."

59. Conservation measures beyond park boundaries was one of the important subjects of discussion at the 1971 conference of Latin American park administrators. At the Second World Conference on National Parks held the following year, Richards ("National Parks") stressed the need to combine the establishment of new national parks with the institution of region-wide conservation measures in rainforest areas.

60. Prance, "Conservation Problems," p. 193.

61. Terborgh, "Preservation of Natural Diversity," p. 715.

62. Diamond, "Island Dilemma," p. 140.

63. FAO, "General Programme," pp. 66–72.

64. Wetterberg, interview, October 29, 1986.

65. Carvalho, "Conservação da Natureza," p. 5; Miller, interview, August 26, 1986. Carvalho had been a Brazilian delegate to several OAS- and UNESCO-sponsored natural resource conferences in the 1960s and was a member of the IUCN's executive council. In large part because of the links he forged between Brazil and the international conservation network, Carvalho shared the 1973 World Wildlife Fund Gold Medal for "highly meritorious services to the conservation of wildlife and natural resources."

66. Economics seemed to reinforce the ecological wisdom: except for the North, most land was already in private hands and expensive enough to preclude all but modest land purchases by the national government.

67. The assignment of preservation responsibilities to the national forest agency was common in Latin America and much of the developing world.

68. IBDF, "Parques Nacionais e Reservas Equivalentes." The report proposed a large reserve on the open plains of the far northern territory of Rio Branco (later Roraima) and another in the cloud forests of the Pico da

Neblina region. It proposed a protected area on the seasonally inundated lands along the main trunk of the Amazon, one in the open forests of the Negro River region, and another along one of the Amazon's southern tributaries. The report (p. 26) did suggest that although the national forests it proposed were to be primarily for timber production, the forests should have an undisturbed core of 50,000 hectares. No justification is given for this number, although it seems to have come from an earlier recommendation by the Brazilian Botanical Society that nature reserves of this size be set up in Amazonia.

69. Wetterberg was not aware of the report during his years in Brazil (Wetterberg, personal communication, July 25, 1988).

Chapter 3

1. Jorge Pádua, interview, May 13, 1986.

2. Lei no. 4.771, September 15, 1965.

3. Lei no. 5.197, January 3, 1967.

4. Carvalho, "Conservação da Natureza," p. 42.

5. Decreto-Lei 1.164, 1971. Foweraker, *Struggle for Land,* p. 101. This was more than half of Amazonia.

6. Flynn, *Brazil: A Political Analysis,* Chapters 3 and 4.

7. Miller, "Replacement of Traditional Elites," pp. 159–160.

8. Deane, "Forest Conservation." All twenty-four state parks and twenty-one state biological reserves established in Brazil by the end of the 1960s were in the southern states (Ludwig, *Brazil: A Handbook,* pp. 304–305).

9. Cintra, "Traditional Brazilian Politics," pp. 154–156; Martins, "The State and the Militarization," pp. 484–485.

10. Brown, "Geographical Patterns."

11. Several like documents for other Latin American countries had evolved out of the Regional Wildlands Project, including Putney, "Estrategia Preliminar para la Conservación de Áreas Silvestres Sobresalientes del Ecuador"; Thelen and Miller, "Guia para la Planificación de Sistemas de Áreas Silvestres, con una Aplicación a los Parques Nacionales de Chile"; and INDERENA, División de Parques Nacionales y Vida Silvestre (Colombia), "Preselección de Áreas del Sistema de Parques Nacionales y Otras Reservas." Wetterberg's was the most geographically and conceptually ambitious, however.

12. Wetterberg et al., "Analysis of Nature Conservation," p. 8.

13. Wetterberg, personal communication, July 25, 1988.

14. Wetterberg et al., "Analysis of Nature Conservation," p. 16. Among those responding from abroad were T.C. Whitmore, a tropical forest specialist at Oxford University; Russell Mittermeier, a primate specialist and an active conservationist; Thomas Lovejoy, World Wildlife Fund-US program director; F.H. Wadsworth, director, U.S. Forest Service's Institute of Tropical Silvaculture; S.L. Krugman, chief of forest genetic research, U.S. Forest

Service; and Ghillean Prance, director of botanical research, New York Botanical Gardens. Respondents from within Brazil included Keith Brown of UNICAMP, who had recently delineated a pattern of Pleistocene forest fragments based on butterflies; Fernando Novaes, chief, Vertebrates Department, Goeldi Museum, Belém; Cory Teixeira de Carvalho, chief, forest animal section, São Paulo Forest Institute; and J. Griffith, professor, Graduate Forestry School, Federal University of Vicosa.

Wetterberg's insistence that the report was only a first, tentative step "toward a firm scientific base for determining conservation priorities in Amazonia" probably encouraged their unreserved support (Jorge Pádua, interview, March 26, 1986). Miller (interview, August 26, 1986) felt that the freshness of the science Wetterberg had used was also important: "There were not yet large groups of scientists out there testing. Perhaps they would have been critical of his approach had they been around."

15. Wetterberg and Jorge Pádua, "Preservação da Natureza," p. 42.

16. Wetterberg and Jorge Pádua, "Preservação da Natureza," pp. 33–37.

17. Wetterberg and Jorge Pádua, "Preservação da Natureza," p. 34. Although INCRA did not guarantee that it would always respect the IBDF's wishes, it did accept the report in principle.

18. Tellingly, determining whether an area was a Pleistocene forest fragment was not a duty of the evaluation teams (Brown, interview, May 9, 1986).

19. In the late nineteenth century, the steadily expanding demand for rubber encouraged caboclos to neglect subsistence activities and concentrate on collecting rubber, which they sold to the itinerant traders, much as they had always sold forest products. When the rubber boom collapsed, the caboclos, trapped within the decaying regional economy, returned to their semi-subsistence lifeway. Bunker ("Forces of Destruction," Table 1) shows that the gross regional income dropped approximately 80 percent between 1909 and 1915, and that the total regional population declined from 1,217,024 to 1,091,545 between 1910 and 1920. Katzman ("Paradoxes of Amazonian Development," p. 447) writes that the collapse of the rubber boom left the caboclo rubber tappers a "stranded population."

20. Bunker ("Power Structures," p. 57), arguing that the caboclo lifeway is more than a residual culture form, suggests that "caboclization" is a dynamic process likely to occur in any economically stagnant areas of Amazonia. The term *seringueiro* refers to a rubber tapper. Normally seringueiros in Amazonia are merely caboclos who concentrate on rubber tapping, although seldom to the total exclusion of other gainful activities that comprise the caboclo lifeway.

21. Foweraker, *Struggle for Land,* p. 137.

22. Pandolfo, interview, July 9, 1984; Hecht, "Cattle Ranching," p. 380.

23. Imperial Law 601, September 18, 1850. Because land in Amazonia had little market value, this law left caboclos fairly secure on the land they occupied while not inconveniencing the dominant commercial interests in the region.

24. Sawyer, "Frontier Expansion."

25. This was especially the case with regard to regularizing land titles in frontier areas. See Mueller, "Frontier Based Agricultural Expansion," p. 150. Bunker discounts this responsibility entirely, perhaps because it was so frequently neglected in practice. In "Forces of Destruction," p. 38, Bunker writes that "There is...no single agency responsible for the protection of the peasants."

26. Schmink, "Land Conflicts," p. 350; Mueller, "Frontier Based Agricultural Expansion," p. 150.

27. Schmink, "Land Conflicts," p. 353. Foweraker (*Struggle for Land*, p. 140) writes that INCRA's "social role is reserved for those occasions when a small multitude is prepared to fight for its right to the land." Perhaps this is the case when powerful development interests are involved, but it was less inclined to ignore this part of its mandate when asked to do so by a relatively powerless agency whose mandate went against the grain of prevailing government ideology.

28. Cantarelli, interview, May 22, 1986.

29. There were still 230 identified tribes remaining in Brazil in 1900, mostly in Amazonia and the Cerrado region to the south of it (Kahn, "Reporter at Large," p. 65). Kahn is the source of the figures for the decline in the number of extant tribes given above. Ramos ("Frontier Expansion," p. 8) estimates that whereas 46 percent of extant Indians had no contact or only minimal contact with national society in 1900, by the early 1980s it was likely only three or four wholly uncontacted groups remained.

30. Dasmann, "National Parks," pp. 166–167.

31. For example, see Meier, *Science and Economic Development,* pp. 208–209.

32. The 1961 Punta del Este Treaty, which confirmed the Alliance for Progress, called for the integration of Indian populations into the "economic, social, and cultural processes of modern life" (Evans, *Decade of Development,* p. 92). Carvalho asserted that "aborigines cannot be kept in a primitive state but must...be encouraged toward full participation in national life." Therefore, "the reconciliation [of native welfare] with the aims of park management is impossible" (Carvalho in Elliott [ed.], *Second World Conference,* Session III, discussion, p. 97).

33. Constantino, "Present Trends," in Elliott (ed.), *Second World Conference,* p. 72.

34. Carvalho, "Conservação da Natureza," p. 33. Nogueira-Neto, interview, February 21, 1986.

35. A few tribes were granted outright ownership of their lands in the nineteenth century, usually for some service to the state. For example, several tribes received title to their lands for aiding the Brazilian army in its war against Paraguay. These were the exceptions, however; most tribes had only a tenuous hold on their lands in the nineteenth and early twentieth

centuries. Brazil's Indian Protection Service had been set up in 1910 to protect Indians from exploitation by private interests, and while the service began with high ideals, inadequate budgets and corruption eventually rendered it incapable of living up to them. It was abolished in 1967 and replaced by FUNAI.

36. One of its directors from this era declared that "Indian programs shall obstruct neither national development nor the axes of penetration for the integration of Amazonia" (Barrett, "Conservation in Amazonia," p. 220).

37. Mueller, "Frontier Based Agricultural Expansion," p. 150.

38. Skillings and Tcheyan, "Economic Development Prospects," p. 35.

39. Nelson, *Development of Tropical Lands,* p. 278; Dasmann, *Ecological Principles,* p. 64.

40. Sternberg, "Development and Conservation," p. 257; Nelson, *Development of Tropical Lands,* p. 131. The FAO had identified livestock production as one of the tropical world's least efficient industries and believed that underdeveloped countries in the tropics could take advantage of that demand if they improved pastures and stock quality.

41. Foweraker, *Struggle for Land,* p. 156; Hecht, "Cattle Ranching," p. 373. Hecht, p. 371 (citing other sources), suggests another motive for government encouragement of Amazon cattle ranching: "Since few other concessions were granted to labor by the regime, cheap food policies (especially for beef) were important priorities."

42. With the rubber boom some individuals did manage to gain legal control of large tracts of land and forced their occupants into wage labor or compulsory rubber collection, but except in and near cities, interest in legal control of land ended with the collapse of the boom, and much land that had been acquired by private owners devolved to the states.

43. Foweraker (*Struggle for Land,* p. 98) described the situation in eastern Pará in the late 1950s, just before the construction of the Belém-Brasília highway, as a "rather sleepy legal scene."

44. Hecht ("Cattle Ranching," p. 377) writes that "if land values increase, then the desire for investment becomes understandable because land tends to hold value in inflationary economies." This was certainly the case in Brazil throughout the 1960s and 1970s. Even in the boom years, inflation remained high enough to make hedges against it seem like reasonable investments.

45. See Schmink, "Land Conflicts," and Foweraker, *Struggle for Land.* See especially Chapter 5, "Law and Lawlessness on the Frontier and the Problem of Bureaucratic Inertia," for a discussion of the chaos surrounding the titling process and the conflicts that arose from it.

46. IBDF/FBCN, *Plano do Sistema: Primera Etapa,* "Alto Xingu, Relatório de Viagem," pp. 213–215. Four- or five-day surveys by two or three scientists were the norm.

47. The IBDF and WWF had recently distributed 100,000 color posters of the otter nationwide, and shortly before the IBDF expedition, two young otters

had been removed from the area and transported to the zoo in Brasília in hopes of beginning a captive breeding program.

48. Jorge Pádua, interview, May 26, 1986. She is the source of the material in the rest of this paragraph.

49. Jorge Pádua, interview, May 13, 1986.

50. Falleros, interview, May 28, 1986. The Department of National Parks was apparently operating under the assumption that there was only minor potential for conflict between Amazon Indians and a conservation program based on Wetterberg's approach. In correspondence with Wetterberg, Betty Meggars, an anthropologist and expert on the Indians of Amazonia, indicated that Indian presence in the areas identified as Pleistocene refuges was not likely to be a serious problem in Brazil, although it might be one in neighboring countries (Wetterberg and Jorge Pádua, "Preservação da Natureza," p. 19).

51. Bunker ("Power Structures") writes that INCRA's power and operating autonomy in Amazonia was derived from its control over federal land and the revenues from land taxes and sales.

52. Jorge Pádua, interview, May 13, 1986.

53. Abele and Connor, "Application of Island Biogeography," p. 89.

54. These included the incursion of predators and the invasion of exotic species from bordering ecosystems and the presence of inhospitable microclimates on the periphery of the reserve. See Diamond, "Island Dilemma," p. 143; MacArthur and Wilson, *Theory of Island Biogeography,* pp. 115–116.

55. The boundary suggestions brought back by the expedition to the upper Xingu region revealed how many considerations could go into finding the right limits for a protected area. The evaluation team suggested using BR 80, the new road being built across northern Mato Grosso, as the southern boundary of a biological reserve in the region. The road was like a natural boundary in that it was clearly identifiable on the ground, and south of it was the vast Xingu Indian reserve, off limits to the IBDF. The team proposed the Xingu River itself for the western boundary, since it was a clear landmark and beyond it was the Jarina Indian reserve. It suggested that the eastern boundary should run along the watershed between the Xingu and the Liberdade rivers. The watershed was not easy to identify in the field because there was little local relief, but since almost all travel in the area was by water, it would act as a barrier to human incursion. For the northern boundary, the team proposed a survey line drawn east-west through the Von Martius Waterfall on the Xingu River. Although this would leave all the northern boundary, except where it crossed the river, without a natural demarcation, it was not deemed a serious problem because most of those entering the area from the north would be traveling by river and would encounter the falls (IBDF/FBCN, *Plano do Sistema: Primera Etapa,* p. 215; Jorge Pádua, interview, May 13, 1986).

56. Jorge Pádua, interview, May 13, 1986; Bernardes Quintão, interview, May 16, 1986.

57. At the Second World Conference on National Parks in 1972, Carvalho
said, "In accordance with suggestions made at the IUCN-sponsored conference at Bareloche in 1968, [Brazilian conservationists] are canvassing
public support for a joint park in the mountainous area on the
Brazil/Venezuela border" (Elliott [ed.], *Second World Conference*, p. 401).

58. Spruce had written of Pico da Neblina in 1908: "It seemed the finest object
for a painter's pencil I had seen in South America. It is impossible to do justice to the scene in words" (quoted in IBDF/FBCN, *Plano do Sistema:
Primera Etapa*, p. 35). A dozen or so technicians, guides, and baggage han-
dlers accompanied the scientists, who had an air force plane at their disposal. The expedition spent two weeks in October 1977 traveling in the
region by plane, truck, boat, and foot in the company of military men, missionaries, and local guides ("Plano de Viagem ao Pico da Neblina,"
pp. 71–73 in IBDF/FBCN, *Plano do Sistema: Primera Etapa*).

59. Daland, *Exploring Brazilian Bureaucracy*, p. 60; Wesson and Fleischer,
Brazil in Transition, p. 127. In 1982, Schmink ("Land Conflicts," p. 355)
wrote, "The bulk of decisions for Amazonia are now carried out within the
presidential palace and the National Security Council, instead of the federal and regional bureaucracies."

60. Ramos ("Indian Peoples," p. 97) reports that a representative from
Roraima Territory proposed removing all Indians from a 150-kilometer
strip along the national boundaries as a matter of national security.

61. Survival International-USA, "Voice of the Yanomami Indians."

62. Jorge Pádua (interview, May 13, 1986) said, "We could not ignore the
Indians in Pico da Neblina, but we figured that [they] would not be a problem for at least twenty or thirty years. We hoped we could then work out
any problems that arose."

63. IBDF/FBCN, *Plano do Sistema: Primera Etapa*, pp. 73–79. IBDF/FBCN,
p. 73, state that the turtle protection in the area was begun in 1976.
However, the more thorough treatment of the subject in IBDF, "Reserva
Biológica de Rio Trombetas, Plano de Manejo," p. 3, states that this protection began more than a decade earlier and that the IBDF took over
responsibility for it in 1970.

64. Assoreira and Carvalho de Vasconcelos, "Viagem Realizada."

65. IBDF/FBCN, "Reserva Biológica de Rio Trombetas, Plano de Manejo,"
p. 5.

66. UNESCO, "Task Force," p. 50.

67. Brown, interview, May 9, 1986.

68. IBDF/FBCN, *Plano do Sistema: Primera Etapa*, pp. 80–84.

69. IBDF/FBCN, *Plano do Sistema: Primera Etapa*, p. 84; Maia, interview,
April 30, 1986. Field reports indicated that approximately 20 percent of
the area's residing families owned their land.

70. Estado do Amazonas, "Parque Nacional do Rio Jaú" (map).

71. Jorge Pádua, interview, May 26, 1986.

72. Nelson (*Development of Tropical Lands,* p. 266) wrote that markets were the principal bottleneck to new land development. Constructing this new road was analogous to unstopping the bottle, and the flow increased after the road was upgraded in 1965.

73. Mueller, "Frontier Based Agricultural Expansion," p. 88.

74. Mueller, "Frontier Based Agricultural Expansion," p. 146. A small farm was defined as under 200 hectares. The area in such farms jumped from 209,800 hectares to 1,566,683 during that period.

75. Myers, "Present Status," p. 111.

76. Jorge Pádua, interview, March 26, 1986.

77. IBDF/FBCN, *Plano do Sistema: Primera Etapa,* pp. 97–101.

78. Falleros, interview, May 28, 1986.

79. IBDF/FBCN, *Plano do Sistema: Primera Etapa,* pp. 63–66.

80. IBDF/FBCN, *Plano do Sistema: Primera Etapa,* pp. 68–72.

81. The field evaluation team saw less tourist potential at the smaller Lago Piratuba, even though it was closer to Belém.

82. IBDF/FBCN, *Plano do Sistema: Primera Etapa,* pp. 86–89.

83. IBDF/FBCN, *Plano do Sistema: Primera Etapa,* pp. 90–94.

84. Wetterberg, interview, December 20, 1985.

85. Jorge Pádua, interview, March 26, 1986.

86. Jorge Pádua, interview, March 26, 1986.

87. Jorge Pádua and Bernardes Quintão, "Parks and Biological Reserves," p. 314.

88. Jorge Pádua, interview, March 26, 1986.

89. For a brief history of the project, see Lewin, "How Big?"

90. Daland, *Exploring Brazilian Bureaucracy,* p. 125.

91. Wetterberg, interview, December 20, 1985. Daland (*Exploring Brazilian Bureaucracy,* p. 218) argued that the frequently broken, frayed, or subverted lines of formal authority in the Brazilian federal bureaucracy encouraged this kind of direct, personal communication outside routine bureaucratic channels.

92. Two national parks outside Amazonia were also established on June 5.

93. Decreto no. 84.017. The decree made it clear that nature protection was the primary goal of the new parks and reserves. It prohibited intensive development for visitors in the biological reserves and permitted it in national parks only where it would not threaten the park's biological resources. It also prohibited dams and other projects that would alter the natural drainage of the protected areas, as well as railroads, roads, aqueducts, and electrical power lines. Although initially proposed as a biological reserve, Jaú was established as a national park.

94. Child, *Geopolitics in South America,* p. 70. Child also writes that the Brazilian ESG and its equivalent in other South American nations with

politically active militaries addressed major problems in national development and policy, a role that in the United States was filled by special study groups or independent think tanks like the Brookings Institution, the Hudson Institute, or the Rand Corporation.

95. Miller, interview, August 26, 1986.

96. Miller, interview, August 26, 1986.

97. Geraldo Budowski, a former Director General of the IUCN, complained about the failure of scientists to get the results of their work to conservation decision-makers. He accused them of being poor at communicating with decision-makers, of being obsessed with ultimate truths, and of using up too much energy in controversy that only confused decision-makers (Budowski, "Opening Address," p. 9). Holdgate et al. ("World Environmental Trends," p. 26) had similar complaints, and many non-scientist conservationists felt the gap between science and policy produced by these tendencies weakened conservation's credentials and retarded its acceptance.

Chapter 4

1. Stillwell, "National Parks of Brazil," p. 406.

2. When INPA instituted its research publication series in 1964, the entire first issue was devoted to reprinting an article by Hans Bluntschli entitled, "Amazonia as a Harmonious Organism," originally published in German in *Geographische Zeitschrift* in 1921. In it, Bluntschli, a Swedish doctor who had traveled through Peruvian Amazonia early in the century, expressed a deeply pantheistic vision of the unity of man and nature that reflected many modern ecological ideas. He praised the lifeways of Amazon Indians for the stability and the respect for nature he thought inherent in them. He condemned the export economy, especially cattle raising, for destroying the forests of the region. Bluntschli especially condemned the intrusion of European influence and urban-based culture, which he saw as promoting social inequality and poverty. "This Amazonia," he wrote (p. 35), "wants to be a child of European culture but it is a caricature. This is the Amazonia of whiskey and zinc roofs; it cannot lead, down its chosen path, to good." Subsequent issues in the INPA series played to similar themes: Amazonia had a basic ecological unity; that unity had to be respected in developing any plans for the region.

3. For a development of this argument with special application to the tropical rainforests, see Committee on Research Priorities, *Research Priorities,* pp. 26–45.

4. Haring, *Empire in Brazil,* pp. 139–141; Burns, *History of Brazil,* chapter 4.

5. Dean, "Forest Conservation."

6. Caldwell, *International Environmental Policy,* p. 189.

7. In 1974, Brooks ("Knowledge and Action," pp. 139–140) wrote, "Today, all the advanced industrial nations are suffering from disillusionment with the failure of science in attacking what are perceived as the most urgent

problems of the future." Some blamed scientists themselves, who were widely thought to be disinterested in real-world issues and who too frequently preferred to produce theoretical work whose internal elegance was balanced by only the remotest possibility of application. Others faulted the way science proceeded at its own unpredictable pace from uncertainty to uncertainty, seldom giving administrators anything firm enough on which to base important decisions. See Meier, *Science and Economic Development*, p. 250; Sachs, *Studies in Political Economy*, pp. 269–270; Ronayne, *Science in Government*, p. 83.

8. Olindo, quoted in Elliot, ed., *Second World Conference*, Session III, discussion, p. 77; Budowski, "Imperialismo Científico."

9. To this end, Cowan drew up a draft "International Convention for Field Studies in Natural History" for the 1968 Latin American Conference on Natural Resources. See Cowan, "Scientific Research," pp. 340–344.

10. Portaria no. 174/81-P, March 11, 1981. Wetterberg (personal communication, July 25, 1988) held that this rule was intended to apply primarily to "consumptive" or "environmentally altering" research.

11. Foresta, *America's National Parks,* Chapter 2. More recently (i.e., in the 1970s) Mario Boza and Alvaro Ugalde had established an impressive set of national parks for Costa Rica and were quick to distill lessons for other Latin American conservationists from their success. They recommended selecting parks with immediate popular appeal—i.e., spectacular scenery or special opportunities for recreation—and with accessibility to large population centers. Once the parks were established, they advised building a mass constituency for them quickly through publicity campaigns promoting park use and the construction of visitor facilities (Boza, "Costa Rica").

12. For example, life expectancy at birth increased from 55 to 61 years between 1960 and 1980. During the same period, the rate of adult literacy increased from 61 to 76 percent, and the percentage of the appropriate age group in primary school jumped from 57 to 93 percent (Balassa et al., *Toward Renewed Economic Growth*, p. 56).

13. At the 1968 Bariloche conference on natural resource management, Fisher ("Parks and Natural Areas," p. 198) had stressed that this was the case for all Latin America.

14. Stillwell, "National Parks of Brazil," p. 405.

15. Only 13 percent of all lands to be acquired for the national parks and 30 percent for the biological reserves were in public ownership by 1975 (UNDP/FAO/IUCN, "General Programme," p. 5).

16. IBDF, "Parques Nacionais e Reservas Equivalentes," p. 63.

17. Jorge Pádua, interview, May 13, 1986.

18. Miller, *Planning National Parks*, pp. 193–194.

19. Wetterberg had raised similar arguments against the possibility of building a large visitor constituency in the UNFAO's "A General Programme," p. 4. He wrote that "Amazon fauna...tends to be overrated as a tourist attraction. Most Amazon species are difficult to observe in their natural habitat

by the untrained observer. Many species, furthermore, are nocturnal and are scarce near populated or heavily visited areas."

20. Decreto no. 84.017, articles 6 and 7. For example, when plans to place a TV tower in Rio's Tijuca National Park were revealed, the Department of National Parks argued that it had no place in the park's management plan and was therefore illegal (an argument it eventually lost).

21. UNFAO, "Wildland Management and Planning," pp. 26–27.

22. Officially, the DN was to provide "leadership and technical support" for the protected areas (UNFAO, "Wildland Management and Planning," pp. 26–27).

23. Bernardes Quintão, interview, May 16, 1986; Guimarães, interview, April 22, 1986.

24. The degree to which this was the case was illustrated by the frequent mention of the fact that the delegado to Pará was a career IBDF administrator, not a political appointee.

25. It appears the delegados were originally established to play a more limited role. The legislation establishing the IBDF, Decreto-lei no. 289, Chapter II, article 1, reads, "IBDF may maintain state or regional representatives, principally for technical ends, when the volume of responsibilities justifies it." It is likely that their power expanded beyond purely technical matters as a result of the play of federal-state politics described in chapter eight.

26. Wetterberg (UNFAO, "A General Programme," p. 18) had written, "The system is appropriate in a country the size of Brazil as long as the state 'delegacias' are permitted to hire staff in accordance with their responsibilities and, in matters related to parks and wildlife, remain under the overall guidance of the central office." Miller (*Planning National Parks*, p. 492) also preferred a simpler plan with a line of authority running directly from the head of a national parks department to the directors of each national park.

27. Foresta, *America's National Parks*, pp. 71–73.

28. Jorge Pádua, interview, May 13, 1986.

29. IBDF/FBCN, *Plano do Sistema: Segunda Etapa*.

30. Jorge Pádua, interview, May 23, 1986.

31. Carvalho, "Conservation of Nature," p. 715.

32. Jorge Pádua, interview, May 23, 1986.

33. The Committee on Research Priorities in Tropical Biology of the American National Research Council concluded that natural reserves were the best approach to the preservation of genetic diversity, and the only one for many organisms (Committee on Research Priorities, *Research Priorities*, p. 56). In fact, some argued taking a species out of its natural environment, which so actively determined its traits, defeated the whole purpose of species conservation.

34. Lovejoy, "Designing Refugia," p. 677; Di Castri and Robertson, "Biosphere Reserve Concept," p. 1.

35. Foweraker, *Struggle for Land,* p. 154.

36. For example, authority for the *várzeas* was divided between INCRA, which controlled the land and issued titles to it; the IBDF, responsible for the forests that grew on them; and SUDEPE, responsible for the waters that flowed over them periodically and for the fish that swam in those waters. Baker ("Administrative Trap," p. 249) writes that such fragmentation causes "each ministry [to] deal only with the elements defined by its terms of reference and will perforce regard these elements of a general problem as [the problem] itself." In 1972, even before most third-world countries had established mechanisms for dealing with the environment, Caldwell (*In Defense of Earth,* pp. 200–201) warned that the need for a comprehensive approach was especially important in environmental management, given the often diffuse nature of environmental problems.

37. Jorge Pádua, interview, May 13, 1986.

38. Pandolfo, interview, July 9, 1984. The division advocated developing Amazonia in line with what it termed the region's "natural calling."

39. Other promising developments included the establishment in 1979 of a federal senate committee to investigate the extent of recent forest clearing in Amazonia, and the IBDF's program, supported by the FAO and the UN Development Programme, to monitor Amazon forest cover with Landsat images provided by U.S. satellites in the same year. With these images, the agency finally had the necessary information to begin enforcing federal clearing regulations throughout Amazonia.

40. Decreto no. 87.585 and 87.587, September 20, 1982.

41. Decreto no. 73.030, October 30, 1973. Nogueira-Neto, "Getting Brazil's Network," p. 27. He had been a member of Brazil's delegation to the 1972 World Conference on National Parks.

42. SEMA, *Programa de Ação;* UNFAO, "General Programme," p. 16.

43. Abele and Connor, "Application of Island Biogeography," p. 93; Terborgh, "Preservation of Natural Diversity," p. 722.

44. UNESCO, "Task Force," p. 12–13, 21.

45. Nogueira-Neto, interview, February 12, 1986. Lovejoy, who had worked with Nogueira-Neto for a decade, characterized him as having "a deep appreciation for science" (Interview, November 26, 1985).

46. For example, two of Island Biogeography Theory's earliest and strongest critics, Abele and Connor ("Application of Island Biogeography," p. 93) wrote that "it is very risky to attempt to predict a priori the best design strategy ... without detailed studies of entire floras and faunas."

47. Nogueira-Neto, interview, February 21, 1986.

48. Nogueira-Neto, letter to Edwin Snider, February 18, 1986.

49. Nogueira-Neto, interview, February 21, 1986.

50. Simões, interview, February 22, 1986.

51. When the agency's investigation of the Juami-Japurá area in western Amazonia turned up only sixteen posseiro families and one legal land title, it was encouraged to further explore the possibility of an ecological station in the area.

52. Nogueira-Neto, interviews, July 20, 1984; February 21, 1986.

53. Figueiredo, interview, March 4, 1986. Nogueira-Neto, interview, July 20, 1984, said, "All the stations begin at my desk." Unless otherwise noted, these interviews are the source for the material in this and the following paragraph.

54. SEMA, *Programa de Ação;* Nogueira-Neto, interview, February 21, 1986.

55. Costantino, "Present Trends," p. 71.

56. Nogueira-Neto, "Getting Brazil's Network," pp. 33–34; SEMA, "Programa de Gerenciamento."

57. Nogueira-Neto, interview, February 21, 1986. The program gained a measure of offsetting credibility from the similarity of its goals to those of the UN's International Biological Program and UNESCO's Biosphere Reserve Initiative. When this regulation was codified into law, it read, ". . . ecological research that will cause changes in the natural environment may be authorized" (Lei no. 6.902, art. 1, para. 2, April 27, 1981).

58. Cowan, "Scientific Research, p. 338, writes that "The principal goal of IBP is a worldwide understanding of the potential productive capacity of the many ecosystems which . . . exist"; UNESCO, "Task Force"; UN Department of Economic and Social Affairs, *Natural Resources,* p. 136.

59. SEMA, "Programa de Gerenciamento"; Simões, interview, February 22, 1986.

60. Nogueira-Neto, interviews, July 20, 1984, and February 21, 1986. These interviews are also the source for the material in the following paragraph.

61. Nogueira-Neto, interview, July 20, 1984.

62. Costa, interview, March 19, 1986. Figueiredo (interview, March 6, 1986) said, "We have good relations with the states because Dr. Paulo is viewed by them as a technocrat, someone outside politics who can be trusted."

63. Freitas, interview, November 13, 1986.

64. Lovejoy, interview, November 26, 1985.

65. Lovejoy, interview, November 26, 1985; Blake (interview, November 1, 1985) said of Nogueira-Neto, "He sees what's important and quietly goes for it."

66. There was some danger in this strategy; if overplayed, it could lead to a nationalistic backlash and a loss rather than gain of domestic support. This happened to Perez Olindo, the leading Kenyan conservationist of the independence era. According to Nash (*Wilderness and the American Mind,* p. 370) Olindo's "repeated recourse to American and European contacts cost him political support, and ultimately his job, in nationalistic Kenya." Nogueira-Neto was careful to make sure this did not happen by balancing

his extensive foreign contacts with nationalist conservation rhetoric at home.

67. Nogueira-Neto and Carvalho, "A Programme of Ecological Stations." Unless otherwise specified, this is the source on the early ecological stations. The island was part of the old Parima Forest Reserve, but it had only existed on paper. SEMA has given several estimates of the size of the Maracá station, ranging from 92,000 to 102,000 hectares.

68. Nogueira-Neto, "Getting Brazil's Network," p. 32.

69. Wetterberg, interview, October 29, 1986.

70. SEMA also held that the islands' proximity to Manaus might permit some limited tourism on them (Nogueira-Neto and Carvalho, "Programme of Ecological Stations," p. 99).

71. Decreto no. 70.030, October 30, 1973, art. 4.

72. Daland (*Exploring Brazilian Bureaucracy*, p. 122) called the Ministry of the Interior "a holding company for a variety of . . . autonomous agencies."

73. Caldwell (*In Defense of Earth*, p. 222) argued that because they were new players in public administration, environmental protection agencies needed especially strong positions within the administrative hierarchy if they were to be effective. Also see Boardman, *International Organization*, p. 176.

74. Jorge Pádua, interview, July 23, 1984.

Chapter 5

1. Schmitter (*Interest Conflict*, p. 235) concluded that the whole Brazilian legal tradition aimed at avoiding definitive state commitments.

2. The federal government assigned miniscule funds to conservation programs and left them hopelessly understaffed. The federal forest codes were ignored, and the forest guard was never created. Although a dozen protected forests were established in the southern states by federal decree in the late 1940s and early 1950s, steps for their protection, or even their demarcation, were seldom taken. See Dean, "Forest Conservation," pp. 64–65; Stillwell, "National Parks of Brazil."

3. De Barros, *Parques Nacionais*, p. 14; Oltremari and Fahrenkrog, "Institutionalization of National Parks," p. 4.

4. Camara, interview, July 4, 1984.

5. Foweraker, *Struggle for Land*, p. 164.

6. Jorge Pádua, interview, May 13, 1986. Schwartzman ("Struggling to be Born") observed that the Brazilian government's interest in science was seldom accompanied by any deep understanding of exactly what science was.

7. Nogueira-Neto, interview, February 21, 1986. "Biota" is the same in English and Portuguese.

8. Skillings and Tcheyan, "Economic Development Prospects."

9. If this was the case, it was not uniquely Brazilian: Boardman (*International Organization,* p.176) writes that conservation measures that involve little real cost and provoke little opposition are attractive political morsels. He cites the near-unanimous congressional and presidential support in the United States for international polar conservation in the early 1970s as an example.

10. Harroy, "International Commission," p.63. According to Jorge Pádua (various interviews) one of the most vocal opponents to her continued concentration of protected natural areas was José Lutzenberger, a nationally prominent environmentalist based in the southernmost state of Rio Grande do Sul. Lutzenberger argued that such a concentration would inevitably lead to the neglect of the rest of the landscape of Amazonia. Harald Sioli, the prominent Amazon scientist, also opposed this emphasis, and for the same reason.

11. Jorge Pádua, various interviews, March–May 1986.

12. Skillings and Tcheyan, "Economic Development Prospects," p. 27; also see Walter and Ugelow, "Environmental Policy," pp. 104–105. Carvalho, "Conservation of Nature," p. 708.

13. PL96–53, August 14, 1979, Section 103/b/3.

14. Skillings, interview, April 23, 1984; Goodland, "Brazil's Environmental Progress."

15. This need for speed in staking out nature's turf was part of international conservation wisdom. It found clear expression at the First World Conference on National Parks in 1962 (Gille, "Role of International Agencies," p. 323, 326), and Miller had subsequently stressed it in his writing.

    In a perverse way, the desire of the proponents of Island Biogeography Theory to see their theory turned into policy encouraged the acceptance of tropical development and deforestation as inevitable. Only under such a view would it make sense to concentrate conservation resources on protected forest isolates whose size and shape were determined by theory. As Diamond ("Island Dilemma," p. 131) wrote, "[C]onsider the fact that we surely cannot save all the rainforest of the Amazon Basin. What fraction of Amazonia must be left to guarantee the survival of [that which should be saved]?" For Jorge Pádua, a commitment to Island Biogeography Theory was also a psychological commitment to the conditions under which the theory would be useful.

16. Clawson, "Park Visits," p. 119.

17. As a Peace Corps volunteer in Chile in the mid-1960s, Wetterberg had been assigned to Vicente Perez Rosales National Park, founded in 1926 yet still undeveloped and little visited. When Wetterberg returned a decade later he was struck by how well used, well managed, and seemingly secure the park had become (Wetterberg, interview, October 29, 1986).

18. Wetterberg, Prance and Lovejoy, "Conservation Progress," p. 5. Jorge Pádua held that just the existence of a federal decree protected an area because it legally committed the federal government to the area's defense.

Moreover, the decree sometimes played into local politics in such a way as to prompt local protection of a natural area as a means to other ends (Jorge Pádua, interview, May 26, 1986).

19. Jorge Pádua, interview, May 13, 1986. The road, much of which crossed through low-lying, seasonally inundated terrain, proved far more difficult to build than initially envisioned, and the project was eventually abandoned. When Jorge Pádua left the IBDF, she became the chief environmental officer for CESP, the São Paulo Energy Company. She founded the Fundação Pro-Natureza, a private conservation organization, in 1986 and remained as president of that organization through the balance of the 1980s. Wetterberg left Brazil in 1978 while the IBDF expeditions to the areas he had identified were underway. Although he remained active in international conservation, first with the American National Park System and later with the U.S. Forest Service, his involvement with Brazilian conservation was minimal after 1978.

20. Lundberg, *Coming World Transformation,* p. 344.

21. See UN, ECLA, *Economic Development,* especially pp. 7–12, 30–34. Also see Meier, *Developmental Planning,* pp. 37–63.

22. Dean, "Forest Conservation."

23. See Nielson, *Golden Donors,* especially Part I, for an account of the evolution and public role of the large American foundations.

24. The Ford Foundation established a Resources and Environment Division, and the Rockefeller Foundation set up an Environmental Studies Division. See Collier and Horowitz, *The Rockefellers,* pp. 304–308 and elsewhere. Also see Barkley and Weissman, "Eco-Establishment."

25. Nisbet, *History of the Idea,* p. 334. Also see Van Doren, *Idea of Progress,* pp. 340–349. Van Doren, p. 340, writes that by the early twentieth century, "the word 'progress' as it is used in ordinary speech usually means little more than technological progress." Also see Cornish, *Study of the Future,* especially Chapter 5. The idea that major revolutions in thinking take place because new ideas are useful to the powerful is a major one in Western thought. It is certainly at the core of Weber's notion of "elective affinity." See Gerth and Mills, *From Max Weber.* Boulding ("Legitimacy of Economics," p. 27) suggests that the acceptance of classical economics as "correct" was largely due to the way it legitimized the rising merchant class of late eighteenth-century England.

26. During the war, the Council on Foreign Relations, the Rockefeller Foundation, and other institutions in the United States which viewed global thinking as their special domain, began to plan for the postwar order, which they assumed would be dominated by the United States and was therefore theirs to define. A consensus on what that world should look like gradually emerged from their work. See Domhoff, *Powers That Be,* pp. 101–108; Arndt, "Development Economics," pp. 24–26.

27. Burns, *History of Brazil,* pp. 420–431.

28. The war encouraged industrial development in Brazil, as it did in much of South America, by cutting off the traditional sources of industrial goods. See Keen and Wasserman, *History of Latin America,* p. 369.

29. Burns, *History of Brazil,* pp. 413–419.

30. Burns, *History of Brazil,* pp. 436–446.

31. Roett, *Brazil: Politics,* p. 118; Schneider, *Political System of Brazil,* pp. 25–26.

32. Pearson, "Latin American Peasant," p. 239.

33. Roett, *Brazil: Politics,* pp. 166–167. For a detailed analysis of this period, see Flynn, *Brazil: A Political Analysis,* Chapter 8.

34. Roett, *Brazil: Politics,* pp. 129–130. The March mayoral election in São Paulo placed a candidate backed by former president Quadros in office. October gubernatorial elections gave the governorships of Minas Gerais and Guanabara to opponents of the military.

35. Wesson and Fleischer, *Brazil in Transition,* p. 25.

36. Haring, *Empire in Brazil,* pp. 139–141. Olivera Lima referred to Positivism as the "Gospel of the Military Academy" (Quoted in Haring, loc. cit.). Lima wrote, perhaps with exaggeration, that the younger officers were more familiar with the teachings of Comte than with conventional military subjects like ballistics and tactics.

37. See Pittman, "Geopolitics in the ABC Countries," Chapter 4, "Brazilian Geopolitical Thought."

38. Wesson and Fleischer, *Brazil in Transition,* pp. 124–125.

39. Schneider, *Political System of Brazil,* p. 95.

40. Evans, *Decade of Development,* pp. 113–115. Also see Janowitz, *Military in the Political Development;* Johnson (ed.), *Role of the Military;* Lieuwen, *Arms and Politics.* In 1961, John F. Kennedy told a gathering of Latin American diplomats that "the new generation of military leaders . . . can not only defend their countries—they can help build them" (Quoted in Leighton and Sanders, "Military Civic Action," p. 103). Castro's recent success in Cuba prompted the United States to encourage the militaries to attack the sources of rural discontent by building schools, digging wells, etc., and, in general, to show a benevolent side of state power. The U.S. quickly incorporated this idea into its training programs for Latin America officers and, through American influence, so did most Latin American military staff colleges.

41. On this last point, see Evans, *Dependent Development.* Daland (*Exploring Brazilian Bureaucracy,* p. 75) writes that "the primary manifest justification for the revolution was to promote economic planning and development in a rational and systematized manner."

42. Evans, "Dependent Development in the Eighties," p. 15.

43. Urquidi, *Challenge of Development,* p. 98. Also see Evans, *Decade of Development,* pp. 110–111.

44. For development theory's insistence that changes in popular attitudes toward work, consumption, and savings were needed, see Meier,

Economic Development, p. 370. For its insistence that value-giving institutions had to be altered, see Millikan and Blackmer, "Resistance and Conflict," and Bryant and White, *Managing Development,* p. 6. For its insistence that universities be brought under the public organs of development, see Urquidi, *Challenge of Development,* p. 98.

45. The Brazilian military was not the first Latin American government to fall back on the rhetoric of apolitical, administrative government as a cover for authoritarianism. Camp ("Political Technocrat in Mexico," p. 111) writes that "the watchwords of the Porfiriato [i.e., the Díaz dictatorship] were 'little politics—much administration'."

46. Flynn, *Brazil: A Political Analysis,* pp. 330–338. For an extensive statement of Furtado's ideas, see his *Economic Development,* various editions.

47. The practical limits of the military's power to impose its will on the political-economic system were illustrated by the corruption that flourished in many states under the "incorruptible" professional administrators that the military had appointed to clean up the corruption that had flourished under former, "political" governors. See Wesson and Fleischer, *Brazil in Transition,* p. 55.

48. Schneider (*Political System of Brazil,* p. 3) writes, "The Brazilian political system and decision process, among the most complex extant, involve an interaction of overlapping political parties, a rich variety of interest groups, and a very large and diffuse bureaucracy." Except for the repression of political parties, this complexity characterized Brazilian public life even under the military government. Schneider, p. 17, wrote that the Brazilian military "had to find some way of striking a balance between the regional, industrial, commercial, coffee-growing, labor, and other interests which share power in Brazil and whose cooperation was necessary for the conduct of government."

49. Grunwald, "Resources in Latin American Development," p. 322.

50. Ministry of Transportation, "Transamazonian Highways," p. 23. Hecht ("Cattle Ranching," p. 370) writes that government programs to settle small farmers on the Amazon frontier "obviated the need for land reform and provided the appearance of a national will to include the rural poor in the government's development strategy." Moran ("Ecological Research," p. 27) writes that the Brazilian government appeared "to brush aside the established use of feasibility studies for a mixture of geopolitical, economic, social, and political reasons." PIN was also in part a response to what one observer called an "emotional accident" (Katzman, "Paradoxes of Amazonian Development," p. 455). President Médici had just taken office when a severe drought struck the Northeast, displacing three and a half million people and raising the specter of widespread famine. Médici personally toured the region, was deeply moved by what he saw, and demanded a program to relieve the suffering in the region.

51. Sachs, *Studies in Political Economy,* p. 243.

52. The discussion of Albuquerque Lima follows Flynn, *Brazil: A Political Analysis,* pp. 426–430. Some of his associates feared that Albuquerque

Lima might attempt to broaden his base of support with a direct appeal to labor, not a pleasing prospect to those who remembered Juan Perón's rise to power in Argentina on just such an appeal two decades earlier.

53. For a brief discussion of this paranoia, see Fearnside, "Brazil's Amazon Settlement Schemes," p. 47. For a more extensive if fragmented treatment, see Pittman, "Geopolitics in the ABC Countries," p. 268 and elsewhere.

54. Reis, *Amazônia e a Cobiça.*

55. Worsnop, "Amazon Basin Development," p. 708. Mahar (*Frontier Development,* p. 18) wrote that real or imagined foreign threats to Brazilian Amazonia "had received an inordinate amount of attention in the years immediately preceding PIN."

56. Roett, *Brazil: Politics,* pp. 196–197.

57. Kleinpenning ("Evaluation of the Brazilian Policy," p. 310) suggests that few in positions of power in Brazil took seriously such threats to national sovereignty in Amazonia. He writes that they appear "to have been used by the Brazilian government to make the opening up and integration of the territory, which was considered necessary for other reasons, more acceptable."

58. UN, ECLA, *Toward a Dynamic Development,* pp. 24–28, 39–40.

59. Schneider, *Political System of Brazil,* p. 6; Roett, *Brazil: Politics,* p. 183.

60. For a discussion of the currents of political power and rivalry that swirled around PIN, see Bunker, *Underdeveloping the Amazon.* For a detailed treatment of PIN's bureaucratic shortcomings, see Moran, *Developing the Amazon.*

61. Sternberg, "Development and Conservation," p. 254.

62. Quoted in Pearson, *Down to Business,* p. 2.

63. Roett, "Brazilian Foreign Policy"; Fishlow, "United States and Brazil," p. 906.

64. Roett, *Brazil: Politics,* p. 198.

65. Most Western-trained members of the managerial and technical elites of the third world had returned home before environmentalism seeped into professional training programs (Caldwell, *International Environmental Policy,* p. 204).

66. Miguel Ozorio de Almeida, quoted by Juda, "International Environmental Concern," p. 95.

67. Caldwell, *International Environmental Policy,* pp. 43–45. Brazil was not the only party to bring a political agenda to the Stockholm Conference. The UN embraced environmentalism at least in part because it realized that such an embrace might improve the standing of the UN in the developed world, where belief in the organization's effectiveness, as well as support for it, was steadily eroding. If the UN could establish a pattern of international cooperation on environmental matters, its peacekeeping mission might be made easier (Kay and Jacobson, "A Framework for Analysis," p. 13 in their (ed.) *Environmental Protection*).

68. Indira Gandhi, for example, argued that while "the rich might look upon development as the cause of environmental destruction, to us it is the primary means of improving the environment for the living" (Sills, "Environmental Movement," p. 34).

69. U.S. Delegation to the U.N. Conference on the Human Environment, "Report."

70. See for example, *The New York Times Index* 1972–1974, for that newspaper's coverage of Brazil's environmental actions and attitudes in the years immediately following the Stockholm Conference. Caldwell, *International Environmental Policy*, p. 53, noted that after the Stockholm Conference, even regimes indifferent to the environment felt obliged to behave in an environmentally responsible fashion as evidence of modernity.

71. Roett, *Brazil: Politics*, p. 200. Brazil's desire for an independent policy course in South America intensified after 1974, when the United States refused to guarantee it would supply processed fuel for its nuclear reactors.

72. Unless otherwise noted, the treatment of the Amazon treaty follows Medina, "Amazonian Pact."

73. Child, *Geopolitics in South America*.

74. Child, *Geopolitics in South America*, p. 5. Pittman ("Geopolitics in the ABC Countries," p. 170) writes that Brazil's neighbors perceived aggressive geopolitical considerations behind the Brazilian military's development of Amazonia, and they saw the development as a direct threat. Child, p. 36, relates how a senior Peruvian military officer compared Brazil's intentions of westward expansion to those of the United States in the nineteenth century and compared his own country's position to that of California.

75. Meira Mattos, *Brasil: Geopolítica*. For a detailed treatment of Meira Mattos's ideas, see Pittman, "Geopolitics in the ABC Countries," pp. 350–385.

76. Pittman, "Geopolitics in the ABC Countries," p. 170; Roett, *Brazil: Politics*, p. 197.

77. *The New York Times*, May 23, 1974, p. 60, col. 1.

78. Medina, "Amazonian Pact," p. 70.

79. There was international precedent for using protected natural areas to strengthen claims to thinly settled areas. In the early twentieth century, Canada had established a vast game refuge in the High Arctic islands as a way of boosting her claims to these thinly settled lands (Environment Canada, "Environment Canada and the North," p. 59). More recently, Argentina had established a string of national parks along its frequently contested Andean border with Chile, a step intended at least in part to strengthen her hold on these areas (Wright, "Park Establishment," p. 767–768). SEMA and the IBDF's conservation programs could therefore serve an older but still important national aim in Amazonia.

80. Faucher, "Paradise That Never Was."

81. See Balassa et al., *Toward Renewed Economic Growth,* selected tables, pp. 44–54.

82. Linz, "Future of an Authoritarian Situation." Faucher, "Paradise That Never Was," p. 25, gives 1976 as the year in which the "local bourgeoisie" lost faith in the military regime.

83. Wesson and Fleischer, *Brazil in Transition,* p. 108.

84. Dean, "Forest Conservation."

85. All three parks established in the 1930s—Serra dos Orgãos in the mountains behind Rio, Itatiaia in the highlands between Rio and São Paulo, and Iguaçu at the site of the most spectacular falls in South America—were easily accessible to the middle classes of the large cities of the South and were intended for their benefit.

86. The military's own security forces were implicated in a failed bombing at a Rio shopping center in 1981 (Roett, *Brazil: Politics,* p. 153).

87. *The Economist,* "Brazil's Morning After," March 12, 1983.

88. Roett, *Brazil: Politics,* p. 201; also see Fishlow, "United States and Brazil," pp. 912–913.

89. Roett, *Brazil: Politics,* pp. 173–174.

90. Portes, "Latin American Class Structures," p. 27; UN, ECLA, *Economic Development,* p. 47; Clawson, "Park Visits," p. 123.

91. Nelson (*Development of Tropical Lands,* p. 280) asserted that "the development of new lands in Latin America is an inevitable and irreversible process that has considerable momentum. There is a political commitment." McDonough (*Power and Ideology,* p. 272) points out the strong association between the development of Amazonia and Brazil's future greatness in the mind of the Brazilian public.

92. Portes, "Latin American Class Structures." Portes, p. 34, defines the informal sector as "those classes defined by their exclusion from fully capitalist relationships of production." The percentage of workers in the informal sector of the U.S. economy fell from half to less than a third in the years between 1900 and 1930. The years between 1950 and 1980 saw roughly comparable increases in economic productivity in South America, but the informal sector dropped only slightly, from 46 to 42 percent of the total labor force. The percentage of the rural work force in the informal sector declined during these decades, but the percent of the urban work force in this sector actually increased considerably, from 13.4 to 19.4 percent.

93. Brazilian per capita GDP dropped from 2,152 1975 dollars in 1980 to 2,072 1975 dollars by 1985. For changes in income distribution, see Wesson and Fleischer, *Brazil in Transition,* p. 169; for declines in per capita GDP, see Balassa et al., *Toward Renewed Economic Growth,* pp. 44–45.

94. The favela population of Rio de Janeiro constituted 7 percent of the city's inhabitants in the 1950s; it made up nearly a third in 1980. São Paulo, with virtually no squatters in 1972, had a million a decade later, with the squatter population growing 30 percent a year.

95. *The Economist,* "Brazil's Morning After," March 12, 1983; Wesson and Fleischer, *Brazil in Transition,* p. 65.

96. *The Economist,* "Brazil's Morning After," March 12, 1983.

97. Roett (*Brazil: Politics,* p. 44) writes that "The highest level of political awareness that the majority of citizens possess, save in a symbolic sense, is of the local community or perhaps the state." The complaints of the Brazilian middle class in the 1980s, centering on poor living standards and the constant erosion of wages through inflation, were the same as those of previous decades and were common to the middle classes in underdeveloped nations throughout the world (Wesson and Fleischer, *Brazil in Transition,* pp. 65–66).

98. *Isto é,* "Pais da Natureza."

99. Trent, personal communication, April 1, 1986.

100. Camara, interview, July 4, 1984.

101. Roett (*Brazil: Politics,* p. 44) writes, "The vast majority of Brazil's citizens remain . . . political subjects."

102. For example, the IBDF delegado in Belo Horizonte, who by all accounts was genuinely interested in promoting forest conservation in the state and who needed public support for his efforts, criticized the local environmentalists for constantly denouncing the IBDF's forest policies without ever offering either informed, specific criticism of his policies or support for his environmental initiatives. Milano, interview, March 21, 1986; Trent, personal communication, April 1, 1986.

103. Schneider, *Political System of Brazil,* pp. 34–35.

104. Evans, "Reinventing the Bourgeoisie," p. S–216; Faucher, "Paradise That Never Was," p. 13.

105. Roett, *Brazil: Politics,* p. 120.

106. Haring, *Empire in Brazil,* p. 139.

107. Stepan, *Beginnings of Brazilian Science,* p. 122.

108. Schwartzman, "Struggling to be Born," pp. 576–577.

109. Meier and Baldwin, *Economic Development,* p. 293.

110. Bryant and White, *Managing Development,* p. 6; Coleman, "Resurrection of Political Economy," p. 34. Meier and Baldwin (*Economic Development,* p. 334) wrote that "the aid of all disciplines is needed, especially history, psychology, sociology, and political science."

111. Schwartzman, "Struggling to be Born," p. 577.

112. Schwartzman ("Struggling to be Born," p. 577) shows how this was part of a broad policy of centralizing science spending under the Ministry of Planning.

113. In an administrative shuffle, the National Research Council and INPA came under Delfim Neto, the economic planner who had led the Brazilian delegation at Stockholm, and whose attitudes towards the environment had not changed since then. Under a minister hostile rather than merely indifferent to ecological research, a sense of beleaguerment spread through

the institute. Herbert Schubart, its director, said, "Our minister does not see conservation interests as his interests; [in fact], he sees conservation as standing in the way of his goals" (Schubart, interview, July 13, 1984).

114. Schubart, interview, July 13, 1984.

115. Rankin, interview, July 13, 1984. There was also very little interest in the Minimum Critical Ecosystem Size project at higher levels of the Brazilian government, and few efforts were made to accommodate it; visas were held up for inscrutable reasons, and scientific equipment was subjected to rigid import controls. Efforts were underway in 1986 within the federal government to change its status from a joint Brazilian-foreign scientific project, which gave it a measure of security under Brazilian law, to a foreign scientific expedition, which would have made it much more subject to bureaucratic caprice.

116. The ministries of finance and planning were given extraordinary powers over the budgets and policies of the other ministries. Since the performance criteria of these "superministries" were tied to national development goals, they were the primary administrative instruments by which a development-oriented discipline was maintained within the federal bureaucracy.

Chapter 6

1. IBDF, "Relatório Pessoal-1985," table 7. At the beginning of 1986 the IBDF employed only twenty-seven professionals that it classified as biologists, and among them, only two were ecologists.

2. Pandolfo, interview, July 9, 1984.

3. Guimarães, interview, April 22, 1986; Jorge Pádua, interview, March 26, 1986.

4. Milano, interview, March 21, 1986.

5. See Wesson and Fleischer, *Brazil in Transition,* pp. 167–178.

6. Milano, interview, March 21, 1986. Wetterberg (personal communication, March 29, 1990) recounted that in the late 1970s the advisory board was an important conduit of information from the IBDF's conservation program to other government agencies, and that the board's ratification of Stage One planning was an important step in the implementation of the IBDF's conservation program.

7. See Wesson and Fleischer, *Brazil in Transition,* pp. 78–79.

8. Milano, interview, February 26, 1986.

9. Bernardes Quintão, interview, March 19, 1986.

10. Milano, interview, March 21, 1986; the author's observations in IBDF headquarters, February–June, 1986. For a discussion of data management problems in third-world bureaucracies, see Bryant and White, *Managing Development,* p. 229.

11. Jesus, various interviews, May 1986. One of the management strengths of the U.S. National Park Service was derived from its policy of circulating

personnel between field and headquarters assignments, thus exposing them to both the administrative and operational sides of running a park system. See Foresta, *America's National Parks*, pp. 87–89.

12. Wesson and Fleischer (*Brazil in Transition*, pp. 54–55) held that the elections of 1982 almost fully restored traditional regional politics in Brazil.

13. Maia, interview, April 30, 1986; Guimarães, interview, April 22, 1986.

14. Jorge Pádua, interview, May 13, 1986; Bernardes Quintão, interview, May 16, 1986.

15. The delegado was generally aware of the problems facing the two protected areas in his state, but he had not visited them or become well acquainted with their problems in the ten months he had been at his post (Guimarães, interview, April 22, 1986).

16. Milano, interview, March 7, 1986.

17. Her reputation was enhanced in 1979 when the Florida Audubon Society awarded her its prize for outstanding young Latin American conservationist.

18. Bernardes Quintão, interview, May 16, 1986.

19. Miller, interview, August 26, 1986; Wendt, interview, October 25, 1985; Wright, interview, January 27, 1986. For a general discussion of this subject, see Elliott (ed.), *Second World Conference*, Session XIV.

20. Wendt, interview, October 25, 1985. What links remained were further frayed by the failure of the FBCN, which for years had acted as a conduit for money from foreign conservation organizations into Brazilian conservation projects, including the IBDF's, to give foreign conservationists what they considered a satisfactory accounting of the funds.

21. Paula, interview, March 13, 1986.

22. IBDF/DN research application files, Brasília.

23. Paula, interview, March 13, 1986. Unless otherwise noted, this interview and one conducted on March 18 are the sources for the material in this and the following two paragraphs.

24. Bernardes Quintão described Stage Two as the "master line" of DN policy while the unit was under her leadership (interview, May 15, 1986).

25. IBDF/FBCN, "Parque Nacional de Sete Cidades: Plano de Manejo," p. 7. Implementing the management plan did, however, involve the elimination of a de facto road network, the removal of a hundred occupying families, and the reintroduction of some native plant species eliminated from the park area by past human action (Wetterberg, personal communication, July 25, 1988).

26. DN employees suspected another reason for the progress at Araguaia. According to them, shortly after Jorge Pádua's resignation over the proposal for a road through this park, money for the plan's implementation began to appear. As one DN employee put it, the higher-ups "felt guilty about what they had done to the park."

27. IBDF/FBCN, "Reserva Biológica de Poço das Antas: Plano de Manejo," p. 9.

28. IBDF/DN, "Parque Nacional de Brasília" (map and visitors' guide).

29. The agency responded to the paralysis of planning with informal estimates of the personnel needed to protect the natural areas in their current state. This provided the best available measure of the adequacy of field staffing under actual circumstances.

30. Wetterberg fully understood this; in the early 1980s, he wrote, "'How much is enough' [has] yet to be established and will undoubtedly be a focal point of discussion during this decade" (Wetterberg, Prance, and Lovejoy, "Conservation Progress," p. 9).

31. Wilcox, "In Situ Conservation," p. 646. Small populations in the wild underwent inbreeding, depression and a narrowing of the genetic base, which reduced a species' long-term survivability; it no longer had the reservoir of genetic possibilities to adapt to whatever demands the future would put on it. See Shaffer, "Minimum Population Sizes"; Soule, "What is Conservation Biology?"

32. Shaffer, "Minimum Population Sizes," p. 132. Shaffer emphasized the intuitive nature of this time frame; it came more out of a sense of the proper pale of the present's responsibility to the future than any scientific calculus, as indeed had Wetterberg's choice of Terborgh's time frame several years earlier.

33. Wilcox, "In Situ Conservation," p. 632; Lovejoy, personal communication, November 27, 1985; Lovejoy, "Discontinuous Wilderness," p. 15; Myers, "Problem of Disappearing Species," p. 233.

34. Lovejoy (personal communication, November 27, 1985) estimated that approximately 15 percent of the Amazon basin should be preserved in a natural state; Miller et al. ("Issues in the Preservation," p. 353) estimated that "a truly comprehensive network of protected areas would require a minimum of 10 percent of the world's area." Because of the interregional species diversity in the tropical rainforest, a larger percentage would be needed there (Miller, interview, August 26, 1986).

35. Rylands and Mittermeier, "Primate Conservation." They pointedly attributed this failure to the IBDF's overreliance on broad theory at the expense of solid field work in selecting its protected areas.

36. Marinho de Abrolhos National Park, also established in 1983, was a marine national park encompassing 91,300 hectares of ocean off the coast of Bahia. Although the Atol das Rocas National Park, centering on the atoll of the same name some 250 kilometers off the northeast coast, had been established in 1979, Marinho de Abrolhos was the first truly maritime national park in the system. There was no mention of it, or of maritime national parks in general, in Stage Two of the system plan, so external initiative likely played a large part in its creation.

37. DN files on external park proposals, unpaged.

38. Rocha, interview, May 29, 1986.

39. Bernardes Quintão, interview, May 16, 1986.

40. Guimarães, interview, April 22, 1986; Milano, interview, March 21, 1986.

41. IBDF/FBCN, *Plano do Sistema: Segunda Etapa,* pp. 128–130; Rocha, interview, March 6, 1986.

42. Milano, interview, March 7, 1986. The DN did, however, feel it could safely ignore the most ambitious land claims of the Indian rights groups: their enormity was likely to rule out their serious consideration at higher levels of government.

43. Rocha, interview, March 6, 1986. Unless otherwise noted, this is the source for the material in the following three paragraphs.

44. Rocha, interview, May 29, 1986.

45. UNESCO, "Action Plan," p. 12. By 1985, Soule ("What is Conservation Biology?" p. 730) could state as a postulate of conservation biology that "nature reserves are inherently disequilibrial for large, rare organisms."

46. Peters and Darling, "Greenhouse Effect."

47. Salati et al., "Origem e Distribuição." According to initial estimates, the percentage of the rain made up of this recycled water varied within the basin from under 20 percent near the Atlantic coast to over 50 percent further west in the interior. Subsequent work indicated these estimates were too low. See Sioli, "Unifying Principles," p. 623.

48. Sioli, "Unifying Principles," p. 624. Lovejoy (personal communication, November 27, 1985) estimated that approximately two-thirds of Amazonia would have to remain under tree cover.

49. Since many rainforest species were poor at dispersal, the clearings for commercial agriculture would have to be kept small. Sioli ("Foreseeable Consequences," p. 268) suggested that rural development planning for Amazonia should include an upper limit on the size of forest clearings. When clearing large areas was inevitable, rare species and unique floral assemblies could be protected in small set-off areas, and corridors of natural vegetation linking protected areas could be left on the landscape. The campos and patches of other naturally occurring vegetation could be used for grazing, as many of them had been for generations. For general discussions of conservation landscapes, see ibid.; Fearnside, "Development Alternatives"; Jordan, "Amazon Rain Forests," p. 399. While influenced by recent scientific discoveries, these efforts to accommodate human prosperity and biological conservation are also part of an older tradition that extends back to Bluntschli's writing in the 1920s (see chapter 4, note 2 above), which was maintained in the IBDF's "Cadernos da Amazônia" publication series in the 1960s and includes Dasmann et al., *Ecological Principles,* which appeared in 1973.

50. Fearnside, "Brazil's Amazon Settlement Schemes," pp. 54–55. The organic material that entered the surface waters of the basin from these semi-inundated lands during flood season was an important source of nutrients for aquatic life, and these lands played an important role in moderating extremes of river flow, so some of them had to be preserved in their natural state if the basin's aquatic ecology was to remain in balance. See Barrow, "Development of the Varzeas," p. 116; Goulding, *Fishes and the Forest.*

51. Meggers, *Amazônia: A Ilusão,* pp. 189–195.

52. Nelson, *Development of Tropical Lands,* p. 265.

53. Falleiros, interview, May 28, 1986.

54. See, for example, the IUCN's seminal *World Conservation Strategy,* published in 1980. This new approach to a fusion of conservation and development went by several names, the most popular of which was "sustainable development," which implied that development that maintained the complexity and productivity of the natural ecosystem could itself be maintained indefinitely. It was a natural next step from the conservation doctrine that had emerged in the 1960s and that Miller refined in South America during the following decade. By the late 1980s, the literature on sustainable development, or ecodevelopment as it was sometimes called, was vast.

55. The idea of coalition-building grew out of experience, particularly efforts to save Africa's colonial legacy of national parks. There, politics simply would not allow native peoples to be ignored. Nor did the immediate exigencies of protecting natural areas; as Myers ("Eternal Values," p. 659) wrote, those areas in which "consumptive forms of exploitation" were allowed enjoyed much better relations with the local communities than did those managed with a strict "hands off" approach. For an example of the heightened sensitivity of the international conservation movement to native rights and interests around the world, see McNeely and Pitt (eds.), *Culture and Conservation.*

56. Martins, "Fighting for Land," p. 101.

57. Bunker, "Forces of Destruction," p. 40.

58. Falleiros, interview, May 26, 1986. See Ramos, "Frontier Expansion," for a detailed discussion. The plight of the Indians was a matter of international as well as national concern by the mid-1980s. See Caufield, "Dam the Amazon."

59. Falleiros, interview, May 26, 1986.

60. See Bunker, "Forces of Destruction."

61. Jorge Pádua, interview, March 26, 1986; Bernardes Quintão, interview, May 16, 1986.

62. The delegado in Pará said, "Managing forest clearing is part of my charge, but I don't have the capacity to watch over it" (Guimarães, interview, April 22, 1986).

63. Bernardes Quintão, interview, May 16, 1986. Jorge Pádua (interview, March 24, 1986) said regarding Salati's findings, "There are no public institutions in Brazil that can respond to this kind of evidence, or act upon it."

64. Camara, interview, July 4, 1984.

65. Brown, interview, May 9, 1986.

66. Wright, personal communication, January 26, 1986. Ironically, the World Conservation Strategy had been developed, at least in part, to appeal to those in the third-world nations who viewed the older, more exclusivist

approach to nature protection as elitist and irrelevant to their own needs for development (Kramer, interview, August 29, 1986).

67. Simon (*Administrative Behavior,* pp. 38–41, 240–244) called such decisions boundedly rational; they make sense in an immediate, limited context, but not necessarily in a broader one.

Chapter 7

1. IBDF/FCBN, *Plano do Sistema: Segunda Etapa,* p. 57; Jorge Pádua, interview, March 26, 1986.

2. Susan Barrett, a landscape architect who helped draw up the management plan as a WWF/IUCN consultant, wrote in "Conservation in Amazonia," pp. 216–217, that "The ability of national parks to attract tourism could be successfully exploited in Amazonia, with benefits in terms of the regional economy, support and funding for the national parks and favorable international opinion. The potential to provide for tourism... is at present being explored at the new [Amazonia] National Park."

3. Stone (*Dreams of Amazonia,* p. 88) wrote, "The poor soils impeded progress around Itaituba, whose small farms, when I saw them in 1983, seemed still not to be producing beyond the subsistence level, despite heavy deforestation."

4. Foweraker, writing of change in Amazonia in his *Struggle for Land,* p. 185, expressed a similar idea in Marxist terms: "Capitalist penetration in Amazonia clearly does not bring about a general modernization of work relations." Miller ("Replacement of the Traditional Elites," p. 163) estimates that by 1981 the gold rush had brought 40,000 free-lance miners to the Tapajós region.

5. R. Ferreira, interview, April 23, 1986.

6. Milano, interview, March 7, 1986.

7. Guards had lived in the park in the early 1980s, but this presence could not be maintained in the face of minimal appropriations, so now the guards and their families lived in Itaituba.

8. R. Ferreira, interview, April 23, 1986. Unless otherwise noted, Ferreira and the author's observations are the sources for the material presented in this section.

9. Rocha, interview, March 6, 1986.

10. Daland (*Exploring Brazilian Bureaucracy,* p. 413) wrote, "The impossibility of effective implementation renders the rational policy process irrelevant. And without rational policy guides, bureaucrats inevitably disregard public goals and subside into incompetence." This was not the case at Amazonia National Park, nor at the majority of the other protected areas in Amazonia. Administrators consistently improvised, conducted their own assessments, and devised fall-back plans to best deal with the situation with available resources. If anything, their sense of isolation, which left them far from support but also far from the normal restraints of office cul-

ture and close supervision, increased their inventiveness and willingness to take the initiative.

11. Since the proposed boundary changes had never been implemented, this land was technically outside the park, but INCRA, still its official custodian, allowed the IBDF to patrol it and to vigorously enforce the laws against clearing public lands.

12. Visitors were allowed to stay in the several small, wooden cabins along the Tapajós that had housed scientists during the earlier flush of research in the park. The director's limited ability to promote tourism was brought home to him when a young German traveler arrived in Itaituba and contacted him about getting to the park. The director told him he could visit the park with the next guard shift if he was willing to wait a few days. The traveler preferred not to wait, so the director offered to ask one of the staff drivers to take him immediately if he was willing to pay for the gas and, since it was the driver's day off, offer the driver some remuneration. The traveler, probably not used to such informal arrangements and suspecting he was being taken advantage of, declined the offer and left Itaituba without visiting the park. The director felt deeply humiliated by the incident: "I am sorry that we are so poor and so ill prepared for visitors that I had to resort to such an arrangement."

13. Milano, interview, March 21, 1986. President Figueiredo also removed several thousand hectares from the northwest corner of the Lago Piratuba reserve. In this case, too, the DN's advice on the exclusion had not been solicited, and it had no advance warning. DN officials speculated that a politically powerful rancher-entrepreneur wanted the land for raising water buffalo and prevailed on the president to remove the area from the reserve, and out of friendship, a belief that it was in the national interest, or both, the president obliged him.

14. IBDF/IUCN, "Reserva Biológica do Rio Trombetas, Plano de Manejo," pp. 51–55.

15. Jorge Pádua, interview, March 26, 1986.

16. IBDF/FBCN, "Reserva Biológica do Rio Trombetas, Plano de Manejo," pp. 47–48.

17. One post was placed near the turtle beaches, where the headquarters would eventually be built; one, a small floating outpost, was placed at the mouth of Lake Erepecu; and a third was built on the banks of the Acapu River where it entered the reserve from the north.

18. IBDF/FBCN, "Reserva Biológica do Rio Trombetas, Plano de Manejo," p. 53. The smoke was a mix of silicate solids, water vapor, sulphur dioxide, and carbon monoxide.

19. Meganck and Goebel ("Shifting Cultivation") reported that this kind of invasion was an old and widespread problem in Latin America. As early as 1946, Mexico's national parks were being invaded by peasants in search of arable land. The South American delegations to the 1972 Second World Conference on National Parks agreed that by then these invasions had

become one of the most widespread and difficult problems facing protected natural areas on the continent. By 1978 an estimated 30,000 settlers were living in Colombia's protected natural areas.

20. Although the power company subsequently commissioned INPA to do an environmental impact study of the dam, it was cold comfort to the director; Electronorte had hired INPA to do an environmental impact study when it began the Tucuruí Dam several years earlier but had ignored the environmental guidelines set forth in the study (Carvalho, interview, April 25, 1986). Unless otherwise noted, Carvalho is the source for the following material in this section.

21. Interviews with IBDF field personnel, March–May, 1986.

22. Protection of the turtle nesting beaches on the Trombetas began in 1965. The IBDF assumed the responsibility in 1970, and once the biological reserve was established, responsibility for the beaches was folded into general responsibilities of the reserve's director, with the understanding that the delegado to Pará would provide additional assistance as needed (IBDF/FBCN, "Reserva Biológica do Rio Trombetas, Plano de Manejo," pp. 3–6).

23. According to the DN, there was something to this argument: the caboclos of the region had become so specialized in turtle poaching that they had lost their farming and other hunting skills (Cantarelli, interview, May 22, 1986).

24. Wesson and Fleischer (*Brazil in Transition,* p. 67) write that the Brazilian church was "perhaps the most progressive branch of Catholicism in the world." During the years of repression, it was the only permitted vehicle of dissent in many places, and it frequently took the side of Amazon caboclos in their disputes with large landowners and the government. The church's position with regard to land conflicts was outlined in a document approved in 1980 by the Brazilian National Bishops' Conference, entitled "The Church and Land Problems." As Schmink ("Land Conflicts," p. 351) points out, the document based its argument for more open, equitable access on the proposition that "land is the gift of God to all men." Many IBDF officials in the field expressed an ambivalence toward the church's involvement in land conflicts: On one hand they were generally and in the abstract sympathetic with the plight of the caboclos and the church's efforts to better their lot; on the other, they considered the church dangerously demagogic when it supported caboclos in what they (the IBDF officials) saw as unreasonable assaults against Amazonia's biological patrimony. The director at the Trombetas reserve conceded that the argument about equal access to reserves was valid from the perspective of class justice—even more than the Partido Trabalhista seemed to realize, since the property owners commonly exploited the surrounding public lands from their inholdings—but he held that the class justice argument missed the crucial point: brazilnut harvesting was a negligible threat to the reserve and dealing with it could wait; a few years of unrestricted turtle harvesting would do irreparable damage.

25. According to the reserve's director, the mayor of Oriximiná was in the brazilnut business, and would not cooperate with the staff.

26. The agricultural frontier in Rondônia would also act as a safety valve for social tensions in rural areas of southern Brazil, where modern farming practices were replacing the older, labor-intensive production methods and displacing many farm workers and small landowners. Mueller ("Frontier Based Agricultural Expansion," p. 143) stresses the importance of this in the government's encouragement of settlement in Rondônia: "Labour displacing changes in the centre-south... forced [the government] to continue implementing colonization schemes.... This is particularly important with regard to Rondônia."

27. Spears ("World Bank") writes that the World Bank had already allocated $20 million to environmental protection in connection with the Polonoroeste project by 1982.

28. Fearnside and Ferreira, "Roads in Rondônia," pp. 358–360; Jorge Pádua, interview, May 13, 1986.

29. IBDF, "Parque Nacional de Pacaás Novos, Mapa de Alteração."

30. Monteiro, interview, May 2, 1986.

31. IBDF/FBCN, *Plano do Sistema: Segunda Etapa,* pp. 139–144; Barragana, interview, May 1, 1986.

32. Jorge Pádua, interview, May 13, 1986. Water buffalo had been introduced from Southern Europe to Marajó Island in the 1890s, and they proved well-adapted to the region; they were more disease resistant in wet environments than regular cattle, were more efficient grazers of wetland grasses, and produced more and richer milk in a humid tropical environment. Buffalo ranching spread from Marajó to other low-lying areas of Amazonia, especially after crossbreeding in the 1950s and 1960s produced strains with improved milk and meat production. By the early 1980s, there were an estimated 400,000 water buffalo in Brazilian Amazonia, and conservation had a new competitor for the low-lying areas of the region. Water buffalo were usually raised on large ranches by innovative and often well connected ranchers, which made them even more formidable competitors (Barrow, "Development of the Várzeas").

33. IBDF, "Reserva Biológica de Guaporé, Plano de Manejo," pp. 79–95.

34. Jorge Pádua, personal communication, August 8, 1988.

35. Santiago, interview, May 3, 1986. Unless otherwise attributed, Santiago and the author's personal observations are the source for the following material in this section.

36. The Guaporé River was patrolled at least weekly where it ran through the reserve. The Rio São Miguel, the western boundary of the reserve, and the Rio Branco further to the east were patrolled at least once a month. The Rio Colorado and the Igarapé Consuelo at the eastern end of the reserve, far from headquarters and difficult to reach from it, were infrequently patrolled (Barragana, interview, May 1, 1986). Unless otherwise noted, Barragana is the source for the following material in this section.

37. IBDF, "Estado de Rondônia: Mapa de Alteração."

38. Less than 15 percent of the settlement area was rated as fair to good for agriculture without high fertilizer inputs (Fearnside, "Settlement in Rondônia," p. 231). The official but overly optimistic target had been full occupancy by 1986.

39. Fearnside and Ferreira, "Roads in Rondônia," p. 358.

40. Falleiros, interview, May 28, 1986.

41. Jorge Pádua and Bernardes Quintão, "Parks and Biological Reserves," p. 312.

42. Falleiros, interview, May 28, 1986. Goodland ("Brazil's Environmental Progress," p. 13) writes that in 1983 the Uru-eu-wau-wau tribe was being contacted for the first time, and all development activity in the area had been suspended until accommodations for it could be arranged.

43. For its part, FUNAI felt that both goals could be achieved at the same time. FUNAI's president in 1979, Adhemar Ribeiro da Silva, argued that past experience had shown that only Indians knew how to preserve their natural environments, so setting aside Indian lands was in fact turning natural areas over to their most experienced and conscientious managers (Ramos, "Development, Integration and the Ethnic Integrity," p. 225).

44. Jorge Pádua, interview, May 13, 1986.

45. IBDF, "Reserva Biológica de Guaporé, Mapa de Alteração."

46. Fearnside and Ferreira ("Roads in Rondônia") write that the state of Rondônia planned to construct two roads through the reserve: one running roughly parallel to the Guaporé River and bisecting its northeast corner and another running from Pimenta Bueno on BR 364 to the Guaporé River, cutting through the middle of the reserve.

47. Sawyer, "Frontier Expansion," pp. 194–198.

48. Jorge Pádua, interview, May 26, 1986.

49. Araujo, interview, April 30, 1986.

50. Estado do Amazonas, "Parque Nacional do Pico da Neblina, Mapa."

51. Araujo, interview, April 30, 1986.

52. Fearnside, "Brazil's Amazon Settlement Schemes," p. 50.

53. Falleiros, interview, May 28, 1986. FUNAI argued that the establishment of the national park in the region would infringe on the Indians' right of unrestricted use of their lands.

54. By the middle of the decade, approximately 7 percent of Brazil was in officially established indigenous areas, and the percentage was even higher in Amazonia.

55. Maia, interview, April 30, 1986.

56. Maia, interview, April 30, 1986.

57. Araujo, interview, April 30, 1986; Nogueira-Neto, interview, February 21, 1986.

58. Araujo, interview, April 30, 1986.

59. Araujo, interview, April 30, 1986.

60. As Bernardes Quintão (interview, May 16, 1986) expressed it, "With the return to democracy, IBDF leadership is more sensitive to popular reactions to their actions."

Chapter 8

1. SEMA's protected areas in Amazonia were also less dominated by rainforest than were the IBDF's. In part, this was a logical outgrowth of SEMA's early decision not to emphasize the representation of major forest regions to the exclusion of other ecosystems, and in part it was due to the fact that most opportunities for acquiring compact, manageable tracts seemed to be in other ecosystems: grasslands, inundated forests, palm forests, cerrado, etc.

2. SEMA, "Organograma-1986." One handled administration, the liaison with CONAMA, and special projects; another oversaw pollution-related activities.

3. Author's observation, SEMA headquarters in Brasília, February–May, 1986.

4. In 1985, 3,000 of the IBDF's 3,700 employees were in the field and under the authority of the delagados. According to Figueiredo, chief of operations for the ecological stations, all but 80 of SEMA's approximately 380 employees were at headquarters in Brasília.

5. Figueiredo, interview, March 19, 1986. Unless otherwise noted, Figueiredo and personal observations are the sources for the material in this and the following paragraph.

6. Nogueira-Neto, "Getting Brazil's Network"; Figueiredo, interview, May 22, 1986. The Jari station also received funds indirectly from the Polamazonia program.

7. Nogueira-Neto, "Getting Brazil's Network," p. 29.

8. SEMA, "Programa de Gerenciamento," unpaged appendix. Costa, interview, March 19, 1986. Costa and personal observations are the source on the following point.

9. SEMA, "Estação Ecológica da Juréia," pp. 27–41; SEMA, "Estação Ecologica do Taim," pp. 29–37; SEMA, "Estação Ecológica de Anavilhanas," pp. 28–32.

10. Simões, interview, March 6, 1986.

11. Lei no. 4.771, September 15, 1965.

12. Decreto no. 289, February 28, 1967, chapter 1, art. 3, sec. 9, instructs the IBDF to comply and enforce compliance [cumprir e frazer cumprir] with the forest code and all legislation pertinent to renewable natural resources, but it was not more specific.

13. Simões, interview, March 6, 1986.

14. CONAMA, Resolução no. 4, September 18, 1985.

15. Simões (interview, March 6, 1986) is the source for the material in this paragraph. SEMA stipulated that only protected areas greater than 100 hectares need be identified by the states and territories.

16. For more detailed discussions of these criticisms, see Boecklen and Gotelli, "Island Biogeographic Theory."

17. Prance, "Review of Phytogeographic Evidence." Lleras ("Monograph on Trigoniaceae") offered support for Prance's pattern of fragments, but by the time Lleras' work appeared, Prance had revised his own thinking.

18. Endler, "Pleistocene Forest Refuges," p. 653. Endler argues that "the simplest explanation [for the geographic distributions of tropical organisms] is that the species are adapting to current geographic differences in the environment within the forest and that subspecies and species accumulate in the large patches of relatively uniform habitats." Endler (p. 641) attributed initial enthusiasm for refuge theory to its elegance rather than to an objective look at the evidence.

19. Pires, "Amazonian Forest," pp. 598–600.

20. Boecklen and Gotelli, "Island Biogeographic Theory," p. 75.

21. Mares, "Conservation in South America," p. 737.

22. Wetterberg, et al., "Conservation Progress," p. 10.

23. Game and Peterkin, "Nature Reserve Selection," pp. 176–177.

24. SEMA, "Estações Ecológicas, Relatório-1986."

25. Figueiredo, interview, May 22, 1986.

26. Nogueira-Neto, "Getting Brazil's Network," p. 28; Figueiredo, interview, May 20, 1986.

27. Figueiredo and Simões (various interviews, February–May 1986) are the sources for the material in this paragraph. One higher-level administrator who had assumed his post in 1982 estimated his real income had dropped 50 percent by 1986.

28. Miller, *Planning National Parks,* p. 558; Wright, interview, January 14, 1986.

29. Nogueira-Neto, letter to Edwin Snider, February 18, 1986.

30. Nogueira-Neto, interview, February 21, 1986.

31. Much of the tract was seasonally inundated, and almost all of it was underlain by poor, sandy soil (Nogueira-Neto and Carvalho, "Programme of Ecological Stations," p. 109).

32. Figueiredo interview, May 20, 1986. The two areas in western Amazonia that SEMA was willing to accept without assured resources for their management seemed exceptions to this rule, but the two, Jutaí-Solimões and Juami-Japurá, seemed safe; they were far from the frontiers of agricultural settlement or from any growth poles. In fact Myers ("Present Status," p. 111) had rated this area of western Amazonia as one of the world's least threatened rainforest regions. The stations also had good, defensible

boundaries, so SEMA risked little in the foreseeable future by assuming responsibility for them.

33. Norgueira-Neto, letter to Edwin Snider, February 18, 1986. He added, "...and is an important ecosystem," but the latter was a flexible standard in practice.

34. The CVRD's chief executive seemed genuinely interested in the environment (Lovejoy, interview, November 26, 1985), and the company was under pressure from the World Bank to make a show of environmental responsibility. Unless otherwise noted, Freitas (interview, November 13, 1986) is the source for the material on the Carajás station.

35. Two of the CVRD areas were undisturbed rainforest, and the third was the site of a unique floral community adapted to the high iron content of the soils of Serra dos Carajás. Bunker ("Power Structures," pp. 69–70) found that a lack of independent power and funding gave EMATER, the Agency for Technical Assistance and Rural Extension Service, a similarly restricted field of action in Amazonia. "[I]ts very dependence on other agencies [largely project grants from the Ministry of Agriculture or payments tied to convênios with SUDAM] limits effective action to the areas where agencies already operate."

36. There was precedent for such a rationale: UNESCO ("Task Force," p. 23) suggested that the global biosphere reserve network should include biologically degraded areas suited for producing "new knowledge for rehabilitating and managing areas which have been subject to deleterious land use practices." Wetterberg ("Analysis of Nature Conservation," p. 6), however, made light of this rationale for acquiring land in Amazonia because he considered very little of Amazonia appropriate for the kind of rehabilitation and intensive land management that the biosphere reserve project had in mind.

37. Unless otherwise noted, Figueiredo (interview, March 19, 1986) is the source on the Cuniã station.

38. There is no mention of the Cuniã station in the 1979 article in which Nogueira-Neto lays out his plans for SEMA's network of protected areas (Nogueira-Neto and Carvalho, "Programme of Ecological Stations").

39. SEMA, initial sketch map of Cuniã management plan.

40. The law covering squatters' rights set a limit of 200 hectares on a squatter's claim, which was intended to prevent large speculators and entrepreneurs from taking advantage of the law. This limit secured the caboclo in his home and its immediate environs, but it did not protect the entire resource base of his lifeway; the caboclo needed access to watercourses for fishing and to large terrestrial areas for hunting and gathering forest products. Trespass was therefore a fact of caboclo life, and there was seldom either the means or the will to prevent it.

41. Fearnside, "Development Alternatives," p. 73.

42. Falleiros, interview, May 28, 1986.

43. Unless otherwise indicated, material in the Maracá section comes from the author's observations in Boa Vista and at the station, and from interviews with Silva and the station guard, May 16, 1986.

44. Figueiredo, interview, May 20, 1986.

45. The management plan called for a weekly westward patrol along the Maracá branch and a slightly longer patrol, conducted with the same frequency, around the eastern tip of the island and westward along the Santa Rosa (SEMA, "Estação Ecológica de Maracá-RR, Memória de Cálculo/86").

46. SEMA, "Estação Ecólogica de Maracá-RR."

47. Author's calculation from information on individual projects made available by SEMA.

48. Royal Geographical Society, "Press Release."

49. SEMA, "Estaçáo Ecológica de Anavilhanas," p. 13.

50. Unless otherwise noted, Ribeiro and Figueiredo (various interviews, March–May 1986) and the author's observations (April 1986) are the sources for the material on Anavilhanas.

51. SEMA, "Estação Ecológica de Anavilhanas, Memória de Cálculo/86."

52. SEMA, "Estação Ecológica de Anavilhanas, Memória de Cálculo/86."

53. The representative held that the caboclos could easily maintain their lifeway by hunting and fishing in the area behind their homesites rather than in the station, and that habit rather than necessity made them reluctant to abandon their old patterns (Ribeiro, interview, April 7, 1986).

54. Rankin, interview, April 14, 1986.

55. Rankin, interview, April 14, 1986.

56. Figueiredo, interview, May 20, 1986.

57. The Ministry of the Interior housed such development-oriented agencies as Polamazonia, the National Housing Bank, the Manaus Free Zone Authority, and all the regional development authorities. Daland (*Exploring Brazilian Bureaucracy,* p. 122) referred to the Ministry of the Interior as "a holding company for a variety of...autonomous agencies." Schneider (*Political System of Brazil,* p. 36) stressed the importance to an autonomous federal agency like SEMA of building its own political constituency.

58. Reed, "National Parks: Atonement," pp. 695–703. Protected natural areas in Amazonia had a double advantage on this score. Not only were these areas less likely to arouse opposition than combatting pollution, but by establishing them in regions where there was little competition for the land, opposition could be further minimized. On this point see Clawson, "Park Visits," p. 119.

59. Jorge Pádua, interview, March 26, 1986; UNFAO, "General Programme," p. 51; Wetterberg et al., "Analysis of Nature Conservation," pp. 18, 22–23.

60. Nogueira-Neto, interview, July 20, 1984. Nogueira-Neto wrote to Wetterberg: "If one of us quits the race, the other will lose" (Wetterberg, personal communication, October 29, 1986).

61. Jorge Pádua, interview, March 26, 1986.

62. See Joyce, "Price of Progress."

63. See *The New York Times,* June 2, 1974, p. 22, for SEMA's early pronouncements on combating pollution. Nogueira-Neto ("Getting Brazil's
Network," p. 29) wrote, "This was a tough decision, but we opted [to
leave] most of the burdens of pollution control to the state agencies and to
the industries that caused the problems."

64. Such a case arose in connection with construction of the Tucuruí Dam in
the early 1980s. Electronorte, the public company constructing the dam,
planned to clear the land behind it with the chemical defoliants 2,4-D and
2,4,5-T (Agent Orange), which would have caused incalcuable environmental damage. After an international outcry was raised, Nogueira-Neto
lent SEMA'a voice and demanded that plans for the spraying be canceled.
See Caufield ("Dam the Amazon," pp. 63–65) for a discussion of the events
surrounding this issue.

65. Wright, interview, January 14, 1986; Joyce, "Price of Progress," p. 48.

66. Nogueira-Neto, "Getting Brazil's Network," pp. 28–29. In fairness,
Nogueira-Neto points out that when this decision was made, the states,
taken together, had more employees officially dealing with pollution than
SEMA ever could have assigned to the problem. Given this, he argued, it
made sense to leave the problem where the personnel were and have SEMA
intervene only when a state was not doing its job (Nogueira-Neto, personal
communication, May 22, 1990).

67. For example, see Nogueira-Neto, "Getting Brazil's Network," and Jorge
Pádua and Carvalho, "New Action."

68. One DN administrator related how he had established an informal working relationship with his counterpart in SEMA on technical matters, but
when that relationship threatened to become routinized, his counterpart
broke it off on orders from above. This was a typical friction-reducing
strategy practiced by potential competitors within the Brazilian federal
bureaucracy. Daland (*Exploring Brazilian Bureaucracy,* p. 227) wrote that
prevailing thought within the Brazilian bureaucracy held that if all communication was eliminated, so was the potential for conflict.

69. Figueiredo, interview, March 6, 1986. Other SEMA administrators knew
preservation was one of the goals of the IBDF's system, but they held it was
preservation toward ill-defined ends—in contrast to SEMA's preservation
for the serious and practical business of science.

70. Klever, interview, February 21, 1986; various conversations with SEMA
officials, February–May 1986.

71. R. Ferreira, interview, April 30, 1986.

72. Rocha, interview, March 6, 1986.

73. Ribeiro, interview, April 7, 1986.

74. Araujo, interview, April 30, 1986. The disadvantages in the field of the distant relationship between the two agencies were mutual. SEMA's Maracá-
Jipioca Ecological Station, comprising two small islands, was situated just
seaward of Lago Piratuba BR, separated from it by a narrow channel.
SEMA had established an active management regime for the station, while

the IBDF had been unable to do so for the Lago Piratuba reserve; yet the forest agency received no help from SEMA.

75. Bramble, personal communication, October 24, 1986.

76. Roett, *Brazil: Politics,* p. 163; Joyce, "Price of Progress," p. 47.

77. Figueiredo, interview, May 20, 1986.

Chapter 9

1. See *The New York Times,* Aug. 28, 1988, sec. I, p. 18, col. 1; Oct. 18, 1988, sec. I, p. 30, col. 1; Dec. 28, 1988, sec. I, p. 26, col. 1; Feb. 3, 1989, sec. I, p. 30, col. 2; March 31, 1989, sec. I, p. 9, col. 1.

2. Faucher ("Paradise That Never Was," p. 25) writes, "The bourgeoisie . . . applied a rather cynical cost/benefit approach to the [military] regime. It opposed the regime from the moment that the concrete benefits did not outweigh the costs associated with authoritarianism."

3. Keen and Wasserman, *History of Latin America,* p. 391. In November 1985, the national congress passed and President Sarney signed an agrarian reform law providing for the distribution of nearly 90 million acres of land over the following four years.

4. Brazil's National Security Council in 1985 recommended a program (subsequently called the Calha Norte project) to substantially increase military presence in, and economic development of, that part of Brazilian Amazonia north of the Amazon and Solimões rivers. See Sternberg, "Manifest Destiny," p. 12.

5. Fearnside, "Development Alternatives"; Goodland, "Brazil's Environmental Progress"; Goulding, *Fishes and the Forest.*

6. Fearnside, "Extractive Reserves."

7. Skillings and Tcheyan, "Economic Development."

8. Page, *Conservation and Economic Efficiency,* p. 200.

9. Caldwell, *Environment and the Global Arena,* p. 118.

10. McNeill, "Historical Perspective," p. 64.

11. Page, *Conservation and Economic Efficiency,* p. 211.

BIBLIOGRAPHY

Abele, L.G., and Edward F. Connor. "Application of Island Biogeography Theory to Refuge Design: Making the Right Decision for the Wrong Reasons," pp. 89–94 in Linn, ed., *First Conference.*

Abele, L.G., and W.K. Patton. "The Size of Coral Heads and the Community Biology of Associated Decapod Crustaceans." *Journal of Biogeography* 3:1 (1976): 34–47.

Adams, Alexander. "How it Began," pp. xxxi–xxxiii in his (ed.) *First World Conference.*

———, ed. *First World Conference on National Parks, Proceedings*, U.S. Department of the Interior, National Park Service. Washington, D.C.: USGPO, 1962.

Adler, J. H. "The World Bank's Concept of Development—An In-House 'Dogmengeschichte'," pp. 30–50 in Bhagwati and Eckaus (eds.), *Development and Planning.*

Aguiar, Neuma, ed. *The Structure of Brazilian Development.* New Brunswick, N.J.: Transaction, 1979.

Anderson, Charles W. "Politics and Development Policy in Central America," pp. 255–262 in Uphoff and Ilchman (eds.), *The Political Economy of Development.*

Arndt, H.W. "Development Economics Before 1945," pp. 13–29 in Bhagwati and Eckaus (eds.), *Development and Planning.*

Assoreira, David, and José Manuel Carvalho de Vasconcelos. "Viagem Realizada a Reserva Biológica do Trombetas em Agosto de 1977." Brasília: IBDF, undated (mimeo).

Attfield, Robin. *The Ethics of Environmental Concern.* Oxford: Basil Blackwell, 1983.

Bacha, Edmar L. "Issues and Evidence on Recent Brazilian Economic Growth." *World Development* 5:1/2 (1977): 47–67.

Baker, Randall. "The Administrative Trap." *Ecologist* 6:7 (1976): 247–251.

Balassa, Bela, et al. *Toward Renewed Economic Growth in Latin America: Summary, Overview, and Recommendations.* Washington, D.C.: Institute for International Economics, 1986.

Barbira-Scazzocchio, Françoise, ed. *Land, People and Planning in Contemporary Amazonia*, Occasional Publication No. 3. Cambridge University: Centre of Latin American Studies, 1980.

Barkley, Katherine, and Steve Weissman. "The Eco-Establishment." *Ramparts* 8:11 (May 1970): 48–49+.

Barnett, Harold J. "Pressures of Growth Upon Environment," pp. 15–20 in Jarrett (ed.), *Environmental Quality.*

———, and Chandler Morse. *Scarcity and Growth.* Baltimore: The Johns Hopkins University Press for Resources for the Future, 1963.

Barrett, S.W. "Conservation in Amazonia," *Biological Conservation* 18 (1980): 209–235.

Barrientos, Fernando. "The Food and Agricultural Organization," pp. 73–84 in IUCN, *Latin American Conference.*

Barros, W. Duarte de. *Parques Nacionais do Brasil.* Rio de Janeiro, 1952.

Barrow, C.J. "Development of the Várzeas (Floodlands) of Brazilian Amazonia," pp. 108–128 in Hemming (ed.), *Change in the Amazon Basin,* Vol.I.

Baumol, W.J. "On the Social Rate of Discount." *American Economic Review*
58 (September 1968): 788–802.

Beckwith, Burnham Putnam. *The Next 500 Years: Scientific Predictions of
Major Social Trends.* New York: Exposition Press, 1967.

Bell, Daniel, ed. *Toward the Year 2000: Work in Progress.* Boston: Houghton
Mifflin, 1968.

Bell, Peter B. "The Ford Foundation as a Transnational Actor," pp. 115–128 in
Keohane and Nye (eds.), *Transnational Relations.*

Beltran, Enrique. "Latin American Cooperation in National Park Matters:
Committee Report," pp. 368–369 in Adams (ed.), *First World Conference.*

Bennett, Alvin LeRoy. *International Organizations.* Englewood Cliffs, N.J.:
Prentice Hall, 1977.

Bhagwati, Jagdish, and Richard S. Eckaus. *Development and Planning: Essays in
Honour of Paul Rosenstein Rodan.* Cambridge, Mass.: The MIT Press, 1973.

Blair, William D., Jr., "The Nature Conservancy: Conservation Through
Cooperation." *Journal of Forest History* 30 (January 1986): 37–40.

Bluntschli, Hans. "A Amazônia como Organismo Harmônico." *Cadernos da
Amazônia* 1 (1964): 9–37.

Boardman, Robert. *International Organization and the Conservation of
Nature.* Bloomington: Indiana University Press, 1981.

Boecklen, William J., and Nicholas J. Gotelli. "Island Biogeographic Theory
and Conservation Practice: Species-Area or Specious-Area Relationships?"
Biological Conservation 29 (1984): 63–80.

Boulding, Kenneth. "The Legitimacy of Economics," pp. 24–30 in Upoff and
Ilchman (eds.), *The Political Economy of Development.*

Boza, Mario Andres. "Costa Rica: A Case Study of Strategy in the Setting Up
of National Parks in a Developing Country," pp. 183–192 in Elliott (ed.),
Second World Conference.

Briggs, Asa. Review of I.F. Clarke's *The Pattern of Expectation, 1644–2001,* in
Futures 11 (October 1979): 426–427.

Brockman, C. Frank. "Supplement to Report of Committee on Problems of
Nomenclature," pp. 424–432 in Adams (ed.), *First World Conference.*

———— and Kai Curry-Lindahl. "Problems of Nomenclature: The Need for
Definitions: Committee Report," pp. 366–367 in Adams (ed.), *First World
Conference.*

Brooks, Harvey. "Knowledge and Action: The Dilemma of Science Policy in the
'70s." *Daedalus* 102:2 (Spring 1973): 125–143.

Brower, David. "A New Decade and a Last Chance: How Bold Shall We Be?"
Sierra Club Bulletin 45 (January 1960):3–4.

Brown, Harrison, James Bonner, and John Weir. *The Next Hundred Years, A
Discussion Prepared For Leaders of American Industry.* New York: The
Viking Press, 1957.

Brown, Keith. "Geographical Patterns of Evolution in Neotropical Lepidoptera:
Systematics and Derivation of Known and New Heliconiini." *Journal of
Entomology* 44:3 (1975): 201–242.

Bruneau, Thomas C., and Philippe Faucher, eds. *Authoritarian Capitalism:
Brazil's Contemporary Economic and Political Development.* Boulder, Colo.:
Westview Press, 1981.

Bryant, Coralie, and Louise G. White. *Managing Development in the Third
World.* Boulder, Colo.: Westview Press, 1982.

Budowski, Geraldo. *Imperialismo Científico*. Mexico City: Ediciones del Instituto Mexicano de Recursos Naturales Renovables, 1972.

———. "Opening Address," pp. 9–12 in IUCN, *The Use of Ecological Guidelines*.

Bunker, Steven G. "The Cost of Modernity: Inappropriate Bureaucracy, Inequality, and Development Program Failure in the Brazilian Amazon." *The Journal of Developing Areas* 16:4 (July 1982): 573–596.

———. "Forces of Destruction in Amazonia." *Environment* 22:7 (September 1980): 14–20+.

———. "Power Structures and Exchange Between Government Agencies in the Expansion of the Agricultural Sector in Para." *Studies in Comparative International Development* 14:1 (Spring 1979): 56–76.

———. *Underdeveloping the Amazon: Extraction, Unequal Exchange and the Failure of the Modern State*. Champaign-Urbana: University of Illinois Press, 1985.

Burgess, Robert L., and David M. Sharpe, eds. *Forest Island Dynamics in Man-Dominated Landscapes*. New York: Springer-Verlag, 1981.

Burns, E. Bradford. *A History of Brazil*, 2d ed. New York: Columbia University Press, 1980.

Cahn, Robert, and Patricia Cahn. "Saved But Threatened." *Audubon* 82:3 (May 1985): 48–51.

Caldwell, Lynton K. "The Changing Structure of International Policy: Needs and Alternatives." *Natural Resources Journal* 12:4 (April 1972): 153–160.

———. *In Defense of Earth: International Protection of the Biosphere*. Bloomington: Indiana University Press, 1972.

———. *International Environmental Policy: Emergence and Dimensions*. Durham, N.C.: Duke University Press, 1984.

Camp, Roderic A. "The Political Technocrat in Mexico and the Survival of the Political System." *Latin American Research Review* 20:1 (1985): 97–118.

Carcasson, R.H. "A Preliminary Survey of the Zoogeography of African Butterflies." *East African Wildlife Journal* 2 (1964): 122–157.

Carvalho, José Candido de Melo. "A Conservação da Natureza e Recursos Naturais na Amazônia Brasileira." *CVRD Revista* 2 (special edition, November 1981): 5–47.

———. "The Conservation of Nature in the Brazilian Amazonia," pp. 707–736 in Sioli (ed.), *The Amazon*.

Castle, Emery, ed. *Contemporary Issues in Natural Resource Economics*. Resources for the Future Reprint 152, Washington, D.C., 1978.

Caufield, Catherine. "Dam the Amazon, Full Speed Ahead." *Natural History* 92 (July 1983): 60–67.

———. "A Reporter at Large: The Rain Forests." *The New Yorker* (January 14, 1985): 41+.

Cehelsky, Marta. *Land Reform in Brazil: The Management of Social Change*. Boulder, Colo.: Westview Press, 1979.

Child, V. Gordon. *Man Makes Himself*. New York: Mentor Books, 1951.

———. *Geopolitics and Conflict in South America: Quarrels Among Neighbors*. New York: Praeger, 1985.

Childe, Jack. "Geopolitical Thinking in Latin America." *Latin American Research Review*, 14:2 (1978): 89–111.

Cintra, Antônio Otávio. "Traditional Brazilian Politics: An Interpretation of Relations Between Center and Periphery," pp. 127–166 in Aguiar (ed.), *Structure of Brazilian Development*.

Clad, James C. "Conservation and Indigenous Peoples: A Study of Convergent Interests," pp. 45–62 in McNeely and Pitt (eds.), *Culture and Conservation*.

Clark, J.G.D. *The Study of Prehistory: An Inaugural Lecture*. London: Cambridge University Press, 1954.

Clawson, Marion, ed. *Natural Resources and International Development*. Baltimore: The Johns Hopkins University Press for Resources for the Future, 1964.

———. "Park Visits in the Coming Decades," pp. 116–126 in Elliott (ed.), *Second World Conference*.

Clement, Roland C. "Conservation Needs in Latin America, Draft Report." National Audubon Society, April 1977.

Cody, Martin L., and Jared M. Diamond, eds. *Ecology and The Evolution of Communities*. Cambridge, Mass.: Belknap Press, 1975.

Coleman, James S. "The Resurrection of Political Economy," pp. 30–39 in Uphoff and Ilchman (eds.), *The Political Economy of Development*.

Collier, Peter, and David Horowitz. *The Rockefellers: An American Dynasty*. New York: Holt, Rinehart and Winston, 1976.

Committee on Research Priorities in Tropical Biology. *Research Priorities in Tropical Biology*. Washington, D.C.: National Academy of Sciences, 1980.

Commoner, Barry. *The Closing Circle*. New York: Bantam Books, 1972.

Costantino, Italo. "Present Trends in Worldwide Development of National Parks," pp. 68–73 in Elliott (ed.), *Second World Conference*.

Coolidge, Harold J. "Future Prospects for International Cooperation in the Field of National Parks and Reserves," pp. 357–361 in Adams (ed.), *First World Conference*.

Cornish, Edward. *The Study of the Future: An Introduction to the Art and Science of Understanding and Shaping Tomorrow's World*. Washington, D.C.: World Future Society, 1977.

Cowan, R.S. "Scientific Research in National Parks," pp. 337–345 in IUCN, *Latin American Conference*.

Crane, Diana. "Transnational Networks in Basic Science," pp. 235–251 in Keohane and Nye (eds.), *Transnational Relations*.

Curry-Lindahl, Kai. "Background and Development of International Conservation Organizations and their Role in the Future." *Environmental Conservation* 5:3 (Autumn 1978): 163–169.

———. "The Conservation Story in Africa During the 1960s." *Biological Conservation* 6:3 (July 1974): 170–178.

Cyert R., and J.G. March. *The Behavioral Theory of the Firm*. Englewood Cliffs, N.J.: Prentice Hall, 1963.

Dahlberg, Kenneth A., et al. *Environment and the Global Arena: Actors, Values, Politics, and Futures*. Durham, N.C.: Duke University Press, 1985.

Daland, Robert T. *Exploring Brazilian Bureaucracy: Performance and Pathology*. Washington, D.C.: University Press of America, 1981.

Darwin, Charles Galton. *The Next Million Years*. New York: Doubleday and Company, 1952.

Dasmann, Raymond. "Development of a Classification System for Protected Natural and Cultural Areas," pp. 388–396 in Elliott (ed.), *Second World Conference*.

———. "National Parks, Nature Conservation and 'Future Primitive.'" *Ecologist* 6:5 (1976): 164–168.

———, John P. Milton, and Peter H. Freeman. *Ecological Principles for Economic Development*. London: John Wiley and Sons, 1973.

Day, Richard H. "Adaptive Economic Theory and Modeling: A Review," pp. 1–14 in Castle (ed.), *Contemporary Issues*.

Dean, Warren. "Forest Conservation in Southeastern Brazil, 1900–1955." *Environmental Review* 9:1 (Spring 1985): 55–69.

Denevan, William E., et al. "Indigenous Agroforestry in the Peruvian Amazon: Bora Indian Management of Swidden Fallows," pp. 137–155 in Hemming (ed.), *Change in the Amazon Basin,* Vol. I.

Diamond, Jared M. "Island Biogeography and Conservation: Strategy and Limitations." *Science* 193 (September 10, 1976): 1027–1029.

———. "The Island Dilemma: Lessons of Modern Biogeographic Studies for the Design of Nature Reserves." *Biological Conservation* 7 (1975): 129–146.

———, and Robert May. "Island Biogeography and the Design of Natural Reserves," pp. 163–186 in Robert May (ed.), *Theoretical Ecology: Principles and Applications.* Philadelphia: W.B. Saunders Company, 1976.

Di Castri, Francesco. "Esquisse Ecologique du Chili." Santiago, Chile, 1972 (mimeo.).

———, and Jane Robertson. "The Biosphere Reserve Concept: 10 Years After." *Parks* 6:4 (January–March 1982): 1–6.

Dickson, David. *The Politics of Alternative Technology.* New York: Universe Books, 1974.

Domhoff, G. William. *The Powers That Be: Processes of Ruling-Class Domination in America.* New York: Random House, 1978.

Dos Santos, Breno Augusto. *Amazônia: Potencial Mineral e Perspectivas de Desenvolvimento.* São Paulo: T.A. Queiroz, 1983.

Doud, Alden Lowell. "International Environmental Developments: Perceptions of Developing and Developed Countries." *Natural Resources Journal* 12:4 (October 1972): 520–529.

Dubos, Rene. *Man Adapting.* New Haven: Yale University Press, , 1965.

Ducke, A., and G.A. Black. "Phytogeographical Notes on the Brazilian Amazon." *Academia Brasileira de Ciência, Anais* 25:1 (1953): 1–46.

Duncan, Otis Dudley. "Social Organization and the Ecosystem," pp. 37–82 in Robert E. L. Farris (ed.), *Handbook of Modern Sociology.* Chicago: Rand McNally and Company, 1964.

The Economist. "The Morning After: A Survey." March 12, 1983, special section, 1–18.

Egler, Frank E. "Pesticides—In Our Ecosystem," pp. 245–267 in Shepard and McKinley (eds.), *Subversive Science.*

Ehrlich, Paul, and Anne H. Ehrlich. *Population, Resources, Environment: Issues in Human Ecology,* 2d ed. San Francisco: Freeman, 1972.

Eidsvik, Harold K. "National Parks and Other Protected Areas: Some Reflections on the Past and Prescriptions for the Future." *Environmental Conservation* 7:3 (Autumn 1980): 185–190.

Ellen, Roy. *Environment, Subsistence, and System: The Ecology of Small-Scale Social Formations.* Cambridge: Cambridge University Press, 1982.

Elliott, Hugh, ed. *Second World Conference on National Parks, September 18–27, 1972, Proceedings.* Morges, Switzerland: IUCN, 1974.

Endler, John A. "Pleistocene Forest Refuges: Fact or Fancy," pp. 641–657 in Prance (ed.), *Biological Diversification.*

Environment Canada. "Environment Canada and the North: A Discussion Paper." Ottawa: Environment Canada, July, 1983 (mimeo.).

Estado do Amazonas, Instituto de Terras e Colonização. "Parque Nacional do Pico da Neblina: Mapa." Manaus, no date (1:250,000).

———. "Parque Nacional do Rio Jaú: Mapa." Manaus, no date (1:250,000).

Evans, Luther, et al. *The Decade of Development: Problems and Issues.* Dobbs Ferry, N.Y.: Oceana Publications, 1966.

Evans, Peter. "Dependent Development in the Eighties," manuscript later published as "State, Local, and Multi-National Capital in Brazil: Prospects for the Stability of the 'Triple Alliance' in the Eighties," pp. 139–168 in Diana Tussie (ed.), *Latin America in the World Economy: New Perspectives*. Hampshire, England: Gower, 1983.

———. *Dependent Development: The Alliance of Multinational, State, and Local Capital in Brazil*. Princeton, N.J.: Princeton University Press, 1979.

———. "Reinventing the Bourgeoisie: State Entrepreneurship and Class Formation in Dependent Capitalist Development." *American Journal of Sociology* 88:Supplement (1982): S210–S247.

Falk, Richard A. *This Endangered Planet: Prospects and Proposals for Human Survival*. New York: Random House, 1972.

———. "Environmental Policy as a World Order Problem." *Natural Resources Journal* 12:4 (April 1972): 161–171.

Farvar, M.T. "The Interaction of Ecological and Social Systems in the Third World," pp. 567–582 in Schofield (ed.), *Earthcare*.

———, and Milton, J.P., eds. *The Careless Technology: Ecology and International Development*. Garden City, N.Y.: Doubleday and Company, 1972.

Faucher, Philippe. "The Paradise That Never Was: The Breakdown of the Brazilian Authoritarian Order," pp. 11–39 in Bruneau and Faucher (eds.), *Authoritarian Capitalism*.

Fearnside, Philip M. "Brazil's Amazon Settlement Schemes: Conflicting Objectives and Human Carrying Capacity." *Habitat International* 8:1 (1984): 45–61.

———. "Deforestation and Decisionmaking in the Development of Brazilian Amazonia." *Interciencia* 10:5 (September–October 1985): 243–247.

———. "Development Alternatives in the Brazilian Amazon: An Ecological Evaluation." *Interciencia* 8:2 (March–April 1983): 65–78.

———. "Extractive Reserves in Brazilian Amazonia." *BioScience* 39:6 (June 1989): 387–393.

———. "Settlement in Rondonia and the Token Role of Science and Technology in Brazil's Amazonian Development Planning." *Interciencia* 11:5 (1986): 229–236.

———, and Gabriel de Lima Ferreira. "Roads in Rondonia: Highway Construction and the Farce of Unprotected Reserves in Brazil's Amazonian Forest." *Environmental Conservation* 11:4 (1984): 358–360.

———, and Judy M. Rankin. "Jari Revisited: Changes and the Outlook for Sustainability in Amazonia's Largest Silvacultural Estate." *Interciencia* 10:3, May–June 1985): 121–129.

Fickett, Lewis P., Jr. *Problems of the Developing Nations: Readings and Case Studies*. New York: Thomas Y. Crowell Company, 1966.

Fisher, Joseph L. "Parks and Natural Areas in the Natural Landscape," pp. 192–199 in IUCN, *Latin American Conference*.

Fishlow, Albert. "The United States and Brazil: The Case of the Missing Relationship." *Foreign Affairs* 60:4 (Spring 1982): 904–923.

Fittkau, E. J., and H. Klinge. "On Biomass and Trophic Structure of the Central Amazonian Rain Forest Ecosystem." *Biotropica* 5:1 (1973): 2–15.

Flenley, John. *The Equatorial Rain Forest: A Geological History*. London: Butterworths, 1979.

Flynn, Peter. *Brazil: A Political Analysis*. Boulder, Colo.: Westview Press, 1979.

Fontaine, Rene C. "International Agencies and Parks," pp. 309–318 in Adams (ed.), *First World Conference*.

Forbes, Stephen A. "The Humanizing of Ecology." *Ecology* 3:2 (1922): 89–92.

Foresta, Ronald A. *America's National Parks and Their Keepers.* Washington, D.C.: Resources for the Future, 1984.

———. "Transformation of the Appalachian Trail." *Geographical Review* 77:1 (January 1987): 76–85.

Forrester, Jay W. *World Dynamics,* Cambridge, Mass.: M.I.T. Press, 1971.

Foweraker, Joe. *The Struggle for Land: A Political Economy of the Pioneer Frontier in Brazil From 1930 to the Present Day.* London: Cambridge University Press, 1981.

Fowles, Jib. "The Problem of Values in Futures Research." *Futures* 9 (August 1977): 303–314.

Fox, Louise M. "Income Distribution in Post-1964 Brazil: New Results." *Journal of Economic History* 43:1 (March 1983): 261–271.

Freeman, Christopher, and Marie Jahoda. *World Futures: The Great Debate.* New York: Universe Books, 1978.

Fundação Universidade do Amazonas. *Proposta de Política Florestal Para a Amazônia Brasileira.* Manaus: Metro Cúbico, 1979.

Furtado, Celso. *Economic Development of Latin America,* 2d ed. London: Cambridge University Press, 1976.

———. *The Economic Growth of Brazil.* Berkeley: University of California Press, 1963.

Game, M., and G.F. Peterken. "Nature Reserve Selection Strategies in the Woodlands of Central Lincolnshire, England." *Biological Conservation* 29 (1984): 157–181.

Garratt, Keith. "The Relationship Between Adjacent Lands and Protected Areas: Issues of Concern for the Protected Area Manager," pp. 65–71 in McNeely and Miller (eds.), *National Parks, Conservation, and Development.*

Gentilli, J. "The Foundation of Australian Bird Geography." *Emu* 49 (1949): 85–130.

Gerth, Hans H., and C. Wright Mills. *From Max Weber: Essays in Sociology.* New York: Oxford University Press, 1968.

Gille, A. "The Role of International Agencies," pp. 319–327 in Adams (ed.), *First World Conference.*

Glacken, Clarence. "Changing Ideas of the Habitable World," pp. 70–92 in Thomas (ed.), *Man's Role.*

Goetel, Walery. "Parks Between Countries," pp. 287–294 in Adams (ed.), *First World Conference.*

Gomez-Pompa, A., C. Vasquez-Yanes, and S. Guevara. "The Tropical Rainforest: A Non-Renewable Resource." *Science* 177 (September 1, 1972): 762–765.

Goodland, Robert. "Brazil's Environmental Progress in Amazonian Development," pp. 5–35 in Hemming (ed.), *Change in the Amazon Basin,* Vol.I.

———. "Tribal Peoples and Economic Development: The Human Ecological Dimension," pp. 13–31 in McNeely and Pitt (eds.), *Culture and Conservation.*

Goodland, Robert, and H.S. Irwin. *Amazon Jungle: Green Hell to Red Desert? An Ecological Discussion of the Environmental Impact of the Highway Construction Program in the Amazon Basin.* New York: Elsevier, 1975.

Goulding, Michael. *The Fishes and the Forest: Explorations in Amazonian Natural History.* Berkeley: University of California Press, 1980.

Goulet, D. *The Cruel Choice: A New Concept in the Theory of Development.* New York: Atheneum, 1971.

Grant, Lindsey. *Thinking Ahead: Foresight in the Political Process.* Washington, D.C.: The Environmental Fund, 1983.

Grunwald, Joseph. "Resource Aspects of Latin American Economic Development," pp. 307–336 in Clawson (ed.), *Natural Resources*.

Guimarães, Roberto P. "Bureaucracy and Ecopolitics in the Third World: Environmental Policy Formation in Brazil." Paper prepared for presentation at the Annual Meeting of the American Political Science Association, September 1–4, 1988, Washington, D.C.

Guppy, Nicholas. "Tropical Deforestation: A Global View." *Foreign Affairs* 62:4 (Spring 1984): 928–965.

Haffer, Jurgen. "Avian Speciation in Amazonian Forest Birds." *Science* 165 (July 11, 1969): 131–137.

———. "General Aspects of the Refuge Theory," pp. 6–26 in Prance (ed.), *Biological Diversification*.

Haring, C.H. *Empire in Brazil: A New World Experiment with Monarchy*. New York: W.W. Norton and Company, 1968.

Harroy, J.P. "The International Commission on National Parks," pp. 62–67 in IUCN, *Latin American Conference*.

Hart, William J. *A Systems Approach to Park Planning*. Morges, Switzerland: IUCN Publication, New Series: Supplementary Paper No. 4, 1966.

Hecht, Susanna B. "Cattle Ranching in Amazonia: Political and Ecological Considerations," pp. 366–398 in Schmink and Wood (eds.), *Frontier Expansion in Amazonia*.

Hemming, John, ed. *Change in the Amazon Basin*. Vol. 1, *Man's Impact on Forests and Rivers*. Vol. 2, *The Frontier After a Decade of Colonisation*. Manchester: Manchester University Press, 1985.

Henderson, Hazel. "Ecologists Versus Economists." *Harvard Business Review* 51 (July–August 1973): 28–36+.

———. "Limitations of Traditional Economics in Making Resource Decisions," pp. 9–28, in George F. Rohrlich (ed.), *Environmental Management: Economic and Social Dimensions*. Cambridge, Mass.: Ballinger Publishing Company, 1976.

Hitch, Charles J., ed. *Resources for an Unknown Future*. Baltimore: The Johns Hopkins University Press for Resources for the Future, 1978.

Holdgate, Martin W., Mohamed Kassas, and Gilbert F. White. "World Environmental Trends Between 1972 and 1982." *Environmental Conservation* 9:1 (Spring 1982): 11–29.

Holdridge, L.R. "Determination of World Plant Formations from Simple Climatic Data." *Science* 105 (1947): 367–368.

———. *Life Zone Ecology*. Rev. ed. San Jose, Costa Rica: Tropical Science Center, 1967.

IBDF. "Parques Nacionais e Reservas Equivalentes no Brasil: Relatório com Vistas a uma Revisão da Política Nacional Nesse Campo." Rio de Janeiro: IBDF, 1969.

———. "Pesquisa em Unidades de Conservação: Relação de Pesquisadores." Brasília: IBDF, 1986, unpaged.

———. Programa de Monitoramento da Cobertura Florestal do Brazil, "Estado de Rondônia: Mapa de Alteração de Cobertura Vegetal Natural." Brasília, 1984 (1:1,000,000).

———. "Parque Nacional de Pacaás Novos: Mapa de Alteração de Cobertura Vegetal Natural." Brasília, n.d. (1986) (1:250,000).

———. "Relatório Pessoal." *Relatório Anual*. Brasília: IBDF, 1986.

———. "Reserva Biológica do Abufari: Proposta de Criação." Brasília, 1982 (1:250,000).

————. "Reserva Biológica de Guaporé: Mapa de Alteração de Cobertura Vegetal Natural." Brasília, n.d. (1986) (1:250,000).

————. "Reserva Biológica de Jaru: Mapa de Alteração de Cobertura Vegetal Natural." Brasília, n.d. (1986) (1:250,000).

IBDF/FBCN. "Parque Nacional da Amazônia (Tapajós): Plano de Manejo." Brasília, 1979.

————. "Parque Nacional de Pacaás Novos: Plano de Manejo." Brasília, 1984 (draft).

————. "Parque Nacional de Sete Cidades: Plano de Manejo." Brasília, 1979.

————. *Plano do Sistema de Unidades de Conservação do Brasil: Primera Etapa.* Brasília, 1979.

————. *Plano do Sistema de Unidades de Conservação do Brasil: Segunda Etapa.* Brasília, 1982.

————. "Reserva Biológica de Jaru: Plano de Manejo." Brasília, 1984 (draft).

————. "Reserva Biológica de Poço das Antas: Plano de Manejo." Brasília, 1981.

————. "Reserva Biológica do Rio Trombetas: Plano de Manejo." Brasília, 1982.

INDERENA, División de Parques Nacionales y Vida Silvestre. "Preselección de Áreas del Sistema de Parques Nacionales y Otras Reservas." Bogota, Colombia, 1974.

Isto é, "Os Pais da Natureza" (June 13, 1984): 32–34.

IUCN. "Biotic Provinces of the World: Further Development of a System for Defining and Classifying Natural Regions for Purposes of Conservation." IUCN Occasional Papers, No. 9. Morges, Switzerland: IUCN, 1973.

————. *Latin American Conference on the Conservation of Renewable Natural Resources, Proceedings.* IUCN Publications New Series No. 13. Morges, Switzerland: IUCN, 1968.

————. *The Use of Ecological Guidelines for Development in the American Humid Tropics, Proceedings.* IUCN Publications New Series No. 31. Morges, Switzerland: IUCN, 1974.

————. *World Conservation Strategy: Living Resource Conservation for Sustainable Development.* Gland, Switzerland: IUCN, 1980.

Jackson, Peter. "WWF and National Parks." *Parks* 3:3 (October–December 1978): 9–11.

James, Preston E., and C.W. Minkel. *Latin America:* 5th ed. New York: John Wiley and Sons, 1986.

Janowitz, Morris. *The Military in the Political Development of New Nations.* Chicago: University of Chicago Press, 1964.

Jarrett, Henry. *Environmental Quality in a Growing Economy.* Essays from the Sixth RFF Forum. Baltimore: The Johns Hopkins University Press for Resources for the Future, 1966.

Johnson, John J. (ed.). *The Role of the Military in Underdeveloped Countries.* Princeton, N.J.: Princeton University Press, 1961.

Jordan, Carl F. "Amazon Rain Forests." *American Scientist* 70 (July–August 1982): 394–401.

Jorge Pádua, Maria Tereza, Alceo Magnanini, and Russell A. Mittermeier. "Brazil's National Parks." *Oryx* 12:4 (June 1974): 452–464.

————, and Angela Tresinari Bernardes Quintão. "Parks and Biological Reserves in the Brazilian Amazon." *Ambio* 11:5 (1982): 309–314.

————, and José Cândido de Melo Carvalho. "New Action in the Field of Conservation." *Environmental Conservation* 6:3 (Autumn 1979): 224.

Joyce, Christopher. "The Price of Progress." *New Scientist* 107 (July 25, 1985): 46–48.

Juda, Lawrence. "International Environmental Concern: Perspectives of and Implications for Developing States," pp. 90–107 in Orr and Soroos (eds.) *Global Predicament.*

Kahn, E.J., Jr. "A Reporter at Large: The Indigenists." *New Yorker* (August 31, 1981): 60+.

Katzman, Martin. "Paradoxes of Amazonian Development in a 'Resource Starved' World." *The Journal of Developing Areas* 10 (July 1976): 445–460.

Kay, David A., and Harold K. Jacobson, eds. *Environmental Protection: The Global Dimension.* Totowa, N.J.: Allanheld, Osmun, , 1983.

Keen, Benjamin, and Mark Wasserman. *A History of Latin America.* 3d ed. Boston: Houghton Mifflin Company, 1988.

Keohane, Robert O., and Joseph S. Nye, Jr. *Transnational Relations and World Politics.* Cambridge, Mass.: Harvard University Press, 1972.

Kleinpenning, J.M.G. "An Evaluation of the Brazilian Policy for the Integration of the Amazon Region (1964–1974)," *Tijdschrift voor Economie en Social Geografie* 68:5 (1977): 297–311.

———. "A Further Evaluation of the Policy for the Integration of the Amazon Region (1974–1976)," *Tijdschrift voor Economie en Social Geografie* 69:1–2 (1978): 78–85.

———, and Sjoukje Volbeda. "Recent Change in Population Size and Distribution," pp. 6–36 in Hemming (ed.) *Change in the Amazon Basin,* Vol. II.

Landsberg, Hans H., Leonard L. Fischman, and Joseph L. Fisher. *Resources in America's Future: Patterns of Requirements and Availability, 1960–2000.* Baltimore: The Johns Hopkins University Press for Resources for the Future, 1963.

Leighton, Richard M., and Ralph Sanders. "Military Civic Action," pp. 103–115 in Fickett (ed.), *Problems of the Developing Nations.*

Leonard, H. Jeffrey. "Confronting Industrial Pollution in Rapidly Industrializing Countries: Myths, Pitfalls and Opportunities." *Ecology Law Quarterly* 12 (1985): 779–816.

Leopold, Aldo. *A Sand County Almanac: With Other Essays on Conservation from 'Round River.'* New York: Oxford University Press, 1966.

Lewin, Roger. "How Big is Big Enough?" *Science* 225 (August 1984): 611–612.

Lieuwen, Edwin. *Arms and Politics in Latin America.* New York: Praeger Publishers, 1961.

Linn, Robert M., ed. *First Conference on Scientific Research in the National Parks, Proceedings.* Vol. 1, U.S. Department of the Interior. Washington, D.C.: USGPO, 1979.

Linz, Juan J. "The Future of an Authoritarian Situation or the Institutionalization of an Authorian Regime: The Case of Brazil," pp. 233–254, in Stepan (ed.), *Authoritarian Brazil.*

Livingston, D.A. "Quaternary Geography in Africa and the Refuge Theory," pp. 523–536 in Prance (ed.), *Biological Diversification.*

Lleras, E. "Monograph on Trigoniaceae." *Flora Neotropica* 19 (1978): 1–73, 1978.

Lovejoy, Thomas E. "Designing Refugia for Tomorrow," pp. 673–679 in Prance (ed.), *Biological Diversification.*

———. "Discontinuous Wilderness: Minimum Areas for Conservation." *Parks* 5:2 (July–September 1980): 13–15.

———. "The Epoch of Biotic Impoverishment." *Great Basin Naturalist Memoirs* (1979): 5–10.

———. "The Science of Amazon Conservation," unpublished manuscript (10 pp.).

———, and D.C. Oren. "Minimum Critical Size of Ecosystems," pp. 7–12 in R.L. Burgess and D.M. Sharpe (eds.), *Forest Island Dynamics in Man-Dominated Landscapes*. New York: Springer-Verlag, 1981.

Lowenthal, David. "The American Scene." *Geographical Review* 58:1 (1968): 61–88.

Ludwig, Armin K. *Brazil: A Handbook of Historical Statistics*. Boston: G.K. Hall and Company, 1985.

Lundberg, Ferdinand. *The Coming World Transformation*. Garden City, N.Y.: Doubleday and Company, 1963.

Lynch, J.F., and N.K. Johnson. "Turnover and Equilibria in Insular Avifaunas with Special Reference to the California Channel Islands." *The Condor* 76 (1974): 370–384.

MacArthur, R.E., and E.O. Wilson. "An Equilibrium Theory of Island Biogeography." *Evolution* 17 (1963): 373–387.

———. *The Theory of Island Biogeography*. Princeton, N.J.: Princeton University Press, 1967.

———, and Kenton R. Miller. *National Parks, Conservation, and Development: The Role of Protected Areas in Sustaining Society*. Proceedings of the World Congress on National Parks, Bali, Indonesia, October 11–22, 1982. Washington, D.C.: Smithsonian Institution Press, 1984.

Maganck, Richard A., and J. Martin Goebel. "Shifting Cultivation: Problems for Parks in Latin America." *Parks* 4:2 (July–September 1979): 4–8.

Maguire, Andrew, and Janet Welsh Brown. *Bordering on Trouble: Resources and Politics in Latin America*. Bethesda, Md.: Adler and Adler, 1986.

Mahar, Dennis J. *Frontier Development Policy in Brazil: A Study of Amazonia*. New York: Praeger Publishers, 1978.

Mandelbaum, K. *The Industrialization of Backward Areas*. Oxford: Oxford University Press, 1945.

Mares, Michael A. "Conservation in South America: Problems, Consequences, and Solutions." *Science* 233 (August 15, 1986): 734–739.

Margoules, C., A.J. Higgs, and R.W. Rafe. "Modern Biogeographic Theory: Are There Any Lessons for Nature Reserve Design?" *Biological Conservation* 24 (1982): 115–128.

Martins, José de Sousa. "Fighting for Land: Indians and Posseiros in Legal Amazonia," pp. 95–105 in Barbeira-Scazzocchio (ed.), *Land, People and Planning*.

———. "The State and the Militarization of the Agrarian Question in Brazil," pp. 463–490 in Schmink and Wood (eds.), *Frontier Expansion in Amazonia*.

Mason, Edward S. "Resources in the Past and for the Future," pp. 1–24 in Hitch (ed.), *Resources for an Uncertain Future*.

May, Robert. "Island Biogeography and the Design of Natural Reserves." *Nature* 254 (March 20, 1975): 177–178.

McConnell, Grant. "The Conservation Movement—Past and Present." *Western Political Quarterly* 7:1 (March 1954): 463–478.

McDonough, Peter. *Power and Ideology in Brazil*. Princeton, N.J.: Princeton University Press, 1981.

McKenzie, R.D. "The Concept of Dominance and World Organization." *American Journal of Sociology* 33:1 (1927): 28–42.

McNeely, Jeffrey A., and David Pitt, eds. *Culture and Conservation: The Human Dimension in Environmental Planning.* London: Croom Helm, 1985.
————. "Culture, the Missing Element," pp. 1–9 in their *Culture and Conservation.*
McNeill, William. "Historical Perspective," pp. 59–67 in Hitch (ed.), *Resources for an Uncertain Future.*
Meadows, Donella H. et al. *The Limits to Growth.* New York: Universe Books, 1972.
Medina, Maria Elena. "The Amazonian Pact, A General Analysis," pp. 78–71 in Barbira-Scazzocchio (ed.), *Land, People and Planning.*
Meganck, Richard, and J. Martin Goebel. "Shifting Cultivation: Problems for Parks in Latin America." *Parks* 4:2 (April–June 1979): 4–8.
Meggers, Betty J. *A Amazônia: A Ilusão de um Paraíso.* Rio de Janeiro: Editora Civilização Brasileira, 1977.
Meier, Gerald M., and Robert E. Baldwin. *Economic Development: Theory, History, Policy.* New York: John Wiley and Sons, 1957.
Meier, Richard L. *Developmental Planning.* New York: McGraw-Hill Book Company, 1965.
————. *Science and Economic Development: New Patterns of Living.* Cambridge, Mass.: The M.I.T. Press, , 1956.
Meira Mattos, Carlos de. *Brasil: Geopolítica e Destino.* Rio de Janeiro: José Olympio Editora, 1979.
————. *Uma Geopolítica Pan Amazônica.* Rio de Janeiro: Jose Olympio Editora, 1980.
Miller, Darrel. "Replacement of Traditional Elites: An Amazon Case Study," pp. 158–171 in Hemming (ed.), *Change in the Amazon Basin,* Vol. II.
Miller, Kenton R. "Parks and Protected Areas: Considerations for the Future." *Ambio* 11:5 (1982): 315–317.
————. *Planning National Parks for Ecodevelopment: Methods and Cases from Latin America.* Center for Strategic Wildlands Management Studies, The School of Natural Resources. Ann Arbor: University of Michigan, 1978.
————, et al. "Issues on the Preservation of Biological Diversity," pp. 337–362 in Repetto (ed.), *The Global Possible.*
Millikan, Max F., and Donald M. Blackmer. "Resistance and Conflict in the Modernization Process," pp. 12–20 in Fickett (ed.), *Problems of the Developing Nations.*
Ministry of Transportation, Brazilian Federal Government. "Transamazonian Highways." Report presented to the Sixth World Meeting of the International Road Federation, Montreal, Canada, October, 1970.
Mishan, E. J. "Ills, Bads, and Disamenities: The Wages of Growth." *Daedalus* 102:4 (Fall 1974): 63–88.
Moran, Emilio F. "The Adaptive System of the Amazonian Caboclo," pp. 136–159 in C. Wagley (ed.), *Man in the Amazon.* Gainesville: University Presses of Florida, 1974.
————. "Ecological, Anthropological, and Agronomic Research in the Amazon Basin." *Latin American Research Review,* 17:1 (1982): 3–41.
————. "Government-Directed Settlement in the 1970s: An Assessment of Transamazon Highway Colonization," pp. 297–317 in his (ed.), *Dilemma of Amazonian Development.*
————, ed. *The Dilemma of Amazonian Development.* Boulder, Colo.: Westview Press, 1983.
Moreau, R. E. "Vicissitudes of the African Biomes in the Pleistocene." *Proceedings of the Zoological Society of London* 144 (1963): 395–421.

Morgan, Lewis Henry. *Ancient Society.* Edited by Eleanor B. Leacock. Cleveland: World Publishing Company, 1963.

Mueller, Charles. "Frontier Based Agricultural Expansion: The Case of Rondonia," pp. 141–153 in Barbira-Scazzocchio (ed.), *Land, People and Planning.*

Mumme, Stephen P., C. Richard Bath, and Valerie J. Assetto. "Political Development and Environmental Policy in Mexico." *Latin American Research Review* 23:1 (1988): 7–34.

Myers, Norman. "Eternal Values of the Park Movement and the Monday Morning World," pp. 634–638 in McNeely and Miller (eds.), *National Parks, Conservation, and Development.*

———. "Forest Refuges and Conservation in Africa," pp. 658–672 in Prance (ed.), *Biological Diversification.*

———. "Islands of Conservation." *New Scientist* 83 (August 23, 1979): 600–602.

———. "The Present Status and Future Prospects of Tropical Moist Forests." *Environmental Conservation* 7:2 (Summer 1980): 101–114.

———. "The Problem of Disappearing Species: What Can be Done?" *Ambio* 9:5 (1980): 229–235.

———. *The Sinking Ark: A New Look at the Problem of Disappearing Species.* Oxford: Pergamon Press, 1979.

Nash, Leonard K. *The Nature of Natural Sciences.* Boston: Little, Brown and Company, 1963.

Nash, Roderick. *Wilderness and the American Mind.* 3d ed. New Haven, Conn.: Yale University Press, 1982.

Nelson, Michael. *The Development of Tropical Lands: Policy Issues in Latin America.* Baltimore: The Johns Hopkins University Press for Resources for the Future, 1973.

Nery da Fonseca, Leopoldo. *Geopolítica.* Rio de Janeiro: Bedeschi, 1940.

Nicholaides, J. J., III, et al. "Continuous Cropping Potential in the Upper Amazon Basin," pp. 337–365 in Schmink and Wood (eds.), *Frontier Expansion in Amazonia.*

Nielsen, Waldemar. *The Golden Donors.* New York: Dutton, 1985.

Nisbet, Robert. *History of the Idea of Progress.* London: Heinemann, 1980.

Nogueira-Neto, Paulo. "Getting Brazil's Network of Ecological Stations on the Ground," pp. 27–34 in *Journal '85: World Resources Institute.* Washington, D.C.: World Resources Institute, 1985.

———. Letter to Edwin W. Snider, Committee for Research and Exploration, National Geographic Society, CARTA/SEMA/GAB No. 109, February 18, 1986.

———, and José Candido de Melo Carvalho. "A Programme of Ecological Stations for Brazil." *Environmental Conservation* 6:2 (Summer 1979): 95–104.

Nurske, R. *Problems of Capital Formation in Underdeveloped Countries.* Oxford: Oxford University Press, 1953.

Odum, Eugene P. "The Strategy of Ecosystem Development." *Science* 164 (April 18, 1969): 262–270.

Oltremari, Juan V., and Eduardo Fahrenkrog. "Institutionalization of National Parks in Chile." *Parks* 3:4 (January–March 1979): 1–4.

Orr, David W., and Marvin S. Soroos, eds. *The Global Predicament: Ecological Prespectives on World Order.* Chapel Hill: University of North Carolina Press, 1979.

Page, Talbot. *Conservation and Economic Efficiency: An Approach to Materials Policy.* Baltimore: The Johns Hopkins University Press for Resources for the Future, 1977.

Pandolfo, Clara. *A Amazônia Brasileira e Suas Potencialidades.* Belém: SUDAM, Departamento de Recursos Naturais, 1979.

Patterson, Thomas T. *Glasgow Unlimited.* London: Cambridge University Press, 1960.

Pearson, Charles S. *Down to Business: Multinational Corporations, the Environment, and Development.* Washington, D.C.: World Resources Institute, 1985.

Pearson, Neale J. "Latin American Peasant Pressure Groups and the Modernization Process," pp. 233–239 in Uphoff and Ilchman (eds.) *Political Economy.*

Peters, Robert L., and Joan D. S. Darling. "The Greenhouse Effect and Nature Reserves." *BioScience* 35 (December 1985): 707–717.

Pfeffermann, Guy, and Richard Webb. "Poverty and Income Distribution in Brazil." *The Review of Income and Wealth* 29:2 (June 1983): 101–124.

Pires, J. Murca. "The Amazonian Forest," pp. 581–602 in Sioli (ed.), *The Amazon.*

Pittman, Howard Taylor. "Geopolitics in the ABC Countries: A Comparison." Ph.D. dissertation, The American University, Washington D.C., 1981.

Polanyi, Karl. *The Great Transformation: The Political and Economic Origins of Our Time.* Boston: Beacon Press, 1957.

Pollard, Sidney. *The Idea of Progress: History and Society.* New York: Basic Books, 1968.

Pompermayer, Malori José. "Strategies of Private Capital in the Brazilian Amazon," pp. 419–438 in Schmink and Wood (eds.), *Frontier Expansion in Amazonia.*

Portes, Alejandro. "Latin American Class Structures: Their Composition and Change During the Last Decades." *Latin American Research Review* 20 (1985): 7–39.

Posey, Darryl. "Cultural Parks and Indigenous Agriculture: Discussion." Smithsonian Institution Conference on Tropical Forest Conservation. Washington, D.C., December 4–6, 1985.

———. "Native and Indigenous Guidelines for Development Strategies: Understanding Biological Diversity Through Ethnoecology," pp. 156–181 in Hemming (ed.), *Change in the Amazon Basin,* Vol. I.

Prance, Ghillean T., ed. *Biological Diversification in the Tropics.* Proceedings of the Fifth International Symposium of the Association for Tropical Biology, Caracas, Venezuela, February 8–13, 1979. New York: Columbia University Press, 1982.

———. "Ciência, Aventura e Fé: Excursão do INPA ao Rio Purus," mss., undated, 13pp.

———. "Conservation Problems in the Amazon Basin," pp. 191–207 in Schofield (ed.), *Earthcare.*

———. "Origin and Evolution of the Amazon Flora." *Interciencia* 3:4 (July–August 1977): 207–222.

———. *The Phytogeographic Subdivisions of Amazonia and Their Consequences on the Selection of Biological Reserves.* Bronx, N.Y.: New York Botanical Garden, 1976.

———. "Phytogeographic Support for the Theory of Pleistocene Forest Refuges Based on Evidence From Distribution Patterns in Caryocaraceae, Chrysobalanaceae, Dichapetalaceae and Lecythidaceae." *Acta Amazonica* 3:3, supplement (December 1973): 1–26.

————. "A Review of the Phytogeographic Evidence for Pleistocene Climate Changes in the Neotropics." *Annals of the Missouri Botanical Garden* 69 (1982): 594–624.

————, and T. S. Elias, eds. *Extinction is Forever: The Status of Threatened and Endangered Plants in the Americas*. Bronx, N.Y.: New York Botanical Garden, 1977.

Price, Kent. Review of Lynton A. Caldwell, *International Environmental Policy*. *Natural Resources Journal* 25:1 (January 1985): 254–257.

Projeto RADAM Brasil. *Levantamento de Recursos Naturais,* vol. 16. Rio de Janeiro: Ministério das Minas e Energia, 1976.

Putney, Alan D. "Estrategia Preliminar para la Conservacion de Areas Silvestres Sobresalientes del Ecuador: Informe Final." Projecto UNCP/FAO/ECU/71/527, Quito, Ecuador, Departamento de Parques Nacionales y Vida Silvestre, Direccion General de Desarrollo Forestal, 1976.

Ramos, Alcida. "Development, Integration and the Ethnic Integrity of Brazilian Indians," pp. 222–229 in Barbira-Scazzocchio (ed.), *Land, People and Planning*.

————. "Frontier Expansion and Indian Peoples in the Brazilian Amazon," pp. 83–104 in Schmink and Wood (eds.), *Frontier Expansion in Amazonia*.

Reed, Nathaniel. "National Parks: Atonement for Environmental Sins," pp. 695–703 in Schofield (ed.), *Earthcare*.

Reis, Arthur Cezar Ferreira. *A Amazônia e a Cobiça Internacional*. São Paulo: Editora Nacional, 1960.

Repetto, Robert, ed. *The Global Possible: Resources, Development, and the New Century*. New Haven, Conn.: Yale University Press, 1985.

Richards, Paul W. "National Parks in Wet Tropical Areas," pp. 219–227 in Elliott (ed.), *Second World Conference*.

————. "Some Problems of Nature Conservation in the Tropics." *Bulletin of the Belgian National Botanical Garden* 41 (1970): 173–187.

————. *The Tropical Rain Forest: An Ecological Study*. London: Cambridge University Press, 1957.

Risner, Marc, and Ronald H. McDonald. "The High Costs of High Dams," pp. 270–307 in McGuire and Brown (eds.), *Bordering on Trouble*.

Rizzini, C. T. "Nota Prévia Sobre a Divisão Fitogeográfica do Brasil." *Revista Brasileira Geográfica* 25:1 (1963): 1–64.

Roberts, Marc J. "On Reforming Economic Growth." *Daedalus* 102:4 (Fall 1974): 109–138.

Rockefeller, Mary, and Laurance Rockefeller. "Parks, Planning, and People: How South America Guards Her Green Legacy." *National Geographic Magazine* 131:1 (January 1967): 74–119.

Roett, Riordan. *Brazil: Politics in a Patrimonial Society*. 3d ed. New York: Praeger, 1984.

————, "Brazilian Foreign Policy: Options in the 1980s," pp. 179–192 in Bruneau and Faucher (eds.), *Authoritarian Capitalism*.

Rolston, Holmes, III. "Duties to Endangered Species." *BioScience* 35:11 (December 1985): 718–726.

Ronayne, Jarlath. *Science in Government*. London: Edward Arnold, 1984.

Rosenau, James N. *The Study of Global Interdependence: Essays on the Transnationalization of World Affairs*. London: Frances Pinter, 1980.

Ross, Eric B. "The Evolution of the Amazon Peasantry." *Journal of Latin American Studies* 10:2 (1978): 193–218.

Rossetti, Jose Paschoal. *Economia Brasileira '83*. São Paulo: Editora Atlas, 1983.

Rostow, Walt Whitman. *The Process of Economic Growth.* New York: Norton, 1952.

Royal Geographic Society (U.K.). "Press Release/Maraca Expedition," undated (early 1987).

Rylands, Anthony, and Russell Mittermeier. "Parks, Reserves and Primate Conservation in Brazilian Amazonia." *Oryx* 17:2 (April 1983): 79–87.

Sachs, Ignacy. "Approaches to a Political Economy of Environment," pp. 294–308 in his *Studies in Political Economy.*

————. *Development and Planning.* London: Cambridge University Press, 1987.

————. *Studies in Political Economy of Development.* Oxford: Pergamon Press, 1980.

Salati, Eneas, José Marques, and Luiz Carlos Molion. "Origim e Distribuição das Chuvas na Amazônia." *Interciencia* 3:4 (July–August 1978): 200–205.

Sandbach, Francis. *Environment, Ideology and Policy.* Montclair, N.J.: Allenheld, Osmun and Company, 1980.

Sanders, Thomas G. "Brazil in 1980: The Emerging Political Model," pp. 193–218 in Bruneau and Faucher (eds.), *Authoritarian Capitalism.*

Santos, Roberto. "Law and Social Change: The Problem of Land in Brazilian Amazonia," pp. 439–462 in Schmink and Wood (eds.), *Frontier Expansion in Amazonia.*

Sauer, Carl O. "The Agency of Man on the Earth," pp. 49–69 in Thomas (ed.), *Man's Role.*

Sawyer, Donald R. "Frontier Expansion and Retraction in Brazil," pp. 180–203 in Schmink and Wood (eds.), *Frontier Expansion in Amazonia.*

Schiff, Ashely L. "Outdoor Recreation Values in the Public Decision Process." *Natural Resources Journal* 6:4 (October 1966): 542–559.

Schlessinger, Arthur, Jr. "The American Character." *Foreign Affairs* 62:1 (Fall 1983): 1–16.

Schmink, Marianne. "Land Conflicts in Amazonia." *American Ethologist* 9 (May 1982): 341–357.

————, and Charles H. Wood (eds.). *Frontier Expansion in Amazonia.* Gainesville: University of Florida Press, 1984.

Schmitter, Philippe. *Interest Conflict and Political Change in Brazil.* Stanford, Calif.: Stanford University Press, 1971.

Schneider, Ronald M. *The Political System of Brazil: Emergence of a 'Modernizing' Authoritarian Regime, 1964–1970.* New York: Columbia University Press, 1971.

Schofield, Edmund A., ed. *Earthcare: Global Protection of Natural Areas.* Proceedings of the Fourteenth Biennial Wilderness Conference. Boulder, Colo.: Westview Press, 1978.

Schrepfer, Susan. "Perspectives on Conservation: Sierra Club Strategies in Mineral King." *Journal of Forest History* 20 (October 1976): 176–190.

Schwartzman, Simon. "Struggling to be Born: The Scientific Community in Brazil." *Minerva*, 16:4 (Winter 1978): 545–580.

Sedjo, Roger A., and Marion Clawson. "How Serious is Tropical Deforestation?" *Journal of Forestry* 81:12 (December 1983): 792–794.

Seitz, John L. *The Politics of Development: An Introduction to Global Issues.* New York: Basil Blackwell, 1988.

SEMA, Coordenadoria de Ecossistemas. "Estação Ecológica de Anavilhanas," Brasília, 1984.

————. "Estação Ecológica da Jureia," Brasília, 1984.

————. "Estação Ecológica de Anavilhanas," Brasília, 1984.

————. "Estação Ecológica de Anavilhanas: Memória de Cálculo/86," Brasília, 1985, unpaged, mimeo.

————. "Estação Ecológica de Maracá-RR," Brasília, 1983, unpaged, mimeo.

————. "Estação Ecológica de Maracá-RR: Memória de Cálculo/86," Brasília, 1985, unpaged mimeo.

————. "Estação Ecológica do Taim," Brasília, 1984.

————. "Programa de Gerenciamento das Unidades de Conservação," Brasília, 1984.

————. Programa de Ação," Brasília, no date.

Shaffer, Mark L. "Minimum Population Sizes for Species Conservation." *BioScience* 31:2 (February 1981): 131–134.

Shepard, Paul, and Daniel McKinley, eds. *The Subversive Science: Essays Toward an Ecology of Man.* Boston: Houghton Mifflin Company, 1969.

Sills, David L. "The Environmental Movement and its Critics." *Human Ecology* 3:1 (1975): 1–41.

Simberloff, D. S. "Equilibrium Theory of Island Biogeography and Ecology." *Annual Review of Ecology and Systemics* 5 (1974): 161–182.

————. "Models in Biogeography," pp. 160–191 in T. J. M. Schopf (ed.), *Models in Paleobiology.* San Francisco: Freeman, Cooper and Company, 1974.

————, and L. G. Abele. "Island Biogeography Theory and Conservation Practice." *Science* 191 (January 23, 1976): 285–286.

Simon, Herbert A. *Administrative Behavior: A Study of Decisionmaking Processes in Administrative Organization.* 3d ed. New York: The Free Press, 1976.

Sioli, Harald (ed.). *The Amazon: Limnology and Landscape Ecology of a Mighty Tropical River and its Basin.* Dordrecht: Dr. W. Junk Publishers, 1984.

————. "Effects of Deforestation in Amazonia," pp. 58–67 in Hemming (ed.), *Change in the Amazon Basin,* Vol. I.

————. "Foreseeable Consequences of Actual Development Schemes and Alternative Ideas," pp. 252–268 in Barbira-Scazzocchio (ed.), *Land, People and Planning.*

————. "Unifying Principles of Amazonian Landscape Ecology and Their Implications," pp. 615–625 in his (ed.) *The Amazon.*

Skillings, Robert F., and Nils O. Tcheyan. "Economic Development of the Amazon Region of Brazil." School of Advanced International Studies, The Johns Hopkins University, Occasional Papers Series no. 9, November 1979.

Soule, Michael E. "What is Conservation Biology?" *BioScience* 35:11 (December 1985): 727–734.

Spears, John. "World Bank Financed Forestry/Agricultural Projects: Examples of Various Strategies That Are Being Used to Relieve Pressure on Tropical Rainforests, Discussion Note." Paper Presented at the Smithsonian Institution Conference on Tropical Forest Conservation, December 4–6, 1985.

Stark, N. "Nutrient Cycling Pathways and Litter." *BioScience* 22:6 (1972): 355–360.

Stepan, Alfred, ed. *Authoritarian Brazil: Origins, Policies, and Future.* New Haven: Yale University Press, 1973.

Stepan, Nancy. *The Beginnings of Brazilian Science: Osvaldo Cruz, Medical Research and Policy, 1890–1920.* New York: Science History Publications, 1976.

Sternberg, Hildgard O'Reilly. "Development and Conservation." *Erdkunde* 27:4 (1973): 253–265.

———. " 'Manifest Destiny' and the Brazilian Amazon: A Backdrop to Contemporary Security and Development Issues." *Conference of Latin Americanist Geographers, Yearbook 1987.*

Stillwell, H. Daniel. "National Parks of Brazil: A Study in Recreation Geography." *Annals of the Association of American Geographers* 53:3 (September 1963): 391–406.

Stone, Roger D. *Dreams of Amazonia.* New York: Viking, 1985.

SUDAM. *Amazônia: Renda Interna: 1959–1978.* Belém: SUDAM, 1982.

———. *Ecologia e Desenvolvimento da Amazonia,* Belém: SUDAM, 1982.

———. *SUDAM Ano 15,* Belém: SUDAM, 1982.

Sullivan, A.L., and M.L. Shaffer. "Biogeography of the Megazoo." *Science* 189 (July 4, 1975): 13–16.

Survival International-USA: News. "The Voice of the Yanomami Indians," 1985, unpaged.

Szulc, Tad. "Brazil's Amazonian Frontier," pp. 191–234 in Maguire and Brown (eds.), *Bordering on Trouble.*

Talbot, Lee M. "The International Role of Parks in Preserving Endangered Species," pp. 295–304 in Adams (ed.), *First World Conference.*

———. "The World's Conservation Strategy." *Environmental Conservation* 7:4 (Winter 1980): 259–268.

Terborgh, John. "Faunal Equilibria and the Design of Wildlife Preserves," pp. 369–380 in F. G. Golley et al. (eds.), *Tropical Ecological Systems.* New York: Springer-Verlag, 1975.

———. "Preservation of Natural Diversity: The Problem of Extinction-Prone Species." *BioScience* 24:12 (December 1974): 715–722.

Thelen, K.D., and Kenton Miller. "Planificación de Sistemas de Áreas Silvestres, Guía para la Planificación de Sistemas de Áreas Silvestres, con una Aplicación a los Parques Nacionales de Chile," Documento Técnico de Trabajo No. 16, FAO/RLAT/TF-109, Santiago, Chile, 1975.

Thomas, William L., Jr., ed. *Man's Role in Changing the Face of the Earth.* Chicago: University of Chicago Press, 1956.

Thompson, D'Arcy Wentworth. *On Growth and Form.* London: University Press, 1917.

Tinker, Jon. "Why Aren't Foresters More Conservationist?" *New Scientist* 63:916 (September 26, 1974): 819–821.

Tosi, J. A. "Zonas de Vida Natural en el Perú: Memoria Explicativa Sobre el Mapa Ecológico del Perú," Boletín Técnico No. 5, Projecto de Cooperación Técnica de la OFA/IIC, Zona Andina, Lima, Peru, 1960.

Tucker, William. *Progress and Privilege: America in the Age of Environmentalism.* Garden City, N.Y.: Anchor Press, 1982.

Udall, Stewart L. "Nature Islands for the World," pp. 1–10 (keynote address) in Adams (ed.), *First World Conference.*

Udvardy, Miklos D. "A Classification of the Biogeographical Provinces of the World." *IUCN* Occasional papers No. 18. Morges, Switzerland: IUCN, 1975.

U.N. Department of Economic and Social Affairs. *Natural Resources in Developing Countries: Investigation, Development and Rational Utilization.* Report of the Advisory Committee on the Application of Science and Technology to Development, United Nations, New York, 1970.

U.N. Economic Commission for Latin America. *The Economic Development of Latin America and its Principal Problems.* New York: UN Department of Economic Affairs, 1950.

———. *Economic Development, Planning and International Co-operation.* Santiago, Chile: United Nations, 1961.

———. *Toward a Dynamic Development Policy for Latin America.* New York: United Nations, 1963.

UNESCO. "Action Plan for Biosphere Reserves." *Nature and Resources* 20:4 (October–December 1984): 12–20.

———. "Task Force on: Criteria and Guidelines for the Choice and Establishment of Biosphere Reserves, Final Report." MAB Report Series No. 22, Paris, 1974.

U.N. Food and Agriculture Organization. "A General Programme for Wildlife Management and Conservation in Brazil." PRODEPEF Technical Report no. 6, UNDP/FAO/IBDF, Brasília, 1978.

———. "Wildland Management and Planning in Brazil." PRODEPEF Technical Report no. 14, UNDP/FAO/IBDF, Brasília, 1978.

U.S. Congress, Joint Economic Committee. *The Analysis and Evaluation of Public Expenditures: The PPB System.* Washington, D.C.: USGPO, 1969.

U.S. Delegation to the UN Conference on the Human Environment. "Report." N.d. [1972].

U.S. Department of State, Office of Food and Natural Resources. *U.S. Strategy Conference on Biological Diversity, November 16–18, 1981, Proceedings,* U.S. Department of State, Washington, April 1982.

U.S. Interagency Task Force on Tropical Forests. *The World's Tropical Forests: A Policy, Strategy, and Program for the United States.* Department of State Publication 9117. Washington, USGPO, 1980.

Uphoff, Norman T., and Warren F. Ilchman, eds. *The Political Economy of Development: Theoretical and Empirical Contributions.* Berkeley: University of California Press, 1972.

Urquidi, Victor L. *The Challenge of Development in Latin America.* New York: Frederick A. Praeger, 1964.

Van Doren, Charles. *The Idea of Progress.* New York: Frederick A. Praeger, 1967.

Vanzolini, P. E. "Zoológica Sistemática, Geografia e a Origem das Espécies," Instituto de Geografia, Universidade de São Paulo, Teses e Monógrafos No. 3, 1970.

———, and E. E. Williams. "South American Anoles: The Geographic Differentiation and Evolution of the *Anolis chrysolepis* Species Group." *Arquivos de Zoológia* 19:1 (1970): 1–240.

Vuilleumer, F., and D. Simberloff. "Ecology vs. History as Determinants of Patchy and Insular Distributions in High Andean Birds," pp. 235–380 in M. K. Hecht et al. (eds.), *Evolutionary Biology,* Vol. 12. New York: Plenum, 1980.

Wagley, Charles, ed. *Man in the Amazon.* Gainesville: University Presses of Florida, 1974.

Walter, Ingo, and Judith Ugelow. "Environmental Policy in Developing Countries." *Ambio* 8:2–3 (1979): 102–109.

Ward, Barbara. *Progress for a Small Planet.* New York: W. W. Norton and Company, 1979.

Weissman, Steve. "Why the Population Bomb is a Rockefeller Baby." *Ramparts* 8:11 (May 1970): 43–47.

Wesson, Robert G., and David V. Fleischer. *Brazil in Transition.* New York: Praeger Publishers, 1983.

Wetterberg, Gary B. "A Case Study: Brazil's Wildlife Management and Conservation Program." Paper Presented at the International Workshop on Wildlife Management in Developing Countries, Peshawar, Pakistan, November 10–12, 1980.

————. "Decade of Progress for South American National Parks 1974–1984."
Washington: U.S. Department of the Interior, National Park Service,
International Affairs Division, 1985.

————. "History and Status of South American National Parks and an Evaluation of Selected Management Options." Ph.D. dissertation, University of
Washington, 1974.

————. "The 1978 Status of National Parks and Equivalent Reserves in South
America." U.S. Department of the Interior, National Park Service,
International Affairs Division, 1980. [English language translation of Gary
Wetterberg et al., "Estado Atual dos Parques Nacionais e Reservas Equiva-
lentes na America do Sul-1978, *Brasil Florestal* 36 (October–December,
1978): 11–36.]

————, et al. "An Analysis of Nature Conservation Priorities in the Amazon,"
PRODEPEF Technical Series no.8, UNDP/FAO/IBDF, Brasília, 1976
[original in Portuguese].

————, Ghillean T. Prance, and Thomas E. Lovejoy. "Conservation Progress in
Amazónia: A Structural Review." *Parks* 6:2 (1981): 5–10.

————, and Maria Tereza Jorge Pádua. "Preservação da Natureza na
Amazonia Brasileira: Situação em 1978, PRODEPEF Série Técnica No. 13,"
IBDF/UNDP/FAO, Brasília, 1978.

Wilcox, Bruce A. "In Situ Conservation of Genetic Resources: Determinants of
Minimum Area Requirements," pp. 639–647 in McNeely and Miller (eds.),
National Parks, Conservation, and Development.

Wilson, Edward O. "The Biological Diversity Crisis," *BioScience* 35:11
(December 1985): 700–706.

————, and E.O. Willis. "Applied Biogeography," pp. 522–534 in Cody and
Diamond (eds.) *Ecology and Evolution.*

Witcomb, Robert F., et al. "Island Biogeography and Conservation: The
Limitations of Small Preserves." Article in preparation in 1976. Washington:
USDA/U.S. Fish and Wildlife Service/Smithsonian Institution.

Wood, Charles H. and John Wilson. "The Magnitude of Migration to the
Brazilian Frontier," pp. 142–152 in Schmink and Wood (eds.) *Frontier
Expansion.*

Woodwell, George M. "On the Limits of Nature," pp. 47–65 in Repetto (ed.),
The Global Possible.

Worsnop, Richard L. "Amazon Basin Development." *Congressional Quarterly
Research Report*, 2:11 (Sept. 17, 1969): 691–708.

Worthington, E. Barton. "The Ecological Century." *Environmental
Conservation* 9:1 (Spring 1982): 65–70.

Wright, R. Michael. "Morne Trois Pitons National Park in Dominica: A Case
Study in Park Establishment in the Developing World." *Ecology Law
Quarterly* 12 (1985): 747–778.

Zinger, C.L., R. Dalsemer, and H. Magargle. "Environmental Volunteers in
America," PB 214 186, U.S. Environmental Protection Agency, Washington,
D.C., 1973.

INDEX

Abele, L.G., 46, 71 ,116; and Island Biogeography Theory, 299n.46
Abufari Biological Reserve, 112, 114, 167, 216
Acapu River, 316n.17
Acre (state): highway from Rondônia to, 179; rubber tapping in, 261; SEMA and, 228
Adler, J.H., 6
Africa: Brazilian interests in, 148–49; conservationism in, 16, 149, 279n.41, 283n.80; national parks of, 314n.55; during Pleistocene era, 285n.18; wildlife preservation in, 16, 282n.74
Agent Orange, Electronorte and, 324n.64
Agency for Technical Assistance and Rural Extension Service (EMATER), 322n.35
Agrarian Reform Institute, Colombian, 19
Agriculture: of Amazonia, 24, 26, 30, 65–66, 72, 114, 130, 144–47, 162, 262, 305n.50, 313n.49 (see also Program of National Integration); bureaucracy and Amazonian, 113; environmentalism and, 149; in Rondônia, 85, 205, 318n.26, 319n.38; swidden, 183; third world, 276n.5; weeds spawned by, 53
Agronomy, INPA research in, 96
Albright, Horace, 282n.74
Albuquerque Lima, Afonso de, 144–46, 305–6n.52
Alliance for Progress, 18, 291n.32
Allopatry, in evolution, 285n.17

Amapá (territory), 29, 70; IBDF delegado in, 168; manganese mining in, 25; politics in, 110; rubber tapping in, 261; soil of, 28
Amazonas (state): conservationism in, 112, 167; development in, 216
Amazonas, Federal University of, 114
Amazon Cooperation, Treaty of, 92, 151–53, 265
Amazon Forest Policy, 256
Amazonia, 2, 3–5, 23–31, 67, 289n.5; biological wealth of, 23, 35; bridges of, 228; colonization of, 26; dams of, 131, 228, 262; development of, 24–25, 151–53, 155–56, 162, 163–76, 178–82, 185–87, 308n.91 (see also Polamazonia; Program of National Integration; Superintendency for Amazon Development); exploitation of, 24–28 (see also Electronorte; Polamazonia); federal responsibility for, 113–14, 299nn.36, 39; forests of (see Rainforests); future of, 256–57, 259–66; under the generals, 144–50, 151, 153, 307n.74 (see also Brazil, military government of); and greenhouse effect, 182; highways to/through, 24, 26 (see also Belém-Brasília Highway; Transamazon Highway); indigenous peoples of (see Indians); international designs on, 145–46, 306nn.55, 57; landownership in, 67, 70, 72–74, 292nn.42, 44, 45; land speculation in, 66; life of, 35, 39–40, 51, 285n.8 (see also Fauna, Amazonian; Plants, Amazonian;